AngularJS by Example

Learn AngularJS by creating your own apps, using practical examples which you can use and adapt

Chandermani

PACKT PUBLISHING

open source*
community experience distilled

BIRMINGHAM - MUMBAI

AngularJS by Example

First published: March 2015

Production reference: 2030315

Published by Packt Publishing Ltd.
Livery Place
35 Livery Street
Birmingham B3 2PB, UK.

ISBN 978-1-78355-381-5

www.packtpub.com

Credits

About the Author

Chandermani is a software craftsman with a passion for technology and is an expert on the web stack. With more than a decade of experience under his belt, he has architected, designed, and developed solutions of all shapes and sizes on the Microsoft platform.

He never believed JavaScript could be a great platform for app development until he saw Angular. Such is his love for this framework that every engagement he is part of has an Angular footprint.

Being an early adopter of the Angular framework, he tries to support the platform in every possible way, whether by writing blog posts on various Angular topics or helping his fellow developers on Stack Overflow, where he is often seen answering questions on AngularJS channels.

A former MSFT employee, he now works for Technovert, where he leads a bunch of awesome developers who build cloud-scale web applications using AngularJS and other new-age frameworks.

Writing this book has just been a surreal experience and I would like to thank my Technovert family who supported me in all possible ways, be it helping me with sample apps, reviewing the content, or offloading some of my professional commitments to make sure I get enough time to write the book.

I especially want to thank Vijay Yalamanchili, who inspired me to take up this endeavor and also made sure there are no impediments while I juggle my professional and book writing commitments.

And finally, I want to express my gratitude toward my family. I know your blessings are always with me.

About the Reviewers

Idan Cohen is a full-stack web developer at HP Software. He has over a decade of experience in large-scale projects on an enterprise level.

He has an unquenchable thirst for cutting-edge technologies and an insatiable hunger for seamless user experience.

Since his military service in an elite technological unit (8200), he has worked with a variety of companies and organizations in the fields of media, telecommunication, and business services.

Ashutosh Das is mainly a backend developer from Bangladesh with experiences of working with Django, Node.js, Laravel, and so on, as well as works with Angular. js. He spends his spare time in GitHub. He works as a freelancer and has a part-time job. He is also a reviewer of the book *Angularjs UI development, Packt Publishing*.

Prasanna Gautam is an engineer who wears many different hats depending on the occasion. He's worked with various web frameworks over the years for both personal and professional projects and finally settled on AngularJS. When this book came up, he wanted to contribute to it from his experience working on AngularJS projects.

Ruoyu Sun is a designer and developer living in Hong Kong. He is passionate about programming and has been contributing to several open source projects. He founded several tech start-ups using a variety of technologies before going into the industry. He is the author of the book *Designing for XOOPS, O'Reilly Media*.

I would like to thank all my friends and family who have always supported me.

Jurgen Van de Moere, born in 1978, grew up in Evergem, Belgium with his parents, sister, and pets. At the age of 6, he started helping his dad, who owned a computer shop, with assembling computers for clients.

While his friends were playing computer games, Jurgen was rather fascinated by writing custom scripts and programs to solve problems that his dad's clients were dealing with. After graduating in latin-mathematics from Sint-Lievenscollege in Ghent, Jurgen continued his education at Ghent University, where he studied computer science.

His Unix username at university was "jvandemo", the nickname he still goes by on the Internet today. In 1999, Jurgen started his professional career at Infoworld. After years of hard work and dedication as a developer and network engineer, he was awarded various management positions in 2005 and 2006.

Being a true developer at heart, he missed writing code, and in 2007, he decided to end his management career to pursue his true passion again: development. Since then, he has been studying and working from his home office in Belgium, where he currently lives with his girlfriend, son, and dogs.

In a rapidly evolving world of data, intensive real-time applications, he now focuses on JavaScript-related technologies with a heavy emphasis on AngularJS and Node.js.

His many private and public contributions have helped form the foundation of numerous successful projects and companies around the world.

If you need help with your project, Jurgen can be reached at hire@jvandemo.com, on his blog at http://www.jvandemo.com, or on Twitter at https://twitter.com/jvandemo.

www.PacktPub.com

Support files, eBooks, discount offers, and more

For support files and downloads related to your book, please visit www.PacktPub.com.

Did you know that Packt offers eBook versions of every book published, with PDF and ePub files available? You can upgrade to the eBook version at www.PacktPub.com and as a print book customer, you are entitled to a discount on the eBook copy. Get in touch with us at service@packtpub.com for more details.

At www.PacktPub.com, you can also read a collection of free technical articles, sign up for a range of free newsletters and receive exclusive discounts and offers on Packt books and eBooks.

https://www2.packtpub.com/books/subscription/packtlib

Do you need instant solutions to your IT questions? PacktLib is Packt's online digital book library. Here, you can search, access, and read Packt's entire library of books.

Why subscribe?

- Fully searchable across every book published by Packt
- Copy and paste, print, and bookmark content
- On demand and accessible via a web browser

Free access for Packt account holders

If you have an account with Packt at www.PacktPub.com, you can use this to access PacktLib today and view 9 entirely free books. Simply use your login credentials for immediate access.

Table of Contents

Preface

The first thing I must do is to congratulate you! You have made an excellent decision in choosing to learn this super awesome JavaScript framework: AngularJS. Rest assured you won't be disappointed, either by AngularJS, or by this book.

JavaScript has come a long way. I remember when I started using JavaScript (around 10 years ago), it was primarily used for doing some client-side form validation and some animation, nothing very serious. Developers hacked their solution using JavaScript without much understanding of the language and its capabilities.

As JavaScript became more mainstream, browsers became more capable, jQuery hit the scene, and developers started testing the limits of the language and browser capabilities.

In recent years, a new breed of JavaScript applications has hit the fancy of the developer community, Single Page Applications (SPAs). These are rich client applications with no page refresh/redirects, bookmarkable URLs and they imbibe the UX design / code patterns such as MVC, MVP, MVVM, or MV*.

AngularJS is one such SPA JavaScript framework. Open sourced by Google and actively developed and supported by a vibrant community around it, this framework has gained a lot of traction. Due to its modular design, powerful features, and great performance it has become a great choice for building business apps over the JavaScript platform.

Through this book, our aim is to teach you how to effectively build apps using the AngularJS platform. We will be building multiple apps on this platform ranging from simple ones to more complex ones.

Learning by example has its advantages; you immediately see the concept explained in action. Also, if you are like me and prefer Do It Yourself (DIY) over too much theory, then this book is a perfect fit for you.

What this book covers

Chapter 1, Getting Started, introduces you to the AngularJS framework. We create a super simple app in AngularJS that highlights some core features of the framework.

Chapter 2, Building Our First App – 7 Minute Workout, will teach us how to build our first real AngularJS app. In the process, we learn more about the framework's MVC constructs and are introduced to scopes and binding capabilities of the framework. We learn about code organization using modules and dependency injection, look at view routing in action, and learn how to use filters.

Chapter 3, More AngularJS Goodness for 7 Minute Workout, focuses on adding the bells and whistles to the 7 Minute Workout app and in the process touches upon into some new Angular capabilities. This chapter covers Angular services, digest cycles, animation support, filters and few other concepts.

Chapter 4, Building Personal Trainer, introduces a new exercise where we morph *7 Minute Workout* into a generic Personal Trainer app. The new app has the capability to create new workout plans other than the original *7 Minute Workout* app. In this chapter, we exclusively focus on AngularJS form capabilities.

Chapter 5, Adding Data Persistence to Personal Trainer, covers retrieving and saving data to the server. We augment our Personal Trainer with data load and data persistence capabilities. Server interaction and data persistence have been ignored in all the previous chapters.

Chapter 6, Working with Directives, explains directives by building some of our own custom directives for the Personal Trainer app. Directives are the most powerful and most misunderstood feature of AngularJS.

Chapter 7, Testing the AngularJS App, highlights how to use the AngularJS testing constructs within Personal Trainer as AngularJS was built with testability in mind.

Chapter 8, Handling Common Scenarios, provides some practical tips and guidance around scenarios that we might encounter while developing apps on this framework. We will cover scenarios such as structuring the app for complex views, inter controller/directive communication, common framework pitfalls, authentication and authorization, code organization for large size apps, and other similar scenarios.

What you need for this book

Since the platform is JavaScript, you need a text editor (preferably an IDE) which you can use to create and edit HTML, CSS, and JavaScript files.

It will be ideal if you are connected to the Internet while working on the samples as some samples link to libraries available online. To work in offline mode, you need to download the libraries and change the reference in the samples.

For *Chapter 5, Adding Data Persistence to Personal Trainer,* which involves client-server interaction, we will be using `MongoLab hosting` which requires an account to be created before it can be used.

The apps build in this book have been developed and tested against Angular version 1.3.3

Who this book is for

If you've always wanted to get started with AngularJS, this is an essential guide designed to help you do exactly that. Start building applications immediately with the featured examples, and uncover a simpler approach to JavaScript web development. You will need some prior experience with HTML, CSS, and JavaScript to get started.

Conventions

In this book, you will find a number of styles of text that distinguish between different kinds of information. Here are some examples of these styles, and an explanation of their meaning.

Code words in text are shown as follows: "The `http-server` module is just one of the many options available out there."

A block of code is set as follows:

```
<div class="container" ng-controller="GuessTheNumberController">
   <!--Truncated Code-->
   <p class="text-info">No of guesses :
      <span class = "badge"> {{noOfTries}}</span>
   <p>
</div>
```

When we wish to draw your attention to a particular part of a code block, the relevant lines or items are set in bold as shown:

```
// outputs the value of property
{{property}}
//outputs the result of boolean comparison. Ternary operator
{{property1 >=0?'positive': 'negative'}}
//call testMethod and outputs the return value
{{testMethod()}}
```

Any command-line input or output is written as follows:

```
npm install http-server -g
```

New terms and **important words** are shown in bold. Words that you see on the screen, in menus or dialog boxes for example, appear in the text like this: "Once the collections are added, add yourself as a user to the database from the **User** tab."

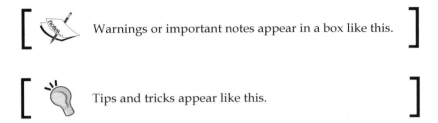

Warnings or important notes appear in a box like this.

Tips and tricks appear like this.

Reader feedback

Feedback from our readers is always welcome. Let us know what you think about this book—what you liked or might have disliked. Reader feedback is important for us to develop titles that you really get the most out of.

To send us general feedback, simply send an e-mail to feedback@packtpub.com, and mention the book title through the subject of your message.

If there is a topic that you have expertise in and you are interested in either writing, or contributing to a book, see our author guide on www.packtpub.com/authors.

Customer support

Now that you are the proud owner of a Packt book, we have a number of things to help you to get the most from your purchase.

Downloading the example code

You can download the example code files for all Packt books you have purchased from your account at http://www.packtpub.com. If you purchased this book elsewhere, you can visit http://www.packtpub.com/support and register to have the files e-mailed directly to you.

Errata

Although we have taken every care to ensure the accuracy of our content, mistakes do happen. If you find a mistake in one of our books—maybe a mistake in the text or the code—we would be grateful if you would report this to us. By doing so, you can save other readers from frustration and help us improve subsequent versions of this book. If you find any errata, please report them by visiting `http://www.packtpub.com/support`, selecting your book, clicking on the **errata submission form** link, and entering the details of your errata. Once your errata are verified, your submission will be accepted and the errata will be uploaded to our website, or added to any list of existing errata, under the Errata section of that title.

Piracy

Piracy of copyright material on the Internet is an ongoing problem across all media. At Packt, we take the protection of our copyright and licenses very seriously. If you come across any illegal copies of our works, in any form, on the Internet, please provide us with the location address or website name immediately so that we can pursue a remedy.

Please contact us at `copyright@packtpub.com` with a link to the suspected pirated material.

We appreciate your help in protecting our authors, and our ability to bring you valuable content.

Questions

You can contact us at `questions@packtpub.com` if you are having a problem with any aspect of the book, and we will do our best to address it.

1
Getting Started

Developing applications in JavaScript is always a challenge. Due to its malleable nature and lack of type checking, building a decent size application in JavaScript is difficult. Moreover, we use JavaScript for all types of processes such as **User Interface** (**UI**) manipulation, client server interaction, and business processing/validations. As a result, we end up with spaghetti code that is difficult to maintain and test.

Libraries such as jQuery do a great job of taking care of various browser quirks and providing constructs that can lead to an overall reduction in lines of code. However, these libraries lack any structural guidance that can help us when the codebase grows.

This is where architectural patterns such as **Model View Controller** (**MVC**) and frameworks such as AngularJS come into the picture. This chapter is dedicated to understanding the concept behind MVC architecture and learning how to put these principles into practice while we build a simple app using AngularJS.

The topics that we will cover in this chapter are as follows:

- **MVC basics**: We will talk in brief about each of the components of the Model-View-Controller pattern.

- **Building our first AngularJS app**: We will build a small game, *Guess the Number!* in AngularJS.

- **Understanding the Model, View, and Controller components**: We will dissect the game that we built to understand the MVC components of AngularJS.

- **Working with scopes**: AngularJS scopes are an important concept to understand. This chapter will introduce us to scopes and the role they play in the framework.

- **An introduction to some AngularJS constructs**: We will introduce some new constructs such as expressions, directives, and interpolations that we used to build the *Guess the Number!* app.

- **App initialization**: We will talk about the app initialization process in AngularJS; this is also known as App bootstrapping.

- Lastly, we will provide some resources and tools that will come in handy during AngularJS development and debugging.

So let's get started with our first topic: MVC.

The basics of Model View Controller

MVC is a UI architectural pattern that has been around for some time. It is based on the premise of separation of responsibility. In MVC, we have the following components:

- **Model**: This stores business data
- **View**: This represents the model in UI
- **Controller**: This is responsible for coordinating between a model and view

Any change in the model is reflected in the view and any change done by the user while interacting with the view is reflected back on the model. Here, the controller acts as a coordinator and is responsible for keeping the model and view in sync.

This is an over-simplified definition of the MVC and if we search the Web, we will find numerous variations of this pattern such as MVP, Front Controller, MVVM, and maybe some others. The net effect of this separation is that the code becomes more organized, more understandable, and maintainable.

For us, the best way to understand MVC is to see it in action and hence, we are going to build our first Hello World app in AngularJS. This app will help us to become familiar with the AngularJS framework and see the MVC paradigm in action.

The customary Hello Angular app (Guess the Number!)

As our first exercise, we want to keep things simple but still showcase the framework capabilities. Therefore, we are going to build a very simple game, *Guess the Number!*. The objective of the game is to guess a computer-generated random number in as few tries as possible.

This is how the game looks:

The gameplay is simple.

We enter the guess in the textbox. To verify whether the guess is correct, we click on **Verify**. The game gives us a hint to improve our next guess. If we are unable to guess or have guessed the number correctly, we can restart the game by clicking on **Restart**.

Before we start working on the game, it is strongly recommended that we run the sample code from a development server instead of loading the app directly from the filesystem. The browser security model has some restrictions on running script content from the local filesystem. Let's quickly look at some easy-to-install options for a development server.

Setting up a development server

The development web server that we choose greatly depends on the platform that we work on and the backend we support. However, for apps in this book that target purely client-side development, any web server will do.

My recommendation would be to use the `http-server` module of Node.js. Since Node.js is available cross-platform, we can install Node.js from `http://nodejs.org/`.

Once Node.js is installed, installing the `http-server` module and running the http server are easy. Open the command line and type the following command:

```
npm install http-server -g
```

This installs the HTTP server at the global level.

To run the server, just navigate to the folder where the app code resides, or open the folder from where we want to serve static files, and type this:

```
http-server
```

And that's it! We have an HTTP server running at `http://localhost:8080` that can serve files from the current directory.

 The `http-server` module does support some startup configurations. Check the documentation at `https://github.com/nodeapps/http-server`.

The `http-server` module is just one of the many options available out there. Depending upon the platform we are on, we can also try Python's `SimpleHTTPServer` module, Mongoose, or any such web server.

Let's build *Guess the Number!*.

Building Guess the Number!

The standard practice when building user interfaces is to build them top-down. Start with designing the UI and then plug in the data and behavior according to the needs. With such an approach, the UI, data, and the behavioral aspects of the app are all tightly coupled, which is a less than ideal situation!

With the MVC paradigm, things work a little differently. There is a conscious effort to design the model beforehand by looking at the UI and expected behavior, and to encapsulate the behavior aspect into the controller, thus minimizing the coupling between the controller implementation and the UI (view) that it supports.

Given these facts, we will start by identifying the model data for our app based on the feature set.

The app model

The model is the data that the view and controller work on. It represents the state of the system projected on the view. To determine the model for our own app, we need to detail the features that the app supports. These features include:

- Supporting the generation of random numbers (`original`)
- Supporting input for a user to guess the value (`guess`)
- Tracking the number of guesses already made (`noOfTries`)
- Giving users hints to improve their guess based on their input (`deviation`)
- Giving a success message if the user guesses the number correctly (`deviation`)

Once we have the feature list, we can now determine what data needs to be tracked and that becomes part of our model. For the preceding feature set, the elements in parentheses denote properties that will support these features and hence represent the app model.

Designing the model for an app is a very crucial process. If it is done right, we can minimize the friction between a model and view and simplify the controller implementation.

While building any app, I urge you to first think about the functionality you want to offer, then the model that can support the functionality, and lastly think about how to build a view for it. This is a good practice irrespective of the library or framework you use to build your app.

The model properties highlighted earlier need to be hosted in a script and then referenced by the view. These model properties will be defined inside a controller and hence it's time to introduce the Angular Controller.

However, before we do that, we first need to create a file for the controller code. Due to the size of the app, we are going to create a single file that will contain everything, from the controller script to the view HTML code. To start with, this is the outline of our app HTML code:

```
<!DOCTYPE html>
<html>
<head>
  <title>Guess The Number !</title>
  <link href="http://netdna.bootstrapcdn.com/bootstrap/
    3.1.1/css/bootstrap.min.css" rel="stylesheet">
</head>
<body>
  <script src="http://ajax.googleapis.com/
    ajax/libs/angularjs/1.3.3/angular.js"></script>
</body>
</html>
```

Downloading the example code

You can download the example code files for all Packt books you have purchased from your account at http://www.packtpub.com. If you purchased this book elsewhere, you can visit http://www.packtpub.com/support and register to have the files e-mailed directly to you.

Create an HTML file and add the preceding HTML code to it. Henceforth, everything that we outline should be appended to this file. The app HTML code itself is self-explanatory. We reference the Twitter Bootstrap CSS in the `<head>` section and the Angular framework inside the `<body>` tag.

 Guess the Number! and all the other apps that are part of this book have been tested against Angular version 1.3.3.

We can now start building the controller.

The controller

The controller manages the model and the view. It is always designed with the view in mind and it is the view's behavior that drives controller functionality. In AngularJS, the controller is a JavaScript class (a constructor function) that hosts the model and exposes some behavior that the view binds to. How it binds to the view will be clear when we discuss the view implementation.

Let's start working on the controller implementation. While defining our model, we have already detailed the functional aspect of the application and we do have a fair idea about how the view should behave. Keeping that in mind, this is how the app controller looks:

```
function GuessTheNumberController($scope) {
    $scope.verifyGuess = function () {
        $scope.deviation = $scope.original - $scope.guess;
        $scope.noOfTries = $scope.noOfTries + 1;
    }
    $scope.initializeGame = function () {
        $scope.noOfTries = 0;
        $scope.original = Math.floor((Math.random() * 1000) + 1);
        $scope.guess = null;
        $scope.deviation = null;
    }
    $scope.initializeGame();
}
```

Add this controller script to the file created earlier after the Angular script declaration inside its own script block.

The `GuessTheNumberController` function sets up some model properties that we described in the *The app model* section and exposes two methods: `verifyGuess` and `intializeGame`.

The `verifyGuess` function verifies whether the guess matches the original value and updates model properties `deviation` and `noOfTries` accordingly. The `initializeGame` function is used to initialize the model properties before the start of the game, and during the game whenever the user clicks on the **Restart** button.

The last statement in the preceding controller calls `initializeGame` to set up the game for the first time.

The overall controller implementation is self-explanatory but the only oddity seems to be the `$scope` object. This `$scope` object has been passed as a parameter to the controller function and all functions and properties are attached to `$scope`. To understand the role of the `$scope` object and how things tie together, we need to start implementing the view.

However, we are still not done with the controller yet. We will revisit the controller once we get the app running and learn a bit more about them.

The app view

The view is nothing but a UI projection of model data. Looking at the *Guess the Number!* UI, we will agree that this UI may not win any **User Experience (UX)** award; still, this HTML is what we call the view.

Let's put some focus on the view and start building it. We have already added the controller to the app file. Add this view code inside the body tag at the top:

```html
<div class="container">
  <h2>Guess the Number !</h2>
  <p class="well lead">Guess the computer generated random number
    between 1 and 1000.</p>
  <label>Your Guess: </label><input type="number"
    ng-model="guess"/>
  <button ng-click="verifyGuess()" class="btn btn-primary
    btn-sm">Verify</button>
  <button ng-click="initializeGame()" class=
    "btn btn-warning btn-sm">Restart</button>
  <p>
    <p ng-show="deviation<0" class="alert alert-warning">Your
      guess is higher.</p>
    <p ng-show="deviation>0" class="alert alert-warning">Your
      guess is lower.</p>
    <p ng-show="deviation===0" class="alert alert-success">Yes!
      That"s it.</p>
  </p>
  <p class="text-info">No of guesses : <span
    class="badge">{{noOfTries}}</span><p>
</div>
```

Lots of interesting stuff here, but before we dissect the view implementation we need to link the view and the controller; in fact, both the view and the controller need to be linked to the Angular framework first.

To let Angular know it needs to process the view HTML, update the existing `<body>` tag with a custom attribute `ng-app`:

```
<body ng-app="app">
```

The `ng-app` attribute tells Angular to treat everything defined inside the HTML tag (with `ng-app` attribute) as an angular app and process it accordingly. The `<body>` tag just mentioned becomes the root of the application.

The `"app"` value of the `ng-app` attribute tells Angular to search for a module named app and load it.

We have a new concept called **module**. Modules in the Angular framework are containers that hold various artifacts that we create or are part of the framework. Any Angular-specific script implementation always goes into one or another module.

Let's define the `"app"` module that the `<body>` tag references. Add the highlighted statement inside the script block containing the controller declaration:

```
angular.module('app',[])
function GuessTheNumberController($scope) {
```

We use the global Angular object that is part of the Angular framework to declare an Angular module. The first parameter is the name of the module and the second is there to provide module dependencies.

We now have a module named app. This module is linked with the view using `ng-app`, hence the Angular framework can now process the view and load the module. However, the link between the controller and the Angular framework (as well as between the view and the controller) is still missing.

To make Angular aware of the controller, we need to register the controller with the module we just created. Update the module declaration now to:

```
angular.module('app',[])
.controller('GuessTheNumberController', GuessTheNumberController);
function GuessTheNumberController($scope) {
```

The `angular.module` function creates a module and returns a module object. This module object has a function `controller` that allows us to register a controller. The first parameter is the name of the controller and the second is the controller implementation itself. With the first two lines from the preceding code, we have declared a module app and registered the `GuessTheNumberController` function with it.

Lastly, we link the controller and the view using another attribute, ng-controller. Update the div (class=container) parameter to:

```
<div class="container" ng-controller="GuessTheNumberController">
```

Well, the app is complete and ready to be tested! Open the file in the browser and start guessing.

 > If you are having trouble running the app, a working HTML is available on my GitHub account http://goo.gl/4j6DG6.

If we glance at the HTML file now, we should be mightily impressed with what we have achieved with these 40 lines. There is no DOM manipulation or model-view synchronization code and still everything works perfectly.

To understand how this app functions in the Angular context, we need to delve deeper into the view HTML as the view acts as an entry point into the app and links everything together.

Let's go back and check the app HTML. It looks like standard HTML with some new attributes (ng-app, ng-controller, ng-model, ng-click, and ng-show) and symbols (,), {, and } ({{ and }}).

In the Angular world, {{ and }} are the interpolation symbols and the ng-* attributes are what we call **directives**. The model properties and functions are either assigned to these directive attributes or referenced inside interpolation symbols. Clearly, interpolation symbols and directive attributes have some behavior attached to them and seem to be linking the view HTML and controller code. Let's try to understand what these directive attributes and interpolation symbols are actually doing.

Interpolation

Look at this HTML fragment from the *Guess the Number!* code:

```
<p class="text-info">No of guesses :
<span class="badge">{{noOfTries}}</span><p>
```

The model properties noOfTries is sandwiched between two interpolation symbols. Interpolation works by replacing the content of the interpolation markup with the value of the expression (noOfTries) inside the interpolation symbol.

Interpolations are declared using the syntax {{expression}}. This expression looks similar to the JavaScript expression but is always evaluated in the context of the linked $scope object. Remember we passed a $scope object to the controller function, as follows:

```
function GuessTheNumberController($scope) {
```

And we then attached the properties noOfTries to the $scope object in the implementation. Clearly, the interpolation expression can reference such properties and link it to the view. Later in this chapter, we will discuss more about the $scope object to understand how the underlying infrastructure works and the link between the controller, $scope, and the view is established.

Another interesting aspect of interpolation is that changes made to model properties are automatically synchronized with the view. Run the app and make some guesses; the noOfTries value changes after every guess and so does the view content.

 Interpolation is an excellent debugging tool in scenarios where we need to see the state of the model. With interpolation, we don't have to put a breakpoint in code just to know the model value. Since interpolation can take an expression, we can pass a function, an object, or a primitive type and see its value.

Interpolations are flexible and can be placed almost anywhere in HTML:

- Inside a tag (<div>{{noOfTries}}</div>)
- As an attribute value (<div class='cls-{{noOfTries}}'>)
- As an attribute name (<input {{myAttributeName}}="">)

Learning interpolation was easy; now let's look at the other framework construct, directives.

Directives

Directives, in AngularJS, are constructs that allow us to extend the standard HTML vocabulary. They help us augment the behavior of the existing HTML elements. Also, they allow us to create our own elements as well! This makes directives the most powerful and the most celebrated feature of the framework. Directives are the way to create and package reusable components in the Angular framework.

For our game, too, we use some Angular directives, including `ng-app`, `ng-controller`, `ng-model`, `ng-click`, and `ng-show`. Each of these directives extends the behavior of the HTML element on which they are defined. Here is what each of these directives do:

- `ng-model`: This sets up a link between the scope property passed in as the attribute value (`guess` in our case) and HTML input element. As we change the input value, the `guess` variable changes; it works the other way round too. In this case, we update the `guess` value in the controller as we do in `intializeGame` function (`$scope.guess = null;`), it clears the input value.

  We can use interpolation to verify if `guess` indeed is changing when `input` changes. Append an interpolation next to `input`, as follows:

  ```
  <input type="number" ng-model="guess"/> {{guess}}
  ```

  Save and refresh the page. If we now enter a numeric value in the input field, the guess interpolation next to it automatically changes.

- `ng-click`: When attached to an HTML element, this directive evaluates the expression passed as an attribute value when the element is clicked. So the **Verify** button causes the `verifyGuess` function to execute and the **Restart** button causes the `initializeGame` method to execute.

- `ng-show`: When attached to an element, this shows or hides the element based on the expression's return value. If true, the element is shown, otherwise it gets hidden. In our case, we use `ng-show` on the three paragraph elements and show/hide them based on the value of `deviation`.

- `ng-controller`: As we have already seen, this directive links the controller implementation with the view.

We will cover `ng-app` later in this chapter.

 Directives are everywhere! They are the most powerful feature of Angular. Using them in HTML is intuitive but creating directives requires a decent understanding of the framework. We have dedicated a complete chapter to directives where we will learn how to create our own directives and use them in views.

Similar to the expression usage in interpolation, directives too can take an expression (although it's not mandatory). All the directives' attributes we have used in the app have an expression assigned to them and like interpolation these expressions are also evaluated in the context of the linked scope. Expressions are like input parameters to a directive.

In Angular, some directives accept interpolated expressions instead of standard expressions, for example, the `ng-src` directive that allows setting the `src` property of the `image` tag dynamically:

```
ng-src="http://www.google.com/images/{{imageName}}"
```

But more often than not we need to provide a non-interpolated expression to the directive. Using an expression with { { } } and without it is not the same and hence we should be always be careful while assigning an expression to the directive attribute.

 Using interpolation expression for a directive that accepts standard expressions is a common mistake that AngularJS newbies make. `ng-click='{{verifyGuess()}}'` is invalid, `ng-click='verifyGuess()'` is correct. When in doubt, always refer to the documentation for the directive to know what is acceptable.

The usage of expressions in interpolation symbols and directives is an important concept to understand and this is what we are going to discuss in the next section on expressions.

Expressions

Expressions in AngularJS are nothing but plain JavaScript code that are evaluated in the context of the *current scope object* with few limitations. The excerpt from the AngularJS documentation (`https://docs.angularjs.org/guide/expression`) highlights the following differences and limitations:

- **Context**: JavaScript expressions are evaluated against the global window. In Angular, expressions are evaluated against a scope object.

- **Forgiving**: In JavaScript, trying to evaluate undefined properties generates `ReferenceError` or `TypeError`. In Angular, expression evaluation is forgiving to `undefined` and `null`.

- **No Control Flow Statements**: You cannot use the following in an Angular expression: conditionals, loops, or exceptions.

- **Filters**: You can use filters within expressions to format data before displaying it.

These limitations still do not stop us from doing some nifty stuff with expressions. As we can see in the following examples, these all are valid expressions:

```
// outputs the value of property
{{property}}

//outputs the result of boolean comparison. Ternary operator
{{property1 >=0?'positive': 'negative'}}

//call testMethod and outputs the return value
{{testMethod()}}

// assign value returned by testMethod to x. Creates "x" on scope
   if not available. Empty output
{{x=testMethod()}}

// calls testMethod() and testMethod2() and assign return values
   to x and y. Empty output
{{x=testMethod();y=testMethod2()}}
```

> Having looked into expressions, I strongly advise you to keep your expressions simple, thus keeping the HTML readable. The ng-show="formHasErrors()" expression is always better than ng-show="unname==null || email==null || emailformatInValid(email) || age < 18".
>
> So, when an expression starts to become complex, move it into a controller function.

That concludes our discussion on expressions. We now have a working app and a fair understanding of the model, view, and controller part of the framework.

Let's dig a bit deeper into the framework and understand how some parts of the app function.

To start with, it is evident now that the ng-controller directive together with interpolation and other directives such as ng-model, ng-show, and ng-click allow us to establish a connection between view and model properties/action methods defined on the controller.

To understand how this connection works, we need to introduce an important new concept: AngularJS data bindings.

AngularJS bindings

To keep the view and the model in sync, Angular creates bindings between view elements and model properties. Bindings are created for the interpolations and directives that we define on the view.

Interpolation bindings are easy to understand. An expression inside the interpolation symbol is evaluated and the return value replaces the interpolation. Whenever the expression value changes, the view is automatically updated.

A directive on the other hand can bind any HTML element attribute with the model depending upon the directive implementation.

For example, the ng-show directive that we have used is as follows:

```
<p ng-show="deviation<0" class="alert alert-warning">Your guess is
    higher.</p>
```

This binds the paragraph's (<p>) class property with the model value deviation. When the expression deviation<0 is false, a CSS class .ng-hide (with style defined as display:none) is appended; when true, the class is removed. This addition and removal of the class results in the previous paragraph element being shown and hidden.

Similarly, the ng-model directive binds the value attribute of the input with the model property it references.

 Angular supports MathML and SVG markup and can perform interpolation on them.

Angular binding setup starts once the browser has rendered the raw HTML file or what we call the view template. The framework then compiles this view template and in the process sets up the necessary binding. It then does the necessary synchronization between the model and the view template that produces the final rendered output. The following screenshot depicts the transformations that happen to the view template after data binding is done for our app:

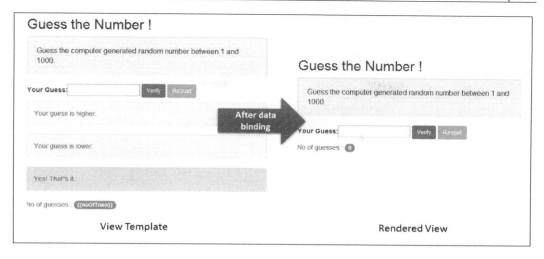

We can ourselves check the view template of the app by removing the ng-app attribute from the body tag and refreshing the app in the browser.

Where Angular differs from other template frameworks is that these bindings between a model and view are live. Angular does not merely merge the model and view templates to create the final HTML. Changes done to the model update the view and any update in the view done by the user is reflected back in the model. AngularJS never regenerates the HTML again; it just works on the relevant part of HTML and updates it on model changes. This data binding capability of the framework together with directives and interpolations makes Angular an exceptional view templating engine too.

An interesting characteristic about these bindings is that they can be one-way or two-way. Depending upon the directive used, the nature of the binding is decided.

In one-way binding, changes to the model are synchronized with the view. Following are examples of one-way binding:

```
<p>
    <p ng-show="deviation<0" class="alert alert-warning">Your
      guess is higher.</p>
    <p ng-show="deviation>0" class="alert alert-warning">Your
      guess is lower.</p>
    <p ng-show="deviation===0" class="alert alert-success">Yes!
      That"s it.</p>
</p>
<p class="text-info">No of guesses : <span
  class="badge">{{noOfTries}}</span><p>
```

Any change to the `noOfTries` and `deviation` properties affects these bindings and consequently the user interface content.

In two-way bindings, not only are changes done to a model reflected in the view, but the reverse also holds true. In our app, the input box defines a two-way binding between the input value and `guess` using the `ng-model` directive:

```
<label>Your Guess: </label><input type="number" ng-model="guess"/>
```

Changing the value in the input box updates `guess` and, if we update the `guess` property in the controller, the view automatically gets updated, as happens in one-way bindings.

The bottom-line is, when adding directives and interpolation to a view, we are essentially instructing Angular to create data bindings that keep the model and view in sync.

The overall bindings in our app look like this:

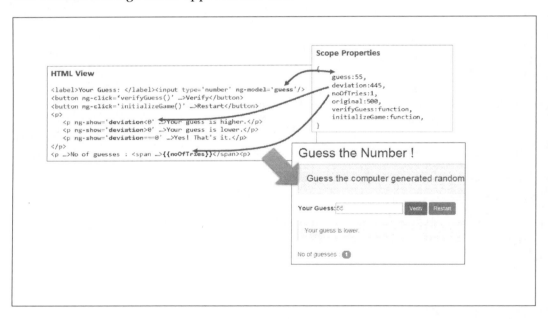

It's time now to revisit the controller implementation and understand the implementation in the light of our newly acquired understanding of Angular bindings.

Revisiting the controller

Now that the app is running, why don't we get a firsthand experience of how the view and controller interact. Put a breakpoint on the JavaScript code inside verifyGuess. Enter a guess and click on **Verify**. The breakpoint will be hit.

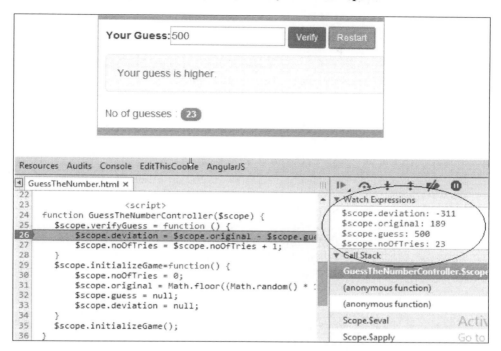

We can see that the value that we added in the input is available on the $scope property guess (see the **Watch Expressions** section in the previous screenshot). Inside the function, we use the guess property and the original property to calculate deviation, and then update the noOfTries property. As we return from the function, the view updates immediately based on model changes.

Let's try to analyze a few important aspects of an AngularJS controller:

- To start with, if you are as observant as I am, you will have noticed that a scope object ($scope) gets passed as a parameter to the controller function (function GuessTheNumberController($scope)), almost magically! We are nowhere calling the controller function and passing any parameter. And you may have guessed it already; if we are not doing it, then the framework must be responsible. How and when is something that we will discuss when we go into scopes in greater detail.

- Also, if you are more observant than me, you will realize that the controller does not reference the view! There are no DOM element references, no DOM selection, or reading or writing. The operations that the controller performs are always on the model data. As a consequence, the controller code is more readable, hence more maintainable (and, of course, testable).

When it comes to writing a controller, the golden rule is never ever, ever, ever reference the DOM element, either using plan JavaScript or with libraries such as jQuery, in the controller. Such code does not belong to the controller.

If you want to do DOM manipulations, use existing directives or create your own.

- In AngularJS, unlike other frameworks, a model does not need to follow any specific structure. We do not have to derive it from any framework class. In fact, any JavaScript object and primitive types can act as a model. The only requirement is that the properties should be declared on a special object exposed by the framework called $scope. This $scope object acts as glue between the model and view and keeps the model and view in sync through Angular bindings (an over-simplification). This $scope object takes up some responsibilities that in traditional MVC frameworks belonged to the controller.

When we talk about a "scope object" or "scope", we're referring to the $scope object. As we will see in the next section, almost every scope object has a constrained existence and hence we simply refer to it as scope.

So far, we have been constantly discussing a scope object or $scope. This is an important concept to understand as it can save us from countless hours of debugging and frustration. The next section is dedicated to learning about scopes and using them.

Scope

Scope, as we described earlier, is a JavaScript object that binds the model properties and behavior (functions) to the HTML view.

An important thing to realize here is that the scope object is not the model but it references our model.

This is a special object for the framework as the complete view behavior is tied to this object. The framework creates these scope objects based on some AngularJS constructs. The framework can create multiple scope objects, depending on how the views are structured. The thing that we should keep in mind is that scope objects are always created in the context of a view element and hence follow a hierarchical arrangement similar to that of HTML elements (with some exceptions).

It will be interesting to see what scopes we have created for our app. To dig into the available scopes, we will use an excellent chrome extension **Batarang**.

To use Batarang, perform the following steps:

1. Download and install this extension from the Chrome web store.
2. Navigate to the app page.
3. Open the Chrome developer console (*F12*).
4. Click on the **AngularJS** tab
5. In this tab, enable the the **Enable** checkbox and we are all set!

> This extension does not work if the file is loaded from a local filesystem (`file:///`). See issue 52 at `https://github.com/angular/angularjs-batarang/issues/52`. I suggest you host the HTML page on any development web server. Refer to the earlier section *Setting up a development server* to learn how to set up a local web server.

If we now open the **Models** tab, we will see two scopes: the **002** and **003** IDs (the IDs may differ in your case) organized in a hierarchical manner, as seen in the following screenshot:

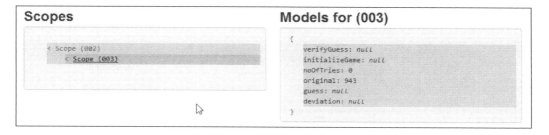

The parent scope (**002**) does not have any model properties but the child scope (**003**) contains all the properties and functions that we have been using as part of our app.

> Whenever we talk about the parent-child scope or scope hierarchy, it actually is an inheritance hierarchy. This implies that the child scope object inherits from the parent scope object (standard JavaScript prototypal inheritance).

It seems that we have been using this very scope (**003**) object to bind the view to the model. We can check this by clicking on the small **<** arrow that precedes each scope name. This should take us to this line in the HTML:

```
<div class="container" ng-controller="GuessTheNumberController">
```

Well, it looks like the scope (**003**) is tied to the previous `div` element and hence is available within the start and end tags of the previous `div`. Any AngularJS view construct that has been declared inside the previous `div` element can access the scope (**003**) properties; in our case, this is the complete application HTML.

We can confirm this by copying the line containing the `{{noOfTries}}` interpolation string and pasting it outside the previous `div` element. The code should look something like this:

```
<div class="container" ng-controller="GuessTheNumberController">
    <!--Truncated Code-->
    <p class="text-info">No of guesses :
        <span class = "badge"> {{noOfTries}}</span>
    <p>
</div>
<p class="text-info">No of guesses :
    <span class="badge">{{noOfTries}}</span><p>
```

If we now refresh the app, we will see two lines that should be tracking the number of tries. Try to guess the number the first tracker will increment but there is no effect on the second one. Please refer to the following screenshot:

Interesting! Isn't it? And it implies that all scope objects are constrained/scoped.

Angular does not create these scopes at random. There is a reason why the *Guess the Number!* app has two scopes. The next section on app bootstrapping covers the underlying cause of multiple scope creation.

We have not talked about the parent scope (**002**) till now. If we try to click the **<** link next to **002** scope, it navigates to the <body> tag with the ng-app directive. This in fact is the *root scope* and was created as part of application bootstrapping. This scope is the parent of all scope objects that are created during the lifetime of applications and is hence called $rootScope. We will throw some more light on this scope object in the next section where we talk about the app initialization process.

Let's summarize the key takeaways from our discussion on scope:

- Scope objects bind the view and model together.
- Scope objects are almost always linked to a view element.
- There can be more than one scope object defined for an application. In fact, in any decent size app there are a number of scopes active during any given time.
- More often than not, child scopes inherit from their parent scope and can access parent scope data.

This was a gentle introduction to scopes and I believe now we should have some basic understanding of scopes. There is more to scopes that we will be covering in the coming chapters. Nonetheless, this should be enough to get us started.

The last topic that we will cover in this chapter is the app initialization process. This will help us understand how and when these scope objects are created and linked to the view HTML.

App bootstrapping

One of the important topics that we have not touched on yet is how AngularJS initializes the app. To answer that, we will have to go back to the HTML view and look at the <body> tag. The <body> tag is as follows:

```
<body ng-app="app">
```

The <body> tag defines an ng-app directive attribute. Wherever Angular encounters this directive, it starts the initialization process. Since we have added ng-app to the <body> tag, everything within the <body> tag becomes part of our AngularJS app.

 This construct makes it possible for an Angular app to coexist with other frameworks, as we can demarcate what part of HTML should use AngularJS.

During this bootstrapping/initialization process Angular does the following:

- It loads the module for the application. Modules are a way for AngularJS to organize and segregate code. As described earlier, these are containers for various Angular artifacts. In fact, even the framework's internal functionality is exposed through such modules.

- It sets up dependency injection (**DI**). DI is not very popular in the JavaScript world but is commonplace in other programming languages. It is basically a mechanism to inject dependencies into components that require it instead of the component creating it itself. For example, in the `GuessTheNumberController` function, we inject the dependency for `$scope`.

  ```
  function GuessTheNumberController($scope) {
  ```

- It creates a `$rootScope` object, which is a scope object available at the global level and not tied to any specific HTML fragment.

> `$rootScope` and `$scope` are instances of the same class (a constructor function). The difference is just the context in which they are available. `$rootScope` is available throughout the HTML (within `ng-app`) whereas `$scope` is always scoped by a specific HTML element.

- It compiles the DOM starting from where `ng-app` is declared. In this compilation process, the framework traverses the DOM, looks for all directives and interpolations, and sets up the binding between the view and model.

- Post compilation, it links the view and scope to produce a live view where changes are synced across the model and viewed in real time as we interact with the app.

This compilation and linking process can also lead to the creation of new scopes, all of which depend on the directive that is being applied to the HTML node. If you have Batarang opened, go back to the lone child scope (**003**) and click on the **<** link. We will again land up here:

```
<div class="container" ng-controller="GuessTheNumberController">
```

Now look at the AngularJS documentation for `ng-controller` (`https://docs.angularjs.org/api/ng/directive/ngController`). There is this quote:

Directive Info

This directive creates new scope.

So, this `ng-controller` declaration when compiled by the framework leads to the creation of a new scope whose visibility is limited within the earlier mentioned `<div>` tag.

 There are a number of other directives in Angular that cause the creation of a new scope; this is precisely the reason why there can be multiple scopes active during the execution of the app.

So now we know how and when these scope objects are created. We also now understand the Angular app initialization process a little better.

The last two sections cover the tools and resources that will come in handy for us while we make some killer apps on AngularJS.

Tools

Tools make our lives easy and we are going to share some tools that will help you with different aspects of AngularJS development, from code writing to debugging:

- **Batarang**: We have mentioned and used Batarang earlier while working with scopes. Batarang is an excellent debugging tool for an AngularJS application and we have explored only a few features of this awesome Chrome extension. We can install it from the Chrome web store (`https://chrome.google.com/webstore/category/apps`).

- **Browser Developer Console**: All current browsers have excellent capabilities when it comes to JavaScript debugging. Since we are working with JavaScript, we can put breakpoints, add a watch, and do everything that is otherwise possible with JavaScript. Remember, a lot of errors with code can be detected just by looking at the browser's console window.

- **jsFiddle** and **Plunker**: jsFiddle (`http://jsfiddle.net/`) and Plunker (`http://plnkr.co/`) are excellent playgrounds for trying out HTML, CSS, and JavaScript code. These tools also have great versioning and sharing capabilities that can come in handy if we want someone's help.

- **IDE extensions**: Many of the popular IDEs on the market have plugins/extensions to make AngularJS development easy for us. Examples include: Sublime Text package (`https://github.com/angular-ui/AngularJS-sublime-package`), JetBrain WebStorm 8 (`http://blog.jetbrains.com/webstorm/2014/03/welcome-webstorm-8/`), and TextMate bundle (`https://github.com/angular-ui/AngularJS.tmbundle`). Search for support for your specific IDE on the Internet to see if there is some helpful stuff available.

Resources

AngularJS is a popular framework and there is a vibrant community to support us in all our endeavors. Together with this book there are also blogs, articles, support forums, and plenty of help. Some of the prominent resources that will be useful are:

- **Framework code and documentation**: Angular documentation (`https://angularjs.org/`) has been criticized a lot in the past but it has got a whole lot better. And there is always the Angular source code, a great source of learning.

- **The AngularJS Google group** (`angular@googlegroups.com`) and the StackOverflow channel (`http://stackoverflow.com/questions/tagged/angularjs`): Head over here if you have any questions or are struck with some issue.

- **AngularJS Google+ Channel** (`https://plus.google.com/+AngularJS`): This is the source of the latest happenings on the framework.

- **Build with Angular** (`https://builtwith.angularjs.org/`): People have been creating some amazing apps using AngularJS. This site showcases such apps and most of them have source code available for us to have a look at.

That's it! The chapter is complete and it's time to summarize what we've learned.

Summary

The journey has started and we have reached the first milestone. Despite this chapter being entitled *Getting Started*, we have covered a lot of concepts that will be necessary for us to know so as to understand the bigger picture. Our learning was derived from our *Guess the Number!* app that we built and dissected throughout the chapter.

We learned about the MVC triad starting from the model and designed the model for our *Guess the Number!* app. We learned how to expose the model over the scope object and how the model drives the view in AngularJS.

We explored the view part of MVC and designed our view. We learned more about AngularJS binding and understood the live nature of these bindings. We explored the new AngularJS view constructs: interpolations and directives, and understood the role expressions play in the framework.

The last MVC element was the controller. We learned about the AngularJS controller and how it works in close sync with the view to provide the necessary behavior. One important consideration that came out of this discussion was that the controller does not directly refer the view or manipulate it.

Once we had a good understanding of AngularJS and the MVC component, we focused our efforts on learning about scopes. We learned how the scope is the glue between the view and the model. We saw scope objects defined inside our game and how changes in the model and view are synced by the framework.

To round things off, we learned about a very important process in AngularJS: app bootstrapping. By exploring the bootstrap process, we were able to connect the dots and answer a number of questions that related to scopes, binding, and app initialization itself.

The groundwork has been done and now we are ready for some serious app development on the AngularJS framework. In the next chapter, we will start working on a more complex exercise and expose ourselves to a number of new AngularJS constructs.

2
Building Our First
App – 7 Minute Workout

I hope the first chapter was intriguing enough and you want to learn more about AngularJS. Believe me we have just scratched the surface. The framework has a lot to offer and it strives to make frontend development with JavaScript a little less painful and a little more enjoyable.

Keeping up with the theme of this book, we will be building a new app in AngularJS and in the process, developing a better understanding of the framework. This app will also help us to explore capabilities of the framework that we have not touched on until now.

The topics we will cover in this chapter include:

- **The 7 Minute Workout problem description**: We detail the functionality of the app that we will build in this chapter.

- **Code organization**: For our first real app, we try to understand how to organize code, specifically AngularJS code.

- **Designing the model**: One of the building blocks for our app is its model. We design the app model based on the app requirements we define.

- **Understanding dependency injection**: One of the core components of AngularJS, DI helps us to keep app elements loosely coupled and testable. We learn about the DI capabilities of the framework in this chapter.

- **Implementing the controller**: We implement the core workout logic using the model created earlier. In the process we also cover some new Angular constructs such as watches and promises.

- **Designing the view**: We create the view for the 7 minute app and integrate it with the controller. We also cover directives such as `ng-src` and `ng-style` that are part of our app view.

- **Creating a single-page app**: AngularJS is all about **single-page apps (SPA)**. We explore the SPA capabilities of the framework by adding a start, workout, and finish page to the app. We also cover route configuration using `$routeProvider` and the routing directive `ng-view`.

- **Working with partial views**: To make the app more professional, we add some additional features. We start with adding exercise details such as a description, steps, and videos to the exercise page. This helps us understand the framework's ability to include partial views using the directive `ng-include`.

- **Implementing a 'workout time remaining" filter**: We learn about AngularJS filters by creating one of our own that tracks the overall workout time. We also go through some framework filters such as date, number, uppercase, and lowercase.

- **Adding the next exercise indicator using ng-if**: We explore the `ng-if` directive and implement a next exercise indicator using `ng-if`.

Let's get started. The first thing we will do is define the scope of our *7 Minute Workout* app.

What is 7 Minute Workout?

I want everyone reading this book to be physically fit. Therefore, this book should serve a dual purpose; not only should it simulate your gray matter, but it should also urge you to look at your physical fitness. What better way to do it than to build an app that targets physical fitness!

7 Minute Workout is an exercise/workout plan that requires us to perform a set of twelve exercises in quick succession within the seven minute time span. *7 Minute Workout* has become quite popular due to its benefits and the short duration of the workout. I cannot confirm or refute the claims but doing any form of strenuous physical activity is better than doing nothing at all. If you are interested in knowing more about the workout, then check on this link: `http://well.blogs.nytimes.com/2013/05/09/the-scientific-7-minute-workout/`.

The technicalities of the app are as follows: we perform a set of twelve exercises, dedicating 30 seconds for each exercise. This is followed by a brief rest period before starting the next exercise. For the app we are building, we will be taking rest periods of 10 seconds each. So the total duration comes out to be a little more than seven minutes.

At the end of the chapter, we will have the 7 Minute Workout app that will look something like this:

Downloading the codebase

The code for this app is available in the companion code package folder of this book under chapter02 on the Packt website (https://www.packtpub.com/). Since we are building the app incrementally, I have created multiple checkpoints that map to folders such as chapter02/checkpoint1, chapter02/checkpoint2, and so on. During the narration, I will highlight the checkpoint folder for reference. These folders will contain the work done on the app up to that point in time.

> The code is also available on GitHub (https://github.com/ chandermani/angularjsbyexample) for everyone to download. Checkpoints are implemented as branches in GitHub. I will also highlight which branch to checkout for each checkpoint we encounter. The *7 Minute Workout* code is available inside repository folder, trainer.

So let's get started!

Code organization

Since we are going to build a decent-size app in AngularJS, it becomes imperative that we define how the code will be structured. For obvious reasons, we cannot take the approach of putting everything into a single file as we did in the first chapter.

The basic folder structure for our web app will look like this:

The css, img, and js folders are self-explanatory. The partials folder will contain HTML views that we will use in the app. The index.html file is the start page for the app. Go ahead and create this folder hierarchy for the app.

Let's now understand how we should organize our JavaScript code.

Organizing the JavaScript code

To effectively organize the script code for our app, we need to be aware of the different AngularJS constructs at our disposal. The following diagram highlights the top-level AngularJS constructs:

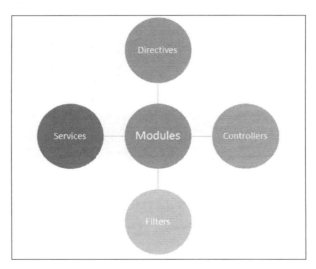

Everything in AngularJS can be categorized into four buckets namely: **controllers**, **directives**, **filters**, and **services**. These constructs are neatly organized using AngularJS modules. We have already talked about controllers and directives, the other two are services and filters.

Services are reusable pieces of code that can be shared across controllers, directives, filters, and services itself. Services are singleton in nature so they also provide a mechanism for sharing data across these constructs.

Filters are a simple concept. Filters in Angular are used to transform model data from one format to another. Filters are mostly used in combination with views. For example, Angular filters such as date and number are used to format date and numeric data that get rendered in the view.

This classification drives our code organization too. We need to organize our own code by segregating components into controllers, directives, filters, and services. Even after this grouping, what options do we have for organizing content at a file and folder level? There are different ways to organize our Angular code in files. The following screenshot depicts three such ways to organize any app code:

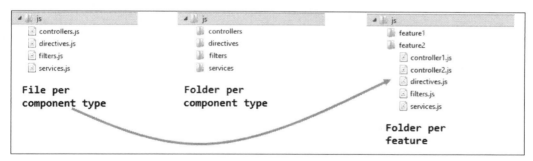

Here are the approaches in detail:

- **File per component**: In this approach, one file for each component type is created. All our controllers go in `controllers.js`, directives in `directives.js`, and so on. This approach works only for small applications where there are a handful of controllers, directives, services, and filters. However, for any decent-size application, maintaining this structure becomes unfeasible.

- **Folder per component**: In this approach, one folder for each component type is created. Here controllers, directives, filters, and services have designated folders. This approach, though far superior to the first approach, has its challenges. Navigating a codebase can become cumbersome as the size of the project grows. Imagine navigating through tens of controllers or services to find a relevant piece of code. Still, this organization can work well with small projects.

- **Folder per feature**: This is a hybrid approach that derives from the first two code organization approaches. In this case, we divide our JavaScript code based on major functional areas or app features. The granularity of these functional areas can vary based on the size of the project and how modular the functional area is. For example, for a **Human Resource (HR)** product, some of the functional areas could be Employees, Timesheet, Attendance, Payroll, and Employee On-Boarding. The advantages of this approach are self-evident. The code becomes more organized, easy to navigate and manageable. Quite frequently, developers or development teams work on specific features and all their activities are limited to a specific feature. The folder per feature organization is ideally suited for such a setup.

> Even while using the third approach, we can have common directives, services, and filters that can potentially be used across features. Common reusable code can be organized in some kind of common folder.
>
> Also keep in mind that this separation of code is logical; we can still access components across the feature set.

For our *7 Minute Workout* app, we are going to take the third approach. This might be too much for this size of app, but it will keep the code well organized. So the folder hierarchy of our JavaScript will look like this:

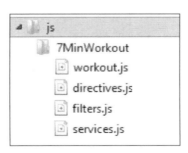

You might have noticed that there is no `controllers.js` file; instead there is a file named `workout.js`. The `workout.js` file will contain the controller code. The convention we are going to follow is to use one controller file per page/view. A feature may have multiple pages/views and hence multiple controller files. Controller separation also makes sense due to the fact that controllers are tightly coupled with the view whereas directives, filters, and services are shared.

There is currently only one major feature/functional area for our app and we will name it 7MinWorkout. In later chapters, as we extend this app, we will add more subfolders (functional areas) to the root `js` folder for all the new features we add. Go ahead and create the `js` and `7MinWorkout` folders if you have not done so already.

 It is recommended that you use at least one development server to run and test your app code.

With the folder structure in place, we can now start designing the app. The first thing that requires our focus is the app model.

The 7 Minute Workout model

Designing the model for this app will require us to first detail the functional aspects of the *7 Minute Workout* app and then derive a model that can satisfy those requirements. Based on the problem statement defined earlier, some of the obvious requirements are:

- Being able to start the workout.
- Providing a visual clue about the current exercise and its progress. This includes:
  - Providing screenshots of the current exercise
  - Providing step-by-step instructions to the user on how to do a specific exercise
  - The time left for the current exercise
- Notifying the user when the workout is completed.

Some valuable requirements that we will add to this app are:

- The ability to pause the current workout.
- Providing information about the next exercise to follow.
- Providing audio clues so that the user can perform the workout without constantly looking at the screen. This includes:
  - A timer click sound
  - Details about the next exercise
  - Signaling that the exercise is about to start
- Showing related videos for the exercise in progress, and the ability to play them.

As we can see, the central theme for this app is workout and exercise. Here, a workout is a set of exercises performed in a specific order for a particular duration. So let's go ahead and define the model for our workout and exercise.

Based on the requirements just mentioned, we will need the following details about an exercise:

- **Name**: This should be unique
- **Title**: This is shown to the user
- A description of the exercise
- Instructions on how to perform the exercise
- Images for the exercise
- The name of the audio clip for the exercise
- Related videos

Based on the preceding description, the exercise model will look something like this:

```
function Exercise(args) {
    this.name = args.name;
    this.title = args.title;
    this.description = args.description;
    this.image = args.image;
    this.related = {};
    this.related.videos = args.videos;
    this.nameSound = args.nameSound;
    this.procedure=args.procedure;
}
```

We use a JavaScript constructor function to define our model class. The `args` parameter can be used to pass initial data when creating new objects for `Exercise`.

For the workout, we need to track:

- **Name**: This should be unique
- **Title**: This is shown to the user
- Exercises that are part of the workout
- The duration for each exercise
- The rest duration between two exercises

So the model class looks like this:

```
function WorkoutPlan(args) {
    this.exercises = [];
    this.name = args.name;
    this.title = args.title;
    this.restBetweenExercise = args.restBetweenExercise;
};
```

The `exercises` array will contain objects in the format `{exercise: new Exercise({}), duration:30}`.

For our *7 Minute Workout* app, we can work without the `WorkoutPlan` model class, but I have jumped ahead as this workout model will come in handy when we extend this sample in the future.

These two classes constitute our model, and we will decide in the future if we need to extend this model as we start implementing the app functionality.

JavaScript does not have the concept of a class. We are simulating class-like usage using the constructor function.

We need to place the preceding model declarations somewhere and the controller seems to be a good fit for it. As we did in *Chapter 1, Getting Started*, we are going to build an AngularJS module to host the controller and model-specific code.

Adding app modules

We touched upon modules in brief in the last chapter. Modules are containers for components that are part of the framework and for components that we create. Modules allow logical separation of components and also permit them to reference each other.

For our *7 Minute Workout* app, all the controllers, directives, services, and filters that we create will be partitioned into multiple AngularJS modules.

To start with, we will add a root module for our app. As a convention, we add all our module declarations in a separate file app.js, which is created in the app's js folder. We make use of the AngularJS Module API to create a new module. Let's add the app.js file in the js folder and add this line at the top:

```
angular.module('app', []);
```

The previous statement creates a module named app (first argument). The second argument is an array of other module dependencies that the app module has. This is empty for the moment as we are only dependent on the framework module. We will talk about dependencies later in this chapter when we discuss the **dependency injection (DI)** framework of AngularJS.

We treat our *7 Minute Workout* app as a feature and hence we will add a module for that too. In the same app.js file, add another module declaration, as follows:

```
angular.module('7minWorkout', []);
```

It's time now to add the controller.

The app controller

To implement the controller, we need to outline the behavior of the application. What we are going to do in *7 Minute Workout* app is:

1. Start the workout.
2. Show the workout in progress and show the progress indicator.
3. After the time elapses for an exercise, show the next exercise.
4. Repeat this process till all exercises are over.

This gives us a fair idea about the controller behavior, so let's start with the implementation.

Add a new JavaScript file workout.js to the 7MinWorkout folder. All code detailed in the line later goes into this file until stated otherwise.

We are going to use the Module API to declare our controller and this is how it looks:

```
angular.module('7minWorkout').controller('WorkoutController',
    function($scope){
});
```

Here, we retrieve the 7minWorkout module that we created earlier in app.js (see the *Adding app modules* section) using the angular.module('7minWorkout') method and then we call the controller method on the module to register our 7minWorkout controller.

The controller method takes two arguments, first being the controller name and the second a constructor function for the controller. We will add our implementation in this function.

> Make a note of the subtleties between creating a module and getting a module.
>
> The following is the code to create a new module:
>
> ```
> angular.module('7minWorkout', []); // creates a new
> module
> ```
>
> This is how you get an existing module:
>
> ```
> angular.module('7minWorkout'); //get an existing module
> ```
>
> The difference is just the extra parameter []. If we use the first syntax multiple times for the same module, it will create the module again and override all existing module dependencies that we may have already configured. This may result in errors like this:
>
> ```
> Argument 'ControllerName' is not a function, got
> undefined.
> ```

The function declaration for the preceding controller takes an argument $scope. When the controller is instantiated, AngularJS injects a scope object into this argument. The mechanism that AngularJS uses to achieve this is the topic of our next discussion.

Dependency injection

Modules provide a way to organize code and act as containers for most of the AngularJS constructs such as controllers, services, directives, and filters. In spite of this segregation, these constructs might make them depend on each other, either inside the same module or across modules.

AngularJS provides a mechanism to manage dependencies between AngularJS constructs in a declarative manner using **dependency injection (DI)**. The DI pattern is popular in many programming languages as DI allows us to manage dependencies between components in a loosely coupled manner. With such a framework in place, dependent objects are managed by a DI container. This makes dependencies swappable and the overall code more decoupled and testable.

Dependency Injection 101

The idea behind DI is that an object does not create/manage its own dependencies; instead the dependencies are provided from the outside. These dependencies are made available either through a constructor, called constructor injection (as with Angular), or by directly setting the object properties, called **property injection**.

Here is a rudimentary example of DI in action. Consider a class Component that requires a Logger object for some logging operation.

```
function Component() {
  var logger = new Logger(); //Logger is now ready to be used.
}
```

The dependency of the Logger class is hardwired inside the component. What if we externalize this dependency? So the class becomes:

```
function Component(l) {
  var logger=l;
}
```

This innocuous-looking change has a major impact. By adding the ability to provide the dependency from an external source, we now have the capability to alter the logging behavior of the Component class without touching it. For example, we have the following lines of code:

```
var c1WithDBLog=new Component(new DBLogger());
var c1WithFileLog=new Component(new FileLogger());
```

We create two Component objects with different logging capabilities without altering the Component class implementation. The c1WithDBLog object logs to a DB and c1WithFileLog to a file (assuming both DBLogger and FileLogger are derived from the Logger class). We can now understand how powerful DI is, in allowing us to change the behavior of a component just by manipulating its dependencies.

Once DI is in place, the responsibility for resolving the dependencies falls on the calling code or client/consumer code that wants to use the Component class.

To make this process less cumbersome for the calling code, we have DI containers/ frameworks. These containers are responsible for constructing the dependencies and providing them to our client/consumer code. The AngularJS DI framework does the same for our controllers, directives, filters, and services.

Dependency injection in Angular

We have already seen an example of DI where the `$scope` object is magically injected into the controller function:

```
angular.module('7minWorkout').controller('WorkoutController',
    function($scope){
```

Here, we instruct AngularJS that whenever it instantiates the controller, it should inject the scope that was created as part of the `ng-controller` directive declaration. The preceding line is an implicit DI. As AngularJS is creating the controller and injecting the dependency, everything is transparent to us. We just use the injected dependencies.

To resolve dependencies, AngularJS uses name matching. For each dependency (a parameter such as `$scope`) defined on the function, Angular tries to locate the dependency from a list of components that have already been registered.

 We register our components using the Module API. The registration of the controller in the previous code is a good example of the DI registration.

This search is done based on the name of the parameter. In the preceding controller function declaration, we need to provide the `$scope` string verbatim for DI to work. We can try this out by changing the function parameter `$scope` in `function($scope)` to `$scope1` and refreshing the browser. The developer console will show the following error:

Error: [$injector:unpr] Unknown provider: $scope1Provider <- $scope1

The approach of using names for dependency resolution has its downsides. One of them is that the previous code breaks when minified.

Handling minification

Minification in JavaScript is the process of removing extra characters for the source code with the aim to reduce the overall size of the codebase. This can lead to the removal of whitespaces/comments, shortening functions/variables, and other such changes. There is a plethora of tools available across all development platforms to minify script files.

A minifier will minify the input parameter names, rendering the AngularJS DI framework useless. Also, since most of the JavaScript code that we use in our production environment is minified, the preceding syntax for injecting dependencies is not very popular. This requires us to explore some other options/syntaxes for injection dependencies.

Dependency annotations

There are two other ways to declare dependencies so that DI does not break after minification.

- **The $inject annotation**: When using the controller function, we can use the `$inject` annotation in the following way:

```
function WorkoutController($scope) {
// Controller implementation
}
WorkoutController['$inject']  =  ['$scope'];
angular.module('app')
.controller('WorkoutController', WorkoutController);
```

We added a static property `$inject` to the constructor function `WorkoutController`. This property points to an array that contains all the dependencies annotated as string values. In our case, there is only one `$scope` object. Note that the dependencies are injected in the controller function based on the order they are declared within `$inject` array.

- **The inline annotation**: An alternate way of dependency declaration is to use inline annotations in the following way:

```
angular.module('7minWorkout')
  .controller('WorkoutController',
    ['$scope', function($scope) {
    }]);
```

The second argument to the controller function is now an array instead of a function. This array contains a list of dependencies annotated using string literals. The last element in the array is the actual controller function (`function($scope)`) with the injected dependencies. Like the `$inject` injection, this too happens based on the annotation order.

Both `$inject` and inline annotations are a bit verbose and at times are prone to mistakes. Be careful and always make sure that the order of annotations matches the order of parameter declaration when used with any Angular construct.

If, on the NodeJS platform, we can use tools such as ng-annotate
(https://github.com/olov/ng-annotate), allowing us to convert
the standard declaration syntax to an inline annotation format. The tool
takes the following code:

```
.controller('WorkoutController', function($scope){
```

Then, it is changed to the following:

```
.controller('WorkoutController', ['$scope',
    function($scope) {
```

Once ng-annotate is plugged into a build system, this process
can be automated allowing us to use the less verbose syntax during
development.

Henceforth, we will be using the inline annotation to declare our controller,
therefore let's change our existing controller declaration inside workout.js
to the previous format.

With this, we have covered the basics of DI in AngularJS. As we build our app, we
will be adding multiple controllers, services, and filters and will use the AngularJS
DI framework to wire them together. For now, let's continue our implementation
of the controller.

Controller implementations

Inside the controller function (function($scope) {), add the declaration for the
model classes (WorkoutPlan and Exercise) that we detailed in *The 7 Minute
Workout model* section.

Then, add declarations of two local variables, as follows:

```
var restExercise;
var workoutPlan;
```

We will see later what they are used for.

Now add some initialization code such as this:

```
var init = function () {
startWorkout();
};
init();
```

We declare the init method and immediately call it. This is just a convention that we will use to signify where the controller execution starts. Inside the init method, we call the startWorkout method that will start the workout. Let's see how to implement this method.

 For all the controller code shared in the following lines, keep adding it inside the controller function before the init method declaration.

The startWorkout method should load the workout data and start the first exercise. The overall method implementation looks like this:

```
var startWorkout = function () {
    workoutPlan = createWorkout();
    restExercise = {
        details: new Exercise({
            name: "rest",
            title: " Relax!",
            description: " Relax a bit!",
          image: "img/rest.png",

        }),
        duration: workoutPlan.restBetweenExercise
    };
    startExercise(workoutPlan.exercises.shift());
};
```

We start by calling the createWorkout() function that loads the overall workout plan. Then, we create a new restExercise exercise object that is not part of the original workout plan to signify the rest period between two exercises. By treating the rest period also as an exercise, we can have uniformity in implementation where we don't have to differentiate between a rest period and an exercise in progress.

The last line starts the first exercise by calling the startExercise method with a parameter signifying the exercise is to start. While doing so, we remove the first exercise from the exercises array and pass it to the function.

We are still missing implementation details for the two functions that are called in the startWorkout function namely: createWorkout and startExercise.

The call to the `createWorkout` method sets up the initial *7 Minute Workout* data. In this function, we first create a `WorkoutPlan` object and then push exercise-related data into its exercises array. The method looks something like this:

```
var createWorkout = function () {
    var workout = new WorkoutPlan({
        name: "7minWorkout",
        title: "7 Minute Workout",
        restBetweenExercise: 10
    });

    workout.exercises.push({
        details: new Exercise({
            name: "jumpingJacks",
            title: "Jumping Jacks",
            description: "Jumping Jacks.",
            image: "img/JumpingJacks.png",
            videos: [],
            variations: [],
            procedure: ""
        }),
        duration: 30
    });
    // (TRUNCATED) Other 11 workout exercise data.
    return workout;
}
```

Exercise data has been truncated in the preceding code. The complete exercise data is available with the companion code in the `checkpoint1` folder under `chapter2`. Copy that data and use it.

GitHub branch: checkpoint2.1 (folder – trainer)

Make note that we are not adding the `Exercise` object directly to the `exercises` array, but a custom object with one property called `details` and the other named `duration`.

The other function `startExercise` looks like this:

```
var startExercise = function (exercisePlan) {
    $scope.currentExercise = exercisePlan;
    $scope.currentExerciseDuration = 0;
    $interval(function () {
```

```
                        ++$scope.currentExerciseDuration;
              }
    , 1000
    , $scope.currentExercise.duration);
    };
```

 Before we discuss the working of the `startExercise` function, there is an important aspect of AngularJS development that we should keep in mind: minimize the number of properties and functions that are attached to the $scope object.

Only properties and functions that are required to be referenced in the view should be attached to the scope object. We have tried to adhere to this principle in our controller implementation too. All the three functions that we have declared previously (`startWorkout`, `createWorkout`, and `startExercise` respectively) are not added to the `$scope` object; instead they are declared as normal functions within the controller.

Coming back to the `startExercise` implementation, let's try to understand what this function is doing.

We start by initializing `currentExercise` and `currentExerciseDuration` on the scope. The `currentExercise` function will track the exercise in progress and `currentExerciseDuration` will track its duration.

To track the progress of the current exercise, we use the `$interval` service of AngularJS.

Tracking the duration of an exercise using the $interval service

The `$interval` service is a wrapper over the `window.setInterval` method. The primary purpose of this service is to call a specific function continuously, at specific intervals.

While invoking `$interval`, we set up a callback function (the first argument) that gets invoked at specific intervals (the second argument) for a specific number of times (the third argument). In our case, we set up an anonymous function that decrements the `currentExerciseDuration` property after every one second (1000 ms) for the number of times defined in `currentExercise.duration` (configured to 30 in each exercise).

Remember that, if we do not provide the third argument to the
$interval service, the callback method will be repeatedly invoked
and the process can only be stopped explicitly by calling the cancel
function of $interval.

We have now used our first AngularJS service $interval. Additionally, as explained
in the Dependency injection section, this service needs to be injected in the controller
before we can use it. So let's do it by changing the controller definition to the following:

```
angular.module('7minWorkout')
    .controller('WorkoutController', ['$scope', '$interval',
        function ($scope, $interval) {
```

Well, injecting dependency was easy!

All names starting with $ such as $scope and $interval are constructs
exposed by the framework. Using this convention, we can distinguish
between dependencies that are provided by the framework and any
custom dependencies that we use or create.

As a good practice, we should not use the $ prefix in any of our service
names.

Time to check how things are looking! We are going to create a makeshift HTML
view and test out our implementation.

Verifying the implementation

The code that we have implemented until now is available in the companion source
code provided with this book. We will use the code located in the checkpoint1
folder under chapter2.

If you have been developing along with the text, your code should be in
sync with the checkpoint1 folder code for these files:

- app.js under the js folder
- workout.js under js/7minworkout

If it is not, update your code. Once the JavaScript files match, you can
copy the index.html file from the app folder under checkpoint1
into your app folder.

GitHub branch: checkpoint2.1 (folder – trainer)

Copy the `index.html` file from the source code package and paste it inside the app folder.

Before we run the `index.html` page, let's inspect the file and see what is in there. Other than the boilerplate HTML stuff, the reference to CSS at the start, the reference to script files at the end, and navbar HTML, there are only a few lines of interest.

```
<body ng-app="app" ng-controller="WorkoutController">
    <pre>Current Exercise: {{currentExercise | json}}</pre>
    <pre>Time Left: {{currentExercise.duration-
        currentExerciseDuration}}</pre>
```

In the preceding code, we use the interpolations to show the current exercise model data (`currentExercise`) and the time left for the exercise (`currentExercise.duration-currentExerciseDuration`). The pipe symbol | followed by `json` is an Angular filter used to format the view data. We will cover filters later in the chapter. Open the `index.html` file in your browser.

It did not work! Instead, interpolation characters are displayed as it is. If we inspect the browser console log (*F12*), there is an error (if you don't see it, refresh the page after you open the browser console). The error message is as follows:

Error: [ng:areq] Argument 'WorkoutController' is not a function, got undefined

What happened? Firstly, we need to verify that our root module `app` loaded correctly and is linked to the view. This link between our root module (`angular.module('app', []);`) and view is established using the attribute `ng-app="app"` defined on the HTML `<body>` tag. Since the match is done based on the module name, the two declarations should match. In our case they do, so this is not the problem and the root module loads perfectly. So what is the issue?

The error message says that Angular is not able to locate the `WorkoutController` function. If we go back to the controller declaration, we find this:

```
angular.module('7minWorkout')
  .controller('WorkoutController', ['$scope', '$interval',
    function ($scope, $interval) {
```

The controller here is declared in a module `7minWorkout` and not in the root module `app`. Because of this, the DI framework is not able to locate the controller definition as the containers are different. To fix this issue, we need to add a module level dependency between our app's root module `app` and the `7minWorkout` module. We do this by updating the module declaration of `app` (in `app.js`) to this:

```
angular.module('app', ['7minWorkout']);
```

In the updated module declaration now, we provide the dependencies in the second array argument. In this case, there is only one dependency—the `7minWorkout` module. Refresh the page after this change and you will see the raw model data as demonstrated in the following screenshot:

```
Current Exercise: {
  "details": {
    "name": "jumpingJacks",
    "title": "Jumping Jacks",
    "description": "A jumping jack or star jump,
    "image": "img/JumpingJacks.png",
    "related": {
      "videos": [
        "//www.youtube.com/embed/dmYwZH_BNd0",
        "//www.youtube.com/embed/BABOdJ-2Z6o",
        "//www.youtube.com/embed/c4DAnQ6DtF8"
      ]
    },
    "procedure": "Assume an erect position, with
                        While in air, bring your
ise your arms up over your head; arms should be s
meet above your head with arms slightly bent"
  },
  "duration": 30
}
```

```
Time Left: 15
```

The model data will update after every passing second! Now we can understand why interpolations are a great debugging tool.

We are not done yet! Wait for long enough on the `index.html` page, and you will realize that the timer stops after 30 seconds and the app does not load the next exercise data. Time to fix it!

Implementing exercise transitions

We still need to implement the logic of transition to the next exercise. Also remember we need to add a rest period between every exercise. We are going to implement a `getNextExercise` function to determine the next exercise to transition to. Here is how the function looks:

```
var getNextExercise = function (currentExercisePlan) {
    var nextExercise = null;
    if (currentExercisePlan === restExercise) {
        nextExercise = workoutPlan.exercises.shift();
    } else {
        if (workoutPlan.exercises.length != 0) {
            nextExercise = restExercise;
        }
    }
    return nextExercise;
};
```

Since we are flipping between resting and exercising, this piece of code does the same. It takes the current exercise in progress and determines what the next exercise should be. If the current exercise is `restExercise` (remember we declared it in `startExercise`), it then pulls the next exercise from the workout exercise array; if not, it then returns `restExercise`. Then checking if (`workoutPlan.exercises. length != 0`) ensures that we do not return any exercise (not even `restExercise`) after the last exercise in the workout is complete. After this, the workout completes its perpetual rest!

Now somebody needs to call this method to get the next exercise and update the `currentExercise` model property. We can achieve this in two ways and the interesting thing is that I will have to introduce two new concepts for this. Let's start with the first approach that we are not going to take eventually but that still highlights an important feature of AngularJS.

Using $watch to watch the models changes

To make a transition to the next exercise, we need a way to monitor the value of `currentExerciseDuration`. Once this value reaches the planned exercise duration, transition to the next exercise is required.

Working through the two app samples we know that AngularJS is capable of updating the view when the model changes using the data binding infrastructure. The nice thing about the framework is that this change tracking feature can be utilized in JavaScript code too!

Exploring $watch

The model tracking infrastructure of Angular is exposed over the `$scope` object. Till now, we have used the scope object just to manage our model properties and nothing else. But this scope object has much more to offer via the scope API functions. One of the functions it provides is `$watch`. This function allows us to register a listener that gets called when the scope property changes. The `$watch` method definition looks like this:

```
$scope.$watch(watchExpression, [listener], [objectEquality]);
```

The first parameter, `watchExpression`, can be either a string expression or a function. If the `watchExpression` value changes, the listener is invoked.

For a string expression, the expression is evaluated in the context of the current scope. This implies that the string expression that we provide should only contain properties/methods that are available on the current scope. If we pass a function as the first argument, AngularJS will call it at predefined times called digest cycles in the AngularJS world. We will learn about digest cycles in the following chapter.

The second parameter listener takes a function. This function is invoked with three parameters namely `newValue`, `oldValue`, and the current scope. This is where we write logic to respond to the changes.

The third parameter is a Boolean argument `objectEquality` that determines how the inequality or change is detected. To start with, Angular not only allows us to watch primitive types such as strings, numeric, Boolean, and dates, but also objects. When `objectEquality` is false, strict comparison is done using the `!==` operator. For objects, this boils down to just reference matching.

However, when `objectEquality` is set to true, AngularJS uses an `angular.equals` framework function to compare the old and new values. The documentation for this method at `https://docs.angularjs.org/api/ng/function/angular.equals` provides details on how the equality is established.

To understand how objects are compared for inequality, it is best to look at some examples.

This gives a watch expression:

```
$scope.$watch('obj',function(n,o){console.log('Data changed!');});
```

These changes to `$scope.obj` will trigger the watch listener:

```
$scope.obj={};  // Logs 'Data changed!'
$scope.obj=obj1; // Logs 'Data changed!'
$scope.obj=null; // Logs 'Data changed!'
```

Whereas these will not:

```
$scope.obj.prop1=value; // Does not log 'Data changed!'
$scope.obj.prop2={}; // Does not log 'Data changed!'
$scope.obj=$scope.obj; // Does not log 'Data changed!'
```

In the preceding scenarios, the framework is not tracking internal object changes.

Instead, let's set the third parameter to `true`:

```
$scope.$watch('obj', function(n,o){console.log('Data
    changed!'},true);
```

All the previous changes will trigger the listener except the last one.

> I have created a jsFiddle link (`http://jsfiddle.net/cmyworld/WL3GT/`) to highlight the differences between the two approaches. jsFiddle uses two objects: `obj` and `obj1`. Also, since Angular change detection is not real-time but dependent upon digest cycle execution, I had to wrap model updates in the `$timeout` service that triggers a digest cycle when time lapses. `$timeout` like `$interval` is an Angular service that calls a function after a specific duration but only once.

If we watch an object with `objectEquality` set to true then keep in mind that the framework does not tell which property in the object has changed. To do this, we need to manually compare the new object (n) and the old object (o).

Do these watches affect performance? Yes, a little. To perform comparison between the new and old values of a model property, Angular needs to track the last value of the model. This extra bookkeeping comes at a cost and each `$watch` instance that we add or is added by the framework does have a small impact on the overall performance. Add to that the fact that, if `objectEquality` is set to `true`, Angular has to now keep a copy of complete objects for the purpose of detecting model changes. This might not be a problem for standard pages, but for large pages containing a multitude of data-bound elements the performance can get affected. Therefore, minimize the use of object equality and keep the number of view bindings under control.

Other than the $watch method that watches an expression on scope, AngularJS also supports watching a collection using the $watchCollection function. The function syntax is:

```
$watchCollection(expression, listener);
```

Here, an expression can be an object or array property on scope. For an object, the listener is fired whenever a new property is added or removed (remember JavaScript allows this). For an array, the listener is fired whenever elements are added, removed, and moved in the array. The listener callback function is called with three parameters:

- newCollection: This denotes new values of a collection.
- oldCollection: This denotes old values of a collection. The values are calculated only if we use this parameter.
- scope: This denotes the current scope object.

With this basic understanding of $watch in place, let's go ahead and add some controller logic.

Implementing transitions using $watch

In our Workout controller, we need to add a watch that tracks currentExerciseDuration. Add the following code to the WorkoutController function:

```
$scope.$watch('currentExerciseDuration', function (nVal) {
    if (nVal == $scope.currentExercise.duration) {
        var next = getNextExercise($scope.currentExercise);
        if (next) {
            startExercise(next);
        } else {
            console.log("Workout complete!")
        }
    }
});
```

We add a watch on currentExerciseDuration and whenever it approaches the total duration of the current exercise (if (nVal == $scope.currentExercise. duration)), we retrieve the next exercise by calling the getNextExercise function and then start that exercise. If the next exercise retrieved is null, then the workout is complete.

With this, we are ready to test our implementation. So, go ahead and refresh the index. Exercises should flip after every 10 or 30 seconds. Great!

But, as we decided earlier, we are not going to use the $watch approach. There is a slightly better way to transition to the next exercise where we do not require setting up any watch. We will be using the AngularJS Promise API to do it.

Using the AngularJS Promise API for exercise transitions

The concept of promise is not unique to AngularJS. Promise specifications have been implemented by multiple JavaScript libraries. AngularJS uses one such implementation that is inspired by Kris Kowal's Q (https://github.com/kriskowal/q). AngularJS exposes the implementation over the $q service that allows us to create and interact with promises. However, the question is what a promise is and why do we require it?

The basics of promises

Browsers execute our JavaScript code on a single thread. This implies that we cannot have any blocking operation as it will freeze the browser and hence counts as a bad user experience. Due to this reason, a number of JavaScript API functions such as functions related to timing events (setTimeout and setInterval) and network operations (XMLHttpRequest) are asynchronous in nature. This asynchronous behavior requires us to use callbacks for every asynchronous call made. Most of us have used the ajax() API of jQuery and provided a function callback for a complete/success variable in the config object.

The problem with callbacks is that they can easily become unmanageable. To understand this, let's look at this example from the Q documentation:

```
step1(function (value1) {
    step2(value1, function(value2) {
        step3(value2, function(value3) {
            step4(value3, function(value4) {
                // Do something with value4
            });
        });
    });
});
```

With a promise library, callbacks such as the one just mentioned can be converted into:

```
Q.fcall(promisedStep1)
.then(promisedStep2)
.then(promisedStep3)
.then(promisedStep4)
.then(function (value4) {
    // Do something with value4
})
.catch(function (error) {
    // Handle any error from all above steps
})
.done();
```

The power of chaining instead of nesting allows us to keep code more organized.

Technically speaking, a promise is an object that provides a value or exception in the future for an operation that it wraps. The Promise API is used to wrap execution of an asynchronous method. A promise-based asynchronous function hence does not take callbacks but instead returns a promise object. This promise object gets resolved some time in the future when the data or error from the asynchronous operation is received.

To consume a promise, the promise API in AngularJS exposes three methods:

- `then(successCallback, errorCallback, notifyCallback)`: This registers callbacks for success, failure, and notification. The following are the parameters:

    ◦ `successCallback`: This is called when the promise is resolved successfully. The callback function is invoked with the resolved value.

    ◦ `errorCallback`: This is called when the promise results in an error and contains the reason for the error.

    ◦ `notifyCallback`: This is called to report the progress of a promise. This is useful for long-running asynchronous methods that can communicate their execution progress.

- `catch(errorCallback)`: This is shorthand for `then(null, errorCallback)`.

- `finally(callback)`: This gets called irrespective of a promise resulting in success or failure.

Chaining of promises is possible because the `then` method itself returns a promise.

We will learn more about promises and how to implement our own promises in the coming chapters. Nonetheless, for now we just need to consume a promise returned by an `$interval` service.

The `$interval` service that we used to decrement the time duration of exercises (`currentExerciseDuration`) itself returns a promise as shown:

```
$interval(function () {
        $scope.currentExerciseDuration =
        $scope.currentExerciseDuration + 1;
    }, 1000, $scope.currentExercise.duration);
```

This promise is resolved after the `$interval` service invokes the callback method (the first argument) for `$scope.currentExercise.duration` (the third argument) and in our case, 30 times is the value for a normal exercise. Therefore, we can use the `then` method of the Promise API to invoke our exercise transition logic in the promise success callback parameter. Here is the updated `startExercise` method with promise implementation highlighted:

```
var startExercise = function (exercisePlan) {
        $scope.currentExercise = exercisePlan;
        $scope.currentExerciseDuration = 0;
        $interval(function () {
            ++$scope.currentExerciseDuration;
        }, 1000, $scope.currentExercise.duration)
        .then(function () {
            var next = getNextExercise(exercisePlan);
            if (next) {
                startExercise(next);
            } else {
                console.log("Workout complete!")
            }
        });
    };
```

The code inside the `then` callback function is the same code that we added when using the $watch-based approach in the last section. Comment the existing `$watch` code and run the app again. We should get the same results. We did it without setting up any watch for the exercise transition.

If you are having a problem with running the code, a work copy is available in `chapter2\checkpoint2` for you to try.
GitHub branch: checkpoint2.2

We have done enough work on the controller for now. If everything is set up correctly, our view should transition between exercises during the workout. Let's concentrate our efforts on the view.

The 7 Minute Workout view

Most of the hard work has already been done while the defining the model and implementing the controller phase. Now we just need to skin the HTML using the super-awesome data binding capabilities of AngularJS. It's going to be simple, sweet, and elegant!

For the *7 Minute Workout* view, we need to show the exercise name, exercise image, a progress indicator, and time remaining. Add the following lines to `index.html` inside the container `div`.

```
<div class="container body-content app-container">
  <div class="row">
    <div id="exercise-pane" class="col-sm-8 col-sm-offset-2">
      <div class="row workout-content">
        <div class="workout-display-div">
          <h1>{{currentExercise.details.title}}</h1>
          <img class="img-responsive"
            ng-src="{{currentExercise.details.image}}" />
          <div class="progress time-progress">
          <div class="progress-bar" role="progressbar"
            aria-valuenow="0" aria-valuemin="0" aria-valuemax=
            "{{currentExercise.duration}}" ng-style="{'width'
            :(currentExerciseDuration/currentExercise.duration)
            * 100 + '%'}">
          </div>
        </div>
        <h1>Time Remaining: {{
          currentExercise.duration-currentExerciseDuration}}</h1>
      </div>
    </div>
  </div>
</div>
</div>
```

There is some styling done using bootstrap CSS and some custom CSS. Other than that we have highlighted the directives and interpolations that are part of the view. Save `index.html` but before we refresh the page, open the companion source code package folder `checkpoint3` under `chapter2`. Make sure your copy of `css\app.css` and `img` folder match. Refresh the page and see the workout app in its full glory!

 In case, your app does not work, you can take the source code from `chapter2\checkpoint3` and run it, or compare what is missing in your own implementation.

GitHub branch: checkpoint2.3

That was pretty impressive. Again very little code was required to achieve so much. Let's see how this view works and what new elements have been incorporated in our view.

We can see that the workout view is driven by a model and the view itself has very little behavior. Since we have used two new directives `ng-src` and `ng-style`, let's discuss them.

Image path binding with ng-src

The image location comes from the exercise model. We use the exercise image path (`currentExercise.details.image`) to bind to the `img` tag using the `ng-src` directive. However, why do we need this directive? We could very well use the `src` attribute of the standard HTML for the img tag instead of `ng-src`:

```
<img class="img-responsive" src =
  "{{currentExercise.details.image}}" />
```

And it still works! Except for one small problem! Remember, Angular takes the template HTML and then applies the scope object to activate the binding. Till Angular completes this process and updates the DOM, the browser continues to render the raw template HTML. In the raw template, the previous `src` attribute points to the `{{currentExercise.details.image}}` string and since it is an `<img>` tag, the browser makes a GET request to this URL literally, which results in a 404 error as seen in the screenshot. We can confirm this in the browser's consoles network log.

When we use `ng-src`, the framework delays the evaluation of the `src` attribute till the model data is available and hence none of the request fails. Therefore, it is always advisable to use `ng-src` with the `<img>` tag if the URL is dynamic and depends upon the model data.

The other directive `ng-style` is used for progress bar style manipulation.

Using ng-style with the Bootstrap progress bar

We use the Bootstrap progress bar (`http://getbootstrap.com/components/#progress`) to provide visual clues about the exercise progress. The progress effect is achieved by changing the CSS `width` property of the progress bar like this: `style="width: 60%;"`. AngularJS has a directive to manipulate the style of any HTML element and the directive is aptly named `ng-style`.

The `ng-style` directive takes an expression that should evaluate to an object, where the key is the CSS style name and the value is the value assigned to the style. For our progress bar, we use this expression:

```
"{'width':(currentExerciseDuration/currentExercise.duration)
    * 100 + '%'}"
```

The `width` CSS property is set to the percentage time elapsed and converted into a string value by concatenating it with `%`.

 Note that we use the object notation ({ }) and not the interpolation notation ({{ }}) in the previous expression.

Remember we can achieve the same effect by using the standard style attribute and interpolation.

```
"{{'width:' + (currentExerciseDuration/currentExercise.duration)
    * 100 + '%'}}"
```

Nevertheless, `ng-style` helps us with its intuitive syntax and if the number of styles to apply is more, the expression used in interpolation can become complex with lots of string concatenation involved.

The `ng-style` directive is a very powerful directive as it allows us to do all types of CSS manipulation and drive them through model changes, as we saw with the progress bar implementation. We should still minimize its usage as inline styling is frowned upon and less maintainable in the long run.

The preferred way to style HTML elements is by using a class attribute. Additionally, if we need dynamic behavior while applying CSS classes, AngularJS has another supporting directive ng-class. In the coming chapters, we will see how to use this directive to dynamically alter page element styles.

The basic *7 Minute Workout* is now complete, so let's start doing a workout now!

We will now add some bells and whistles to the app to make it look more professional and in the process discover a little more about the framework.

Adding start and finish pages

The *7 Minute Workout* app starts when we load the page but it ends with the last exercise sticking to the screen permanently. Not a very elegant solution. Why don't we add a start and finish page to the app? This will make the app more professional and allow us to understand the single page nomenclature of AngularJS.

Understanding SPAs

Single page applications (**SPAs**) are browser-based apps devoid of any full page refresh. In such apps, once the initial HTML is loaded, any future page navigations are retrieved using AJAX as HTML fragments and injected into the already loaded view. Google Mail is a great example of a SPA. SPAs supply a great user experience as the user gets what resembles a desktop app, with no constant post-backs and page refreshes that are typically associated with traditional web apps.

One of the primary intentions of AngularJS was to make SPA development easy. Therefore, it contains a host of features to support the SPA development. Let's explore them and add our app pages too.

View layouts for SPAs using ng-view

To use the SPA capabilities of the framework, the view HTML needs to be augmented with some new constructs. Let's alter the index.html file and make it ready for use as a SPA view template. Add this piece of HTML inside the <body> tag, after the navbar declaration:

```
<div class="container body-content app-container">
        <div ng-view></div>
</div>
```

In the preceding HTML, we are setting up a nested `div` structure. The inner `div` has a new directive declaration, `ng-view`. The immediate question is, what does this directive do?

Well, HTML elements with this `ng-view` directive act as a container that hosts partial HTML templates received from the server. In our case, the content of the start, workout, and finish pages will be added as inner HTML to this `div`. This will happen when we navigate across these three pages.

For the framework to know which template to load at what time (inside the `ng-view` `div` element), it works with an Angular service named `$route`. This `$route` service is responsible for providing routing and deep-linking capabilities in AngularJS.

However, before we can use the `$route` service, we need to configure it. Let's try to configure the service to make things clearer.

Defining 7 Minute Workout routes

The standard Angular `$route` service is not part of the core Angular module but defined in another module `ngRoute`. Hence, we need to import it in a similar manner to the way we imported the `7minWorkout` module. So go ahead and update the `app.js` file with the `ngRoute` module dependency.

```
angular.module('app', ['ngRoute', '7minWorkout']);
```

We will also need to reference the module's JavaScript file as it is not part of the standard framework file `angular.js`. Add reference to the `angular-route.js` file after the reference to `angular.js` in `index.html`.

```
<script src="http://ajax.googleapis.com/ajax/libs/angularjs/1.3.3/
  angular.js"></script>
<script src="http://ajax.googleapis.com/ajax/libs/angularjs/1.3.3/
  angular-route.js"></script>
```

The last part to configure is the actual routes. We need to configure the routes for each of the three pages. Once configured, the routing service will match routes and provide enough information to the `ng-view` directive to help it render the correct partial view.

In the AngularJS world, any configurations required before the app becomes usable are defined using the module API's `config` method. Components defined in any module can use this method's callback to do some type of initialization.

Load the `app.js` file and update the module declaration code for the app module to:

```
angular.module('app', ['ngRoute', '7minWorkout']).
config(function ($routeProvider) {
    $routeProvider.when('/start', {
        templateUrl: 'partials/start.html'
    });
    $routeProvider.when('/workout', {
        templateUrl: 'partials/workout.html',
        controller: 'WorkoutController'
    });
    $routeProvider.when('/finish', {
        templateUrl: 'partials/finish.html'
    });
    $routeProvider.otherwise({
        redirectTo: '/start'
    });
});
```

Before we discuss the preceding code, let's understand a bit more about module initialization and the role of the `config` function in it.

The config/run phase and module initialization

AngularJS does not have a single entry point where it can wire up the complete application. Instead, once the DOM is ready and the framework is loaded, it looks for the `ng-app` directive and starts module initialization. This module initialization process not only loads the module declared by `ng-app` but also all its dependent modules and any dependencies that the linked modules have, like a chain. Every module goes through two stages as it becomes available for consumption. It starts with:

- **config**: Services in modules that require initial setup are configured during this stage. `$routeProvider` is a good example of this. Every app will require a different set of routes before it can be used; therefore, these routes are configured at the config stage. Limited DI capabilities are available at this stage. We cannot inject services or filters as dependencies at the present time. `$routeProvider` injection works as it is a special class of services called providers. We will learn more about these special service classes such as providers, values, and constants in forth coming chapters.

- **run**: At this stage, the application is fully configured and ready to be used. The DI framework can be completely utilized at this stage. Similar to the `config` function, the Module API also provides a `run` method callback. We can use this method to initialize stuff that we need during application execution.

With this basic understanding of module initialization stages and the role of the config stage, let's get back to our route configuration code.

The `config` function just mentioned takes a callback function that gets called during the config stage. The function is called with the `$routeProvider` dependency. We define three main routes here and one fall back route using the `$routeProvider` API.

We call the `when` function of `$routeProvider` that takes two arguments:

- `path`: This is a bookmarkable URL to a partial view. In our code, the first `when` configures `/start` as a route and is accessible in the browser under the `http://<hostname>/index.html#/start` URL.

- `routeConfig`: This parameter takes route configurations. There are a number of configuration options available but we have just used two of them. `templateUrl` defines the remote path from where AngularJS will load the HTML template. The `controller` function defines the Angular controller that will be instantiated and attached to the HTML view when the browser hits this route. We are not attaching any controller to start and finish routes as they are mere static HTML content.

The other method `$routeProvider` is otherwise used for a wildcard route match. If the route does not match any of the routes defined (`/start`, `/workout`, and `/finish`), then, by default, it redirects the user to the `/start` route in the browser; in other words, it loads the start page. We can verify this by providing routes such as `http://<hostname>/index.html#/abc`.

The following screenshot tries to highlight what role the index.html, ng-view, and $route services play:

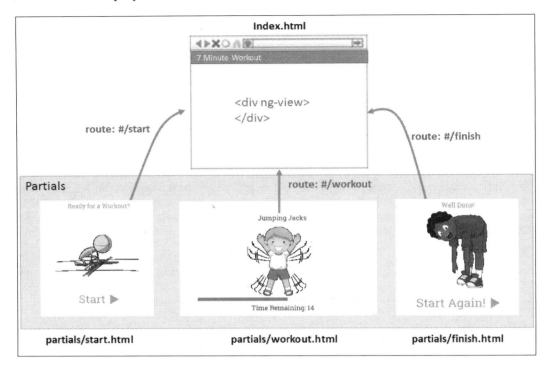

Since we have defined three partial HTML files in the route, it's time to add them to the partial folder. Copy the start.html and finish.html files from the chapter2/ checkpoint4/partials (*GitHub Branch: checkpoint2.4*) and create a new file, workout.html.

Move all the code in the div fragment <div class="row"> from index.html into workout.html. Also remove the ng-controller declaration from the body tag. The body tag should now read as follows:

```
<body ng-app="app">
```

The ng-controller declaration from the body tag should be removed as we have already directed Angular to inject the WorkoutController controller function when navigating to the #/workout route during our route configuration (see the preceding $routeProvider config route).

This is a common mistake that many newbies make. If we specify the controller to load in the `$routeProvider` configuration and also apply the `ng-controller` directive on the related template HTML. Angular will create two controllers and you may experience all types of weird behaviors such as duplicate method calls, Ajax calls, and others.

Go ahead and refresh the index page. If you have followed our guidance, you will land on the page with the URL such as `http://<hostname>/index.html#/start`. This is our apps start page. Click on the **Start** button and you will navigate to the workout page (`href='#/workout'`); the workout will start. To check how the finish page looks, you need to change the URL in the browser. Change the fragment after # character to `/finish`.

As of now, when the workout finishes, transitioning to the finish page does not happen. We have not implemented this transition. The navigation from the start page to workout was embedded in a tag (`href='#/workout'`). Transition to the finish page will be done inside the controller.

View navigation in the controller using $location

If you thought we would use the `$route` service for navigation in our controller, you are a tad wrong. The `$route` service (`https://docs.angularjs.org/api/ngRoute/service/$route`) has no method to change the current route. Nonetheless, the `$route` service has a dependency on another service, `$location`. We will use the `$location` service to transition to the finish page.

Here is how the AngularJS documentation (`https://docs.angularjs.org/api/ng/service/$location`) describes $location service:

> *The $location service parses the URL in the browser address bar (based on the window.location) and makes the URL available to your application. Changes to the URL in the address bar are reflected into $location service and changes to $location are reflected into the browser address bar.*

Open `workout.js` and replace the `console.log("Workout complete!")` line with this:

```
$location.path('/finish');
```

Make note of the difference in terms when referencing the paths. In the anchor (`<a>`) tag, we used `href='#/wokout'`, whereas we are not using the # symbol with the `$location.path` function.

As always, we should add the dependency of the `$location` service to `WorkoutController`, as follows:

```
angular.module('7minWorkout')
   .controller('WorkoutController', ['$scope', '$interval',
      '$location', function ($scope, $interval, $location) {
```

Since we have started our discussion on the `$location` service, let's explore the capabilities of the `$location` service in more depth.

Working with the $location service

The `$location` service is responsible for providing client-side navigation for our app. If routes are configured for an app, the location service intercepts the browser address changes, hence stopping browser postbacks/refreshes.

If we examine the browser addresses for these routes, they contain an extra # character and the address appears in the following manner:

`http://<hostname>/index.html#/start` (or **`#/workout`** or **`#/finish`**)

The # character in the URL is something we may have used to bookmark sections within the page, but the `$location` service is using this bookmark-type URL to provide correct route information. This is called the **hashbang** mode of addressing.

We can get rid of # if we enable HTML5 mode configuration. This setting change has to be done at the config stage using the `html5Mode` method of the `$locationProvider` API. Let's call this method inside the module `config` function:

```
$locationProvider.html5Mode(true);
```

The addresses will now look like:

```
http://<hostname>/start (or /workout or /finish)
```

However, there is a caveat. It only works as long as we don't refresh the page and we do not type in the address of our browser directly. To have a true URL, rewrite as shown in the preceding code. We need to add support for it on the server side too. Remember when we are refreshing the page, we are reloading the Angular app from the start too so URLs mentioned previously will give `404` errors as Angular `$location` cannot intercept page refreshes.

The $location service also enables us to extract and manipulate parts of address fragments. The following diagram describes the various fragments of an address and how to reference and manipulate them.

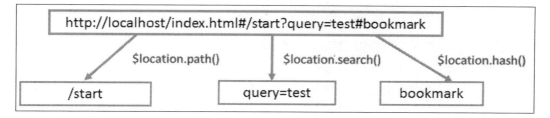

We have already made use of the path function to navigate to the finish page. That is pretty much all we'll say about the $location service for now.

At the end we have converted our simple *7 Minute Workout* into an SPA. Now we can see how easy it was to create an SPA using AngularJS. We get all the benefit of standard web apps: unique bookmarkable URLs for each view (page) and the ability to move back and forward using the browser's back and forward buttons but without those annoying page refreshes. If we show some patience after the last exercise completes, the finish page will indeed load.

An up-to-date implementation is available in chapter2\checkpoint4. *GitHub Branch: checkpoint2.4*

The app looks a little better now, so let's continue to improve the app.

Learning more about an exercise

For people who are doing this workout for the first time, it will be good to detail each step involved for each exercise. We can also add reference to some YouTube videos for each exercise to help the user understand the exercise better.

We are going to add the exercise description and instructions on the left panel and call it the description panel. We will add a reference to YouTube videos on the right panel, the video panel. To make things more modular and learn some new concepts, we are going to create independent views for each description panel and YouTube video panel.

The model data for this is already available. The description and procedure properties in the Exercise model (see *Exercise declaration in workout.js*) provide the necessary details about the exercise. The `related.videos` array contains some related YouTube videos.

Adding descriptions and video panels

Let's start by adding the exercise description panel. Add a new file `description-panel.html` to the partial folder. Add the following content to the file:

```html
<div>
    <div class="panel panel-default">
        <div class="panel-heading">
            <h3 class="panel-title">Description</h3>
        </div>
        <div class="panel-body">
            {{currentExercise.details.description}}
        </div>
    </div>
    <div class="panel panel-default">
        <div class="panel-heading">
            <h3 class="panel-title">Steps</h3>
        </div>
        <div class="panel-body">
            {{currentExercise.details.procedure}}
        </div>
    </div>
</div>
```

The previous partial code needs to be referenced in the workout page. Open `workout.html` and add a new fragment, before the exercise pane `div` (`id='exercise-pane'`), and also update the style of exercise pane `div`. Refer to the following highlighted code:

```html
<div id="description-panel" class="col-sm-2" ng-include =
  "'partials/description-panel.html'"> </div>
<div id="exercise-pane" class="col-sm-7">
   // Existing html
</div>
```

To add the video panel content, we will not create a file as we did for the description panel. Instead, we will declare the video panel template inline and include it in the workout.

In the `workout.html` file, after the exercise pane `div`, add this declaration:

```
<div id="exercise-pane" class="col-sm-7">
   // Existing html
</div>
<div id="video-panel" class="col-sm-2" ng-include = "'
   video-panel.html'"></div>
```

Lastly, add this script section following the preceding `div` (`id="video-pane"`):

```
<script type="text/ng-template" id="video-panel.html">
 <div class="panel panel-default">
    <div class="panel-heading">
       <h3 class="panel-title">Videos</h3>
    </div>
    <div class="panel-body">
       <div ng-repeat="video in
         currentExercise.details.related.videos">
          <iframe width="330" height="220" src="{{video}}"
             frameborder="0" allowfullscreen></iframe>
       </div>
    </div>
 </div>
</script>
```

This script defines our video panel view template.

Now go ahead and load the workout page (`#/workout`) and you should see the exercise description and instructions on the left pane.

As you will see, for some reason the videos still do not show up. The browser console log shows the following errors:

Error: [$interpolate:interr] Can't interpolate: {{video}} Error: [$sce:insecurl] Blocked loading resource from url not allowed by $sceDelegate policy. URL: //www. youtube.com/embed/MMV3v4ap4ro

http://errors.angularjs.org/1.2.15/$sce/insecurl?p0=%2F%2Fwww.youtube. com%2Fembed%2FMMV3v4ap4ro

The great thing about AngularJS error reporting is that the Angular error contains a URL that we can navigate to to learn more about the error. In our current setup, the videos do not load due to a security feature of AngularJS called **Strict Contextual Escaping (SCE)**.

This feature restricts the loading of contents/resources into the HTML view from untrusted sources. By default, only data from the same origin is trusted. The same origin is defined as the same domain, protocol, and port as the application document.

To include video content from YouTube, we need to configure explicit trust for the `http://www.youtube.com/` domain.

This configuration has to be done at the config stage using `$sceDelegateProvider`. To do this, open `app.js` and inject the `$sceDelegateProvider` dependency into the `config` function for the `app` module:

```
angular.module('app', ['ngRoute', '7minWorkout']).
config(function ($routeProvider, $sceDelegateProvider) {
```

Add this code inside the `config` function after the route declarations:

```
$sceDelegateProvider.resourceUrlWhitelist([
    // Allow same origin resource loads.
    'self',
    'http://*.youtube.com/**']);
});
```

In the preceding code, we use the `resourceUrlWhitelist` function to configure the domains we trust. The `self` parameter refers to the same origin. The second array elements add trust for `http://www.youtube.com/` and its subdomains. How * and ** are interpreted has been described in the AngularJS documentation for SCE at `https://docs.angularjs.org/api/ng/service/$sce`, as follows:

> *: matches zero or more occurrences of any character other than one of the following 6 characters: ':', '/', '.', '?', '&' and ';'. It's a useful wildcard for use in a whitelist.*

> ***: matches zero or more occurrences of any character. As such, it's not not appropriate to use in for a scheme, domain, etc. as it would match too much. (e.g. http://**.example.com/ would match http://evil.com/?ignore=.example.com/ and that might not have been the intention.) Its usage at the very end of the path is ok. (e.g. http://foo.example.com/templates/**).*

Once `$sceDelegateProvider` is configured, the videos from YouTube should load. Refresh the workout page to verify that videos show up on the right pane.

 The preceding code is available in `chapter2\checkpoint5` for you to verify.

GitHub Branch: checkpoint2.5

What we have done here is define two new views and include them in our workout HTML using a new directive: `ng-include`.

Working with ng-include

The `ng-include` directive, like the `ng-view` directive, allows us to embed HTML content, but unlike `ng-view` it is not tied to the current route of the app. Both `ng-view` and `ng-include` can load the template HTML from:

- **Remote file location**: This is a URL. This is the case with our first `ng-include` directive that loads HTML from the `description-panel.html` file under partials.

- **Embedded scripts**: We use this approach with the second `ng-include` directive. The content of the second `ng-include` directive is embedded within the page itself, inside a `script` tag:

  `<script type="text/ng-template" id="video-panel.html">`

  The `ng-include` directive references this script HTML using its ID (`ng-include = "'video-panel.html'"`). We are free to use any ID value and it need not end with `.html`.

 The template script declaration should have the type set to `text/ng-template`; if not, the framework will not locate it.

The `ng-include` directive is a perfect way to split a page into smaller, more manageable chunks of HTML content. By doing this, we can achieve some level of reusability as these chunks can be embedded across views or multiple times within a single view.

Now the question arises of whether we should embed the view as script blocks or load the partial views from a server. Loading partials from the server involves one extra call but, once Angular gets the partial template, it caches it for future use. Therefore, the performance hit is very small. Including templates inline can make the page more bloated, at least while designing the view.

AngularJS uses the $templateCache service to cache the partials that it loads during the lifetime of the application. All partials that we reference in ng-view and ng-include are cached for future use.

The $templateCache service is injectable and we can use $templateCache to cache templates manually, such as $templateCache.put('myTemplate', 'Sample template content'). We can now reference this template in ng-view or ng-include.

In general, if the partial view is small, it is fine to include it in the parent view as a script block (the inline embedded approach). If the partial view code starts to grow, using a separate file makes more sense (the server view).

Note that, in both ng-include directives, we have used quoted string values ('partials/description-panel.html' and 'video-panel.html'). This is required as ng-include expects an expression and as always expressions are evaluated in the context of the current scope. To provide a constant value, we need to quote it.

The use of expressions to specify a path for ng-include makes it a very powerful directive. We can control which HTML fragments are loaded from the controller. We can define a property or function on the scope and bind that to the ng-include value. Now any change to the bound property will change the bound HTML template. For example, consider this include function:

```
<div ng-include='template'></div>
```

In the controller, we can do something like this:

```
if(someCondition) {
  $scope.template='view1'  // Loads view1 into the above div
}
else
{
  $scope.template='view2'  // Loads view2 into the above div
}
```

The ng-include directive creates a new scope that inherits (prototypal inheritance) from its parent scope. This implies that the parent scope properties are visible to the child scope and hence the HTML templates can reference these properties seamlessly. We can verify this as we reference the scope properties defined in WorkoutController in the partials/description-panel.html and video-panel.html partials.

Another interesting directive that we have used in our video panel partials is `ng-repeat`. The job of the `ng-repeat` directive is to append a fragment of HTML repeatedly, based on elements in an array or the properties of an object.

Working with ng-repeat

The `ng-repeat` directive is a powerful and a frequently used directive. As the name suggests, it repeats! It duplicates an HTML fragment based on an array or object properties. We use it to generate YouTube video output in the right pane:

```
<div ng-repeat="video in currentExercise.details.related.videos">
  <iframe width="330" height="220" src="{{video}}" frameborder=
  "0" allowfullscreen></iframe>
</div>
```

The `ng-repeat` directive looks a bit different from standard Angular expressions. It supports the following expression formats:

- **Items in expression**: We use this format for our video panel. The expression should return an array that can be enumerated over. On each iteration of `ng-repeat`, the current iterated item is assigned to items as with the video variable mentioned earlier.

- **(key,value) in expression**: This syntax is used when the expression returns an object. In JavaScript, objects are nothing but key/value hash pairs, where we reference the value using the key. This format of `ng-repeat` is useful to iterate over properties of an object.

- **Items in an expression track by tracking_expression**: `ng-repeat` responsible for iterating over a collection and repeatedly rendering DOM content. When items are added, removed, or moved in the underlying collection, it does some performance optimization so that it does not have to re-create the entire DOM again based on these model changes. It adds a tracking expression in the form of `$$hashKey` (a unique key) to every element that we bind to `ng-repeat`. Now, when we add or remove or move elements in the collection, `ng-repeat` can add/remove and move only those specific elements. So basically tracking expressions is used to track array element identities.

We can provide our own tracking expression for Angular using the `tracking_expression` argument. This expression can be a property on the collection object. For example, if we have a task collection returned from a server, we can use its ID property in the following way:

```
task in tasks track by task.id
```

With this change, Angular will use the id property of a task to track elements in the array. This also implies that the property must be unique or we will get the following error:

[ngRepeat:dupes] Duplicates in a repeater are not allowed. Use 'track by' expression to specify unique keys. Repeater: task in tasks track by task.id, Duplicate key: 1

Also see jsFiddle http://jsfiddle.net/cmyworld/n972k/ to understand how track is used in AngularJS.

The ng-repeat directive, like ng-include, also creates a new scope. However, unlike ng-include, it creates it every time it renders a new element. So, for an array of n items, n scopes will get created. Just like ng-include, scopes created by ng-repeat also inherit from the parent scope.

It will be interesting to see how many scopes are active on the workout page. Let's use the Batarang chrome plugin for this again. Navigate to the workout page (#/workout), open the Batarang plugin, and enable it (instructions are available in the previous chapter). The scope hierarchy for the workout page should look something like this:

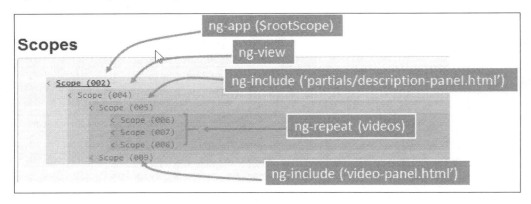

As we can see, ng-view, ng-include, and ng-repeat all create new scopes that inherit from the parent scope. If we wait a bit and let the exercise transition happen, we will see new scopes getting created and old ones getting destroyed (observe their IDs 002,004). This screenshot was taken during the first exercise (jumping jack). We can also look at the model properties attached to each scope in Batarang by clicking on the scope links (such as Scope (006)).

The previous screenshot also highlights what has caused the new scope to be created. Starting from $rootScope, which is the parent of all the scopes, a scope hierarchy has been created. In this scope hierarchy, the properties/functions defined on the parent scope are available to the child scope to consume. We can confirm this by looking at the two ng-include partials. These partials are referring to a property currentExercise that has been defined on the parent scope (004).

This feature is complete. Let's now add another capability to our app and learn about another great feature of AngularJS: filters.

Displaying the remaining workout time using filters

It will be nice if we can tell the user the time left to complete the workout and not just the duration of every exercise. We can add a countdown timer somewhere in the exercise pane that shows the overall time remaining.

The approach that we are going to take here is to define a scope variable workoutTimeRemaining. This variable will be initialized with the total time at the start of the workout and will reduce with every passing second till it reaches zero.

Since workoutTimeRemaining is a numeric value but we want to display a timer in the format (hh:mm:ss), we need to do a conversion between the seconds data and the time format. AngularJS filters are a great option for implementing such features.

Creating a seconds-to-time filter

Instead of using a filter, we could implement the same logic in a method such as convertToTime(seconds) and bind this method to the UI using something like <h2>{{convertToTime(workoutTimeRemaining)}}</h2>; it would have worked perfectly. However, there is a better way and that is by implementing our own filter. Before that, let's learn a bit more about these filters.

Understanding AngularJS filters

The primary aim of an Angular filter is to format the value of an expression displayed to the user. Filters can be used across views, services, controllers, and directives. The framework comes with multiple predefined filters such as date, number, lowercase, uppercase, and others. This is how we use a filter in a view:

```
{{ expression | filterName : inputParam1 }}
```

An expression is followed by the pipe symbol |, which is followed by the filter name and then an optional parameter (inputParam1) separated by a colon (:). Here are some examples of the date filter. Given this date 7 August 2014, 10:30:50 in the current time zone:

```
$scope.myDate=new Date(2014,7,7,10,30,50);

<br>{{myDate}} <!--2014-08-07T05:00:50.000Z-->
<br>{{myDate | date}}  <!--Aug 7, 2014-->
<br>{{myDate | date : 'medium'}}  <!--Aug 7, 2014 10:30:50 AM-->
<br>{{myDate | date : 'short'}}  <!--8/7/14 10:30 AM-->
<br>{{myDate | date : 'd-M-yy EEEE'}} <!--7-8-14 Thursday-->
```

It is not very often that we use filters inside services, controllers, or directives but if we do need to do it, we have two options. Let's say we want to format the same date inside a controller:

- In the first option, we inject dateFilter (make a note of the extra Filter string that we have added to the filter name) into our controller using DI:

```
function MyController($scope, dateFilter)
```

And then use the date filter to format the date:

```
$scope.myDate1 = dateFilter(new Date(2014,8,7),"MMM d,
   yyyy");
```

- The second option is to use an inbuilt $filter service. Here we inject the $filter service:

```
function MyController($scope, $filter)
```

And then use this service to get the date filter and call it:

```
$scope.myDate2 = $filter("date")(new Date(2014,8,7),"MMM d,
   yyyy");
```

The final result is the same.

Angular has a number of inbuilt filters that come in handy during view rendering. Some of the most used filters are:

- **date**: As we have seen earlier in the chapter, the date filter is used to format the date in a specific format. This filter supports quite a number of formats and is locale-aware too. Look at the documentation for the date filter for more details: `https://docs.angularjs.org/api/ng/filter/date`.

- **uppercase and lowercase**: These two filters, as the name suggests, change the case of the string input.

- **number**: This filter is used to format string data as numeric. If the input is not a number, nothing is rendered.

- **filter**: This very confusing filter is used to filter an array based on a predicate expression. It is often used with the `ng-repeat` directive such as:

  ```
  exercise in workout.exercises | filter: 'push'
  ```

  This code will filter all exercises where any string property on an exercise object contains the word push. Filter supports a number of additional options and more details are available in the official documentation at `https://docs.angularjs.org/api/ng/filter/filter`.

Filters are an excellent mechanism for transforming the source model into different formats without changing the model data itself. Whenever we have a requirement to present data in a specific format, rather than changing the model data to suit the presentation needs we should use AngularJS filters to achieve this. The next sections provide a great example of this where we implement a filter that converts second into hh:mm:ss format.

Implementing the secondsToTime filter

Our filter `secondsToTime` will convert a numeric value into hh:mm:ss format. Open the `filters.js` file and add the following code to it:

```
angular.module('7minWorkout').filter('secondsToTime', function () {
    return function (input) {
        var sec = parseInt(input, 10);
        if (isNaN(sec)) return "00:00:00";

        var hours = Math.floor(sec / 3600);
        var minutes = Math.floor((sec - (hours * 3600)) / 60);
        var seconds = sec - (hours * 3600) - (minutes * 60);

        return ("0" + hours).substr(-2) + ':'
                + ("0" + minutes).substr(-2) + ':'
```

```
                + ("0" + seconds).substr(-2);
    }
  });
```

We again use the Module API to first retrieve the `7minWorkout` module. We then invoke the Module API method filter. The function takes two arguments: the name of the filter and a filter function. Our filter function does not take any dependency but we have the capability to add dependencies to this function. The function should return a factory function that is called by the framework with the input value. This function (`function (input)`) in turn should return the transformed value.

The implementation is quite straightforward as we convert seconds into hours, minutes, and seconds. Then we concatenate the result into a string value and return the value. The `0` addition on the left for each hour, minute, and seconds variable is to format the value with a leading `0` in case the calculated value for hours, minutes, or seconds is less than 10.

Before we use this filter in our view, we need to implement the workout time remaining logic in our controller. Let's do that. Open the `workout.js` file and update the `WorkoutPlan` constructor function by adding a new function `totalWorkoutDuration`:

```
function WorkoutPlan(args) {
  //existing WorkoutPlan constructor function code
  this.totalWorkoutDuration = function () {
    if (this.exercises.length == 0) return 0;
    var total = 0;
    angular.forEach(this.exercises, function (exercise) {
        total = total + exercise.duration;
    });
    return this.restBetweenExercise * (this.exercises.length - 1)
      + total;
}
```

This method calculates the total time of the workout by adding up the time duration for each exercise plus the number of rest durations. We use a new AngularJS library function `forEach` to iterate over the workout exercise array. The `angular.forEach` library takes an array as the first argument and a function that gets invoked for every item in the array.

Now locate the `startWorkout` function and update it by adding these two sections:

```
var startWorkout = function () {
  workoutPlan = createWorkout();
```

```
$scope.workoutTimeRemaining =
    workoutPlan.totalWorkoutDuration();

    // Existing code. Removed for clarity

    $interval(function () {
        $scope.workoutTimeRemaining = $scope.workoutTimeRemaining
            - 1;
    }, 1000, $scope.workoutTimeRemaining);

    startExercise(workoutPlan.exercises.shift());
};
```

We assign `totalWorkoutDuration` for the workout plan to `$scope.workoutTimeRemaining` and at the end of the method before calling `startExercise`, we add another `$interval` service to decrement this value after every second, for a total of `workoutTimeRemaining` times.

That was easy and quick. Now it's time to update the view. Go to `workout.html` and add the highlighted line in the following code:

```
<div class="workout-display-div">
  <h4>Workout Remaining - {{workoutTimeRemaining |
    secondsToTime}}</h4>
  <h1>{{currentExercise.details.title}}</h1>
```

Now, every time the expression `workoutTimeRemaining` changes, the filter will execute again and the view will get updated. Save the file and refresh the browser. We should see a countdown timer for the workout!

Wait a minute. The total workout duration shown is 7 minutes 50 seconds not 7 minutes. Well, that's not a problem with our calculation even though the total workout duration indeed is 7:50 minutes. Basically, this is a sub-8 minute workout so we call it *7 Minute Workout*!

The app so far is available in `chapter2\checkpoint6` for your reference.
GitHub Branch: checkpoint2.6

Before we conclude this chapter, we are going to add one last enhancement that will add to the usability of the app. We will show the name of the next exercise during the rest periods.

Adding the next exercise indicator using ng-if

It will be nice for the user to be told what the next exercise is during the short rest period after each exercise. This will help in preparing for the next exercise. So let's add it.

To implement this feature, we would simply output the title of the exercise from the first element in the `workoutPlan.exercises` array in a label during the rest stage. This is possible because transitioning to the next exercise involves removing the `exercise` object from the `workoutPlan.exercises` array and returning it. Therefore, the array is shrinking after each exercise and the first element in the array always points to the exercise that is due. With this basic understanding in place, let's start the implementation.

We will show the next exercise next to the **Time Remaining countdown** section. Change the workout div (`class="workout-display-div"`) to include the highlighted content.

```
<div class="workout-display-div">
  <!-- Exiting html -->
  <div class="progress time-progress">
     <!-- Exiting html -->
  </div>
  <div class="row">
     <h3 class="col-sm-6 text-left">Time Remaining:
       <strong>{{currentExercise.duration-currentExerciseDuration
       }}</strong></h3>
     <h3 class="col-sm-6 text-right" ng-if=
       "currentExercise.details.name=='rest'">Next up:
       <strong>{{workoutPlan.exercises[0].details.title}
       }}</strong></h3>
  </div>
</div>
```

We wrap the existing `Time Remaining` h1 and add another h3 to show the next exercise inside a new div (`class="row"`) and update some styles. Also, there is a new directive ng-if in the second h3.

The ng-if directive is used to add or remove a specific section of DOM based on whether the expression provided to it returns true or false. The DOM element gets added when the expression evaluates to true. We use this expression with our ng-if declaration:

```
ng-if="currentExercise.details.name=='rest'"
```

The condition checks whether we are currently at the rest phase. We are using the rest exercise name property to do the match.

Other than that, in the same h3 we have an interpolation that shows the name of the exercise from the first element of the `workoutPlan.exercises` array.

The ng-if directive belongs to the same category of directives that show/hide content based on a condition. We covered the ng-show directive in the previous chapter and there is another directive, ng-hide, that does the opposite of what ng-show does. The difference between ng-if and ng-show/ng-hide is that ng-if creates and destroys the DOM element, whereas ng-show/ng-hide achieves the same effect by just changing the display CSS property of the HTML element to none.

With ng-if, whenever the expression changes from false to true, a complete re-initialization of the ng-if content happens. A new scope is created and watches are set up for data binding. If the inner HTML has ng-controller or directives defined, those are recreated and so are child scopes, as requested by these controllers and directives. The reverse happens when the expression changes from true to false. All this is destroyed. Therefore, using ng-if can sometimes become an expensive operation if it wraps a large chunk of content and the expression attached to ng-if changes very often.

There is another directive that belongs to this league: ng-switch. When defined on the parent HTML, it can swap child HTML elements based on the ng-switch expression. Consider this example:

```
<div id="parent"  ng-switch on="userType">
    <div ng-switch-when="admin">I am the Admin!</div>
    <div ng-switch-when="powerUser">I am the Power User!</div>
    <div ng-switch-default>I am a normal user!</div>
</div>
```

Here, we bind the expression `userType` to `ng-switch`. Based on the value of `userType` (`admin`, `powerUser`, or any other), one of the inner `div` elements will be rendered. The `ng-switch-default` directive is a wildcard match/fallback match and it gets rendered when `userType` is neither `admin` nor `powerUser`.

We are not done yet as the `{{workoutPlan.exercises[0].details.title}}` interpolation refers to the `workoutPlan` object, but this property is not available on the current scope in `WorkoutController`. To fix this, open the `workout.js` file and replace all instances of `workoutPlan` with `$scope.workoutPlan`. And finally, remove the following line:

```
var workoutPlan;
```

Refresh the workout page; during the rest phase, we should see the next workout content. It should look something like the following screenshot:

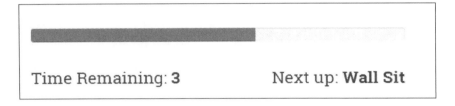

The app so far is available in `chapter2\checkpoint7` for your reference.

GitHub branch: checkpoint2.7

Well, it's time to conclude the chapter and summarize our learnings.

Summary

We started this chapter with the aim of creating an AngularJS app that is more complex than the sample we created in the first chapter. The *7 Minute Workout* app fitted the bill and we learned a lot about the AngularJS framework while building this app.

We started with defining the functionality of the *7 Minute Workout* app. We then focused our efforts on defining the code structure for the app. In the process, we learned about the building blocks of AngularJS namely controllers, directives, filters, and services and how these components need to be organized in our codebase.

To build the app, we started by defining the model of the app. Once the model was in place, we started the controller implementation. While implementing the controller we learned about DI, services, the AngularJS watch infrastructure, and the AngularJS Promise API.

Once we had a fully functional controller, we created a supporting view for the app. We used some new directives: `ng-src` and `ng-style`. The `ng-src` directive helped us to bind the exercise image to an HTML `img` tag. The `ng-style` directive was used to change the style of the progress bar dynamically.

To add some improvements to the app, we then converted it into a **single-page application (SPA)**. We added three pages (start, workout, and finish) to the app. During this implementation, we learned about AngularJS SPA constructs, including `ng-view`, `$route`, and `$location`. We also learned about these module execution stages: `config` and `run`.

Once the basic SPA was set up, we added some enhancements to the workout page in terms of exercise descriptions and videos. We used the `ng-include` directive to achieve this. During this task, we also covered the `ng-repeat` directive that was used to iterate over the video array and render them.

Then, we covered one of the core constructs of Angular filters. We saw how to use filters such as the date filter and how to create one.

Lastly, we learned about the `ng-if` directive that is used to conditionally render DOM elements based on an expression. We used it to render notifications of the next exercise next exercise during exercise rest periods.

We have created the basic *7 Minute Workout* app. For a better user experience, we have added some small enhancements to it too but we are still missing some good-to-have features that would make our app more usable—such as causing the workout to pause, audio clues for exercise progress, and things like that. We will be building these features in the coming chapters as we learn more about the framework.

3
More AngularJS Goodness for 7 Minute Workout

If the previous chapter was about building our first useful app in AngularJS, then this chapter is about adding a whole lot of AngularJS goodness to it. The *7 Minute Workout* app still has some rough edges/limitations that we can fix and make the overall app experience better. This chapter is all about adding those enhancements and features. As always, this app building process should provide us with enough opportunities to foster our understanding of the framework and learn new things about it.

The topics we will cover in this chapter include:

- **Exercise steps formatting**: We try to fix data of exercise procedure steps by formatting the step text as HTML.

- **Audio support**: We add audio support to the workout. Audio clues are used to track the progress of the current exercise. This helps the user to use the app without constantly staring at the display screen.

- **Pause/resume exercises**: Pause/resume is another important feature that the app lacks. We add workout pausing and resuming capabilities to the app. In the process, we learn about the keyboard and mouse events supported by Angular. We also cover one of the most useful directives in Angular that is `ng-class`.

- **Enhancing the Workout Video panel**: We redo the apps video panel for a better user experience. We learn about a popular AngularJS library `ui.bootstrap` and use its modal dialog directive for viewing videos in the popup.

- **AngularJS animation**: Angular has a set of directives that make adding animation easy. We explore how modern browsers do animation using CSS transitions and keyframe animation constructs. We enable CSS-based animation on some of our app directives. Finally, we also touch upon JavaScript-based animation.

- **Workout history tracking**: One of the building blocks of AngularJS, **Services**, is covered in more detail in this chapter. We implement a history tracking service that tracks workout history for the last 20 workouts. We cover all recipes of service creation from value, constant, to service, factory, and provider. We also add a history view. We discover a bit more about the `ng-repeat` directive and two super useful filters: `filter` and `orderBy`.

In case you have not read *Chapter 2, Building Our First App – 7 Minute Workout*, I would recommend you check out the *Summary* section at the end of the last chapter to understand what has been accomplished.

On a side note, I expect you to be using using the *7 Minute Workout* pattern on a regular basis and working on your physical fitness. If not, take a 7 minute exercise break and exercise now. I insist!

Hope the workout was fun! Now let's get back to some serious business. Let's start with formatting the exercise steps.

We are starting from where we left off in *Chapter 2, Building Our First App – 7 Minute Workout*. The `checkpoint7` code can serve as the base for this chapter. Copy the code from `chapter2\checkpoint7` before we start to work on app updates.

The code is also available on GitHub (`https://github.com/chandermani/angularjsbyexample`) for everyone to download. Checkpoints are implemented as branches in GitHub.

The branch to download is:

GitHub branch: checkpoint2.7 (folder – trainer)

Formatting the exercise steps

One of the sore points in the current app is the formatting of the exercise steps. It is plain difficult to read these steps.

The steps should either have a line break (`<br/>`), or formatted as an HTML list for easy readability. This seems to be a straightforward task and we can just go ahead and change the data that is bounded to the `currentExercise.details.procedure` interpolation or write a filter than can add some HTML formatting using the line delimiting convention (`.`). For quick verification, let's update the first exercise steps in `workout.js` by adding break (`<br/>`) after each line:

```
procedure: "Assume an erect position, with feet …\
    <br/>Slightly bend your knees, and propel yourself …\
    <br/>While in air, bring your legs out to the side about …\
```

Now refresh the workout page. The output does not match our expectation

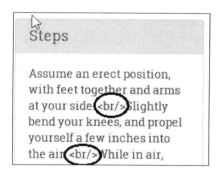

The break tags were literally rendered in the browser. Angular did not render the interpolation as HTML; instead it escaped the HTML characters.

The reason behind this behavior is **strict contextual escaping** (SCE) again! Do you remember the YouTube video rendering issues? In the last chapter, we had to configure the behavior of SCE using `$sceDelegateProvider` so that the YouTube videos are rendered in the workout page.

Well, as it turns out in Angular, SCE does not allow us to render arbitrary HTML content using interpolation. This is done to save us from all sort of attacks that are possible with arbitrary HTML injection in a page such as **cross-site scripting** (**XSS**) and clickjacking. AngularJS is configured to be secure by default.

Till now, we have used `ng-include` and `ng-view` to inject HTML templates from local and remote sources but we have not rendered model data as HTML.

If we cannot use interpolation to bind HTML model data, there must a directive that we can use. The `ng-bind-html` directive is what we are looking for.

Understanding ng-bind-html

As the name suggests, the `ng-bind-html` directive is used to bind model data as HTML. If data contains HTML fragments, the AngularJS templating engine will honor them and render the content as HTML.

Behind the scenes, `ng-bind-html` uses the `$sanitize` service to sanitize the HTML content. The `$sanitize` service parses the HTML tokens and only allows whitelisted tokens to be rendered and removes the others. This includes removal of embedded script content such as `onclick="this.doSomethingEvil()"` from the rendered HTML.

We can override this behavior if we trust the HTML source and want to add the HTML as it is to the document element. We do this by calling the `$sce.trustAsHtml` function in the controller and assigning the return value to a scope variable:

```
$scope.trustedHtml=$sce.trustAsHtml('<div
  onclick="this.doSomethingGood() />');
```

And then bind it using `ng-bind-html`:

```
<div ng-bind-html="trustedHtml"></div>
```

A working example of this process is available in the AngularJS documentation for the `$sanitize` service (`https://docs.angularjs.org/api/ngSanitize/service/$sanitize`). I have also forked the example Plunker (`http://plnkr.co/edit/IRNK3peirZaK6FqCynGo?p=preview`) so that we can play with it and get a better understanding of how input sanitization works.

Some of the key takeaways from the previous discussion are as follows:

*   When it comes to rendering random HTML, AngularJS is secure by default. It escapes HTML content by default.
*   If we want to include model content as HTML, we need to use the `ng-bind-html` directive. The directive too is restrictive in terms of how the HTML content is rendered and what is considered safe HTML.

- If we trust the source of the HTML content completely, we can use the `$sce` service to establish explicit trust using the `trustAsHtml` function.

Let's return to our app implementation, as we have realized we need to use `ng-bind -html` to render our exercise steps.

Using ng-bind-html with data of the exercise steps

Here is how we are going to enable exercise step formatting:

1. Open the `description-panel.html` file and change the last `div` element with the `panel-body` class from:

   ```
   <div class="panel-body">
       {{currentExercise.details.procedure}}
   </div>
   ```

   To

   ```
   <div class="panel-body" ng-bind-html
     ="currentExercise.details.procedure">
   </div>
   ```

   Since `ng-bind-html` uses the `$sanitize` service that is not part of the core Angular module but is part of the `ngSanitize` module, we need to include the new module dependency.

   The process is similar to what we did when we included the `ngRoute` dependency in *Chapter 2, Building Our First App – 7 Minute Workout.*

2. Open `index.html` and add reference to the script file `angular-sanitize.js` after `angular-route.js`, as follows:

   ```
   <script src="http://ajax.googleapis.com/ajax/libs/angularjs/1.3.3/
     angular-sanitize.js"></script>
   ```

3. Update the module dependency in `app.js` as follows:

   ```
   angular.module('app', ['ngRoute', 'ngSanitize',
     '7minWorkout']).
   ```

That's it. Since we are not using the `$sanitize` service directly, we do not need to update our controller.

Refresh the page and the steps will have line breaks:

> **Steps**
>
> Assume an erect position,
> with feet together and arms
> at your side.
> Slightly bend your knees,
> and propel yourself a few
> inches into the air.
> While in air, bring your legs
> out to the side about
> shoulder width or slightly
> wider.

 The app so far is available in `chapter3\checkpoint1` in the companion codebase for us to verify.

GitHub branch: checkpoint3.1 (folder – trainer)

In the preceding implementation, we added HTML line breaks (`<br>`) to the model content (`Exercise.procedure`) itself. Another approach could be to keep the content intact and instead use a filter to format the content. We can create a filter that converts a bunch of sentences delimited by a dot (.) or a newline (\r\n) into HTML content with either a line break or list.

I leave it up to you to try the filter-based approach. The filter usage should look something like this:

```
<div class="panel-body" ng-bind-html=
   "currentExercise.details.procedure | myLineBreakFilter">
```

That pretty much covers how to bind HTML content from a model in AngularJS. It's time now to add an essential and handy feature to our app, *audio support*.

Tracking exercise progress with audio clips

For our *7 Minute Workout* app, adding sound support is vital. One cannot exercise while constantly staring at the screen. Audio clues will help the user to perform the workout effectively as he/she can just follow the audio instructions.

Here is how we are going to support exercise tracking using audio clues:

- A ticking clock sound tracks the progress during the exercise
- A half-way indicator sounds, indicating that the exercise is halfway through
- An exercise-completion audio clip plays when the exercise is about to end
- An audio clip plays during the rest phase and informs users about the next exercise

Modern browsers have good support for audio. The `<audio>` tag of HTML5 provides a mechanism to embed audio into our HTML content. We will use it to embed and play our audio clips during different times in the app.

AngularJS does not have any inherent support to play/manage audio content. We may be tempted to think that we can just go ahead and directly access the HTML audio element in our controller and implement the desired behavior. Yes, we can do that. In fact, this would have been a perfectly acceptable solution if we had been using plain JavaScript or jQuery. However, remember there is a sacrosanct rule in Angular: "Thou shalt not manipulate DOM in the AngularJS controller" and we should never break it. So let's back off and think about what else can be done.

We touched upon the concept of directives in *Chapter 1, Getting Started*, and we also learned that the DOM manipulation work belongs to AngularJS directives. Since the base framework does not have a directive to support audio, the options we are left with are: writing our own directive or using a third-party directive that wraps HTML5 audio. We will take the easier route and use a third-party directive `angular -media-player` (https://github.com/mrgamer/angular-media-player). Another reason we do not plan to create our own directive is that the topic of directive creation is a non-trivial pursuit and will require us to get into the intricacies of how directives work. We will cover more about directives in the chapter that we have dedicated exclusively for them.

The popularity of AngularJS has benefitted everyone using it. No framework can cater to the ever-evolving needs of the developer community. This void is filled by the numerous directives, services, and filters created by the community and open-sourced for everyone to use. We use one such directive `angular-media-player`. It is always advisable to look for such readymade components first before implementing our own.

Additionally, we should pledge to give back to the community by making public any reusable components that we create in Angular.

Let's get started with the implementation.

Implementing audio support

We have already detailed when a specific audio clip is played in the last section. If we look at the current implementation for the controller, the `currentExercise` and `currentExerciseDuration` controller properties and the `startWorkout` and `startExercise` functions are the elements of interest to us.

The workout exercises created inside `createWorkout` at the moment do not reference the exercise name pronunciation audio clips (`nameSound`). Update the `createWorkout` function with the updated version of code from `chapter3\checkpoint2\js\7MinWorkout\workout.js` before proceeding.

GitHub branch: checkpoint3.2 (folder – trainer)

After the update, each exercise would have a property as follows:

`nameSound: "content/jumpingjacks.wav"`

We can use the `startWorkout` method to start the overall time ticker sound. Then, we can alter the `startExercise` method and fix the `$interval` call that increments `currentExerciseDuration` to include logic to play audio when we reach half way.

Not very elegant! We will have to alter the core workout logic just to add support for audio. There is a better way. Why don't we create a separate controller for audio and workout synchronization? The new controller will be responsible for tracking exercise progress and will play the appropriate audio clip during the exercise. Things will be clearer once we start the implementation.

To start with, download and reference the `angular-media-player` directive. The steps involved are:

1. Download `angular-media-player.js` from `https://github.com/mrgamer/angular-media-player/tree/master/dist`.

2. Create a folder vendor inside the `js` folder and copy the previous file.

3. Add a reference to the preceding script file in `index.html` after the framework script declarations:

```
<script src="js/vendor/angular-media-player.js"></script>
```

4. Lastly, inject the `mediaPlayer` module with the existing module dependencies in `app.js`:

```
angular.module('app', [..., '7minWorkout', 'mediaPlayer']).
```

Open `workout.html` and add this HTML fragment inside exercise `div` (`id="exercise-pane"`) at the very top:

```
<span ng-controller="WorkoutAudioController">
  <audio media-player="ticksAudio" loop autoplay src="content/tick10s.
mp3"></audio>
  <audio media-player="nextUpAudio" src="content/nextup.mp3"></audio>
  <audio media-player="nextUpExerciseAudio"
playlist="exercisesAudio"></audio>
  <audio media-player="halfWayAudio" src="content/15seconds.wav"></
audio>
  <audio media-player="aboutToCompleteAudio" src="content/321.wav"></
audio>
</span>
```

In the preceding HTML, there is one audio element for each of the scenarios we need to support:

- `ticksAudio`: This is used for the ticking clock sound
- `nextUpAudio`: This is used for the next audio sound
- `nextUpExerciseAudio`: This is the exercise name audio
- `halfWayAudio`: This gets played half-way through the exercise
- `aboutToCompleteAudio`: This gets played when the exercise is about to end

The `media-player` directive is added to each `audio` tag. This directive then adds a property with the same name as the one assigned to the `media-player` attribute on the current scope. So the `media-player = "aboutToCompleteAudio"` declaration adds a scope property `aboutToCompleteAudio`.

We use these properties to manage the audio player in `WorkoutAudioController`.

Other than the audio directives, there is also an `ng-controller` declaration for `WorkoutAudioController` on the `span` container.

With the view in place, we need to implement the controller.

Implementing WorkoutAudioController

There is something different that we have done in the previous view. We have an `ng-controller` declaration for `WorkoutAudioController` inside the existing parent controller context `WorkoutController`.

> `WorkoutController` gets instantiated as part of route resolution as we saw in *Chapter 2, Building Our First App – 7 Minute Workout*, where we defined a route, as follows:
>
> ```
> $routeProvider.when('/workout', { templateUrl:
>     'partials/workout.html', controller:
>     'WorkoutController' });
> ```
>
> Since `WorkoutController` is linked to `ng-view`, we have effectively nested `WorkoutAudioController` inside `WorkoutController`.

This effectively creates a child MVC component within the parent MVC component. Also, since the `ng-controller` directive creates a new scope, the child MVC component has its own scope to play with. The following screenshot highlights this hierarchy:

```
Scope (ng-view \ WorkoutController)

  $id: 2
  workoutPlan: Object
  workoutTimeRemaining: 463
  currentExerciseIndex: 0
  cur
    d      Scope (WorkoutAudioController)
    du
  cur        $id: 3
             exercisesAudio: Array[12]
             ticksAudio: Object
             nextUpAudio: Object
             nextUpExerciseAudio: Object
             halfWayAudio: Object
             aboutToCompleteAudio: Object
```

This new scope inherits (prototypal inheritance) from the parent scope, and has access to the model state defined on parent $scope. Such segregation of functionality helps in better organization of code and makes implementation simple. As views and controllers start to become complex, there are always opportunities to split a large view into smaller manageable subviews that can have their own model and controller as we are doing with our workout audio view and controller.

We could have moved the view template (the span container) for audio into a separate file and included it in the workout.html file using ng-include (as done for description-panel.html), hence achieving a true separation of components. However, for now we are just decorating the span with the ng-controller attribute.

Let's add the WorkoutAudioController function to the workout.js file itself. Open workout.js and start with adding the WorkoutAudioController declaration and some customary code after the WorkoutController implementation:

```
angular.module('7minWorkout')
  .controller('WorkoutAudioController', ['$scope', '$timeout',
    function ($scope, $timeout)     {
    $scope.exercisesAudio = [];
    var init = function () {
    }
    init();
}]);
```

The standard controller declaration has a skeleton init method and the exercisesAudio property, which will store all audio clips for each exercise defined in Exercise.nameSound.

When should this array be filled? Well, when the workout (workoutPlan) data is loaded. When does that happen? WorkoutAudioController does not know when it happens, but it can use the AngularJS watch infrastructure to find out. Since the WorkoutAudioController scope has access to the workoutPlan property defined on the parent controller scope, it can watch the property for changes. This is what we are going to do. Add this code after the declaration of the exercisesAudio array in WorkoutAudioController:

```
var workoutPlanwatch = $scope.$watch('workoutPlan', function
(newValue, oldValue) {
    if (newValue) {   // newValue==workoutPlan
        angular.forEach( $scope.workoutPlan.exercises,
        function (exercise) {
            $scope.exercisesAudio.push({
```

```
                    src: exercise.details.nameSound,
                    type: "audio/wav"
                });
            });
            workoutPlanwatch();  //unbind the watch.
    }
});
```

This watch loads all the exercise name audio clips into the `exercisesAudio` array once `workoutPlan` is loaded.

One interesting statement here is:

```
workoutPlanwatch();
```

As the comment suggests, it is a mechanism to remove the watch from an already watched scope property. We do it by storing the return value of the `$scope.$watch` function call, which is a function reference. We then can call this function whenever we want to remove the watch, which is the case after the first loading of `workoutPlan` data. Remember the workout data is not going to change during the workout.

Similarly, to track the progress of the exercise, we need to watch for the `currentExercise` and `currentExerciseDuration` properties. Add these two watches following the previous watch:

```
$scope.$watch('currentExercise', function (newValue, oldValue) {
    if (newValue && newValue !== oldValue) {
        if ($scope.currentExercise.details.name == 'rest') {
            $timeout(function () { $scope.nextUpAudio.play();}
, 2000);
            $timeout(function () {
                      $scope.nextUpExerciseAudio.play(
                      $scope.currentExerciseIndex + 1, true);}
, 3000);
        }
    }
});

$scope.$watch('currentExerciseDuration', function (newValue,
  oldValue) {
if (newValue) {
if (newValue == Math.floor($scope.currentExercise.duration / 2)
  && $scope.currentExercise.details.name !== 'rest') {
        $scope.halfWayAudio.play();
        }
    else if (newValue == $scope.currentExercise.duration - 3) {
```

```
            $scope.aboutToCompleteAudio.play();
        }
    }
});
```

The first watch on `currentExercise` is used to play the audio of the next exercise in line during the rest periods. Since the audio for the next exercise is a combination of two audio clips, one that echoes *next-up* and another that echoes the exercise name (from the array that we have built previously using the `workoutPlan` watch), we play them one after another. This is how the audio declaration for the the next-up audio looks:

```
<audio media-player="nextUpAudio"
  src="content/nextup.mp3"></audio>
<audio media-player="nextUpExerciseAudio"
  playlist="exercisesAudio"></audio>
```

The first one is like other audio elements that take the audio using the `src` attribute. However, the `nextUpExerciseAudio` value takes `playlist`, which is an array of audio sources. During every rest period, we play the audio from one of the array elements by calling:

```
$scope.nextUpExerciseAudio.play($scope.currentExerciseIndex
  + 1, true);}
```

To play the audio content in succession, we use `$timeout` to control the audio playback order. One plays after 2 seconds and the next after 3 seconds.

The second watch on `currentExerciseDuration` gets invoked every second and plays specific audio elements at mid-time and before the exercise ends.

 The `media-player` directive exposes a number of functions/properties on the object that it adds to the current scope. We have only used the `play` method. The `media-player` documentation has more details on other supported functions/properties.

Now is the time to verify the implementation, but before we do that we need to include the audio clips that we have referenced in the code. The audio files are located in the `audio` folder of the app inside `chapter3/checkpoint2/app/content`.

Copy the audio clips and refresh the workout page. Now we have full-fledged audio support in *7 Minute Workout*. Wait a minute, there is a small issue! The next up exercise audio is off by one. To verify this, wait for the first exercise to complete and the rest period to start. The next up exercise audio does not match with the exercise that is coming up next, it is one step ahead. Let's fix it.

Exploring the audio synchronization issue

To fix the audio synchronization issue, let's first debug and identify what is causing the problem.

Put a breakpoint inside `workoutPlan` watch (inside the `if` condition) and start the workout. Wait for the breakpoint to hit. When it hits, check the value of `workoutPlan.exercises`:

```
 init();
};

ar.module('7minWorkout')
ntroller('WorkoutAudioContr(
  $scope.exercisesAudio = [].

 var workoutPlanwatch = $sc(
     if (newValue) {
         angular.forEach($scope.workoutPlan.exercises, function (exercise) {
             $scope.exercisesAudio.push({ src: exercise.details.nameSound, type:
```

```
WorkoutPla
▶ exercises: Array[11]
  name: "7minWorkout"
  restBetweenExercise: 10                    ime
  title: "7 Minute Workout"
▶ totalWorkoutDuration: function () {
▶   proto  : WorkoutPlan                     lue
```

The first time this watch is triggered (`newValue` is not null), the `workoutPlan.exercises` array has 11 elements as seen in the previous screenshot. Nonetheless, we added 12 exercises when we loaded the plan for the first time in `startWorkout`. This is causing the synchronization issue between the next-up audio and the exercise order. However, why do we have one element fewer?

The first line inside the `startWorkout` function does the necessary assignment to `workoutPlan`:

```
$scope.workoutPlan = createWorkout();
```

If our understanding of watches is correct, then the watch should get triggered as soon as we assign `$scope.workoutPlan` a value—in other words, whenever `$scope.workoutPlan` changes.

This is not the case, and it can be confirmed by debugging the `startWorkout` function. The watch does not trigger while we are inside `startWorkout` and well beyond that. The last line of `startWorkout` is:

```
startExercise($scope.workoutPlan.exercises.shift());
```

By removing an item from the `exercises` array, we are one item short when the watch actually triggers.

As it turns out, change detection/tracking does not work in real-time. Clearly, our understanding of watches is not 100 percent correct!

To fix this innocuous looking problem, we will have to dig deeper into the inner working of Angular and then fix parts of our workout implementation.

> The next section (*AngularJS dirty checking and digest cycles*) explores the internal workings of the Angular framework that can become a bit overwhelming if we have just started learning this framework. Feel free to skip this section and revisit it in the future. We will summarize our understanding of Angular dirty checking and digest cycle execution at the end of the section, before we actually fix the audio synchronization issue.

AngularJS dirty checking and digest cycles

Let's step back and try to understand how the AngularJS watch infrastructure works. How is it able to update HTML DOM on model data changes? Remember HTML directives and interpolations too use the same watch infrastructure.

The properties that we watch in Angular are standard JavaScript objects/values and since JavaScript properties (at least till now) are not observable, there is no way for Angular to know when the model data changed.

This raises the fundamental question: how does AngularJS detect these changes?

Well, AngularJS detects changes only when the `$scope.$apply(exp)` function is invoked. This function can take an argument `exp` that it evaluates in the current scope context. Internally, `$apply` evaluates `exp` and then calls the `$rootScope.$digest()` function.

The call to `$digest()` triggers the model change detection process. The immediate question that comes to mind is: "when is `$apply` called and who calls it?" Before we can answer this question, it would be good to know what happens in the digest cycle.

The invoking of the `$digest()` function on `$rootScope` in the Angular world is called the **digest cycle**. It is termed as *cycle* because it is a repeating process. What happens during the *digest loop* is that Angular internally starts two smaller loops as follows:

- **The $evalAsync loop**: `$evalAsync` is a method on the `$scope` object that allows us to evaluate an expression in an asynchronous manner before the next digest loop runs. Whenever we register some work with `$evalAsync`, it goes into a list. During the `$evalAsync` loop, items in this list are evaluated till the list is empty and this ends the loop. We seldom need it; in fact I have never used it.

- **The $watch list loop**. All the watches that we register, or are registered by the framework directives and interpolations, are evaluated in this loop.

To detect the model changes, Angular does something called as **dirty checking**. This involves comparing the old value of the model property with the current value to detect any changes. For this comparison to work, Angular needs to do some book keeping that involves keeping track of the model value during the last digest cycle.

If the framework detects any model changes from the last digest cycle, the corresponding model watch is triggered. Interestingly, this watch triggering can lead to a change in model data again, hence triggering another watch.

For example, if the `$watch` callback updates some model data on the scope that is being watched by another watch expression, another watch will get triggered.

Angular keeps reevaluating the watch expression until no watch gets triggered or, in other words, the model becomes stable. At this moment, the watch list loop ends.

To safeguard against an infinite loop, the watch list loop runs only 10 times after which an error is thrown and this loop is terminated. We will see an error like this in the developer console:

```
Uncaught Error: 10 $digest() iterations reached.
Aborting!
```

We should be careful when updating the scope data in a watch. The update should not result in an infinite cycle. For example, if we update the same property that is being watched inside the watch callback, we will get an error.

When both the `$evalAsync` and `$watch` loops are complete, AngularJS updates the HTML DOM and the digest cycle itself ends.

An important thing that needs to be highlighted here is that the digest cycle evaluates every model property being watched in any scope across the application. This may seem inefficient at first as on each digest cycle we evaluate each and every property being watched irrespective of where the changes are made, but this works very well in real life.

See the answer at http://stackoverflow.com/questions/9682092/databinding-in-angularjs/9693933#9693933 by Misko (creator of Angular!) to know why it is not such a bad idea to implement dirty checking in this manner.

The only missing piece of the model change tracking jigsaw is: when is `$scope.$apply` called or when does the digest cycle run? Till now we have never invoked the `$scope.$apply` method anywhere.

Angular made a very plausible assumption about when the model can change. It assumes model data can get updated on events such as user interaction (via the mouse and keyboard), form field updates, Ajax calls, or timer functions such as `setTimeout` and `setInteval`. It then provided a set of directives and services that wrap these events and internally call `$scope.$apply` when such events occur.

Here is a source code snippet (simplified) from the `ng-click` directive in AngularJS:

```
element.on("click", function(event) {
  scope.$apply(function() {
    fn(scope, {$event:event});
  });
});
```

The `element.on` method is a jQuery- (or jqlite)-based method that adds an event handler for click events. When the mouse click event occurs, the event handler calls `scope.$apply`, hence triggering the digest cycle. It is precisely for this reason that we do not litter our implementation with calls to `$scope.$apply()` everywhere.

Summarizing our learnings

To recap:

- An Angular watch does not trigger as soon as a model being watched changes.

- A watch is only triggered during a digest cycle. A digest cycle is in an iterative process during which Angular compares the old and new values of the watched expression for changes. If the value changes, the watch is triggered. Angular does this for all watches that we create and the ones created by the framework to support data binding.

- A digest cycle is triggered by calling `$scope.$apply`. The framework calls `$scope.$apply` at various times during the app execution. For example, when a button is clicked, or when `$interval` lapses.

The concept of the digest cycle is very important to understand once we get into serious AngularJS development. This can save us countless hours of debugging and frustration that accompanies it. In the next section, we will make use of this newfound understanding of the digest cycle to fix the audio synchronization issue.

Fixing the next-up exercise's audio synchronization issue

Now that we know what the digest cycle is, and that change detection is not real-time, things start to make sense. The workoutPlan watch did not trigger between these two calls in startWorkout:

```
var startWorkout = function () {
    $scope.workoutPlan = createWorkout();
    // Existing code
    startExercise($scope.workoutPlan.exercises.shift());
}
```

Here, the exercise and exercise audio arrays went out of sync. Let's fix it.

Removing elements from the exercise array after each exercise is a suboptimal implementation as we have to build this array every time the workout starts. It will be better if we do not alter the array once the exercise starts and instead use the currentExerciseIndex property with the exercises array to always locate the current exercise in progress.

Go ahead and copy the updated WorkoutController functions: startWorkout, startExercise, and getNextExercise from workout.js located in chapter2/checkpoint2/app/js/7MinWorkout.

The updated functions now are using the currentExerciseIndex instead of removing items from the exercises array.

There is a fix required in workout.html too. Update the highlighted code:

```
<h3 class="col-sm-6 text-right" ng-if=
  "currentExercise.details.name=='rest'">Next up:
  <strong>{{workoutPlan.exercises[currentExerciseIndex +
  1].details.title}}</strong></h3>
```

Now, the upcoming audio should be in sync with the next exercise. We can verify it by running the workout again and listening to the upcoming exercise audio during the rest period.

Chapter3\Checkpoint2 has the working version of the code that we have implemented so far.

GitHub branch: checkpoint3.2 (folder – trainer)

Other than learning about dirty checking and digest cycles, we have learned other important things in this section too. Let's summarize them as follows:

- We have extended the workout functionality without altering the main `WorkoutController` function in any way.

- Nested controllers allow us to manage subviews independently of each other and such views are only dependent on their parent view for scope data.

  This means that changes to scope properties/schemas on the parent can affect these child views. For example, our `WorkoutAudioController` function is dependent on properties with these names: `currentExercise` and `currentExerciseDuration` and if we decide to rename/remove any of them, we need to fix the audio view and the controller.

  This also implies that we cannot move the workout audio-related view outside the parent view due to the dependency on model data. If we want something truly reusable, we will have to look at creating our own directive.

- DOM manipulation should be restricted to directives and we should never do DOM manipulation in a controller.

With audio support out of the way, we are one step closer to a fully functional app. One of the missing features that will be an essential addition to our app is the exercise pause feature.

Pausing exercises

If you have used the app and done some physical workout along with it, you will be missing the exercise pause functionality badly. The workout just does not stop till it reaches the end. We need to fix this behavior.

To pause the exercise, we need to stop the timer and stop all the sound components. Also, we need to add a button somewhere in the view that allows us to pause and resume the workout. We plan to do this by drawing a button overlay over the exercise area in the center of the page. When clicked, it will toggle the exercise state between paused and running. We will also add keyboard support to pause and resume the workout using the key binding *p* or *P*. Let's start with fixing our controller.

Implementing pause/resume in WorkoutController

To pause a running exercise, we need to stop the interval callbacks that are occurring after every second. The $interval service provides a mechanism to cancel the $interval using the promise returned (remember, as discussed in the previous chapter, the $interval service call returns a promise). Therefore, our goal will be to cancel the $interval service when we pause and set up this again when we resume. Perform the following steps:

1. Open the workout.js file and declare an exerciseIntervalPromise variable inside WorkoutController that will track the $interval promise.

2. Remove the $interval call that is used to decrement $scope.workoutTimeRemaining. We will be using a single timer to track the overall workout progress and individual exercise progress.

3. Refactor the startExercise method, remove the $interval call (including the then callback implementation) completely, and replace it with a single line:

```
var startExercise = function (exercisePlan) {
  // existing code
    exerciseIntervalPromise = startExerciseTimeTracking();
};
```

4. Add the startExerciseTimeTracking() method:

```
var startExerciseTimeTracking = function () {
    var promise = $interval(function () {
        ++$scope.currentExerciseDuration;
        --$scope.workoutTimeRemaining;
    }, 1000, $scope.currentExercise.duration
      - $scope.currentExerciseDuration);

    promise.then(function () {
        var next = getNextExercise($scope.currentExercise);
        if (next) {
            startExercise(next);
        } else {
            $location.path('/finish');
        }});
    return promise;
}
```

All the logic to support starting/resuming an exercise has now been moved into this method. The code looks similar to what was there in the startExercise function, except the $interval promise is returned from the function in this case.

Also, instead of having a separate $interval service for tracking the overall workout time remaining, we are now using a single $interval to increment currentExerciseDuration and decrement workoutTimeRemaining. This refactoring helps us to simplify the pause logic as we do not need to cancel and start two $interval services. The number of times the $interval callback will be triggered also has a different expression now:

```
$scope.currentExercise.duration - $scope.currentExerciseDuration
```

The currentExercise.duration is the total duration of the exercise, and currentExerciseDuration signifies how long we have been doing the exercise. The difference is the time remaining.

Lastly, add methods for pausing and resuming after the startExerciseTimeTracking function:

```
$scope.pauseWorkout = function () {
    $interval.cancel(exerciseIntervalPromise);
    $scope.workoutPaused = true;
};
$scope.resumeWorkout = function () {
    exerciseIntervalPromise = startExerciseTimeTracking();
    $scope.workoutPaused = false;
};
$scope.pauseResumeToggle = function () {
    if ($scope.workoutPaused) {
        $scope.resumeWorkout();
    } else {
        $scope.pauseWorkout();
    }
}
```

The pauseWorkout function pauses the workout by cancelling the existing interval by calling the $interval.cancel function. The cancel method takes the exerciseIntervalPromise object (set in the startExercise function) that is the interval promise to cancel.

The resumeWorkout method sets up the interval again by calling the startExerciseTimeTracking() function again. Both these methods set the state of the workout by setting the wokoutPaused variable.

The `pauseResumeToggle` function acts as a toggle switch that can pause and resume the workout alternately. We will be using this method in our view binding. So let's shift our focus to the view implementation.

Adding the view fragment for pausing/resuming

We need to show a pause/resume overlay `div` when the mouse hovers over the central exercise area. A naïve way to add this feature would be to use the `ng-mouse*` directives. However, let's do it this way and learn a bit or two about the `ng-mouse*` directives.

Pausing/resuming overlays using mouse events

Open `workout.html` and update the exercise `div` with this:

```
<div id="exercise-pane" class="col-sm-7" ng-mouseenter =
  "showPauseOverlay=true" ng-mouseleave="showPauseOverlay=false">
```

Inside the preceding `div` element and just before the `WorkoutAudioController` span, add this:

```
<div id="pause-overlay" ng-click="pauseResumeToggle()" ng-
show="showPauseOverlay" >
  <span class="glyphicon glyphicon-pause pause absolute-center"
     ng-class="{'glyphicon-pause' : !workoutPaused, 'glyphicon-play' :
workoutPaused}"></span>
</div>
```

Also, go ahead and update the `app.css` file in the CSS folder with the updated file available in `chapter3/checkpoint3/app/css`. We have updated `app.css` with styles related to pause the `overlay div` element.

Now open the `app.css` file and comment the CSS property **opacity** for style `#pause-overlay`. Additionally, comment the style defined for `#pause-overlay:hover`.

In the first `div` (id=exercise-pane) function, we have used some new `ng-mouse*` directives available in AngularJS. These directives wrap the standard JavaScript mouse event. As the name suggests, the `ng-mouseenter` directives evaluate the expression when the mouse enters the element on which the directive is defined. The `ng-mouseleave` directive is just the reverse. We use these directives to set the scope property `showPauseOverlay` true or false based on the location of the mouse. Based on the `showPauseOverlay` value, the `ng-show="showPauseOverlay"` shows/hides the pause overlay.

Refresh the workout page and we should see a **pause** button overlay over the exercise area. We can click on it to pause and resume the workout.

Other directives such as ng-mousedown, ng-mousemove, and ng-mouseover are there to support the corresponding mouse events.

Be very careful with directives such as mouseover and mousemove. Depending upon how the HTML is set up, these directives can have a severe impact on the performance of the page as these events are rapidly raised on mouse movements that cause repeated evaluation of the attached directive expression.

We seldom require using the ng-mouse* directives. Even the preceding implementation can be done in a far better way without using ng-mouseenter or ng-mouseleave directives.

Pausing/resuming overlays with plain CSS

If you are a CSS ninja, you must be shaking your head in disgust after looking at the earlier implementation. We don't need the mouse events to show/hide an overlay. CSS has an inbuilt pseudo selector `:hover` for it, a far superior mechanism for showing overlays as compared to mouse-event bindings.

Let's get rid of all the `ng-mouse*` directive that we used and the `showPauseOverlay` variable. Remove the mouse-related directive declarations from the `exercise-pane` portion of `div` and `ng-show` directive from `pause-overlay` div. Also uncomment the styles that we commented in `app.css` in the last section. We will achieve the same effect but this time with plain CSS.

Let's talk about other elements of the pause/resume `div` (id="pause-overlay") overlay, which we have not touched on till now. On clicking on this `div` element, we call the `pauseResumeToggle` function that changes the state of the exercise. We have also used the `ng-class` directive to dynamically add/remove CSS classes based on the state of the exercise. The `ng-class` directive is a pretty useful directive that is used quite frequently, so why not learn a little more about it?

CSS class manipulation using ng-class

The `ng-class` directive allows us to dynamically set the class on an element based on some condition. The `ng-class` directive takes an expression that can be in one of the three formats:

- **A string**: Classes get applied on the base on the string tokens. Each space -delimited token is treated as a class. The following is an example:

  ```
  $scope.cls="class1 class2 class3"
  ng-class="cls" // Will apply the above three classes.
  ```

- **An array**: Each element in an array should be a string. The following is an example:

  ```
  $scope.cls=["class1", "class2", "class3"]
  ng-class="cls" // Will apply the above three classes.
  ```

- **An object**: Since objects in JavaScript are just a bunch of key-value maps, when we use the object expression, the key gets applied as a class if the value part evaluates to true. We use this syntax in our implementation:

  ```
  ng-class="{'glyphicon-pause' : !workoutPaused,
    'glyphicon-play' : workoutPaused}"
  ```

In this case, the `glyphicon-pause` (the pause icon) class is added when `workoutPaused` is `false`, and `glyphicon-play` (the play icon) is added when `workoutPaused` is `true`. Here, `glyphicon-pause`/`glyphicon-play` is the CSS name for Bootstrap font glyphs. Check the Bootstrap site for these glyphs `http://getbootstrap.com/components/`. The end result is based on the workout state, the appropriate icon is shown.

The ng-class directive is a *super* useful directive, and anytime we want to support dynamic behavior with CSS, this is the directive to use.

Let's re-verify that the pause functionality is working fine after the changes. Reload the workout page and try to pause the workout. Everything seems to be working fine except... the audio did not stop. Well, we did not tell it to stop so it did not! Let's fix this behavior too.

Stopping audio on pause

We need to extend our `WorkoutAudioController` function so that it can react to the exercise being paused. The approach here again will be to add a watch on the parent scope property `workoutPaused`. Open `workout.js` and inside the `WorkoutAudioController`, add this watch code before the `init` function declaration:

```
$scope.$watch('workoutPaused', function (newValue, oldValue) {
    if (newValue) {
        $scope.ticksAudio.pause();
        $scope.nextUpAudio.pause();
        $scope.nextUpExerciseAudio.pause();
        $scope.halfWayAudio.pause();
        $scope.aboutToCompleteAudio.pause();
    } else {
        $scope.ticksAudio.play();
        if ($scope.halfWayAudio.currentTime > 0 &&
          $scope.halfWayAudio.currentTime <
            $scope.halfWayAudio.duration)
      $scope.halfWayAudio.play();
    if ($scope.aboutToCompleteAudio.currentTime > 0 &&
        $scope.aboutToCompleteAudio.currentTime <
          $scope.aboutToCompleteAudio.duration)
        $scope.aboutToCompleteAudio.play();
    }
});
```

When the workout pauses, we pause all the audio elements irrespective of whether they are playing or not. Resuming is a tricky affair. Only if the *halfway* audio and *about to complete* audio are playing at the time of the pause do need to continue them. The conditional statements perform the same check. For the time being, we do not bother with the upcoming exercise audio.

Go ahead and refresh the workout page and try to pause the workout now. This time the audio should also pause.

Our decision to create a `WorkoutAudioController` object is serving us well. We have been able to react to a pause/resume state change in the audio controller instead of littering the main workout controller with extra code.

Let's add some more goodness to the pause/resume functionality by adding keyboard support.

Using the keyboard to pause/resume exercises

We plan to use the *p* or *P* key to toggle between the pause and resume state. If AngularJS has mouse-event support, then it will definitely have support for keyboard events too. Yes indeed and we are going to use the `ng-keypress` directive for this.

Go ahead and change the app container `div` (class="workout-app-container") to:

```
<div class="row workout-app-container" tabindex="1"
  ng-keypress="onKeyPressed($event)">
```

The first thing that we have done here is add the `tabindex` attribute to the `div` element. This is required as keyboard events are captured by elements that can have focus. Focus for HTML input elements makes sense but for read-only elements such as `div` having keyboard focus requires `tabindex` to be set.

The previous code captures the keypress event at the div level. If we have to capture such an event at a global level (the document level), we need to have a mechanism to propagate the captured event to child controllers such as WorkoutController.

We will not be covering how to actually capture keyboard events at the document level, but point you to these excellent resources for more information:

- https://github.com/drahak/angular-hotkeys
- http://chieffancypants.github.io/angular-hotkeys/
- http://stackoverflow.com/questions/15044494/what-is-angularjs-way-to-create-global-keyboard-shortcuts

These libraries work by creating services/directives to capture keyboard events.

Secondly, we add the ng-keypress directive and in the expression, call the onKeyPress function, passing in a special object $event.

$event is the native JavaScript event object that contains a number of details about the cause and source of the event. All directives that react to events can pass this $event object around. This includes all ng-mouse*, ng-key*, ng-click, and ng-dblclick directives and some other directives.

Open the workout.js file and add the method implementation for onKeyPressed:

```
$scope.onKeyPressed = function (event) {
    if (event.which == 80 || event.which == 112) { // 'p' or 'P'
        $scope.pauseResumeToggle();
    }
};
```

The code is quite self-explanatory; we check for the keycode value in event.which and if it is *p* or *P*, we toggle the workout state by calling pauseResumeToggle().

There are two other directives available for keyboard-related events namely, ng-keydown and ng-keyup. As the name suggests, these directives evaluate the assigned expression on keydown and keyup events.

The updated implementation is available in `checkpoint3` folder under `chapter3`.

GitHub branch: checkpoint3.3 (folder – trainer)

The *7 Minute Workout* app is getting into better shape. Let's add another enhancement to this series by improving the video panel loading and playback support.

Enhancing the workout video panel

The current video panel implementation can at best be termed as amateurish. The size of the default player is small. When we play the video, the workout does not pause. The video playback is interrupted on exercise transitions. Also, the overall video load experience adds a noticeable lag at the start of every exercise routine which we all would have noticed. This is a clear indication that this approach to video playback needs some fixing.

Since we can now pause the workout, pausing the workout on video playback can be implemented. Regarding the size of the player and the general lag at the start of every exercise, we can fix it by showing the image thumbnail for the exercise video instead of loading the video player itself. When the user clicks on the thumbnail, we load a pop up/dialog that has a bigger size video player that plays the selected video. Sounds like a plan! Let's implement it.

Refactoring the video panel and controller

To start with, let's refactor out the view template for the video panel into a separate file as we did for the description panel. Open the `workout.html` file and remove the script declaration for the video panel template (`<script type="text/ng-template" id="video-panel.html">...</script>`).

Change the `ng-include` directive to point to the new video template:

```
<div id="video-panel" class="col-sm-3"
  ng-include="'partials/video-panel.html'">
```

Make note of the path change for the `ng-include` attribute; the template file will now reside in the `partials` folder similar to `description-panel.html`.

Next, we add the `video-panel.html` file from `partial` to our app. Go ahead and copy this file from the companion codebase `chapter3/checkpoint4/app/partials`.

Other than some style fixes, there are two notable changes done to the video panel template in `video-panel.html`. The first one is a declaration of the new controller:

```
<div class="panel panel-info"
ng-controller="WorkoutVideosController">
```

As we refactor out the video functionality, we are going to create a new controller, WorkoutVideosController.

The second change is as follows:

```
<img height="220" ng-src="
  https://i.ytimg.com/vi/{{video}}/hqdefault.jpg" />
```

The earlier version of the template used iframe to load the video with the src attribute set to interpolation {{video}} with the complete video URL. With the preceding change, the video property does not point directly to a YouTube video; instead it just contains the identifier for the video (such as dmYwZH_BNd0).

 We have referenced this *Stack Overflow* post http://stackoverflow.com/questions/2068344/how-do-i-get-a-youtube-video-thumbnail-from-the-youtube-api, to determine the thumbnail image URL for our videos.

video-panel.html also contains a view template embedded in script tag:

```
<script type="text/ng-template" id="youtube-modal">...<script>
```

We will be using this template to show the video in a pop-up dialog later.

Since we plan to use the video identifier instead of the absolute URL, workout data needs to be fixed in workout.js. Rather than doing it manually, copy the updated workout data from the workout.js file in chapter2\checkpoint4\app\js\7MinWorkout. The only major change here is the videos array that earlier contained absolute URLs but now has video IDs like this:

```
videos: ["dmYwZH_BNd0", "BABOdJ-2Z6o", "c4DAnQ6DtF8"],
```

If we comment out the ng-controller="WorkoutVideosController" attribute in the video-panel.html file and refresh the workout page, we should have a better page load experience, devoid of any noticeable lags. Instead of videos, we now render images.

 Remember to uncomment the declaration ng-controller="WorkoutVideosController" before proceeding further.

However, we have lost the video replay functionality! Let's fix this too.

Video playback in the pop-up dialog

The plan here is to open a dialog when the user clicks on the video image and plays the video in the dialog. Once again, we are going to look at a third-party control/component that can help us here. Well, we have a very able and popular library to support modal pop-up dialogs in Angular, the `ui.bootstrap` dialog (`http://angular-ui.github.io/bootstrap/`). This library consists of a set of directives that are part of Bootstrap JavaScript components. If you are a fan of Twitter Bootstrap, then this library is a perfect drop-in replacement that we can use.

 The `ui.bootstrap` dialog is part of a larger package `angular-ui` (`http://angular-ui.github.io/`) that contains a number of AngularJS components ready to be used within our projects.

Similar to the Bootstrap modal popup, `ui.bootstrap` too has a modal dialog and we are going to use it.

Integrating the ui.bootstrap modal dialog

To start with, we need to reference the `ui.bootstrap` library in our app. Go ahead and add the reference to `ui.bootstrap` in the `index.html` script section after the framework script declarations:

```
<script src="//cdnjs.cloudflare.com/ajax/libs/
    angular-ui-bootstrap/0.10.0/ui-bootstrap-tpls.js"></script>
```

Import the `ui.bootstrap` module in `app.js`:

```
angular.module('app', ['ngRoute', 'ngSanitize',
    '7minWorkout', 'mediaPlayer', 'ui.bootstrap']).
```

The `ui.bootstrap` module is now ready for consumption.

Now we need to add a new JavaScript file to implement the video popup. Copy the `workoutvideos.js` file from `chapter3\checkpoint4\app\js\7MinWorkout`. Also, add a reference to the file in `index.html` after the `workout.js` reference:

```
<script src="js/7MinWorkout/workoutvideos.js"></script>
```

Let's try to understand the important parts of `workoutvideos.js`.

We start with declaring the controller. Nothing new here, we are already familiar with how to create a controller using the Module API. The only point of interest here is the injection of the `$modal` service:

```
angular.module('7minWorkout')
    .controller('WorkoutVideosController', ['$scope', '$modal',
        function ($scope, $modal) {
```

The `ui.bootstrap` modal dialog is controlled by the `$modal` service. We were expecting a directive for the modal dialog that we could manage through the controller. As it turns out, the same role here is played by the `$modal` service. When invoked, it dynamically injects a directive (`<div modal-window></div>`) into the view HTML which finally shows up as popup.

 In Angular, services normally do not interact with view elements. The `$modal` service is an exception to this rule. Internally, this service uses the `$modalStack` service that does DOM manipulation.

In `WorkoutVideosController`, we define the `playVideo` method that uses the `$modal` service to load the video in the popup. The first thing we do in the `playVideo` method is to pause the workout. Then, we call the `$modal.open` method to open the popup.

The `$modal.open` function takes a number of arguments that affect the content and behavior of the modal popup. Here is our implementation:

```
var dailog = $modal.open({
    templateUrl: 'youtube-modal',
    controller: VideoPlayerController,
    scope:$scope.$new(true),
    resolve: {
        video: function () {
            return '//www.youtube.com/embed/' + videoId;
        }
    },
    size: 'lg'
}).result['finally'](function () {
    $scope.resumeWorkout();
});
```

Here is a rundown of the arguments:

* `templateUrl`: This is the path to the template content. In our case, we have embedded the modal template in the `script` tag of the `video-panel.html` file:

    ```
    <script type="text/ng-template" id="youtube-modal">
    ```

Instead of the template URL, we can provide inline HTML content to the dialog service by using a different argument template. Not a very useful option as readability of the template HTML is severely affected.

- `controller`: Like a true MVC component, this dialog allows us to attach a controller to the dialog scope. We reference the `VideoPlayController` controller function that we have declared inline. Every time the modal dialog is opened, a new `VideoPlayController` object is instantiated and linked to the modal dialog view (defined using the `templateUrl` path just mentioned).

We have declared the controller inline as it has no use outside the dialog. Instead, if `VideoPlayController` was declared using the Module API `controller` function, we will have to use alternate controller syntax such as `controller: 'VideoPlayerController', //` `Using quotes ''`.

- `scope`: This parameter can be used to provide a specific scope to the modal dialog view. By default, the modal dialog creates a new scope that inherits from `$rootScope`. By assigning the `scope` configuration to `$scope.$new(true)`, we are creating a new isolated scope. This scope will be available inside the dialog context when it opens.

The `$new` function on the scope object allows us to create a new scope in code. We rarely need to create our own scope objects as they are mostly created as part of directive execution, but at times the `$new` function can come in handy, as in this case.

Calling `$new` without an argument creates a new scope that inherits (prototypal inheritance) from the scope on which the function is invoked.

Having the `true` parameter in `$new` instructs the scope API to create an isolated scope.

In AngularJS, isolated scopes are scopes that do not inherit from their parent scope and hence do not have access to parent scope properties. Isolated scopes help in keeping the parent and child scopes independent of each other, hence making the child component more reusable across the app. The video player dialog is a simple example of this. The dialog is only dependent upon the resolved YouTube video URL and can be used anywhere in the application where there is a requirement to play a specific video.

We will cover isolated scopes in greater depth in the chapter dedicated to AngularJS directives.

- `resolve`: Since we have declared our modal scope to be an isolated scope, we need a mechanism to pass the selected video from the parent scope to the isolated modal dialog scope. The `resolve` argument solves this parameter passing problem.

  The `resolve` argument is an interesting parameter. It takes an object where each property is a function and when injected with the key name (property name) into the dialog controller, it is resolved to the function's return value.

  For example, the `resolve` object has one property video that returns the concatenated value of the YouTube video URL with the video ID (passed to the `playVideo` function as `videoId`). We use the property name `video` and inject it into `VideoPlayerController`. Whenever the dialog is loaded, the `video` function is invoked and the return value is injected in the `VideoPlayerController` as the property name `video` itself.

  The `resolve` object hash is a good mechanism for passing specific data to the modal dialog keeping the dialog reusable as long as the correct parameters are passed.

- `size`: Used to specify the size of the dialog. We use `large(lg)`, the other option is `small(sm)`.

There are a few more options available for the `$modal.open` function. Refer to the documentation for `ui.bootstrap.modal` (`http://angular-ui.github.io/bootstrap/#/modal`) for more details.

The return value of the `$modal.open` function also interests us and this is how we use it:

```
.result['finally'](function () {
  $scope.resumeWorkout();
});
```

The `result` property on the returned object is a promise that gets resolved when the dialog closes. The `finally` function callback is invoked irrespective of whether the result promise is resolved or rejected and in the callback we just resume the workout.

The `result` property is not the only property on the object returned by `$modal.open`. Let's understand the use of these properties:

- `close(data)`: This function can close the dialog. The data argument is optional and can be used to pass a value from the modal dialog to the parent components that invoked it.

- `dismiss(reason)`: This is similar to the `close` function, but it allows us to cancel the dialog.

- `result`: As detailed previously, this is a promise that gets resolved when we close the dialog. If the dialog is closed using the `close(data)` method, the value is resolved to the `data` value. If `dismiss(reason)` is called, the promise is rejected with the `reason` value. Remember, these callbacks are available on the `then` method of the `promise` object and look something like this:

```
result.then(function(result){...}, function(reason){...});
```

If we had resumed the workout using `then` instead of `finally`, the code would have looked like this:

```
.result.then(function (result) {
    $scope.resumeWorkout();        // on success
}, function (reason) {
    $scope.resumeWorkout(); // on failure
});
```

Since `finally` gets called irrespective of whether the promise is resolved or rejected, we save some code duplication.

 We have to use the object indexer syntax (`result['finally']`) to invoke `finally` as `finally` is a keyword in JavaScript.

- `opened`: This is also a promise that is resolved when the modal dialog is opened and the dialog template has been downloaded and rendered. This promise can be used to perform some activity once the dialog is fully loaded.

The return value of `$modal.open` comes in handy when we desire to control the modal dialog from outside the dialog itself. For example, we can call `dialog.close()` to forcefully close the dialog popup from `WorkoutVideosController`.

The implementation of `VideoPlayerController` is simple:

```
var VideoPlayerController = function ($scope, $modalInstance, video) {
    $scope.video = video;
    $scope.ok = function () {
        $modalInstance.close();
    };
};
```

We inject three dependencies: the standard `$scope`, `$modalInstance`, and video.

The `$modalInstance` service is used to control the opened instance of the dialog as we can see in the `$scope.ok` function. This is the same object that is returned when the `$modal.open` method is called. The method and properties for `$modalInstance` have already been detailed earlier in the section. We just use the `close` method to close the dialog.

The `video` object is the YouTube link that we have injected using the video property of the `resolve` object while calling `$modal.open`. We assign the video link received to the modal scope and then the view template (`youtube-modal`) binds to this video link:

```
<iframe width="100%" height="480" src="{{video}}" frameborder="0"
    allowfullscreen></iframe>
```

Before we forget, since we have defined the `VideoPlayController` as a normal function, we need to make sure it is minification-safe. Hence, we add a `$inject` property on the `VideoPlayController` object with the required dependencies:

```
VideoPlayerController["$inject"] = ['$scope', '$modalInstance',
    'video'];
```

Remember we covered the `$inject` annotation syntaxes in *Chapter 2, Building Our First App – 7 Minute Workout*.

Let's try out our implementation. Load the workout page and click on the video image. The video should load into a modal popup:

The complete code so far is available in `chapter3\checkpoint4`. I will again encourage you to look at this code if you are having issues with your own implementation.

GitHub Branch: checkpoint3.4 (folder – trainer)

The app is definitely looking better now. Next, let's add some razzmatazz to our app by adding a pinch of animation to it!

Animations with AngularJS

HTML animations can either be done using css, or by using some JavaScript library such as jQuery. Given that CSS3 has inherited support for animation, using CSS is a preferred way of implementing animation in our apps. With the use of CSS3 transitions and animation constructs, we can achieve some impressive animation effects.

In AngularJS, a set of directives has been built in such a way that adding animation to these directives is easy. Directives such as ng-repeat, ng-include, ng-view, ng-if, ng-switch, ng-class, and ng-show/ng-hide have build-in support for animation.

What does it mean when we say the directive supports animation?

Well, from the CSS perspective, it implies that the previous directive dynamically adds and removes classes to the HTML element on which they are defined at specific times during directive execution. How this helps in CSS animation will be clear when we discuss CSS animation in our next section.

From a script-based animation perspective, we can use the module animate function to animate the previous directives using libraries such as jQuery.

Let's look at both CSS and script-based animation and then understand what Angular has to offer.

AngularJS CSS animation

CSS animation is all about animating from one style configuration to another using some animation effect. The animation effect can be achieved by using any of the following two mechanisms:

- **Transition**: This is where we define a start CSS state, the end CSS state, and the transition effect (animation) to use. The effect is defined using the style property transition. The following CSS style is an example:

```
.my-class {
  -webkit-transition:0.5s linear all;
  transition:0.5s linear all;
  background:black;
}
```

```
.my-class:hover {
    background:blue;
}
```

When the preceding styles are applied to an HTML element, it changes the background color of the element from black to blue on hover with a transition effect defined by the `transition` property.

Such animations are not just limited to pseudo selector such as hover. Let's add this style:

```
.my-class.animate {
    background:blue;
}
```

When this style is added, a similar effect as demonstrated previously can be achieved by dynamically adding the `animate` class to an HTML element which already has `my-class` applied.

- **Animation**: This is where we define the start CSS state, the keyframe configuration that defines the time duration of the animation, and other details about how the animation should progress. For example, these CSS styles have the same effect as a CSS transition:

```
.my-class {
    background:black;
}
.my-class:hover {
    background:blue;
    animation: color 1s linear;
    -webkit-animation: color 1s linear;
}
@keyframes color {
    from {
        background: black;
    }
    to {
        background: blue;
    }
}
```

The basic difference between transition and animation is that we do not need two CSS states defined in the case of animation. In the first example, transition happens when the CSS on the element changes from `.my-class` to `.my-class:hover`, whereas in the second example, animation starts when the CSS state is `.my-class:hover`, so there is no end CSS concept with animation.

The `animation` property on `.my-class:hover` allows us to configure the timing and duration of the animation but not the actual appearance. The appearance is controlled by `@keyframes`. In the preceding code, `color` is the name of the animation and `@keyframes color` defines the appearance.

 We will not be covering CSS-based animation in detail here. There are many good articles and blog posts that cover these topics in depth. To start with, we can refer to MDN documentation for transition (`https://developer.mozilla.org/en-US/docs/Web/Guide/CSS/Using_CSS_transitions`) and for animation (`https://developer.mozilla.org/en-US/docs/Web/Guide/CSS/Using_CSS_animations`).

To facilitate animations, AngularJS directives add some specific classes to the HTML element.

Directives that add, remove, and move DOM elements, including `ng-repeat`, `ng-include`, `ng-view`, `ng-if`, and `ng-switch`, add one of the three sets of classes during different times:

- `ng-enter` and `ng-enter-active`: These are added when directive adds HTML elements to the DOM.
- `ng-leave` and `ng-leave-active`: These are added before an HTML element is removed from the DOM.
- `ng-move` and `ng-move-active`: These are added when an element is moved in the DOM. This is applicable to the `ng-repeat` directive only.

The `ng-<event>` directive signifies the start and `ng-<event>-active` signifies the end of CSS states. We can use this `ng-<event>\ng-<event>-active` pair for transition-based animation and `ng-<event>` only for keyframe-based animation.

Directives such as `ng-class`, `ng-show`, and `ng-hide` work a little differently. The starting and ending class names are a bit different. The following table details the different class names that get applied for these directives:

Event	Start CSS	End CSS	Directive
Hiding an element	`.ng-hide-add`	`ng-hide-add-active`	`ng-show`, `ng-hide`
Showing an element	`.ng-hide-remove`	`ng-hide-add-remove-active`	`ng-show`, `ng-hide`

Event	Start CSS	End CSS	Directive
Adding a class to an element	`<class>-add`	`<class>-add-active`	`ng-class` and `class="{{expression}}"`
Removing a class from an element	`<class>-remove`	`<class>-remove-active`	`ng-class` and `class="{{expression}}"`

Make note that even interpolation-based class changes (`class="{{expression}}"`) are included for animation support.

Another important aspect of animation that we should be aware of is that the start and end classes added are not permanent. These classes are added for the duration of the animation and removed thereafter. AngularJS respects the transition duration and removes the classes only after the animation is over.

Let's now look at JavaScript-based animation before we begin implementing animation for our app.

AngularJS JavaScript animation

The idea here too remains the same but instead of using CSS-based animation, we use JavaScript to do animation. This is the CSS:

```
.my-class {
  background:black;
}
.my-class:hover {
  background:blue;
}
```

We can do something that resembles JavaScript-based animation when we use jQuery (it requires a plugin such as `http://www.bitstorm.org/jquery/color-animation/`):

```
$(".my-class").hover( function()
  {$(this).animate({backgroundColor:blue},1000,"linear");
```

To integrate script-based animation with Angular, the framework provides the Module API method `animation`:

```
animation(name, animationFactory);
```

The first argument is the name of the animation and the second parameter, `animationFactory`, is an object with the callback function that gets called when Angular adds or removes classes (such as `ng-enter` and `ng-leave`) as explained in the CSS section earlier in the chapter.

It works something like this. Given here is an AngularJS construct that supports animation such as `ng-repeat`:

```
<div ng-repeat="item in items" class='repeat-animation'>
```

We can enable animation by using the Module API animation method:

```
myApp.animation('.repeat-animation', function() {
  return {
    enter : function(element, done) { //ng-enter or element added
    //Called when ng-enter is applied
    jQuery(element).css({
          opacity:0
      });
      jQuery(element).animate({
opacity:1
      }, done);
    }
  }
});
```

Here, we animate when `ng-enter` is applied from the opacity value from 0 to 1. This happens when an element is added to the `ng-repeat` directive. Also, Angular uses the class name of the HTML element to match and run the animation. In the preceding example, any HTML element with the `.repeat-animation` class will trigger the previous animation when it is created.

For the `enter` function, the `element` parameter contains the element on which the directive has been applied and `done` is a function that should be called to tell Angular that the animation is complete. Always remember to call this `done` function. The preceding jQuery `animate` function takes `done` as a parameter and calls it when the animation is complete.

Other than the `enter` function, we can add callbacks for `leave`, `move`, `beforeAddClass`, `addClass`, `beforeRemoveClass`, and `removeClass`. Check the AngularJS documentation on the ngAnimate module at `https://code.angularjs.org/1.2.15/docs/api/ngAnimate` for more details. Also, a more comprehensive treatment for AngularJS animation is available on the blog post at `http://www.yearofmoo.com/2013/08/remastered-animation-in-angularjs-1-2.html`.

Armed with an understanding of animation now, let's get back to our app and add some animation to it.

Adding animation to 7 Minute Workout

Time to add some animation support for our app! The AngularJS `ngAnimate` module contains the support for Angular animation. Since it is not a core module, we need to inject this module and include its script.

Add this reference to the angular animate script in `index.html`:

```
<script src="http://ajax.googleapis.com/ajax/libs/angularjs/1.3.3/
    angular-animate.js"></script>
```

Add module dependency for the `ngAnimate` module in `app.js`:

```
angular.module('app', ['ngRoute', 'ngSanitize', '7minWorkout',
    'mediaPlayer', 'ui.bootstrap', 'ngAnimate']).
```

We are all set to go.

The first animation we are going to enable is the `ng-view` transition, sliding in from the right. Adding this animation is all about adding the appropriate CSS in our `app.css` file. Open it and add:

```
div[ng-view] {
    position: absolute;
    width: 100%;
    height: 100%;
}
div[ng-view] .ng-enter,
div[ng-view] .ng-leave {
    -webkit-transition: all 1s ease;
    -moz-transition: all 1s ease;
    -o-transition: all 1s ease;
    transition: all 1s ease;
}
div[ng-view] .ng-enter {
    left: 100%;      /*initial css for view transition in*/
}
div[ng-view] .ng-leave {
    left: 0;         /*initial css for view transition out*/
}
div[ng-view] .ng-enter-active {
    left: 0;         /*final css for view transition in*/
}
div[ng-view] .ng-leave-active {
    left: -100%;     /*final css for view transition out*/
}
```

This basically is transition-based animation. We first define the common styles and then specific styles for the initial and final CSS states. It is important to realize that the div[ng-view] .ng-enter class is applied for the new view being loaded and div[ng-view] .ng-leave for the view being destroyed.

For the loading view, we transition from 100% to 0% for the left parameter.

For the view that is being removed, we start from left 0% and transition to left -100%

Try out the new changes by loading the start page and navigate to the workout or finish page. We get a nice right-to-left animation effect!

Let's add a keyframe-based animation for videos as it is using ng-repeat, which supports animation. This time we are going to use an excellent third-party CSS library animate.css (http://daneden.github.io/animate.css/) that defines some common CSS keyframe animations. Execute the following steps:

1. Add the reference to the library in index.html after the bootstrap.min.css declaration:

   ```
   <link href="//cdnjs.cloudflare.com/ajax/
   libs/animate.css/3.1.0/animate.min.css" rel="stylesheet" />
   ```

2. Update the video-panel.html file and add a custom class video-image to the ng-repeat element:

   ```
   <div ng-repeat="video in currentExercise.details.related.videos"
   ng-click="playVideo(video)" class="row video-image">
   ```

3. Update the app.css file to animate the ng-repeat directive:

   ```
   .video-image.ng-enter,
   .video-image.ng-move {
       -webkit-animation: bounceIn 1s;
       -moz-animation: bounceIn 1s;
       -ms-animation: bounceIn 1s;
       animation: bounceIn 1s;
   }
   .video-image.ng-leave {
       -webkit-animation: bounceOut 1s;
       -moz-animation: bounceOut 1s;
       -ms-animation: bounceOut 1s;
       animation: bounceOut 1s;
   }
   ```

The setup here is far simpler as compared to transition-based animation. Most of the code is around vendor-specific prefixes.

We define animation effect `bounceIn` for the `ng-enter` and `ng-move` states and `bounceOut` for the `ng-leave` state. Much cleaner and simpler!

To verify the implementation, open the workout and wait for the first exercise to complete to see the bounce-out effect and the next exercise to load for the bounce -in effect.

 The app implementation so far is available in companion code `chapter3\checkpoint5`.

GitHub Branch: checkpoint3.5 (folder – trainer)

While using animation, we should not go overboard and add too much of it as it makes the app look amateurish. We have added enough animation to our app and now it's time to move to our next topic.

One area that we still have not explored is Angular services. We have used some Angular services, but we have little understanding of how services work and what it takes to create a service. The next section is dedicated to this very topic.

Workout history tracking using Angular services

What if we can track the workout history? When did we last exercise? Did we complete it? How much time did we spend?

Tracing workout history requires us to track workout progress. Somehow, we need to track when the workout starts and stops. This tracking data then needs to be persisted somewhere.

One way to implement this history tracking is to extend our `WorkoutController` function with the desired functionality. This approach is less than ideal, and we have already seen how to make use of another controller (such as `WorkoutAudioController`) and delegate all the related features to it.

In this case, historical data tracking does not require a controller, so instead we will be using a *service* to track historical data and share it across all app controllers. Before we start our journey of implementing the workout tracking service, let's learn a bit more about AngularJS services.

AngularJS services primer

Services are one of the fundamental constructs available in AngularJS. As described earlier, services in Angular are reusable (mostly non-UI) components that can be shared across controllers, directives, filters, and other services. We have already used a number of inbuilt Angular services such as $interval, $location, and $timeout.

A service in AngularJS is:

- **A reusable piece of code that is used across AngularJS constructs**: For example, services such as $location, $interval, $timeout, and $modal are components that perform a specific type of work and can be injected anywhere. Services normally do not interact with DOM.

 The $modal service is an exception to this rule as it does manipulate DOM to inject modal dialog related HTML.

- **Singleton in nature**: The singleton nature of the service means that the service object injected by the DI framework is the same across all AngularJS constructs. Once the AngularJS DI framework creates the service for the first time, it caches the service for future use and never recreates it. For example, wherever we inject the $location service, we always get the same $location object.

- **Created on demand**: The DI framework only creates the service when it is requested for the first time. This implies that if we create a service and never inject it in any controller, directive, filter, or service, then the service will never be instantiated.

- **Can be used to share state across the application**: Due to the singleton nature of the service, services are a mechanism to share data across all AngularJS constructs. For example, if we inject a service into multiple controllers, and update the service state in one of the controllers, other controllers will get the updated state as well. This happens because service objects are singleton, and hence everyone gets the same service reference to play with.

Let's learn how to create a service.

Creating AngularJS services

AngularJS provides five recipes (ways) to create a service. These recipes are named constant, value, service, factory, and provider. The end result is still a service object that is consumable across the application. We can create these service objects by either using the Module API or the $provide service (which itself is a service!).

The Module API itself internally uses the `$provide` service. We will be using the Module API for our sample code.

Let's try to understand each of the five ways of creating a service. The first ones that are constant and value are somewhat similar.

Creating services with the constant and value services

Both the *constant* and *value* services are used to create values/objects in Angular. With the Module API, we can use the `constant` and `value` functions respectively to create a constant and value service. For example, here are the syntaxes:

```
angular.module('app').constant('myObject', {prop1:"val1",
  prop2:"val2"});
```

or

```
angular.module('app').value('myObject', {prop1:"val1",
  prop2:"val2"});
```

The preceding code creates a service with the name `myObject`. To use this service, we just need to inject it:

```
angular.module('app').controller('MyCtrl',['$scope','myObject',
function($scope, myObject) {
    $scope.data=myObject.prop1; //Will assign "val1" to data
});
```

 Angular framework service names by convention are prefixed with the $ sign (`$interval`, `$location`) to easily differentiate these from user-defined services. While creating our own service, we should not prefix the $ sign to our service names, to avoid confusion.

The one difference between the constant and value service is that the constant service can be injected at the configuration stage of the app whereas the value service cannot.

In the previous chapter, we talked about the configration and run stage of every AngularJS module. The configuration stage is used for the initialization of our service components before they can be used. During the configuration stage, the standard DI does not work as at this point services and other components are still being configured before they become injectable. The constant service is something that we can still inject even during the configuration stage. We can simply inject the `myObject` service in the `config` function:

```
angular.module('app').config(function(myObject){
```

> We should use the constant service if we want some data to be available at the configuration stage of the module initialization too.

Another thing to keep in mind is that the constant and value services do not take any dependencies so we cannot inject any.

Creating services using a service

These are services created using the module service method and look something like this:

```
angular.module('app').service('MyService1',['dep1',function(dep1)
    {
        this.prop1="val1";
        this.prop2="val2";
        this.prop3=dep1.doWork();
    }]);
```

The previous service is invoked like a constructor function by the framework and cached for the lifetime of the app. As explained earlier, the service is created on demand when requested for the first time. To contrast it with plain JavaScript, creating a service using the service function is equivalent to creating an object using the constructor function:

```
new MyService(dep1);
```

Services created using the *service* recipe can take dependencies (dep1). The next way to create a service is to use *factory*.

Creating services with a factory service

This mechanism of service creation uses a `factory` function. This function is responsible for creating the service and returning it. Angular invokes this `factory` function and caches the return value of this function as a `service` object: factory implementation looks like this:

```
angular.module('app').factory('MyService2', ['dep1', function (dep1) {
    var service = {
        prop1: "val1",
        prop2: "val2",
        prop3: dep1.doWork()
    };
    return service;
});
```

In the previous code, the `factory` function creates a `service` object, configures it, and then returns the object. The difference between the service and factory function is that, in the first case, Angular creates the `service` object treating the service as the `constructor` function, whereas the case of the factory service, we create the object and provide it to the framework to cache.

 Remember to return a value from the `factory` function or the service will be injected as undefined.

The factory way of creating a service is the most commonly used method as it provides a little more control over how the `service` object is constructed.

The last and the most sophisticated recipe of creating a service is provider.

Creating services with a provider service

The *provider* recipe gives us the maximum control over how a service is created and configured. All the previous ways of creating a service are basically pre-configured provider recipes to keep the syntax simple to understand. The provider mechanism of creating a service is seldom used, as we already have easier and more intuitive ways to create these sharable services.

In this method, the framework first creates a custom object that we define. This object should have a property `$get` (which itself is injectable) that should be the `factory` function as mentioned earlier. The return value of the `$get` function is the service instance of the desired service. If it all sounds gibberish, this example will help us understand the provider syntax:

```
angular.module('app').provider('myService3', function () {
    var prop1;
    this.setIntialProp1Value = function (value) {
        prop1 = value; // some initialization if required
    };
    this.$get = function (dep1) {
        var service = {
            prop1: prop1,
            prop2: dep1.doWork(),
            prop3: function () {}
        };
        return service;
    };
});
```

We define this piece of code as a provider service, `myService3`. Angular will create an object of this provider and call the `$get` factory function on it to create the actual service object. Note that we are injecting dependencies in the `$get` method, and not in the provider service declaration.

The final outcome is the same as `myService1` and `myService2` except that the provider allows us to configure the service creation at the configuration stage. The following code shows how we can configure the initial value of the `prop1` property of the `myService3` service:

```
angular.module('app').config(function (myService3Provider) {
    myService3Provider.setIntialProp1Value("providerVal");
});
```

Here, we call the initial `setIntialProp1Value` method on the provider, which affects the value of `prop1` (it sets it to `providerVal`) when the service is actually created. Also, make a note of the name of the dependency we have passed; it is `myService3Provider` and not `myService3`. Remember this convention or the configuration dependency injection will not work.

> I have created a fiddle to show how each of the constant, value, service, factory, and provider services are created. You can experiment with these service constructs here at `http://jsfiddle.net/cmyworld/k3jjk/`.

When should we use the provider recipe? Well, the provider syntax is useful only if we need to set up/initialize parts of the service before the service can be consumed. The `$route` service is a good example of it. We use the underlying `$routeProvider` to configure the routes before they can be used in the app.

With this understanding of AngularJS services, it is time for us to implement workout history tracking.

Implementing workout history tracking

The first task here is to define the service for tracking data. The service will provide a mechanism to start tracking when the workout starts and end tracking when the workout ends.

The WorkoutHistoryTracker service

We start with defining the service. Open the `services.js` file and add the initial service declaration as follows:

```
angular.module('7minWorkout')
    .factory('workoutHistoryTracker', ['$rootScope', function
    ($rootScope) {
        var maxHistoryItems = 20;    //Track for last 20 exercise
        var workoutHistory = [];
        var currentWorkoutLog = null;
        var service = {};
        return service;
}]);
```

We use the factory recipe to create our service and the dependency that we inject is $rootScope. Let's quickly go through some guidelines around using scope in the service.

Services and scopes

From a scope perspective, services have no association with scopes. Services are reusable pieces of components which are mostly non-UI centric and hence do not interact with DOM. Since a scope is always contextually bound to the view, passing $scope as a dependency to a service neither makes sense, nor is it allowed. Also, a scope's lifetime is linked to the associated DOM element. When the DOM is removed, the linked scope is also destroyed whereas services being singleton are only destroyed when the app is refreshed. Therefore, the only dependency injection allowed in a service from a scope perspective is $rootScope, which has a lifetime similar to the service lifetime.

We now understand that injecting current scope ($scope) in a service is not allowed. Even calling a service method by passing the current $scope value as a parameter is a bad idea. Calls such as the following in controller should be avoided:

```
myService.updateUser($scope);
```

Instead, pass data explicitly, which conveys the intent better.

```
myService.updateUser({first:$scope.first, last:$scope.last,
    age:$scope.age});
```

If we pass the current controller scope to the service, there is always a possibility that the service keeps the reference to this scope. Since services are singleton, this can lead to memory leaks as a scope does not get disposed of due to its reference inside the service.

Service implementation continued...

Continuing with the implementation, we will track the last 20 workouts done. The workoutHistory array will store the workout history. The currentWorkoutLog array tracks the current workout in progress.

Add two methods: `startTracking` and `endTracking` on the service object, as follows:

```
service.startTracking = function () {
    currentWorkoutLog = { startedOn: new Date().toISOString(),
completed: false,
exercisesDone: 0 };
    if (workoutHistory.length >= maxHistoryItems) {
        workoutHistory.shift();
    }
    workoutHistory.push(currentWorkoutLog);
};

service.endTracking = function (completed) {
    currentWorkoutLog.completed = completed;
    currentWorkoutLog.endedOn = new Date().toISOString();
    currentWorkoutLog = null;
};
```

The controller will call these methods to start and stop tracking of the exercise.

In the `startTracking` function, we start with creating a new workout log with the current time set. If the `workoutHistory` array has reached its limits, we delete the oldest entry before adding the new workout entry to `workoutHistory`.

The `endTracking` function marks the workout as completed based on the input variable. It also sets the end date of the workout and clears the `currentWorkoutLog` variable.

Add another service function `getHistory` that returns the `workoutHistory` array:

```
service.getHistory = function () {
  return workoutHistory;
}
```

Lastly, add an event subscriber:

```
$rootScope.$on("$routeChangeSuccess", function (e, args) {
    if (currentWorkoutLog) {
        service.endTracking(false); // End the current tracking if in
progress the route changes.
    }
});
```

Events in Angular are a new concept that we will touch upon later during the implementation. For now, it will be enough to say that this piece of code is used to end exercise tracking when the application route changes.

Passing a false value to the `endTracking` function marks the workout as incomplete.

Lastly, include the `services.js` reference in `index.html` after the `filters.js` reference.

```
<script src="js/7MinWorkout/services.js"></script>
```

We are now ready to integrate the service with our `WorkoutController` function.

Integrating the WorkoutHistoryTracker service with a controller

Open `workout.js` and inject the `workoutHistoryTracker` service dependency into the controller declaration:

```
.controller('WorkoutController', ['$scope', '$interval',
  '$location', '$timeout', 'workoutHistoryTracker', function (
  $scope, $interval, $location, $timeout, workoutHistoryTracker) {
```

The preceding injections are no different from the other services that we have injected so far.

Now add this line inside the `startWorkout` function just before the call to `startExercise`:

```
workoutHistoryTracker.startTracking();
$scope.currentExerciseIndex = -1;
startExercise($scope.workoutPlan.exercises[0]);
```

We simply start workout tracking when the workout starts.

We now need to stop tracking at some point. Find the function `startExerciseTimeTracking` and replace `$location.path('/finish');` with `workoutComplete();`. Then, go ahead and add the `workoutComplete` method:

```
var workoutComplete = function () {
workoutHistoryTracker.endTracking(true);
$location.path('/finish');
}
```

When the workout is complete, the `workoutComplete` function is invoked and calls the `workoutHistoryTracker.endTracking();` function to end tracking before navigating to the finish page.

With this, we have now integrated some basic workout tracking in our app. To verify tracking works as expected, let's add a view that shows the tracking history in a table/grid.

Adding the workout history view

We are going to implement the history page as a pop-up dialog. The link to the dialog will be available on the top `nav` object of the application, aligned to the right edge of the browser. Since we are adding the link to the top `nav` object, it can be accessed across pages.

Copy the updated `index.html` file from the companion code in `chapter3/checkpoint6/app`. Other than some style fixes, the two major changes to the `index.html` file are the addition of a new controller:

```
<body ng-app="app" ng-controller="RootController">
```

Add the history link:

```
<ul class="nav navbar-nav navbar-right"> <li>
  <a ng-click="showWorkoutHistory()" title="Workout
  History">History</a>
</li></ul>
```

As the previous declaration suggests, we need to add a new controller `RootController` to the app. Since it is declared alongside the `ng-app` directive, this controller will act as a parent controller for all the controllers in the app. The current implementation of `RootController` opens the modal dialog to show the workout history.

Copy the `root.js` file from `chapter3\checkpoint6\app\js` and place it in the same folder where the `app.js` file resides.

`RootController` implementation is similar to `WorkoutVideosController`. The only point of interest in the current `RootController` implementation is the use of the `workoutHistoryTracker` service to load and show workout history:

```
var WorkoutHistoryController = function ($scope, $modalInstance,
  workoutHistoryTracker) {
  $scope.search = {};
$scope.search.completed = '';
    $scope.history = workoutHistoryTracker.getHistory();
    $scope.ok = function () {
        $modalInstance.close();
    };
};
```

Remember, we get the same service instance for `workoutHistoryTracker` as the one passed in to `WorkoutController` (because services are singleton), and hence the `getHistory` method will return the same data that was created/updated during workout execution.

Add a reference to the `root.js` file in `index.html` after the `app.js` reference (if not already added):

```
<script src="js/root.js"></script>
```

Next we need to add the view. Copy the view HTML from `chapter3\checkpoint6\app\partials\workout-history.html` into the partial folder.

We will not delve deeply into workout history view implementation yet. It basically has a table to show workout history and a radio button filter to filter content based on whether the exercise was completed or not.

Run the app and we should see the **History** link in the top navigation bar. If we click on it, a popup should open that looks something like this:

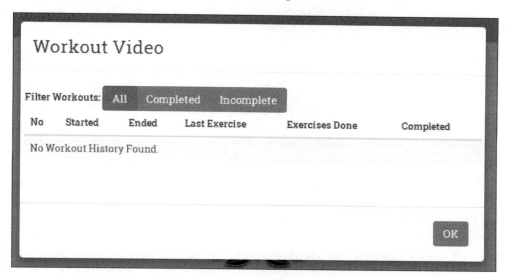

Since there is no workout data, there is no history. Start the workout and click on the link again and we will see some data in the grid, as seen in the following screenshot:

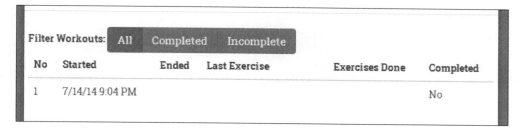

If we now navigate to the start or finish page by changing the URL or wait for the workout to finish and then check the history, we will see the end time for the exercise too.

 Check code in `chapter3/checkpoint6/app` if you are having problems running the app.

GitHub branch: checkpoint3.6 (folder – trainer)

We now have some rudimentary history tracking enabled that logs the start and end time of a workout. The `WorkoutController` function starts the tracking when the workout starts and ends it when the workout ends. Also, if we manually navigate away from the workout page, then the `workoutHistoryTracker` service itself stops tracking the running workout and marks it as incomplete. The service makes use of the eventing infrastructure to detect whether the route has changed. The implementation looks like this:

```
$rootScope.$on("$routeChangeSuccess", function (e, args) {
if (currentWorkoutLog) {
        service.endTracking(false);
}});
```

To understand the preceding piece of code, we will need to understand the AngularJS eventing primitives.

AngularJS eventing

Events are implementation of the observer design pattern. They allow us to decouple publishing and subscribing components. Events are common in every framework and language. JavaScript too has support for events where we can subscribe to events raised by DOM elements such as a button click, input focus, and many others. We can even create custom events in JavaScript using the native `Event` object.

AngularJS too supports a mechanism to raise and consume events using the scope object. These events might sound similar to DOM element events but these custom events have a very specific purpose/meaning within our app. For example, we can raise events for the start of an exercise, start of a workout, workout completion, or workout aborted. In fact, a number of Angular services themselves raise events signifying something relevant has occurred, allowing the subscribers of the event to react to the change.

This eventing infrastructure is completely built over the scope object. The API consists of three functions:

- `$scope.$emit(eventName, args)`
- `$scope.$broadcast(eventName, args)`
- `$scope.$on(eventName, listener(e, args))`

`$scope.$emit` and `$scope.$broadcast` are functions to publish events. The first argument that these functions take is the name of the event. We are free to use any string value for the name. It is always advisable to use strings that signify what happened, such as `workoutCompleted`. The second argument is used to pass any custom data to the event handler.

`$scope.$on` is used to subscribe to events raised either using either `$scope.$emit` or `$scope.$broadcast`. The match between the event publisher and subscriber is done using the `eventName` argument. The second argument is the listener that gets invoked when the event occurs.

The `listener` function is called by the framework with two arguments, the event and the arguments passed when the event was raised. Since we have already used the `$on` function in our service, let's try to dissect how it works. In this line:

```
$rootScope.$on("$routeChangeSuccess", function (e, args) {
```

We define the event handler on `$rootScope` as we can only inject `$rootScope` in a service and since `$rootScope` too is a scope, subscription works. We subscribe to an event $routeChangeSuccess. However, who raises this event?

One thing is pretty evident from the event name: that this event is raised when the app route changes. Also, who is responsible for managing routes, the `$route` service? The `$route` services raises this event when the route change is complete. The service also raises two other events: `$routeChangeError` and `$routeUpdate`. Refer to the `$route` documentation for more details about the events.

Since `$route` is a service, it also has access to `$rootScope` only, so it calls:

```
$rootScope.$broadcast('$routeChangeSuccess', next, last);
```

The `next` and `last` parameters are the old and the new route definitions. The `$routeChangeSuccess` event signifies successful transition from the last to next route. The `last`/`next` objects are route objects that we added when defining the route using `$routeProvider`.

The `$route` service previously mentioned uses the `$broadcast` method, but why `$broadcast` and why not `$emit`? The difference lies in the way `$broadcast` and `$emit` propagate events.

To understand the subtle difference between these methods, let's look at this diagram which shows a random scope hierarchy that can exist in any AngularJS app and how events travel:

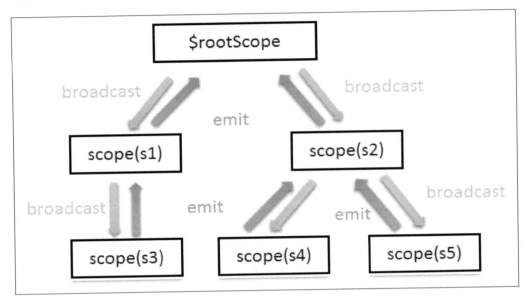

`$rootScope` is the overall parent of all scopes. Other scopes come into existence when a directive asks for a new scope. Directives such as `ng-include`, `ng-view`, `ng-controller`, and many other directives cause new scopes to be rendered. For the previous scope hierarchy, this occurs:

- The `$emit` function sends the event or message up the scope hierarchy, from the source of the event or scope on which the event is raised to the parent scope related to the parent DOM element. This mechanism is useful when a child component wants to interact with its parent component without creating any dependency. Based on the previous diagram, if we do a `$scope.$emit` implemention on scope `s4`, then scope `s2` and `$rootScope` can catch the event with `$scope.$on`, but scope `s5`, `s3`, or `s1` cannot. For emitted events, we have the ability to stop propagation of the event.

- `$broadcast` is just the opposite of `$emit`. As shown in the image, `$broadcast` happens down the scope hierarchy from the parent to all its child scopes and its child scopes and so on. Unlike `$emit`, a `$broadcast` event cannot be cancelled. If scope `s2` does a broadcast, scope `s4` and `s5` can catch it but scope `s1`, `s5`, and `$rootScope` cannot.

Since `$rootScope` is the parent of all scopes, any broadcast done from `$rootScope` can be received by each and every scope of the application. A number of services such as `$route` use `$rootScope.$broadcast` to publish event messages. This way any scope can subscribe to the event message and react to it. The `$routeChangeSuccess` event in the `$route` service is a good example of such an event.

For obvious reasons, `$emit` from `$rootScope` does not work for global event propagation (like `$routeChangeSuccess`) as `$emit` propagates the events up the hierarchy, but, since `$rootScope` is at the top of the hierarchy, the propagation stops there itself.

> Since `$rootScope.$broadcast` is received by each and every scope within the app, too many of these broadcasts on the root scope can have a detrimental effect on the application's performance. Look at this `jsPerf` (`http://jsperf.com/rootscope-emit-vs-rootscope -broadcast`) test case to understand the impact.

We can summarize the different `$broadcast` and `$emit` functions in two sentences:

- `$emit` is what goes up
- `$broadcast` is what propagates down

Eventing is yet another mechanism to share data across controllers, services, and directives but its primary intent is not data sharing. Events as the name suggests signify something relevant happened in the app and let other components react to it.

That sums up the eventing infrastructure of AngularJS. Let's turn our focus back to our app where we plan to utilize our newfound understanding of the eventing.

Enriching history tracking with AngularJS eventing

The `$routeChangeSuccess` event implementation in `workoutHistoryTracker` makes more sense now. We just want to stop workout tracking as the user has moved away from the workout page.

The missing pieces on our history tracking interface are two columns, one detailing the last exercise in progress and the other providing information about the total number of exercises done.

This information is available inside `WorkoutController` when the workout is in progress and it needs to be shared with the `workoutHistoryTracker` service somehow.

One way to do it would be to add another function to the service such as `trackWorkoutUpdate(exercise)` and call it whenever the exercise changes, passing in the exercise information for the new exercise.

Or we can raise an event from `WorkoutController` whenever the exercise changes, catch that event on the `$rootScope` object in the service, and update the tracking data. The advantage of an event-based approach is that in the future, if we add new components to our app that require exercise change tracking, no change in the `WorkoutController` implementation will be required.

We will be taking the eventing approach here. Open `workout.js` and inside the `startExercise` function, update the `if` condition to this:

```
if (exercisePlan.details.name != 'rest') {
  $scope.currentExerciseIndex++;
  $scope.$emit("event:workout:exerciseStarted",
    exercisePlan.details);
}
```

Here, we emit an event (that moves up) with the name `event:workout:exerciseStarted`. It is always a good idea to add some context around the source of the event in the event name. We pass in the current exercise data to the event.

In `services.js`, add the corresponding event handler to the service implementation:

```
$rootScope.$on("event:workout:exerciseStarted", function (e, args) {
currentWorkoutLog.lastExercise = args.title;
    ++currentWorkoutLog.exercisesDone;
});
```

The code is self-explanatory as we subscribe to the same event and update workout history data with the last exercise done and the number of total exercises completed. The `args` argument points to the `exercisePlan.details` object that is passed when the event is raised with `$emit`.

One small improvement we can do here is that, rather than using a string value in an event name, which can lead to typos or copy paste issues, we can get these names from a constant or value service, something like this:

```
angular.module('7minWorkout').value("appEvents", {
    workout: { exerciseStarted: "event:workout:exerciseStarted" }
});
```

Add the preceding code to the end of `services.js`.

Inject this value service in the `workoutHistoryTracker` service and `WorkoutController` and use it in event publishing and subscription:

```
$scope.$emit(appEvents.workout.exerciseStarted,
    exercisePlan.details); // in WorkoutController

$rootScope.$on(appEvents.workout.exerciseStarted, function (e,
    args) {// in workoutHistoryTracker service
```

The value service `appEvents` acts as a single source of reference for all events published and subscribed throughout the app.

We can now verify our implementation after starting a new workout and checking the history table. We should see data in the two columns: **Last Exercise** and **Exercises Done**:

No	Started	Ended	Last Exercise	Exercises Done	Completed
1	7/16/14 7:31 AM		Push Up	3	No

It might seem that we are done with workout history tracking but there is still a minor issue. If we refresh the browser window, the complete workout data is lost. We can confirm this by refreshing the browser and looking at the history grid; it will be empty!

Well, the data got lost because we are not persisting it. It is just in memory as a JavaScript array. What options do we have for persistence?

We can do persistence on a server. This is a viable option but, since we have not touched on the client-server interaction part in Angular, let's skip this option for now.

The other option is to use the browser's local storage. All modern browsers have support for the persisting user data in browser storage.

The advantage of this storage mechanism is that data is persisted even if we close the browser. The disadvantage is that the store is not shared across the browser; each browser has its own store. For now, we can live with this limitation and use browser storage to store our workout history data.

Persisting workout history in browser storage

To implement browser storage integration with our service, we will again look for a community solution and the one we plan to use is AngularJS-local-storage (https://github.com/grevory/angular-local-storage). This is a simple module that has a service wrapper over the browser local storage API.

I hope now we are quite used to adding module dependencies and dependency injection at service, filter, and controller level.

Go ahead and add the LocalStorageModule dependency to our app module in app.js.

Then open services.js and inject the dependency localStorageService into workoutHistoryTracker.

Add two declarations at the top of our workoutHistoryTracker service with other declarations:

```
var maxHistoryItems = 20
, storageKey = "workouthistory"
, workoutHistory = localStorageService.get(storageKey) || []
```

Add this line at the end of the startTracking function:

```
localStorageService.add(storageKey, workoutHistory);
```

Add this line at the end of the event handler for event appEvents.workout. exerciseStarted:

```
localStorageService.add(storageKey, workoutHistory);
```

Finally, add this line to the end of the endTracking function:

```
localStorageService.add(storageKey, workoutHistory);
```

Again pretty simple stuff! When the service is instantiated, we check if there is some workout history available by calling the get method of localStorageService passing in the key to our entry. If there is no historical data, we just assign an empty array to workoutHistory.

Thereafter, in each relevant function implementation, we update the historical data by calling an add function on localStorageService. Since the local storage does not have the concept of updates, adding the same data with the same key again overwrites the original data, which is similar to an update. Also, note that we update the complete array, not a specific row in the local storage.

The historical data is now being persisted and we can verify this by generating some workout history and refreshing the page. If our implementation was spot on, the data will not be lost.

> The current state of the app is available in the `checkpoint7` folder under `chapter3`. Check it out if you are having issues with running the app.
>
> *GitHub Branch: checkpoint3.7 (folder – trainer)*

The workout history view (`workout-history.html`) has some new constructs that we have not touched so far. With the history tracking implementation out of the way, it is a good time to look at these new view constructs.

Filtering workout history.

The first in line are the radio inputs that we have added to filter exercises.

The snippet for showing radio button filters looks like this:

```
<label><input type="radio" name="searchFilter"
  ng-model="search.completed" value="">All</label>
<label><input type="radio" name="searchFilter"
  ng-model="search.completed" value="true">Completed</label>
<label><input type="radio" name="searchFilter"
  ng-model="search.completed" value="false">Incomplete</label>
```

We use the `ng-model` directive to bind the `input` value attribute to the model property `search.completed`. This implies that, if we select a radio button with text `All`, the model property `search.completed` will be empty. The `search.completed` property will be `true` for the second radio and `false` for the third radio selection.

> Radio input also supports additional custom directives such as `ng-value` and `ng-change`. We will be covering these directives in more detail in an upcoming chapter where we learn about Angular support for the `forms` and `input` elements.

The idea here is to use the radio buttons to set the `$scope.search.completed` property. Now to understand how we use the `search.completed` property, we need to dissect the new avatar of `ng-repeat`.

Filtering and ordering using ng-repeat

The `ng-repeat` expression that we have used here seems to be more complex than the one that was used for showing video list. It looks like this:

```
<tr ng-repeat="historyItem in history | filter:search | orderBy:'-
    startedOn'">
```

As we know, the symbol | is used to represent a filter in an expression. In the preceding `ng-repeat` expression, we have added two filters one after another and this is how we interpret the complete filter expression.

Take the history array and apply the filter `filter` with a search expression that contains data to search for. On the resultant (filtered) array, again apply a filter to reorder the array elements based on the model property `startedOn`.

 Remember, ng-repeat supports objects for iteration too, but the filters filter and orderBy only work on arrays.

From the previous expression, we can see how the result of one filter acts as an input for another filter and what we finally get is a filtered data set that has passed through both the filters. The `filter` search filter alters the count of the source array whereas the `orderBy` filter reorders the elements.

Let's explore these filters in more detail and understand how to use them

The filter object of AngularJS filters

We touched upon `filter` in the last chapter. The `filter` object is a very versatile and powerful filter and provides a number of options to search and filter an array. The general `filter` syntax is:

```
{{ filter_expression | filter : expression : comparator}}
```

The `filter` object can take three types of expressions (the first filter parameter expression), as follows:

- **Strings**: The array searches for this string value. If it is an array of objects, each property in the array that is of the string type is searched. If we prefix it with ! (`!string`) then the condition is reversed.
- **Objects**: This syntax is used for more advanced searches. In the preceding `ng-repeat`, we use object search syntax. The value of our `search` object is `{completed:''}`, `{completed:true}`, or `{completed:false}` based on the radio options selected. When we apply this search expression to the filter, it

tries to find all the objects in the history where `historyItem.completed = search.completed`.

Using the object notation, we restrict our search to specific properties on the target array elements, unlike the `string` expression that only cares about the property value and not the name of the property.

We can search based on multiple properties too. For example, a search expression such as `{completed:true, lastExercise:"Plank"}`, will filter all exercises that were completed where the last exercise was `Plank`. Remember that in a multi-condition filter, every condition must be satisfied for an item to be filtered.

- `function(value)`: We can pass a predicate function, which is called for each array element and the element is passed in as value parameter. If the function returns true, it's a match else a mismatch.

The `comparator` parameter defined in the previous filter syntax is used to control how comparison is done for a search.

- `function(actual, expected)`: The `actual` value is the original array value and `expected` is the filter expression. For example, in our case, we have this:

```
<tr ng-repeat="historyItem in history | filter:search |
    orderBy:'-startedOn'">
```

Each `historyItem` is passed into `actual` and the `search` value into `expected`. The function should return `true` for the item to be included in the filtered results.

- `true`: A strict match is done using `angular.equals(actual, expected)`.
- `false|undefined`: This does a case-insensitive match. By default, comparison is case-insensitive.

The other filter that we have used is an `orderBy` filter.

The AngularJS orderBy filter

The `orderBy` filter is used to sort the array elements before they are rendered in the view. Remember, the order in the original array remains intact. We use the `orderBy` filter to sort the workout history array using the `startedOn` property.

The general syntax of `order` by looks like this:

```
{{ orderBy_expression | orderBy : expression : reverse}}
```

The expression parameter can take these:

- **Strings**: This is used to sort an array based on its element property name. We can prefix + or - to the string expression, which affects the sort order. We use the expression -startedOn to sort the workout history array in decreasing order of the startedOn date.

  Since we are using a constant expression for search, we have added quotes (') around -startedOn. If we don't quote the expression and use:

  ```
  <tr ng-repeat="historyItem in history | filter:search | orderBy:-
  startedOn">
  ```

  AngularJS would look for a property name startedOn on the scope object.

- function(element): This sorts the return value of the function. Such expression can be used to perform custom sorting. The element parameter is the item within the original array. To understand this, consider an example array:

  ```
  $scope.students = [
      {name: "Alex", subject1: '60', subject2: "80"},
      {name: "Tim", subject1: '75', subject2: "30"},
      {name: "Jim", subject1: '50', subject2: "90"}];
  ```

  If we want to sort this array based on the total score of a student, we will use a function:

  ```
  $scope.total = function(student){
    return student.subject1 + student.subject2;

  }
  ```

  Then, use it in the filter:

  ```
  ng-repeat="student in students | orderBy:total"
  ```

- Arrays: This can be an array of string or functions. This is equivalent to *n*-level sorting. For example, if the orderBy expression is ["startedOn", "exercisesDone"], the sorting is first done on the startedOn property. If two values match the next level, sorting is done on exerciseDone. Here too, we can again prefix - or + to affect the sort order.

Rendering a list of items with support for sorting and filtering is a very common requirement across all business apps. These are feature-rich filters that are flexible enough to suit most sorting and filtering needs and are extensively used across Angular apps.

There is another interesting interpolation that has been used inside the ng-repeat directive:

```
<td>{{$index+1}}</td>
```

Special ng-repeat properties

The `ng-repeat` directive adds some special properties on the scope object of current iteration. Remember, `ng-repeat` creates a new scope on each iteration! These are as follows:

- `$index`: This has the current iteration index (zero based)
- `$first`: This is true if it is the first iteration
- `$middle`: This is true if it is neither the first nor last iteration
- `$last`: This is true if it is the last iteration
- `$even`: This is true for even iterations
- `$odd`: This is true for odd iterations

These special properties can come in handy in some scenarios. For example, we used the `$index` property to show the serial number in the first column of the history grid.

Another example could be this:

```
ng-class="{'even-class':$even, 'odd-class':$odd}"
```

This expression applies `even-class` to the HTML element for even rows and `odd-class` for odd rows.

With this, we have reached the end of another chapter. We have added a number of small and large enhancements to the app and learned a lot. It's time now to wrap up the chapter.

Summary

Bit by bit, piece by piece, we are adding a number of enhancements to the *7 Minute Workout* app that are imperative for any professional app. There is still scope for new features and improvements but the core app works just fine and can be used without any major hiccups.

We started our journey by fixing the exercise step content formatting issue, where we learned about how to use `ng-bind-html` to bind HTML data and the role `$sce` service plays when it comes to keeping our HTML safe.

We then added audio support in our app. In the process, we learned how to extend the app's functionality without altering the existing controller; instead, we created a new MVC subcomponent.

While adding audio support, we also learned about the change tracking infrastructure of AngularJS and got introduced to concepts such as dirty checking and digest cycles.

Pausing and resuming exercises was another useful feature that we added. We learned about the keyboard and mouse-based directives that Angular provides, including `ng-mouse*`, `ng-key*`, `ng-click`, and some others.

Video panel loading had some lags that led to lags in the overall application. We fixed the video panel lag and added modal popups for video viewing. We again refactored our video player implementation by introducing another controller in the implementation. This resulted in the creation of another MVC sub component.

Next, we explored animation support in AngularJS and added some animation effects in our workout app. We explored all types of animation models, including transition effects, keyframe animation, and JavaScript-based animation.

Lastly, we implemented workout history tracking. This involved us in writing an Angular service that tracked historical data. This complete section was dedicated to understanding one of the fundamental building blocks for Angular, services. We learned about various mechanisms to create services, including constant, value, service, factory, and provider.

During implementation of the history tracking view, we also discovered a great deal about the `ng-repeat` construct and two related filters: `filter` and `orderBy`.

What next? We are going to build a new app *Personal Trainer*. This app will allow us to build our own *custom* workouts. Once we have the capability of creating our own workout, we are going to morph the *7 Minute Workout* app into a generic *Workout Runner* app that can run workouts that we build using *Personal Trainer*.

For the next chapter, we will showcase AngularJS form capabilities while we build a UI that allows us to create, update, and view our own custom workouts/exercises.

4
Building Personal Trainer

The *7 Minute Workout* app has been an excellent opportunity for us to learn about AngularJS. Working through the app, we have covered a number of AngularJS constructs. Still, there are areas such as AngularJS form (HTML) support and client-server communication that remain unexplored. This is partially due to the fact that *7 Minute Workout* from a functional standpoint had limited touchpoints with the end user. Interactions were limited to starting, stopping, and pausing the workout. Also, the app neither consumes, nor produces any data (except workout history).

In this chapter, we plan to delve deeper into one of the two aforementioned areas, AngularJS form support. Keeping up with the health and fitness theme (no pun intended), we plan to build a *Personal Trainer* app. The new app will be an extension to *7 Minute Workout*, allowing us to build our own customized workout plans that are not limited to the *7 Minute Workout* plans that we already have.

The topics we will cover in this chapter include:

- **Defining Personal Trainer requirements**: Since we are building a new app in this chapter, we start with defining the app requirements.

- **Defining the Personal Trainer model**: Any app design starts with defining its model. We define the model for *Personal Trainer*, which is similar to the *7 Minute Workout* app built earlier.

- **Defining the Personal Trainer layout and navigation**: We define the layout, navigation patterns, and views for the new app. We also set up a navigation system that is integrated with AngularJS routes and the main view.

- **Adding support pages**: Before we focus on the form capability and build a workout builder view, we build some supporting pages/views for workout and exercise listing.

- **Defining the workout builder view**: We lay out the workout builder view to manage workouts.

- **Building forms**: We make extensive use of HTML forms and input elements to create custom workouts. In the process, we learn more about Angular forms. The concepts that we cover include:

  ○ **ng-model and NgModelController**: We learn about the directive `ng-model` of the primary `form` object and associated controller `NgModelController`.

  ○ **Data formatting and parsing**: We explore the `NgModelController` formatter and parser pipeline architecture and implementation. We also create our own parser/formatter.

  ○ **Input validation**: We learn about the validation capabilities of AngularJS and the role `ng-model` and `NgModelController` play here.

  ○ **Input and form states**: Forms and input controls expose state information that can be used to provide a better user experience.

  ○ **Common form scenario**: We go through some common form usage scenarios and how to handle them in AngularJS.

  ○ **Dynamically generated form input**: We look at the `ng-form` directive and how to use the directive to manage dynamic generated input.

- **Nuances of scope inheritance**: Scope inheritance in Angular has some nuances that are important to understand and work around. We dedicate a section to learn about them.

Time to get started!

The Personal Trainer app – the problem scope

The *7 Minute Workout* app is good, but what if we could create an app that allows us to build more such workout routines customized to our fitness level and intensity requirements? With this flexibility, we can build any type of workout whether it is 7 minutes, 8 minutes, 15 minutes, or any other variations. The opportunities are limitless.

With this premise, let's embark on the journey of building our own *Personal Trainer* app that helps us to create and manage training/workout plans according to our specific needs. Let's start with defining the requirements for the app.

The new *Personal Trainer* app will now encompass the existing *7 Minute Workout* app. The component that supports workout creation will be referred to as "Workout Builder". The *7 Minute Workout* app itself will also be referred to as "Workout Runner". In the coming chapters, we will fix *Workout Runner*, allowing it to run any workout created using *Workout Builder*.

Personal Trainer requirements

Based on the notion of managing workouts and exercises, these are some of the requirements that our *Personal Trainer* app should fulfil including:

- The ability to list all available workouts.
- The ability to create and edit a workout. While creating and editing a workout, it should have:
    - The ability to add workout attributes including name, title, description, and rest duration
    - The ability to add/remove multiple exercises for workouts
    - The ability to order exercises in the workout
    - The ability to save workout data
- The ability to list all available exercises.
- The ability to create and edit an exercise. While creating and editing an exercise, it should have:
    - The ability to add exercise attributes such as name, title, description, and procedure
    - The ability to add pictures for the exercise
    - The ability to add related videos for the exercise
    - The ability to add audio clues for the exercise

All the requirements seem to be self-explanatory; hence, let's start with the design of the application. As customary, we first need to think about the model that can support these requirements.

The Personal Trainer model

No surprises here! The *Personal Trainer* model itself was defined when we created the *7 Minute Workout* app. The two central concepts of workout and exercise hold good for *Personal Trainer* too.

The only problem with the existing workout model is in the way it has been implemented. Since the model definition is inside `WorkoutController` (`workout.js`), we are in no position to reuse the same model for *Personal Trainer*.

We can either recreate a similar model for *Personal Trainer* (which does not feel right), or we can refactor the existing code in a way that the model classes (constructor functions) can be shared. Like any sane developer, we will be going with the second option. Let's understand how we can share the model across the application.

Sharing the workout model

JavaScript is a malleable language. You do not need to define any type upfront to use it. We don't have to declare our model to use it. We can very well create the model using the standard object notation ({ }) any time we need. Still, we define the constructor function for our model. Defining an explicit model structure helps us in clearly communicating what we are working against.

To share these model classes, we plan to do something unconventional. We are going to expose the model as an AngularJS service using the *factory* template. Things will be clear once we do this refactoring.

To start with, download the base version of the new *Personal Trainer* app from the companion codebase in `chapter4/checkpoint1`.

The code is also available on GitHub (`https://github.com/chandermani/angularjsbyexample`) for everyone to download. Checkpoints are implemented as branches in GitHub.

The branch to download is as follows:

GitHub Branch: checkpoint4.1 (folder – trainer)

This code has the complete *7 Minute Workout* (*Workout Runner*) app. We have added some more content to support the new *Personal Trainer* app. Some of the relevant updates are:

- Adding the new `WorkoutBuilder` module. This module contains implementations pertaining to *Personal Trainer*. Check `app.js` for the module declaration.

- Updating layout and styles of the app: Check `app.css` and `index.html` fixes.

- Adding some blank HTML partials for *Personal Trainer* in the `workoutbuilder` folder under `app/partials/`.

- Defining some new routes for *Personal Trainer*. We cover route setup for the app in the coming section.

Let's get back to defining the model.

The model as a service

In the last chapter, we dedicated a complete section to learning about AngularJS services, and one thing we learned there was that services are useful for sharing data across controllers and other AngularJS constructs. We essentially do not have data but a blueprint that describes the shape of the data. The plan, hence, is to use services to expose the model structure. Open the `model.js` file present in the `shared` folder under `app/js`.

 The `model.js` file has been added in the `shared` folder as the service is shared across the *Workout Builder* and *Workout Runner* apps. In future too, all shared components will be added to this `shared` folder.

The new model definition for `Exercise` looks like this:

```
angular.module('app').factory('Exercise', function () {
    function Exercise(args) {
        //Existing fields
    }
    return Exercise;
});
```

We define a new factory service `Exercise` on the `app` module (the main module of our app). The service implementation declares the `Exercise` constructor function that is the same as the one used in *7 Minute Workout* (*Workout Runner*) and then returns the function object.

Make note that we do not use this:

```
return new Exercise({});
```

Instead, we use this:

```
return Exercise;
```

Since services are singleton in nature, if we use the first option we are stuck with a single instance of the `Exercise` object. By doing `return Exercise`, we are actually returning a constructor function reference. Now we can inject the Exercise service anywhere and also use `new Exercise({})` to create the model object.

> The name of the constructor function (here `function Exercise(args)`) is irrelevant. What matters is the name of the service as we create objects with the name of the service. It is better to assign the same names to the service and the model constructor function to avoid any confusion.

Look at the other model `WorkoutPlan`; a similar implementation has been done for this too.

That's all on the model design front. The next thing we are going to do is define the structure for the new app.

The Personal Trainer layout

The skeleton structure of *Personal Trainer* looks like this:

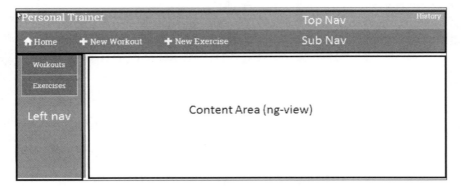

This has the following components:

- **Top Nav**: This contains the app branding title and history link.
- **Sub Nav**: This has navigation elements that change based on the active view (the view shown is `ng-view`).
- **Left nav**: This contains elements that are dependent upon the active view.
- **Content Area**: This is the main view. This is where most of the action happens. We will create/edit exercises and workouts and show a list of exercises and workouts here.

Look at the source code files, there is a new folder `workoutbuilder` under `app/partials`. It has view files for each element that we have described previously with some placeholder content. We will be building these views as we go along in this chapter.

However, firstly we need to link up these views within the app. This requires us to define the navigation patterns for the app and accordingly define the app routes.

The Personal Trainer navigation with routes

The navigation pattern that we plan to use for the app is the `list-detail` pattern. We create list pages for `exercises` and `workouts` available in the app. Clicking on any list item takes us to the detail view for the item where we can perform all CRUD operations (create/read/update/delete). The following routes adhere to this pattern:

Route	Description
`#/builder`	This just redirects to `#builder/workouts`.
`#/builder/workouts`	This lists all the available workouts. This is the landing page for *Personal Trainer*.
`#/builder/workouts/new`	This creates a new workout.
`#/builder/workouts/:id`	This edits an existing workout with the specific ID.
`#/builder/exercises`	This lists all the available exercises.
`#/builder/exercises/new`	This creates a new exercise.
`#/builder/exercises/:id`	This edits an existing exercise with the specific ID.

The route configurations in `app.js` define these new routes.

We have also tried to integrate top navigation and left navigation elements into the preceding route definitions that are not supported out-of-the-box. The next section talks about this integration.

Integrating left and top navigation

The basic idea around integrating left and top navigation into the app is to provide context-aware subviews that change based on the active view. For example, when we are on a list page as opposed to editing an item, we may want to show different elements in the navigation. An e-commerce site is a great example of this. Imagine Amazon's search result page and product detail page. As the context changes from a list of products to a specific product, the navigation elements that are loaded also change.

To integrate left and top navigation into *Workout Builder*, we have extended the app at a number of locations. To start with, look at the new routes in app.js. Some of these routes contain custom properties that are not part of the standard route configuration object created using when (https://code.angularjs.org/1.3.3/docs/api/ngRoute/provider/$routeProvider):

```
$routeProvider.when('/builder/workouts', {
templateUrl: 'partials/workoutbuilder/workouts.html',
controller: 'WorkoutListController',
leftNav: 'partials/workoutbuilder/left-nav-main.html',
topNav: 'partials/workoutbuilder/top-nav.html'
});
```

Open the index.html file and pay attention to the highlighted code:

```
<div class="navbar navbar-default navbar-fixed-top top-navbar">
    <!--Existing html-->
    <div id="top-nav-container" class="second-top-nav">
        <div id="top-nav" ng-include="currentRoute.topNav"></div>
    </div>
</div>
<div class="container-fluid">
  <div id="content-container" class="row">
    <div class="col-sm-2 left-nav-bar"
      ng-if="currentRoute.leftNav">
      <div id="left-nav" ng-include="currentRoute.leftNav"></div>
      </div>
      <div class="col-sm-10 col-sm-offset-2">
          <div id="page-content" ng-view></div>
      </div>
  </div>
</div>
```

The index.html file has been updated and now defines three areas, one each for top and left navigation, and one for the main view.

Looking back at route configuration, the `templateUrl` property in the route definition references the view template that is loaded in the `ng-view` directive of the `div` element. We try to simulate something similar to what Angular does for our left and top navigation.

The value of the `topNav` property is used to load the top navigation view in the `top-nav` `div` element (`"id = top-nav"`) using the `ng-include` directive. We do the same for left navigation too. The `ng-if` directive in the `left-nav` section is used to hide left navigation if the current route configuration does not define the `leftNav` property. We will shortly see how to set up the `currentRoute` property used in the `ng-include` expression mentioned previously.

With this configuration in place, we can associate different left and top navigation views with different pages. In the preceding route configuration for the workout list, the left navigation comes from `left-nav-main.html` and top navigation from `top-nav.html`. Look at the other route configuration too, to learn what other navigation templates we have configured.

The last part of this integration is setting up the `currentRoute` property and binding it to `ng-include`. Angular sets up the `ng-view` template using the route configuration `templateUrl` property, but it does not know or care about the `topNav` and `leftNav` properties that we have added. We need to write some custom code that binds the navigation URLs with the respective `ng-includes` directives.

To do this linkup, open `root.js` and add these event handler lines to `RootController`:

```
$scope.$on('$routeChangeSuccess', function (e, current, previous) {
  $scope.currentRoute = current;
});
```

We subscribe to the `$routeChangeSuccess` event raised by the `$route` service. As the name suggests, the event is raised when the route change is complete or the main view is loaded. The current and previous parameters are the route configuration objects for the loaded and the previous view respectively. These are the same objects that we configured inside the `$routeProvider.then` function. Once we assign the `current` object to `currentRoute`, it is just a matter of referencing the route properties in `ng-include` (`currentRoute.topNav` or `currentRoute.leftNav`) and the correct template for left and top navigation are loaded. Look at the highlighted code of the `index.html` file outlined previously.

The reason this event handler is in `RootController` is because `RootController` is defined outside the `ng-view` directive and encompasses nearly the complete index page. Hence, it is a good place to plug common functionality used across child views.

Go ahead and load the workout builder page `#/builder`. We will be redirected to the `workouts` page under `#/builder`. This page lists all the available workouts.

The redirect to the workouts page happens due to this route definition:

```
$routeProvider.when('/builder',{redirectTo:'/builder/workouts'});
```

The workout list page is currently empty but the left and top navigation links work. Click on the **New Workout** or **New Exercise** link on top nav and the app loads the create `workout/exercise` pages. The left navigation associated with the list pages (`left-nav-main.html`) has two links: **Workouts** and **Exercises**, to switch between the workout and exercise list.

With a little customization, we have been able to create a decent navigation system that reacts to the main view change and loads the correct views in left and top navigation. Along the same lines, we can always add footer and multiple subviews to our app if desired.

> For more complex needs, there is a compelling offering from the community called `ui-router` (`http://angular-ui.github.io/ui-router/site`). It supports complex routing scenarios and nested views. With `ui-router`, we are not limited to a single `ng-view`.

The skeleton layout, views, and navigation are now in place and it's time to add some meat to the implementation. The exercise and workout list is something that is easy to implement, so let's take that first.

> Since one of our main focus points in this chapter is to explore the HTML form capabilities of AngularJS, we plan to fast-forward through material that we already have covered and know well.

Implementing the workout and exercise list

Even before we start implementing the workout and exercise list pages, we need a data store for exercise and workout data. The current plan is to have an in-memory data store and expose it using an Angular service. In the coming chapter, where we talk about server interaction, we will move this data to a server store for long-term persistence. For now, the in-memory store will suffice. Let's add the store implementation.

WorkoutService as a workout and exercise repository

The plan here is to create a `WorkoutService` instance that is responsible for exposing the exercise and workout data across the two applications. The main responsibilities of the service include:

- **Exercise-related CRUD operations**: Get all exercises, get a specific exercise based on its name, create an exercise, update an exercise, and delete it
- **Workout-related CRUD operations**: These are similar to the exercise-related operations, but targeted toward the workout entity

Open the companion codebases, copy the `services.js` and `directives.js` files from the `shared` folder under `chapter4/checkpoint2/app/js`, and add them to the shared folder locally. Add references to these files to the `index.html` script reference section too.

 The `directives.js` file contains a directive to show confirmed messages when trying to delete a workout. We will be using it in the workout builder view.

There is nothing new here that we have not seen. The basic outline of the service looks like this:

```
angular.module('app')
    .factory("WorkoutService", ['WorkoutPlan', 'Exercise',
      function (WorkoutPlan, Exercise) {
        var service = {};
        var workouts = [];
        var exercises = [];
        service.getExercises = function () {//implementation}
        service.getWorkouts = function (){//implementation}
        //Some initialization code to load existing data.
        return service;
    }]);
```

We create the `WorkoutService` object on the main module app and inject the model services: `WorkoutPlan` and `Exercise`. The two methods: `getExercises` and `getWorkouts`, as the names suggest, return the list of exercises and workouts respectively. Since we plan to use the in-memory store to store workout and exercise data, the `exercises` and `workouts` arrays store this data. As we go along, we will be adding more functions to the service.

Time to add the controller and view implementation for the workout and exercise list!

Exercise and workout list controllers

Copy the `exercise.js` and `workout.js` files from the `workoutbuilder` folder under `chapter4/checkpoint2/app/js/`. Also, go ahead and update `index.html` with the references to these two files, at the end of the script declaration area. Again some standard stuff here! Here is the description of the files:

- `workout.js`: This defines the `WorkoutListController` controller that loads workout data using `WorkoutService`. The `$scope.goto` function implements navigation to the workout detail page. This navigation happens when we double-click on an item in the workout list. The selected workout name is passed as part of the route/URL to the workout detail page.

- `exercises.js`: This has two controllers defined that are: `ExercisesNavController` and `ExerciseListController`.

  `ExerciseListController` is used by the exercise list view.

  `ExerciseNavController` is there to support the `left-nav-exercises.html` view, and just loads the exercise data. If we look at the route definition, this view is loaded in the left navigation when we create/edit a workout.

Lastly, we need to implement the list views that have so far been empty!

Exercise and workout list views

Copy the `workouts.html` and `localhost exercises.html` views from the `workoutbuilder` folder under `chapter4/checkpoint2/app/partials`.

Both the views use `ng-repeat` to list out the exercises and workouts. The `ng-dblclick` directive is used to navigate to the respective detail page by double-clicking on the list item.

Go ahead and refresh the builder page (`#/builder`); one workout is listed, the *7 Minute Workout*. Click on the **Exercises** link on the left navigation to load the 12 exercises that we have already configured in `WorkoutService`.

 The code implementation so far is available in the `checkpoint2` folder under `chapter4` for us to validate against.
GitHub branch: checkpoint4.2 (folder – trainer)

The easy stuff is out of the way. Time to add the ability to load, save, and update exercise/workout data!

Building a workout

The core functionality *Personal Trainer* provides is around workout and exercise building. Everything is there to support these two functions. In this section, we focus on building and editing workouts using AngularJS.

The `WorkoutPlan` model has already been defined, so we are aware of the elements that constitute a workout. The workout builder page facilitates user input and lets us build/persist workout data.

Once complete, the workout builder page will look like this:

The page has a left navigation that lists out all the exercises that can be added to the workout. Clicking on the arrow icon on the right adds the exercise to the end of the workout.

The center area is designated for workout building. It consists of exercise tiles laid out in order from top to bottom and a form that allows the user to provide other details about the workout such as name, title, description, and rest duration.

This page operates in two modes:

- **Create/New**: This mode is used for creating a new workout. The URL is #/builder/workouts/new.
- **Edit**: This mode is used for editing the existing workout. The URL is #/builder/workouts/:id, where :id maps to the name of the workout.

With this understanding of the page elements and layout, it's time to build each of these elements. We will start with left nav (navigation).

Building left nav

Left nav for the **Workout Builder** app shows the list of exercises that the user can add to the workout by clicking on the arrow next to the name of the exercise. Copy the left nav implementation from left-nav-exercises.html located in the companion codebase folder workoutbuilder under chapter4\checkpoint3\app\partials\ locally. A simple view looks like this:

```
<div id="left-nav-exercises" ng-controller="ExercisesNavController">
    <h4>Exercises</h4>
    <div ng-repeat="exercise in exercises|orderBy:'title'"
      class="row">
        <button class="btn btn-info col-sm-12" ng-click
          ="addExercise(exercise)">{{exercise.title}}<span class
          ="glyphicon glyphicon-chevron-right"></span></button>
    </div>
</div>
```

The view implementation contains ng-repeat used to list out all the exercises and the ng-controller directive pointing to ExercisesNavController. The ng-click directive refers to the function (addExercise) that adds the clicked exercise to the workout.

We have already added ExercisesNavController to exercise.js earlier in this chapter. This controller loads all the available exercises used to bind the ng-repeat directive. The missing piece is the implementation of the addExercise(exercise) function.

Implementing the add exercise functionality from left nav is a bit tricky. The views are different; hence, the scope of left nav and the scope of the main view (loaded as part of the route in `ng-view`) is different. There is not even a parent-child hierarchy to share data.

We always want to keep the UI section as decoupled as possible, hence the option we have here is to either use AngularJS events (`$broadcast` or `$emit`), or create a service to share data. We covered both techniques in the previous chapter while working on *7 Minute Workout*.

For our current implementation, we will go the service way and introduce a new service into the picture that is `WorkoutBuilderService`. The reason for going the service way will be clear when we work on the actual workout, save/update logic, and implement the relevant controllers.

The ultimate aim of the `WorkoutBuilderService` service is to co-ordinate between the `WorkoutService` (that retrieves and persists the workout) and the controllers (such as `ExercisesNavController` and others we will add later), while the workout is being built, hence reducing the amount of code in the controller to the bare minimum.

Adding the WorkoutBuilderService service

`WorkoutBuilderService` tracks the state of the workout being worked on. It:

- Tracks the current workout
- Creates a new workout
- Loads the existing workout
- Saves the workout

`WorkoutBuilderService` has a dependency on `WorkoutService` to provide persistence and querying capabilities.

Copy the `services.js` file and from the `WorkoutBuilder` folder under `chapter4/checkpoint3/app/js`, add a reference for `services.js` in the `index.html` file after existing script references.

Let's look at some relevant parts of the service.

Unlike `WorkoutService`, `WorkoutBuilderService` has a dependency on model services: `WorkoutPlan` and `Exercise`. `WorkoutBuilderService` also needs to track the workout being built. We use the `buildingWorkout` property for this. The tracking starts when we call the `startBuilding` method on the service:

```
service.startBuilding = function (name) {
  if (name) { //We are going to edit an existing workout
  buildingWorkout =
    WorkoutService.getWorkout(name);
    newWorkout = false;
  }
  else {
  buildingWorkout = new WorkoutPlan({});
  newWorkout = true;
}
  return buildingWorkout;
};
```

The basic idea behind this tracking function is to set up a `WorkoutPlan` object (`buildingWorkout`) that will be made available to views that manipulate the workout details. The `startBuilding` function takes the workout name as a parameter. If the name is not provided, it implies we are creating a new workout, and hence a new `WorkoutPlan` object is created and assigned; if not, we load the workout details by calling `WorkoutService.getWorkout(name)`. In any case, the `buildingWorkout` property has the workout being worked on.

The `newWorkout` object signifies whether the workout is new or an existing one. It is used to differentiate between the save and update case when the `save` method on this service is called.

The rest of the methods, that is, `removeExercise`, `addExercise`, and `moveExerciseTo` are self-explanatory and affect the exercise list that is part of the workout (`buildingWorkout`).

`WorkoutBuilderService` is calling a new function `getWorkout` on `WorkoutService` which we have not added yet. Go ahead and copy the `getWorkout` implementation from the `services.js` file under `chapter4/checkpoint3/app/js/shared`. We will not dwell into the new service code as the implementation is quite simple.

Let's get back to left nav and implement the remaining functionality.

Adding exercises using exercise nav

To add exercises to the workout we are building, we just need to inject the dependency of `WorkoutBuilderService` into the `ExercisesNavController` and call the service method `addExercise`:

```
$scope.addExercise = function (exercise) {
    WorkoutBuilderService.addExercise(exercise);
}
```

Internally, `WorkoutBuilderService.addExercise` updates the `buildingWorkout` model data with the new exercise.

The preceding implementation is a classic case of sharing data between independent MVC components. The shared service exposes the data in a controlled manner to any view that requests it. While sharing data, it is always a good practice to expose the state/data using functions instead of directly exposing the data object. We can see that in our controller and service implementations too. `ExerciseNavController` does not update the workout data directly; in fact it does not have direct access to the workout being built. Instead, it relies upon the service method `addExercise` to change the current workout's exercise list.

Since the service is shared, there are pitfalls to be aware of. As services are injectable through the system, we cannot stop any component from taking dependency on any service and calling its functions in an inconsistent manner, leading to undesired results or bugs. For example, the `WorkoutBuilderService` needs to be initialized by calling `startBuilding` before `addExercise` is called. What happens if a controller calls `addExercise` before the initialization takes place?

Next, we implement the workout builder controller (`WorkoutDetailController`). As we work on this controller, the integration between the service, the left nav controller, and workout builder controller will be self-evident.

Implementing WorkoutDetailController

`WorkoutDetailController` is responsible for managing a workout. This includes creating, editing, and viewing the workout. Due to the introduction of `WorkoutBuilderService`, the overall complexity of this controller has reduced. Other than the primary responsibility of integrating with the view, `WorkoutDetailController` will delegate most of the other work to `WorkoutBuilderService`.

WorkoutDetailController is associated with two routes/views namely /builder/
workouts/new and /builder/workouts/:id. This handles both creating and editing
workout scenarios. The first job of the controller is to load or create the workout that
it needs to manipulate. We plan to use Angular's routing framework to pass this data
to WorkoutDetailController.

Go ahead and update two routes (app.js) by adding the highlighted content:

```
$routeProvider.when('/builder/workouts/new', {
    <!—existing route data-->
    controller: 'WorkoutDetailController',
    resolve: {
        selectedWorkout: ['WorkoutBuilderService', function
          (WorkoutBuilderService) {
            return WorkoutBuilderService.startBuilding();
        }],
    }});
$routeProvider.when('/builder/workouts/:id', {;
    <!—existing route data-->
    controller: 'WorkoutDetailController',
    resolve: {
      selectedWorkout: ['WorkoutBuilderService', '$route',
        function (WorkoutBuilderService, $route) {
      return WorkoutBuilderService.startBuilding(
        $route.current.params.id);
        }],
    }});
```

The updated route definition uses a new route configuration property resolve.
Remember we have already used a similar property resolve in the previous chapter
when we worked with the $modal dialog service and passed the video URL to the
modal dialog to play:

```
resolve: {
  video: function () {
    return '//www.youtube.com/embed/' + videoId;}},
```

Here too, resolve behaves in a similar manner.

Let's try to learn a bit more about the resolve object as it is a handy feature.

Route resolving

The `resolve` property is part of the *route configuration object*, and provides a mechanism to pass data and/or services to a specific controller. This is the same controller that is instantiated as part of a route change (specified in the `controller` property of the route configuration object). The `resolve object` property can be one of the following:

- **A string constant**: The string name should be an AngularJS service. This is not very useful or often used as AngularJS already provides the ability to inject a service into the controller.

- **A function**: In this case, the return value of the function can be injected into the controller with the property name. If the function returns a *promise* (we discussed promises in *Chapter 2, Building Our First App – 7 Minute Workout*), the route is not resolved and the view is not loaded till the promise itself is resolved. Once the promise is resolved, the resolved value is injected into the controller. If the promise fails, the `$routeChangeError` event is raised on `$rootScope` and the route does not change.

We add a property `selectedWorkout` (that points to a function) to resolve an object in both routes. This function, when executed during the route change, starts the workout building process by calling the `WorkoutBuilderService.startBuilding` function.

For the new workout route, we do not pass any parameter:

```
WorkoutBuilderService.startBuilding();
```

For the edit route (route with `:id`), we pass the workout name in a route/URL:

```
WorkoutBuilderService.startBuilding($route.current.params.id);
```

The return value of `selectedWorkout` is the workout returned by `WorkoutBuilderService.startBuilding`.

> The previous `$route.current` property contains useful details about the current route. The `params` object contains values for all placeholder tokens that are part of the route. Our edit route (`/builder/workouts/:id`) has only one token ID, hence `params.id` will point to the value of the last fragment of the workout edit route.
>
> These tokens are also available through an Angular service `$routeParams`. We will cover `$routeParams` later in the chapter. We did not use `startBuilding($routeParams.id)` here, as this service is not read during the `resolve` function call.

Note that any function properties of the `resolve` object can take dependencies similar to an AngularJS controller. Have a look at the `selectedWorkout` declaration:

```
selectedWorkout: ['WorkoutBuilderService', function
  (WorkoutBuilderService) {
```

We take a dependency on `WorkoutBuilderService`.

Using the `resolve` configuration to load the selected workout has another advantage. We can handle routes that are not found.

Resolving routes not found!

With dynamically generated routes, there is always a chance of a route being invalid. For example, the workout edit route, such as `builder/workouts/abc` or `builder/workouts/xyz`, points to workout names (`abc` and `xyz`) that don't exist. In such a scenario, the workout builder page does not make sense.

The `resolve` configuration can help here. If a workout with a given name is not found, we can redirect the user back to the workout list page. Let's see how. Open `app.js` and add the highlighted code, to edit the workout route:

```
$routeProvider.when('/builder/workouts/:id', {
    //existing code
    resolve: {
        selectedWorkout: ['WorkoutBuilderService', '$route',
  '$location', function (WorkoutBuilderService, $route, $location) {
  var workout =
  WorkoutBuilderService.startBuilding($route.current.params.id);
            if (!workout) {
                $location.path('/builder/workouts');
            }
            return workout;
        }],
    }
```

We try to load the workout with a specific ID (workout name) and if not found, redirect the user back to the workout list page. Since we are using the `$location` service, we need to add it as a dependency in the `selectWorkout` function.

There is another use case the `resolve` object can handle that involves asynchronous server interaction using promises. We will cover this scenario in the next chapter. For now, let's continue with the `WorkoutDetailController` implementation.

Implementing WorkoutDetailController continued...

To implement `ExerciseDetailController`, we inject the current workout being built using DI. We have already set up the preceding `resolve` object to get the workout. Add a new controller declaration to `workout.js` (located in the `WorkoutBuilder` folder under `app\js`) after the `WorkoutListController` declaration:

```
angular.module('WorkoutBuilder').controller('WorkoutDetailControll
er', ['$scope', 'WorkoutBuilderService', 'selectedWorkout', function
($scope, WorkoutBuilderService, selectedWorkout) {
  var init = function () {
  $scope.workout = selectedWorkout; // Resolved workout
  };
  init();
}]);
```

The `$scope.workout` object tracks the workout we are working on.

For now, this is enough for the controller implementation. Let's update the skeleton workout builder view.

Implementing the workout builder view

Go back a few pages and check the layout of workout builder page. The page is divided into two sections, the section on the left contains the exercises in the workout and the section on the right contains a form to enter other details about the workout.

Copy content from the `workout.html` file under `chapter4/checkpoint3/app/partials/workoutbuilder` to your local view code. Now run the app, navigate to `#/builder/workouts`, and double-click on the *7 Minute Workout* tile. This should load the *7 Minute Workout* details with a view similar to the one shown at the start of the section *Building a workout*.

In the event of any problem, you can refer to the `checkpoint3` code under `chapter4` that contains a working implementation of *Workout Builder*.

GitHub branch: checkpoint4.3 (folder – trainer)

We will be dedicating a lot of time to this view so let's understand some specifics here.

The exercise list div (id="exercise-list") lists outs the exercises that are part of the workout in order. To render the exercise list, we use a template for each exercise item and render it using ng-include="'workout-exercise-tile'" inside ng-repeat. The template HTML is available at the end of the same file. Functionally, this template has:

- The delete button to delete the exercise
- Reorder buttons to move the exercise up and down the list as well as to the top and bottom

The second div element for workout data (id="workout-data") contains the HTML input element for details such as name, title, and rest duration and a button to save and reset the workout changes.

The complete thing has been wrapped inside the HTML form element so that we can make use of the form-related capabilities that AngularJS provides. Nonetheless, what are these capabilities?

AngularJS forms

Forms are such an integral part of HTML development that any framework that targets client-side development just cannot ignore them. AngularJS provides a small but well-defined set of constructs that make standard form-based operations easier.

If we think carefully, any form of interaction boils down to:

- Allowing user input
- Validating those inputs against business rules
- Submitting the data to the backend server

AngularJS has something to offer for all the preceding use cases.

> Angular 1.3 forms have a number of new features and improvements over their predecessors (Angular 1.2.x). While working on the app, we will highlight any feature that is exclusive to version 1.3.
>
> Since the framework is constantly updated, it is always advisable to refer to the framework documentation on a specific version to find out what capabilities are supported.

For user input, it allows us to create two-way bindings between the form input elements and the underlying model, hence avoiding any boilerplate code that we may have to write for model input synchronization.

It also provides constructs to validate input before it is can be submitted.

Lastly, Angular provides $http and $resource services for client-server interaction and persisting data to the server.

Since the first two use cases are our main focus in this chapter, let's learn more about AngularJS user input and data validation support.

AngularJS form constructs

The primary form-related constructs in AngularJS are:

- The form directive and the corresponding FormController object
- The ng-model directive and the corresponding NgModelController object

For the ng-model directive to work correctly, another set of directives is required, which include:

- input: HTML input extended using directive
- textarea: HTML textarea extended using directive
- select: HTML dropdown extended using directive

 What we see here is Angular extending the existing HTML elements by implementing directives over them.

The first directive that requires our focus is the ng-model directive. Let's explore this directive and understand how it works.

The ng-model directive

One of the primary roles of the ng-model directive is to support two-way binding between user input and the underlying model. With such a setup, changes in a model are reflected in the view, and updates to the view too are reflected back on the underlying model. Most of the other directives that we have covered so far only support one-way binding from models to views. This is also due to the fact that ng-model is only applied to elements that allow user input.

The ng-model directive works with the input, textarea, and select HTML elements as these are primarily responsible for user input. Let's look at these elements in more detail.

Using ng-model with input and textarea

We used the ng-model directive for the first time when creating the Guess the Number! game (*Chapter 1, Getting Started*) where the input (type=number) element was used for numerical entries.

Open workout.html and look for ng-model. Here too, it has only been applied to HTML elements that allow user data input. These include input, textarea, and select. The workout name input setup looks like this:

```
<input type="text" name="workoutName" id="workout-name"
  ng-model="workout.name">
```

The preceding ng-model directive sets up a two-way binding between the input and model property workout.name.

Angular supports most of the HTML5 input types, including text, date, time, week, month, number, URL, e-mail, radio, and checkbox. This simply means binding between a model and any of these input types just works out-of-the-box.

The textarea element too works the same as input:

```
<textarea name="description" ng-model="workout.description" . .
  . > </textarea>
```

Here we bind textarea to workout.description. Under the cover, there are directives for each input, textarea, and select, which co-ordinates with the ng-model directive to achieve two-way binding.

> It is important to understand that the ng-model directive is there to update the model. When the actual update is done, it is influenced by the supporting directives: input, textarea, and select. For example, when ng-model is used with input, the change and input events (yes, input is the name of an event too) are subscribed by the input directive, and model data is updated when these events are triggered. This effectively creates a two-way binding between the model data and the HTML element on which ng-model is declared.

Why don't we verify this binding work? Add a model interpolation expression against any of the linked input such as this one:

```
<input type="text" ... ng-model="workout.name">{{workout.name}}
```

Open the workout builder page, and type something in the input, and see how the interpolation is updated instantaneously. The magic of two-way binding!

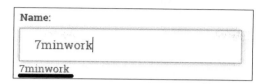

Using ng-model with select is a bit different as we can set up the select options in multiple ways.

Using ng-model with select

Let's look at how select has been set up:

```
<select … name="duration" ng-model="exercise.duration"
ng-options="duration.value as duration.title for duration in
    durations"></select>
```

There are no inner option tags! Instead, there is a ng-options attribute. If you recall the ng-repeat expression, the ng-options expression looks similar. It allows us to bind an object or array to select. The ng-options directive here binds to an array, durations. The array looks like this:

```
$scope.durations = [{ title: "15 seconds", value: 15 },
                    { title: "30 seconds", value: 30 }, ...]
```

The ng-options directive supports multiple formats of data binding. The format we use is:

```
[selected] as [label] for [value] in array
```

Where:

- selected: What (duration.value) gets assigned to ng-model (exercise. duration) when the item is selected
- label: What is shown (duration.title) in the dropdown
- value: This is an item (duration) in the array that binds to a select option

The selected parameter is optional and only required if we want to set a subproperty of a selected item to ng-model, which we do want. If it sounds confusing, update the ng-options expression in the view to:

```
ng-options="duration.title for duration in durations"
```

Then, add the {{exercise.duration}} interpolation just after the select end tag (</select>). Refresh the workout builder page and try to select a time duration from the drop-down box. The interpolation value is an object instead of the integer time. See the following screenshot:

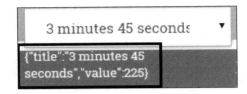

Revert the ng-options expression and try again, this time the interpolation should have the correct time duration.

 The ng-options directive also supports binding to an object property and multiple expression formats. Check the documentation on select to know more about these options at https://code.angularjs.org/1.3.3/docs/api/ng/directive/select

The ng-options directive gives us great flexibility when it comes to binding an object or array to select. However, we can still use the traditional option tag instead of ng-options. The same select tag if implemented with the option tag would look like this:

```
<select ... ng-model="exercise.duration">
  <option value="{{duration.value}}"
    label="{{duration.title}}"
    ng-repeat="duration in durations"
    ng-selected="exercise.duration==duration.value">
    {{duration.title}}
  </option>
</select>
```

In this case, the option tags are generated using ng-repeat. Also, the ng-model directive binds to the option value property ({{duration.value}}). The ng-selected directive is used to bind the initial value of the model data to the view.

Clearly ng-options is a better alternative to option as it provides more flexibility and is a little less verbose. Given that the option tag approach only works with string values, it is always advisable to use ng-options.

Like `input`, `select` too supports two-way binding. We saw how changing `select` updates a model, but the model to view binding may not be apparent. To verify if a model to a view binding works, open the *7 Minute Workout* app and verify the duration dropdowns. Each one has a value that is consistent with model value (`30 seconds`).

AngularJS does an awesome job in keeping the model and view in sync using `ng-model`. Change the model and see the view updated, change the view and watch the model updated instantaneously. Starting from Angular 1.3, things just got even better. In 1.3, we can even control when the updates to the view are reflected on the model.

 If you are using Angular 1.2.x or earlier, you can safely skip the next section.

Controlling model updates with ng-model-options (Angular 1.3)

The `ng-model-options` directive is pretty useful if we want to control when the model should be updated on view changes. To understand what it has to offer, let's try out some of its options.

Let's take the same `workoutName` input and try it out. Update the `workoutName` input to this:

```
<input type="text" … ng-model="workout.name"
  ng-model-options="{updateOn:'blur'}">{{workout.name}}
```

Open the workout builder page and enter some content in `workoutName` input. Model interpolation does not update as we type, but only when we leave the input—interesting!

The `updateOn` expression allows us to customize on what event model data should be updated, and we can configure multiple events here (space-delimited).

Change previous `updateOn` to:

```
ng-model-options="{updateOn:'blur mouseleave'}"
```

The model is now updated on `blur`, as well as when the mouse leaves the input. To experience the `mouseleave` event, start typing with the mouse cursor inside the `workoutName` input and then move the mouse out. The model interpolation changes to reflect what we have typed!

Another interesting feature that `ng-model-options` provides is what we call a **debounce effect**. Again, the best way to learn about it is by using it. Update the `ng-model-options` value to this:

```
ng-model-options = "{updateOn:'default blur'
  , debounce: {'default': 1000, 'blur': 0}}"
```

Refresh the workout builder page and change the workout name. The model does not get updated as you type, but it eventually does (after one second) without us leaving the field.

This debounce mechanism dictates how long Angular waits after an event to update the underlying model. The `default` keyword previously used is a special string that signifies the default event of the control.

As we type, the debounce setup waits for a second before applying model changes. However, in the case of `blur`, changes are reflected immediately.

Wondering why we require these options? Well, there are indeed some use cases where these options help. Assume we want to remotely validate if a username entered by a user exists. In a standard setup, every keypress would result in a remote call for validating a name. Instead, if we do a model update on `blur`, only one remote call would suffice. Type ahead input too can utilize these options (especially the debounce option) to reduce the number of remote requests.

 I would recommend that we stick to the standard behavior and avoid `ng-model-options` unless there is a specific need to control model update timing, as highlighted earlier.

The `ng-model-options` directive has some other interesting options that we will not be covering here. Look at the platform documentation at `https://docs.angularjs.org/api/ng/directive/ngModelOptions` to learn more about them.

So far, we have looked at `ng-model` from the data binding perspective, but `ng-model` has some other uses too.

ng-model – beyond data binding

The `ng-model` directive in itself is a mini MVC component that has its own controller. Through this controller, it exposes an API to format and validate model data.

Let's try to understand what happens when we create a form and add an input with `ng-model`. Consider this screenshot that is based on `workout.html` form layout:

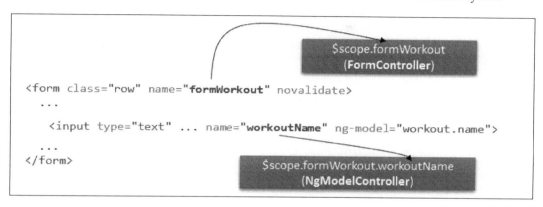

As we can see from the preceding screenshot, when Angular encounters the `form` tag, it executes the `form` directive. This directive creates an instance of a special Angular class `FormController` that is made available to us on the current scope. See the previous screenshot. `$scope.formWorkout` is a `FormController` object and its name derives from a form name (`name="formWorkout"`). The `form` controller (the `FormController` object) provides an API to check and manipulate the state of the form.

On similar lines, when AngularJS encounters the `ng-model` directives, it creates a `model` controller (an instance of the `ngModelController` class). If the element with `ng-model` is defined inside a named form, the model controller instance is available as a property of the `form` controller (see `$scope.formWorkout.workoutName` in the screenshot).

Similar to `FormController`, `NgModelController` too provides an API to manipulate the model data. The next few sections cover the form, the model directives, and their respective controllers in more detail.

One question that we may have is, "Why do we need to know about `form`, `ng-model` directives?" Or do we really need to learn about `FormController` and `NgModelController` in detail? These are valid questions that we should address before getting into specifics.

We need to know about the `form` and `ng-model` directives from the usage perspective.

The `FormController` class is a useful utility class to manage the HTML form state.

`NgModelController` is commonly used to check the validation state of the input element. It is desirable to understand the inner working of a model controller as the complete validation framework, data parsing, and formatting are dependent on the `NgModelController` implementation.

Once we have a clear understanding of how these controllers work, life becomes a little easier when dealing with Angular form quirks.

Understanding NgModelController

`NgModelController` is the command center for the `ng-model` directive. It provides an API to:

- Format and parse model data
- Validate model data

To support formatting, parsing, and data validation, AngularJS implements a pipeline architecture (`http://en.wikipedia.org/wiki/Pipeline_%28software%29`). In a pipeline setup, data/control passes from one component to another in a linear fashion. There is uniformity of interface when it comes to the components that are part of a pipeline. The output from one component feeds into the next component in pipeline, so on and so forth.

AngularJS model controller defines two pipelines:

- **Formatter**: This pipeline is used as `$formatters`. It is an array of formatter functions that are called one after another when the model value changes. The return value of one formatter function acts as an input to another. At the end of pipeline execution, the value returned by last formatter is rendered in the view. A formatter function takes one parameter, value, and should return the same or a transformed value.

- **Parser**: This pipeline is used as `$parsers`. This is also an array of parser functions. Parser pipeline is executed when the view element is updated by the user and model data needs to be synchronized (the reverse of when the formatter pipeline is executed). Similar to formatters, parsers too are called in sequence one after another, passing in the view data. Any parser can update the data before passing to the next parser in line. The last return value gets assigned to the underlying model.

The following screenshot helps us visualize the formatter and parser pipelines in the context of model and view:

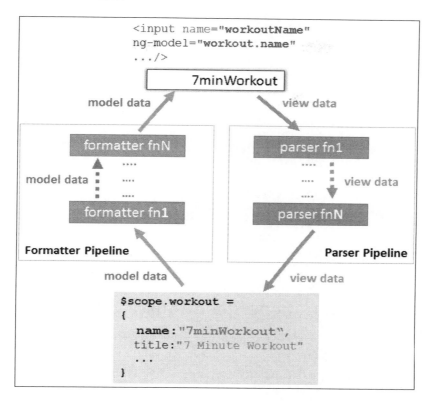

Having such a complex architecture for such a simple concept of model-view synchronization seems to be an overkill, but that is not the case. In fact, the pipeline architecture provides enough flexibility and extensibility. The complete AngularJS validation infrastructure is built upon formatter and parser pipelines.

 Angular 1.3 does not employ these pipelines for validation. Validating user input in Angular 1.3 happens after execution of formatter/parser pipelines.

As the name suggests, these pipelines make formatting a model and parsing view data easier. For example, if we want to format model data as uppercase in the input textbox, we can simply define the following formatter (code courtesy: *API docs* https://code.angularjs.org/1.3.3/docs/api/ng/type/ngModel. NgModelController):

```
function upperCase(value) {
    if (value) { return value.toUpperCase();}
}
ngModel.$formatters.push(upperCase);
```

An important consequence of using pipeline architecture with ng-model is that the order in which the pipeline functions are registered affects the overall behavior of the pipeline and hence ng-model. This holds true for both formatter and parser pipelines. Any pipeline function can short-circuit (clear) or update the value it receives during its execution, affecting the behavior of subsequent pipeline functions.

To understand the parser and formatter pipeline better, let's implement a sample formatter and parser function that can convert a decimal value to an integer value for our restBetweenExercise input textbox.

Implementing a decimal-to-integer formatter and parser

The rest between exercise input takes the rest duration (in seconds) between two exercises. Therefore, it does not make sense to save a decimal value for such input. Let's create a formatter and parser to sanitize the user input and model data.

Our formatter and parser functions work on similar lines, both converting the input value into integer format. Add the following watch function to WorkoutDetailController:

```
var restWatch = $scope.$watch('formWorkout.restBetweenExercise',
  function (newValue) {
if (newValue) {
      newValue.$parsers.unshift(function (value) {
        return isNaN(parseInt(value)) ? value : parseInt(value);
      });
      newValue.$formatters.push(function (value) {
        return isNaN(parseInt(value)) ? value : parseInt(value);
      });
      restWatch(); //De-register the watch after first time.
    }
});
```

We register our formatter and parser once the `restBetweenExercise` model controller is created. The watch has been registered just to know when the model controller instance is created.

The expression inside the parser/formatter function is as follows:

```
return isNaN(parseInt(value)) ? value : parseInt(value);
```

It checks for the result of `parseInt`; if it is **NaN** (**not a number**), then it returns the value as it is, otherwise it returns the parsed value. Observe that we are not clearing the value if it is not a number, instead we are returning it as it is. Other formatters/parsers in the pipeline can take care of non-numeric values.

Also, we register our parser at the start of the parser pipeline by calling `unshift` and formatter at the end of the pipeline by calling `push`.

We can now test it out. Add the model data interpolation next to the **Rest Time** label:

```
Rest Time (in seconds):{{workout.restBetweenExercise}}
```

Load the workout builder page, enter a numeric non-integer value, and check the interpolation. It contains the integer part only. See the following screenshot:

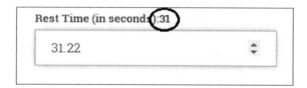

This is our parser in action! To test the formatter, we need to provide a model property with a decimal value. We can set the model value in the controller `init` function where we assign the selected workout, something like this:

```
$scope.workout.restBetweenExercise = 25.53;
```

Load the workout builder page and we should see the following output:

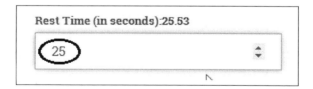

This is our formatter in action!

We now have a fair understanding of formatter and parser pipeline, and have created a set of formatter/parser set too.

Formatters and parsers can be useful in a number of scenarios when dealing with user input. For example, we can implement a parser that takes the rest time input in hh:mm:ss format and converts it into seconds in the model. A formatter can be created to do the reverse.

It's time now to look at AngularJS validation infrastructure.

AngularJS validation

As the saying goes "never trust user input", and Angular has us covered here! It has a rich validation support that makes sure data is sanitized before submission.

In AngularJS, we have built-in support for validating input types including text, numbers, e-mails, URLs, radios, checkboxes, and a few others. Depending on the input type, we set the parameters (such as `<intput type='email'`). Correct validations are automatically setup by Angular.

Other than validations based on input type, there is also support for validation attributes including the standard `required`, `min`, `max`, and custom attributes such as `ng-pattern`, `ng-minlength`, and `ng-maxlength`.

Let's add the `required` validation to workout name (`name="workoutName"`) input and see how it works. Update the workout name input to this:

```
<input type="text" name="workoutName" class="form-control"
  id="workout-name" placeholder="Enter workout name. Must be
  unique." ng-model="workout.name" required>
```

Now the input needs to have a value, else validation fails. However, how can we know if validation has failed? `NgModelController` comes to our rescue here. It can provide the validation state of the input. Let's add a message label after the input and verify this:

```
<label ng-show="formWorkout.workoutName.$error.required" ng-
class="{'text-danger': formWorkout.workoutName.$error.required}">
  Workout name is required and it should be unique.</label>
```

Load the new workout page (`#/buider/workouts/new`) now and the error label appears as shown in the following screenshot:

Name:

Enter workout name. Must be unic

Workout name is required and it should be unique.

Every model controller (such as `formWorkout.workoutName` shown previously) has a property `$error` that contains a list of all errors for the specific `ng-model` directive. The `$error` key (the property name) is the name of the validation (required in our case) that is failing and the value is `true`. If the key is not present on the `$error` object, it implies the input does not have the corresponding validation error. We use the `$error.required` error key to show the validation error and set an error class style.

Adding such a basic validation was easy, but there is a small issue here. The validation message is shown as soon as we load the form, not an ideal user experience. For a better user experience, the message should show up only after the user interacts with the input and not before that. AngularJS can help here too.

The AngularJS model state

Every element that uses `ng-model` — including `input`, `textarea`, and `select` — has some states defined on the associated model controller:

- `$pristine`: The value of this is `true` as long as the user does not interact with the input. Any updates to the input field and `$pristine` is set to `false`. Once `false`, it never flips, unless we call the `$setPristine()` function on the model controller.

- `$dirty`: This is the reverse of `$pristine`. This is `true` when the input data has been updated. This gets reset to `false` if `$setPristine()` is called.

- `$touched`: This is part of Angular 1.3. This is `true` if the control ever had focus.

- `$untouched`: This is part of Angular 1.3. This is `true` if the control has never lost focus. This is just the reverse of `$touched`.

- `$valid`: This is `true` if there are validations defined on the input element and none of them are failing.

- `$invalid`: This is `true` if any of the validations defined on the element are failing.

`$pristine\$dirty` or `$touched\$untouched` is a useful property that can help us decide when error labels are shown. Change the `ng-show` directive expression for the preceding label to this:

```
ng-show="formWorkout.workoutName.$dirty &&
    formWorkout.workoutName.$error.required"
```

Now reload the page, the error message is gone! Nonetheless, remember the control is still invalid.

As we can see, having a model state gives us great flexibility while managing the view, but the advantages don't end here. Based on the model state, Angular also adds some CSS classes to an input element. These include the following:

- `ng-valid`: This is used if the model is valid.
- `ng-invalid`: This is used if the model is invalid.
- `ng-pristine`: This is used if the model is pristine.
- `ng-dirty`: This is used if the model is dirty.
- `ng-untouched`: This is part of Angular 1.3. This is used when the input is never visited.
- `ng-touched`: This is part of Angular 1.3. This is used when the input has focus.
- `ng-invalid-<errorkey>`: This is used for a specific failed validation.
- `ng-valid-<errorkey>`: This is used for a specific validation that does not have failure.

To verify it, just load the workout builder page and inspect the `workoutName` input element in the developer console:

```
<input type="text" name="workoutName" class=" form-control ng-pristine
ng-untouched ng-invalid ng-invalid-required" ...>
```

Add some content to input and tab out. The CSS changes to this:

```
<input type="text" name="workoutName" class=" form-control
    ng-dirty ng-valid ng-valid-required ng-touched" ...>
```

These CSS class transitions are tremendously useful if we want to apply visual clues to the element depending on its state. For example, look at this snippet:

```
input.ng-invalid {  border:2px solid red; }
```

It draws a red border around any input control that has invalid data.

As we add more validations to *Workout Builder*, observe (in the developer console) how these classes are added and removed as the user interacts with the input element.

Now that we have an understanding of model states and how to use them, let's get back to our discussion on validations.

Workout builder validation

The workout data needs to be validated for a number of conditions. Let's get the complete set of validations from the `workout.html` file located in the `workoutbuilder` folder under `chapter4/checkpoint4/app/partials`. Copy the inner content from `<div id="workout-data" class="col-sm-3">` and replace the existing content inside the corresponding `div` element locally.

Also, comment out the formatter/parser watch that we created earlier to convert numeric data to integer values. We plan to do validations on the same field and those validations might interfere with the formatter/parser.

The `workout.html` view now has a number of new validations including, `required`, `min`, `ng-pattern`, `ng-minlength`, and `ng-maxlength`. Multiple validation error messages have also been associated with failing validations.

Let's test out one such validation (the `restBetweenExercise` model field) and understand some subtleties around AngularJS validations. Change the label `Rest Time` again to this:

```
Rest Time (in seconds): {{ workout.restBetweenExercise }}
```

Open the new workout builder page and enter some content in the input field of **Rest Time**. If we enter a numeric value, the model data updates immediately and gets reflected in the label, but, if we try to enter a negative value or non-numeric data, the model property is cleared. There are some important conclusions that we can derive from this behavior:

- Updates to a model and model validation happen instantaneously, not on input blur

- Once validations are in place, AngularJS does not allow invalid values to be assigned to the model from view

- This holds good the other way around too. Invalid model data does not show up in the view either

> It is possible to alter this behavior in Angular 1.3. As we saw earlier, ng-model-options allow us to control when the model is updated.
>
> An option that we did not cover earlier but will make more sense now is the property allowInvalid available on ng-model-options. If this is set to true, invalid view values are reflected on the model.

We can confirm the last finding too by setting the restBetweenExecise value to an invalid value. Update the init method set of WorkoutDetailController:

```
$scope.workout.restBetweenExercise = -33;
```

Now load a new workout builder view again. The value in the corresponding input is empty but the restBetweenExercise model has a value, as shown here:

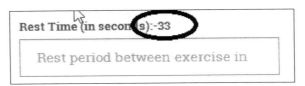

To understand what happened, we need to understand how AngularJS does validation. This discussion however needs to be divided into two parts: one corresponding to pre-Angular 1.3 and the other to Angular 1.3.

Angular 1.3 differs a bit from its predecessors, hence this division. If you are still using pre-Angular 1.3, you can skip the section dedicated to validation in Angular 1.3.

How validation works (pre-Angular 1.3)

In AngularJS, validations are done using the parser/formatter pipelines. As detailed earlier, these pipelines are a series of functions called one after another and allowing us to format/parse data.

Angular too uses these pipelines to register validation functions within the pipeline. Whenever we use a specific input type (email, url, number), or we apply validation such as required, min, or max, Angular adds corresponding validation functions to the two pipelines.

These validation functions (inside the pipeline) test the input value against a condition and return `undefined` if the validation fails, otherwise, pass the value along to the next in the pipeline. The end effect is that model or view data is cleared on validation failures.

For example, have a look at the `restBetweenExercise` input:

```
<input type="number" ng-model="workout.restBetweenExercise"
  min="1" ng-pattern="/^-?\d+$/" required ...>
```

> We could have implemented a positive integer value check by only applying `ng-pattern="/^\d+$/"`. Using two validators (`min` and `ng-pattern`) to achieve the same effect, allows us to showcase the different types of validations Angular supports.

It has checks for number, format, required, and minimum values. If we inspect the `$formatters` and `$parsers` pipeline for this input, a total of six formatters and five parsers are registered (a mere observation, not a documented fact). One of the validation functions that do regular expression-based validation (`ng-pattern`) is registered in both the formatter and parser pipelines and its implementation looks like this (from AngularJS source code 1.2.15):

```
function(value) {
    return validateRegex(pattern, value);
};
```

The `validateRegex` function returns `undefined` if the regex validation fails, hence clearing the value.

The following diagram depicts the behavior of the parser pipeline when data is invalid:

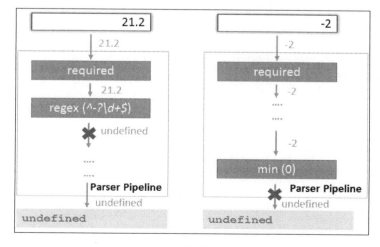

In the preceding screenshot, the first validation fails at the regex parser and the second at `min` value parser.

The formatter validation pipeline that maps model data to a view behaves in a similar manner to the parser pipeline. An important consequence of this behavior is that, if data in the model is invalid, it does not show up in the view and the view element is empty. Due to this, we cannot know the initial state of a model if the data is invalid and there is no validation error to guide us.

How validation works (Angular 1.3)

One of the major differences between pre-Angular 1.3 and 1.3 is that the validation functions of 1.3 are not part of parser/formatter pipelines. Validators in 1.3 are registered on the model controller property object `$validators`. Angular calls each function defined on the `$validators` property to validate the data.

Another difference is that validator functions in 1.3 return a Boolean value to signify if the validation passed or failed. In pre-Angular 1.3, the original value was returned if validation passed, and `undefined` when validation failed. To contrast the approach, look at the regex validator (`ng-pattern`) implementation in Angular 1.3.3:

```
function(value) {
        return ctrl.$isEmpty(value) || isUndefined(regexp)
                            || regexp.test(value);
};
```

This function returns a Boolean result.

Due to the way validators are set up in Angular 1.3, there are some important implications:

- Formatters and parsers always run before validators get a chance to validate input. In pre-Angular 1.3, we could control the order.

- In the case of a parser pipeline (the one that converts a view value to a model) specifically, if there is failure during parsing, the validator pipeline is not called.

- In pre-Angular 1.3, a failed validator in the pipeline used to clear the input value, and the subsequent validators received `undefined`. In 1.3, each validator gets a chance to validate the input value irrespective of the outcome of other validations.

Look at the following diagram that highlights the data flow for Angular 1.3 validators:

Hope this discussion clears things up in terms of how validation in AngularJS works. Having this understanding is essential for us while we build bigger and more complex forms for our apps.

Angular 1.3 has another form of benefit. It can help us manage validation messages for failed validations more effectively. Angular 1.3 introduces two new directives: `ng-messages` and `ng-message`, to manage validation messages. Let's learn how these directives work.

Managing validation error messages with ng-messages (Angular 1.3)

Some inputs contain a lot of validations and controlling when a validation message shows up can become complex. For example, the `restBetweenExercise` inputs have a number of validations. To highlight failed validation, there are four error labels that look like this:

```
<label ng-show="formWorkout.restBetweenExercise.$dirty &&
    formWorkout.restBetweenExercise.$error.required" class=
    "text-danger">Time duration is required.</label>
```

Angular 1.3 provides a better mechanism to show/hide an error message based on the state of the control. It exposes two directives: `ng-messages` and `ng-message` that allow us to show/hide error messages, but with a less verbose syntax.

The `restBetweenExercise` error messages with the `ng-messages` directive look like this:

```
<div ng-messages="formWorkout.restBetweenExercise.$error"
ng-if="formWorkout.restBetweenExercise.$dirty">
    <label ng-message="required" class="text-danger">
Time duration is required.</label>
    <label ng-message="number" class="text-danger">
Time duration should be numeric.</label>
    <label ng-message="min" class="text-danger">
Only positive integer value allowed.</label>
    <label ng-message="pattern" class="text-danger">
Only integer value allowed.</label>
</div>
```

To try it out, comment the existing validation labels for `restBetweenExercise`, and add the preceding code after the `restBetweenExercise` input.

These directives belong to a new Angular module `ngMessages`, hence a script reference to `angular-messages.js` needs to be added to `index.html`:

```
<script src="http://ajax.googleapis.com/ajax/libs/angularjs/
  1.3.3/angular-messages.js"></script>
```

And the module needs to be referenced in `app.js`, as follows:

```
angular.module('app', ['ngRoute', . . . , 'ngMessages']).
```

Open the workout builder page and play around with the `restBetweenExercise` input. The validation messages are now being managed by the `ng-messages` directive.

The `ng-messages` directive basically watches the state of an object (object properties) and shows/hides the message (using `ng-message`) based on the state changes.

The `ng-messages` directive is normally used with the `$error` property of the model controller. Whenever an error key on the `$error` object is true, the corresponding `ng-message` is displayed. For example, empty input for `restBetweenExercise` has only one `$error` key:

```
{ "required": true }
```

Hence the following error label shows up:

```
<label ng-message="required" class="text-danger">
   Time duration is required.</label>
```

Interestingly, if we enter a negative decimal value such as -22.45, the $error now has this:

```
{ "min": true, "pattern": true }
```

However, only the min object-related message is shown. This is the standard behavior of the ng-messages directive whereas it only shows the first failed validation. To show all the failed validations, we need to add another property to the ng-messages HTML:

```
<div ng-messages=". . ." ng-messages-multiple>
```

The ng-messages directive also supports message reuse and message override, which becomes relevant when working on large apps that have numerous messages. We would not be covering this topic, but it is recommended that you look at the framework documentation on ng-messages (https://code.angularjs. org/1.3.3/docs/api/ngMessages) to learn more about this scenario.

The ng-messages directive is a pretty useful directive and if you are on Angular 1.3, it's better to use the ng-messages directive to show validation errors instead of the standard ng-show/ng-hide-based approach.

> The chapter4\checkpoint4 path contains the complete implementation done thus far, including all validations added for workout.
>
> *GitHub branch: checkpoint4.4 (folder – trainer)*

Let's now do something a little more interesting and a bit more complex. Let's implement a custom validation for an exercise count!

Custom validation for an exercise count

A workout without any exercise is of no use. There should at least be one exercise in the workout and we should validate this restriction.

The problem with exercise count validation is that it is not something that the user inputs directly and the framework validates. Nonetheless, we still want a mechanism to validate the exercise count in a manner similar to other validations on this form.

Since Angular validations are built over ng-model, our custom solution too will depend on it. Add these lines inside the exercise list div element (id="exercise-list") at the very top:

```
<span name="exerciseCount" ng-model = "workout.exercises.length"> </span>
  <div class="alert alert-danger" ng-show =
    "formWorkout.exerciseCount.$dirty &&
    formWorkout.exerciseCount.$error.count">
  The workout should have at least one exercise!
</div>
```

The previous span has an ng-model attribute pointing to exercise count. Quite interesting!

A standard HTML span does not support a name attribute. Add to that, the ng-model directive on span too makes no sense as the user is not directly manipulating the exercise count. Still, we have defined both the name and ng-model attribute on the span object.

Remember what we learned in the *ng-model – beyond data binding* section? When Angular encounters ng-model on an element inside a form, it creates an NgModelController object and exposes it on the scope using the name attribute (exerciseCount). The span setup is there to just get hold of the model controller so that the exercise count validator can be registered.

We are not using the ng-model directive in its true sense here. There is no two-way binding involved. We are only interested in using the model controller API to do custom validation.

Let's see how to implement the custom validation logic. Add these two watches to WorkoutDetailController:

```
$scope.$watch('formWorkout.exerciseCount', function (newValue) {
    if (newValue) {
        newValue.$setValidity("count",
            $scope.workout.exercises.length > 0);
```

```
        }});

    $scope.$watch('workout.exercises.length',
        function (newValue, oldValue) {
            if (newValue != oldValue) {
                $scope.formWorkout.exerciseCount.$dirty = true;
                $scope.formWorkout.$setDirty();
                $scope.formWorkout.exerciseCount
    .$setValidity("count", newValue > 0);
            }});
```

The first watch is on `formWorkout.exerciseCount`, an instance of `NgModelController`. This watch contains the initialization code for the exercise count validation. The watch is required because the `WorkoutDetailController` completes execution before the `ng-model` directive gets the chance to instantiate and attach the `exerciseCount` model controller to `formWorkout`. This watch gets fired once the model controller is available. We check for the number of exercises in the workout and set the validity of the model using the API method:

```
    newValue.$setValidity("count",
        $scope.workout.exercises.length > 0);
```

The `$setValidity` function is used to set the validation key (`"count"`) on the `$error` object for a failed validation. The second parameter signifies whether the validation defined by the key (the first parameter) is valid. A `false` value implies the validation has failed. The previous HTML uses `formWorkout.exerciseCount.$error.count` to show the error message accordingly.

Next, we need a mechanism to re-evaluate our validation logic when exercises are added or removed from the workout. The second watch takes care of this. Whenever the length of the `exercises` array changes, the watch is fired.

The watch implementation sets the form and the `exerciseCount` model controller, `$dirty`, as the `exercises` array has changed. Finally, the watch re-evaluates the count validation by calling `$setValidity`. If the workout has no exercise, the expression `$scope.workout.exercises.length > 0` returns `false`, causing the count validation to fail.

Since we are implementing our own custom validation, we need to explicitly set the `$dirty` flag at both the form and element level. Form controllers have an API specifically for that `$setDirty` property, but in the model controller we just set the `$dirty` property directly.

Open the new workout builder page, add an exercise, and remove it; we should see the error **The workout should have at least one exercise!**.

> Implementing custom validation directly inside the controller is not a standard practice. What we have here is an ad hoc setup for validation. A custom validator is otherwise implemented using validator functions, which are registered with the model controller's parser and formatter pipelines for validation.
>
> Also, given the fact that custom validations are implemented using directives, we plan to postpone this discussion to later chapters. We implement one such validation in *Chapter 6, Working with Directives*. The validation checks the uniqueness of the workout name field and returns an error if a workout already exists with the specific name.
>
> In case you are having issues with validation, code updates so far are available in the checkpoint5 folder under chapter4 in the companion codebase.
>
> *GitHub Branch: checkpoint4.5 (folder – trainer)*

What we did using custom validation could have been easily done by using an error label and ng-class without involving any of the model validation infrastructure. By hooking our custom validation into the existing validation infrastructure, we do derive some benefits. We can now determine errors with a specific model and errors with the overall form in a consistent and familiar manner.

To understand how model validation rolls up into form validation, we need to understand what form-level validation has to offer. However, even before that, we need to implement saving the workout, and call it from the workout form.

Saving the workout

The workout that we are building needs to be persisted (in-memory only). The first thing that we need to do is extend the WorkoutService and WorkoutBuilderService objects.

WorkoutService needs two new methods: addWorkout and updateWorkout:

```
service.updateWorkout = function (workout) {
    var workoutIndex;
    for (var i = 0; i < workouts.length; i++) {
        if (workouts[i].name === workout.name) {
            workouts[i] = workout;
```

```
            break;
        }
    }

    return workout;
};

service.addWorkout = function (workout) {
    if (workout.name) {
        workouts.push(workout);
        return workout;
    }
}
```

The `addWorkouts` object does a basic check on the workout name and then pushes the workout into the workout array. Since there is no backing store involved, if we refresh the page, the data is lost. We will fix this in the next chapter where we persist the data to a server.

The `updateWorkout` object looks for a workout with the same name in the existing workouts array and if found, updates and replaces it.

We only add one save method to `WorkoutBuilderService` as we are tracking the context in which workout construction is going on:

```
service.save = function () {
    var workout = newWorkout ?
        WorkoutService.addWorkout(buildingWorkout):
            WorkoutService.updateWorkout(buildingWorkout);
    newWorkout = false;
    return workout;
};
```

The `save` method calls `WorkoutService`, `addWorkout`, or `updateWorkout` based on whether a new workout is being created or an existing one is being edited.

From a service perspective, that should be enough. Time to integrate the ability to save workouts into `WorkoutDetailController` and learn more about the `form` directive!

The AngularJS form directive and form validation

Forms in Angular have a different role to play as compared to traditional forms that post data to the server. We can confirm that by looking at our form definition:

```
<form class="row" name="formWorkout" novalidate>
```

It is missing the standard `action` attribute.

 The `novalidate` attribute on the `form` directive tells the browser not to do inbuilt input validations.

The standard form behavior of posting data to the server using full-page post-back does not make sense with a SPA framework such as AngularJS. In Angular, all server requests are made through AJAX invocations originating from controllers, directives, or services.

The form here plays a different role. When the form encapsulates a set of input elements (such as `input`, `textarea`, and `select`) it provides an API for:

- Determining the state of the form, such as whether the form is *dirty* or *pristine* based on the input controls on it
- Checking validation errors at the form or control level

 If you still want the standard `form` behavior, add the `action` attribute to the form, but this will definitely cause a full-page refresh.

Similar to `input`, `textarea`, and `select`, `form` too is a directive that on execution creates a special `FormController` object and adds it to the current scope. The earlier `form` declaration creates a controller with the name `formWorkout` in the `WorkoutDetailController` scope.

Before we look at the form controller API in more detail, let's add the `save` method to *Workout Builder* to save the workout when the **Save** button is clicked. Add this code to `WorkoutDetailController`:

```
$scope.save = function () {
    if ($scope.formWorkout.$invalid) return;
    $scope.workout = WorkoutBuilderService.save();
    $scope.formWorkout.$setPristine();
}
```

We check the validation state of the form using its `$invalid` property and then call the `WorkoutBuilderService.save` method if the form state is valid. Finally, we set the form to pristine state by calling the `$setPristine` method on the form controller.

Except for the new form controller, the rest of the API is pretty standard. Let's look at the controller API in a little more detail.

The FormController API

`FormController` plays a similar role for form HTML, as `NgModelController` plays for input elements. It provides useful functions and properties to manage the state of the form. We already have used some API functions and properties in the previous `save` method. The API includes the following functions:

- `$addControl(modelController)`: This API method is used to register a model controller (`NgModelController`) with the form. The input-related directives call this internally. When we register a model controller with a form, changes in the model controller affect the state of the form and hence the form controller. If the model controller marks input as dirty, the form becomes dirty. If there are validation errors in the model controller, then it results in the form state changing to invalid as well.

- `$removeControl(modelController)`: When we remove the model controller from the form controller, it no longer tracks the model controller state.

- `$setValidity(validationKey, status, childController)`: This is similar to the `$setValidity` API of `NgModelController` but is used to set the validation state of the model controller from the form controller.

- `$setDirty()`: This is used to mark the form dirty.

- `$setPristine()`: This is used to make the form pristine. This is often used to mark the form pristine after persisting the data to server on save. When the form loads for the first time, it is in the pristine state.

> The `$setPristine` call propagates to all model controllers registered with the form, so all child inputs are also set back to the pristine state. We call this function in our `WorkoutDetailController.save` function too.

- `$setUntouched()`: This is part of Angular 1.3. This is used to mark the form untouched. This is mostly called in sync with `$setPristine`, after data is saved.

Other than the state manipulation API, there are some handy properties that can be used to determine the state of the form. These include $pristine, $dirty, $valid, $invalid, and $error. Except for the $error property, the rest are similar to model controller properties.

We use the $dirty property with the workout title:

```
<h2 class="col-sm-5 col-sm-offset-1">{{workout.title}}
{{formWorkout.$dirty?'*':''}} ...
```

It appends an asterisks (*) symbol after the title when the form is dirty.

 One excellent use case for $pristine\$dirty properties is to warn the user when he/she navigates away from a form that is dirty, to save any changes.

We use the $invalid property of the form controller to verify if there are validation errors before we perform a save in WorkoutDetailController.

The $error property on the form controller is a bit more complex. It aggregates all failures across all contained inputs. The $error key (property name) corresponds to the failing error condition and the value is an array of controllers that are invalid. For a model controller, the value was just true or false. If we put a breakpoint on the $scope.save function on a new workout page, and click on **Save**, the $error object looks something like this:

```
▼ $scope.formWorkout.$error: Object
  ▶ count: Array[1]
  ▶ required: Array[3]
```

The count error is for the custom validation we did for the exercise count. Three other validation errors are pertaining to empty inputs. Play around with the input elements and check how the formWorkout.$error object behaves. See how consistent it is with the individual model controller errors.

With this, we have covered most of the FormController API. The workout can now be saved, and later reopened for editing from workout the list page (#/builder/workouts).

Since forms are so commonplace in HTML development, there are some standard use cases and quirks that we encounter while using them with Angular. The next few sections talk about these quirks and use cases.

The first one is related to validation/error messages not shown when the form is submitted.

Fixing the saving of forms and validation messages

To observe the first quirk, open a new workout builder page and directly click on the **Save** button. Nothing is saved as the form is invalid, but validations on individual form input do not show up at all. It now becomes difficult to know what elements have caused validation failure. The reason behind this behavior is pretty obvious. If we look at the error message bindings for any input element, it looks like this:

```
ng-show="formWorkout.workoutName.$dirty &&
    formWorkout.workoutName.$error.required"
```

Remember that earlier in the chapter, we explicitly disabled showing validation messages till the user has touched the input control. The same issue has come back to bite us and we need to fix it now.

If we look at the model controller API, we do not have a function to mark the model dirty, in fact we have a method that is the other way around, $setPristine. Changing/manipulating the $dirty property directly is not desirable as this and similar properties such as $pristine, $valid, and $invalid are there to determine the state of the model controller and not to update its state.

 We broke this rule earlier when we implemented the exercise count validation. We explicitly set the $dirty flag as there was no other alternative available.

Therefore, setting the $dirty flag is ruled out; instead we plan to employ a nifty trick. Let's introduce a new variable, submitted. This variable is set to true on the **Save** button click. Update the save implementation by adding the highlighted code:

```
$scope.save = function () {
    $scope.submitted = true; // Will force validations
    if ($scope.formWorkout.$invalid) return;
    $scope.workout = WorkoutBuilderService.save();
    $scope.formWorkout.$setPristine();
    $scope.submitted = false;
}
```

Nonetheless, how does this help? Well, there is another part to this fix that requires us to change the error message related to the ng-show expression. The expression now changes to:

```
ng-show="(submitted || formWorkout.workoutName.$dirty) &&
    formWorkout.workoutName.$error.required"
```

With this fix, the error message is shown when the control is dirty or form **Submit** button is pressed (submitted is true). This expression fix now has to be applied to every ng-show directive where $dirty check is done.

Angular 1.3 has this feature inbuilt. The form controller in Angular 1.3 already has $submitted, and its behavior matches our own implementation.

Look up Angular documentation on form and FormController to learn more about the $submitted property.

Time to refactor the code as the expression has become a little complex. Add a hasError method in WorkoutDetailController:

```
$scope.hasError = function (modelController, error) {
   return (modelController.$dirty || $scope.submitted) && error;
}
```

The function does a similar check to the previous one in ng-show, but here we pass, in the controller, the error state parameter. The ng-show expression now becomes:

```
ng-show = "hasError(formWorkout.workoutName,
   formWorkout.workoutName.$error.required)"
```

Apply similar updates to all ng-show directives where $dirty is used.

If we now open the new workout builder page and click on the **Save** button, we should see all validation messages on the input controls:

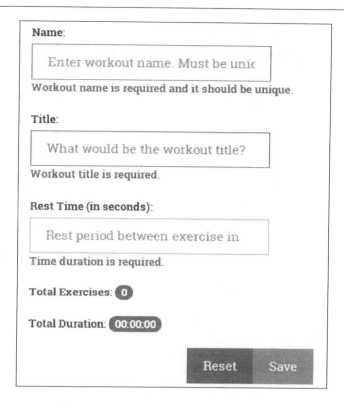

Another common issue that we might encounter when we use AngularJS services and share data is unwanted model updates. To demonstrate this:

1. Open the existing *7 Minute Workout* app, delete some of the exercises, and update some fields.

2. Then, navigate away from the page by clicking on the **Home** link on the top nav.

3. Now open the *7 Minute Workout* app again.

The changes have persisted! However, we did not save the workout.

Fixing unwarranted model updates

Why did model changes persist in spite of not saving them? Any guesses? To give you a hint, the issue is not with the form or controller implementation, but the service implementation. Look at the `getWorkout(name)` function under `shared\services.js`.

Time's up! Let's understand why. The `getWorkout(name)` implementation looks like this:

```
var result = null;
angular.forEach(service.getWorkouts(), function (workout) {
  if (workout.name === name) result = workout;
});
return result;
```

We iterate over the workout list and return the workout that matches the workout name. There lies the problem!

We return an element from the workout array (by calling `service.getWorkouts()`) and then bind it directly in the workout builder page. Due to this, any change to the workout in the workout builder affects the actual workout data. To fix the problem, we just need to return a copy of the workout instead of the original.

Update the `getWorkout` method implementation by changing the `if` condition to this:

```
if (workout.name === name) result = angular.copy(workout);
```

That's it! Go ahead and try updating the existing workout and navigate away. This time, changes are not persisted when we leave the page and come back.

>
> This issue is also due to the `get` methods (`getWorkout` and `getWorkouts`) working on local data. If data is retrieved from a remote server every time, we will not encounter this problem.

Resetting the form to its initial state is another common requirement that we should add to our *Workout Builder* app.

Resetting the form

The standard way of resetting the form is to call the reset method on the form object such as `document.forms["formWorkout"].reset()` or to use `input type="reset"`, which clears all the form inputs. The drawback of this approach is that fields are completely cleared, instead of reverting back to their original content.

For *Workout Builder*, we will reset the form to its initial state using a similar approach outlined in the last section. Open `workout.js`, update `WorkoutDetailController`, and add the `reset` method:

```
$scope.reset = function () {
  $scope.workout =
WorkoutBuilderService.startBuilding($routeParams.id);
  $scope.formWorkout.$setPristine();
  $scope.submitted = false;
};
```

We reset the `workout` object, set the form to pristine and the `submitted` variable to `false` for future validation. The `startBuilding` function internally calls the `getWorkout` method on `WorkoutService`. As we saw in the last section, `getWorkout` always returns a new copy of a workout, which finally gets assigned to `$scope.workout` as just mentioned, causing the form to reset to its original state.

However, what about the `$routeParams` reference given in the preceding code? `$routeParams` is an AngularJS service that complements the `$route` service and contains data about specific URL fragments. Since we have used it in `save`, why not formally introduce it and learn a bit more about it?

AngularJS $routeParams

The `$routeParams` service contains route fragment values derived from the current route, for routes that are dynamic in nature. To understand it better, let's look at the route configuration for *Workout Builder* in the edit mode:

```
$routeProvider.when('/builder/workouts/:id', {
```

The previous route has a variable part `:id` that changes based on the name of the workout. For *7 Minute Workout*, the route is this:

```
/builder/workout/7minuteworkout
```

The `$routeParams` service maps the literal string value `7minuteworkout` to the `id` property and makes the data available to any controller/service (in this case, `$routeParams.id`).

In the case of a new workout, the route is `/builder/workouts/new`, and does not use any placeholder. Therefore, `$routeParams.id` is undefined in this case.

Coming back to the `reset` implementation, remember to add `$routeParams` dependency to the `WorkoutDetailController` declaration for the `reset` function to work correctly.

Finally, to bind the method to the form element, add a `reset` button to the form after the `save` button declaration:

```
<button class="btn btn-primary pull-right"
  ng-click="reset()">Reset</button>
```

We can now try it out. Create a new workout or open the existing one. Make some changes and click on **Reset**. The form should be reset to the state when it was loaded.

The reset is done, what next? We have still not implemented validation for the exercise duration of exercises that are dynamically added to the workout. Let's take care of this scenario too.

Dynamically generated inputs and forms

For dynamically generated form elements, as we have in the exercise list section, we still want to validate data entered by the user. AngularJS falls short in this scenario as the obvious validation mechanism does not work.

Ideally something like this should work for our exercise list in `ng-repeat`:

```
<input type="number" name="{{exercise.name}}-duration"  ng-
model="exercise.duration"/>
```

Sadly, this does not work. AngularJS literally creates a model controller with the name `{{exercise.name}}-duration`. The reason is that the `name` attribute on the form and input (with `ng-model`) do not support interpolations. There is still an open issue on this (visit `https://github.com/angular/angular.js/issues/1404` for more information).

 This issue has been fixed in Angular 1.3. The approach detailed later and that uses nested forms is still a better approach. With nested forms, we do not need to use interpolation expression for `ng-model` or validation messages (such as `formworkout[{{exercise.name}}-duration]).$error`.

The mechanism or workaround that Angular gives us to support dynamically generated inputs is the `ng-form` directive. This directive behaves in a similar manner to the `form` directive. It allows us to create nested forms and do individual form-level validation, with each form having its own set of inputs. Let's add `ng-form` and validate exercise duration.

Validating exercise duration with ng-form

Change the exercise list item template script (`id="workout-exercise-tile"`) and wrap the `select` tag into an `ng-form` directive together with a validation label:

```
<ng-form name="formDuration">
  <select class="select-duration form-control" name="duration"
  ng-model="exercise.duration" ng-options="duration.value as
    duration.title for duration in durations" required>
    <option value="">Select Duration</option>
  </select>
  <label ng-show=
    "hasError(formDuration.duration,
     formDuration.duration.$error.required)"
     class="text-danger">Time duration is required.</label>
</ng-form>
```

The `ng-form` directive behaves similarly to `form`. It creates a form controller and adds it to the scope with the name `formDuration`. All validations within the `ng-form` happen in the context of the `formDuration` form controller as we can see in the previous binding expressions. This is possible because `ng-repeat` creates a new scope for each item it generates.

Other than the `formDuration` added to the `ng-repeat` scope, internally the `formDuration` controller is also registered with the parent form controller (`formWorkout`) using the controller API function `$addControl`.

Due to this, the validation state and dirty/pristine state of the child forms roll up into the parent form controller (`formWorkout`). This implies:

- If there are validation errors at the child form controller, even the parent form controller state becomes invalid (`$invalid` returns true for parent)

- If the child form controller is set to dirty, the parent form controller is also marked dirty

- Conversely, if we call `$setPristine` on the parent form controller, all child form controllers are also reset to the pristine stage

Refresh the workout builder page again and now the validation on exercise duration also works and integrates well with the parent formWorkout controller. If there is any error in the exercise duration input, the formWorkout controller is also marked invalid.

If you are having problems with the implementation, check checkpoint6 folder under chapter4 for a working implementation of what we have achieved thus far.

Checkpoint6 also contains implementation for *Delete Workout* that we will not cover. Look at the code and see where it has been extended to support the delete functionality

GitHub branch: checkpoint4.6 (folder – trainer)

Other than workout persistence, we now have a fully functional workout builder. A good time to start building some customized workouts!

We have now reached a point where we should feel comfortable working with Angular. The only major topics left are client-server interaction, directives, and unit testing. However, from what we have learned thus far, we have enough ammunition to build something decent. Purposefully, we have overlooked one important topic that is critical for us to understand before we take up any serious Angular development: *scope inheritance*.

We need to understand the nuances of scope inheritance (prototypal inheritance). Scope inheritance behavior can stump even the most experienced developers. To learn about it, we need to revisit the concept of scopes, but this time from an inheritance hierarchy perspective.

Revisiting Angular scopes

To refresh our memory, scopes in Angular are created mostly as part of directive execution. Angular creates a new scope(s) whenever it encounters directives that request for a new scope. The ng-controller, ng-view, and ng-repeat directives are good examples of such directives.

Depending upon how these directives are declared in HTML, the scope hierarchy is also affected. For nested directives that request for the new scope, more often than not, the child directive scope inherits from the parent directive scope. This inheritance adheres to the standard JavaScript prototypal inheritance.

Some directives request for an isolated scope on execution. Such scopes do not inherit from their parent scope object.

Prototypal inheritance in JavaScript can catch developers off-guard, especially the ones who come from an object-oriented background (lot of us do). In prototypal inheritance, an object inherits from other objects, as there is no concept of classes here.

 There is a good tutorial available online at `http://javascript.info/tutorial/inheritance`, in case you are interested in exploring prototypal inheritance in depth.

Prototypal inheritance on the surface seems to work similarly to class-based inheritance. An object derives from other objects, and hence can use the parent objects' properties and functions. Nonetheless, there is a big difference when it comes to updating/writing to properties.

In prototypal inheritance, the parent object and preceding prototypal chain are consulted for reads, but not for writes.

Interesting! Let's try to understand this hypothesis with examples. All the following examples use the Angular scope object.

 You can try these snippets in jsFiddle. Here is a basic fiddle for this at `http://jsfiddle.net/cmyworld/9ak1gahe/`. Remember to open the browser debugger console to see the log messages.

Consider this piece of code and corresponding scope setup:

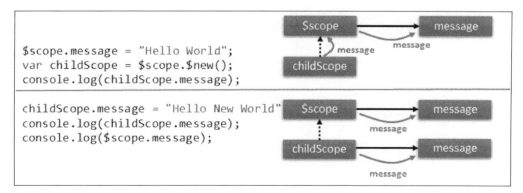

$scope.$new is a scope API function that creates the new child scope that inherits prototypically from the $scope object.

The first console.log logs the message property (Hello World) defined on the parent $scope. During reads, JavaScript looks for a message property on the childScope object. Since childScope does not have this property, it traverses up the hierarchy (the parent object) in search of message, and finds it on the parent $scope object.

The subsequent assignment childScope.message = "Hello New World";, should have then overwritten the message variable on the parent object, but it does not! Instead, a new message property is created on childScope, and it shadows the parent $scope.message property. Clearly, reads traverse the prototypal chain but writes do not.

This premise holds good for the primitive property (number, Boolean, date, and string) and object assignments, but if the property is declared on an object (declared on the parent object), changes to it on the child scope are reflected in the parent object too. Consider this variation to the preceding example:

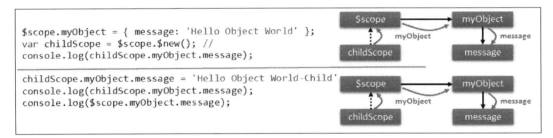

```
$scope.myObject = { message: 'Hello Object World' };
var childScope = $scope.$new(); //
console.log(childScope.myObject.message);

childScope.myObject.message = 'Hello Object World-Child';
console.log(childScope.myObject.message);
console.log($scope.myObject.message);
```

This time no new property is created on the childScope object, and the last two console.log functions print the same message ('Hello Object World - Child').

The write did not happen on childScope this time due to a subtle read here. JavaScript had to first look for the myObject property before it could resolve the message reference. The myObject property was found on parent $scope and that was used.

Consider another variation:

```
$scope.myObject = { message: 'Hello Object World' };
var childScope = $scope.$new(); //creates a child scope

childScope.myObject= {message:'Hello Object World - Child'};
console.log(childScope.myObject.message);
console.log($scope.myObject.message);
```

This time, like the first case, a new property `myObject` is created on `childScope`. `$scope.myObject` and `childScope.myObject` are two different objects and can be manipulated independently.

Now that we understand the subtleties, what are the implications? This behavior affects two-way binding and property assignments.

Strangely enough, we have not faced this issue, in spite of our working on forms that have a number of these two-way bindings (`ng-model`). There are two good reasons for this:

- The complete form container has only one scope (except the exercise list scopes that are created due to `ng-repeat`), which is the scope created as part of `ng-view`.

- None of the `ng-model` expressions that we have used bind to a primitive object. Each one binds to an object property, such as `ng-model="workout.name"`.

 Always use the . notation (bind to object property) while binding to `ng-model` to avoid prototypal inheritance nuances.

It is not very difficult to create something that highlights this two-way binding issue, in the context of real angular controllers and directives. Look at this jsFiddle http://jsfiddle.net/cmyworld/kkrmux2f. There are two sets of input, both used to enter user-specific data. The first set of inputs has the two-way binding issue, whereas the second set works just fine.

Let's try another case: and this time on the workout builder view.

The use case is, whenever the user clicks on any of the exercise tiles that are part of the workout, we need to show the exercise description between the tiles and the input fields. Simple enough?

Let's begin the pursuit. Update the `exercises-list` `div` style to this:

```
<div id="exercises-list" class="col-sm-4 col-sm-offset-1">
```

Add a new `div` element for the exercise description just around the `workout-data` parameter of `div`:

```
<div id="exercise-description" class="col-sm-1">
  {{selectedExercise.details.description}}</div>
<div id="workout-data" class="col-sm-3">
```

Finally, update the `workout.exercises ng-repeat` directive to this:

```
<div ng-repeat="exercise in workout.exercises" class="
    exercise-item" ng-click="selectedExercise=exercise">
```

The `exercise-description` parameter of `div` has an interpolation to a variable `selectedExercise` that should contain the current selected exercise. We assign `selectedExercise` when the exercise tile is clicked, inside the `ng-click` expression.

The implementation looks correct but it does not work. Open the *7 Minute Workout* app and try it yourself. Clicking on any of the workout tiles has no effect. Again, the reason is prototypal inheritance!

When we used `selectedExercise=exercise` in `ng-repeat`, the property got created on a scope that was created as part of the `ng-repeat` execution, and not on the original scope.

How can we fix this? Well, one option is to change the `ng-click` directive to this:

```
ng-click="$parent.selectedExercise=exercise"
```

Make the change, and refresh the page, and try clicking again. This time it works, as shown here:

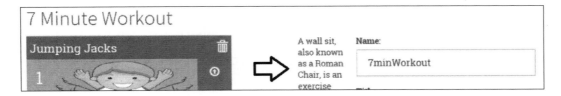

`$parent` is a special property on every `$scope` object that points to the parent scope from which the scope was created.

While the usage of `$parent` does solve this problem, it is not the recommended way to achieve this fix. The fix is brittle and whenever a new scope is added (this can be due to the addition of a new directive at some point in the future) in the HTML hierarchy, the `$parent` link might not point to the correct parent scope. In such a scenario, we have to fix the expression again, leading to undesired results such as, `$parent.$parent.$parent.selectedExercise`.

The correct way to fix this would be to create an object with a selected exercise property to track the exercise. In `WorkoutDetailController`, add a variable to track the selected exercise at the top:

```
$scope.selected = {};
```

Change the interpolation for the description to this:

```
{{selected.exercise.details.description}}
```

Change the `ng-click` expression to this:

```
ng-click="selected.exercise=exercise"
```

We have a perfectly working solution for our use case. This time, we track the selected exercise as a sub property (`exercise`) of `selected` object and hence things just work.

That's it on scopes inheritances and the nuances around it. A very important topic that is essential to grasp to be a pro Angular dev.

 Another excellent discussion on this topic is available under this Angular wiki article at `https://github.com/angular/angular.js/wiki/Understanding-Scopes`. An essential and highly informative read!

Looking back at the goals that we had for *Personal Trainer*, we still have stuff pending. Adding/editing new exercises needs to be implemented and lastly the *Personal Trainer* app needs to integrate with the implementation of *7 Minute Workout* (*Workout Runner*). The *Workout Runner* app needs to support the running of any workout that we build using *Personal Trainer*.

We will be ending this chapter here. But one of the earlier tasks of creating an exercise builder is something I will urge everyone to go ahead and implement. The solution is similar to *Workout Builder* except the data elements are exercise-specific. It will be a good exercise for us to reinforce our learnings.

 Once done, you can compare your implementations with the one available in `chapter4/checkpoint7`.

GitHub branch: checkpoint4.7 (folder – trainer)

Integrating the *Personal Trainer* app with *7 Minute Workout* is something we will take up in the next chapter.

Time to summarize what we have learned thus far!

Summary

We now have a *Personal Trainer* app. The process of converting a specific *7 Minute Workout* app to a generic *Personal Trainer* app has helped us learn a number of new concepts.

We started the chapter by defining the new app requirements. Then, we designed the model as a shared service.

We defined some new views and corresponding routes for the *Personal Trainer* app. We also used the existing routing infrastructure to set up a navigation system by extending routes. We then turned our focus to workout building.

One of the primary technological focuses in this chapter was AngularJS forms. The workout builder view employed a number of form input elements and we implemented all common form scenarios.

We worked with the `ng-model` directive, explored the `NgModelController` API, and learned about formatter and parser pipelines and the role these pipelines play in formatting, parsing, and data validation.

We explored Angular validation in depth, and implemented a custom validation using the `NgModelController` API.

We covered nested forms and how to manage dynamically generated input controls using the `ng-form` directive.

Lastly, we learned about the nuances of scope inheritance, and how to avoid some scope inheritance gotchas while building apps with Angular.

The next chapter is all about client-server interaction. The workouts that we create need to be persisted. In the next chapter, we build a persistence layer that allows us to save workout data on the server.

Before we conclude this chapter, here is a friendly reminder. If you have not completed the exercise building routine for *Personal Trainer*, go ahead and do it. It's always a great and fulfilling experience to try out new stuff unassisted. You can always compare your implementation with what has been provided in the companion codebase.

5
Adding Data Persistence to Personal Trainer

It's now time to talk to the server! There is no fun in creating a workout, adding exercises, and saving it, to later realize that all our efforts are lost because the data is not persisted anywhere. We need to fix this.

Seldom are applications self-contained. Any consumer app, irrespective of the size, has parts that interact with elements outside its boundary. And with web-based applications, the interaction is mostly with a server. Apps interact with the server to authenticate, authorize, store/retrieve data, validate data, and perform other such operations.

This chapter explores the constructs that AngularJS provides for client-server interaction. In the process, we add a persistence layer to Personal Trainer that loads and saves data to a backend server.

The topics we cover in this chapter include:

- **Provisioning a backend to persist workout data**: We set up a MongoLab account and use its REST API to access and store workout data.

- **Understanding the $http service**: $http is the core service in Angular to for interacting with a server over HTTP. You learn how to make all types of GET, POST, PUT, and DELETE requests with the $http service.

- **Implementing, loading, and saving workout data**: We use the $http service to load and store workout data into MongoLab databases.

- **Creating and consuming promises**: We touched upon promises in the earlier chapters. In this chapter, not only do we consume promises (part of HTTP invocation) but we also see how to create and resolve our own promises.

- **Working with cross-domain access**: As we are interacting with a MongoLab server in a different domain, you learn about browser restrictions on cross-domain access. You also learn how JSONP and CORS help us make cross-domain access easy and about AngularJS JSONP support.

- **Using the $resource service for RESTful endpoints**: The $resource service is an abstraction built over $http to support the RESTful server endpoints. You learn about the $resource service and its usage.

- **Loading and saving exercise data with $resource**: We change parts of the system to employ the $resource service to load and save exercise data.

- **Request/response interceptors**: You learn about interceptors and how they are used to intercept calls in a request/response pipeline and alter the remote invocation flow.

- **Request/response transformers**: Similar to interceptors, transformers function at the message payload level. We explore the working of transformers with examples.

Let's get the ball rolling.

AngularJS and server interactions

Any client-server interaction typically boils down to sending HTTP requests to a server and receiving responses from a server. For heavy apps of JavaScript, we depend on the AJAX request/response mechanism to communicate with the server. To support AJAX-based communication, AngularJS exposes two framework services:

- $http: This is the primary component to interact with a remote server using AJAX. We can compare it to the ajax function of jQuery as it does something similar.

- $resource: This is an abstraction build over $http to make communication with RESTful (http://en.wikipedia.org/wiki/Representational_state_transfer) services easier.

Before we delve much into the preceding service we need to set up our server platform that stores the data and allows us to manage it.

Setting up the persistence store

For data persistence, we use a document database, MongoDB (https://www.mongodb.org/), hosted over MongoLab (https://mongolab.com/) as our data store. The reason we zeroed in MongoLab is because it provides an interface to interact with the database directly. This saves us the effort of setting up server middleware to support the MongoDB interaction.

It is never a good idea to expose the data store/database directly to the client, but, in this case, since your primary aim is to learn about AngularJS and client-server interaction, we take this liberty and will directly access the MongoDB instance hosted in MongoLab.

There is also a new breed of apps that are built over **noBackend** solutions. In such a setup, frontend developers build apps without the knowledge of the exact backend involved. Server interaction is limited to making API calls to the backend. If you are interested in knowing more about these noBackend solutions, do checkout `http://nobackend.org/`.

Our first task is to provision an account on MongoLab and create a database:

1. Go to `https://mongolab.com` and sign up for a MongoLab account by following the instructions on the website.

2. Once the account is provisioned, login and create a new Mongo database by clicking on the **Create New** button in the home page.

   On the database creation screen, you need to make some selection to provision the database. See the following screenshot to select the free database tier and other options:

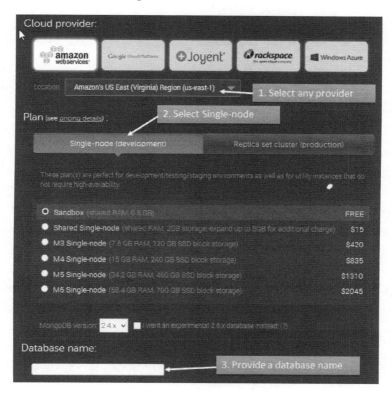

3. Create the database and make a note of the database name that you create.

4. Once the database is provisioned, open the database and add two collections to it from the **Collection** tab:

   ○ `exercises`: This stores all *Personal Trainer* exercises

   ○ `workouts`: This stores all *Personal Trainer* workouts

   Collections in the MongoDB world equate to a database table.

> MongoDB belongs to a breed of databases termed **document databases**. The central concepts here are documents, attributes, and their linkages. And, unlike traditional databases, the schema is not rigid.
>
> We will not be covering what document databases are and how to perform data modeling for document-based stores in this book. *Personal Trainer* has a limited storage requirement and we manage it using the preceding two document collections. We may not even be using the document database in its true sense.

5. Once the collections are added, add yourself as a user to the database from the **User** tab.

6. The next step is to determine the API key for the MongoLab account. The provisioned API key has to be appended to every request made to MongoLab. To get the API key, perform the following steps:

   1. Click on the username (not the account name) in the top-right corner to open the user profile.

   2. In the section titled **API Key**, the current API key is displayed; copy it.

The datastore schema is complete; we now need to seed these collections.

Seeding the database

The *Personal Trainer* app already has a predefined workout and a list of 12 exercises. We need to seed the collections with this data.

Open `seed.js` from `chapter5/checkpoint1/app/js` from the companion codebase. It contains the seed JSON script and detailed instructions on how to seed data into the MongoLab database instance.

Once seeded, the database will have one workout in the workouts collection and 12 exercises in the exercises collection. Verify this on the MongoLab site, the collections should show this:

Everything has been set up now, let's start our discussion with the $http service and implement workout/exercise persistence for the *Personal Trainer* app.

$http service basics

The $http service is the primary service for making an AJAX request in AngularJS. The $http service provides an API to perform all HTTP operations (actions) such as GET, POST, PUT, DELETE, and some others.

HTTP communication is asynchronous in nature. When making HTTP requests, a browser does not wait for the response to arrive before continuing processing. Instead, we need to register some callback functions that are invoked in the future when the response arrives from the server. The AngularJS Promise API helps us streamline this asynchronous communication and we use it extensively while working with the $http service, as you will see later in this chapter.

The basic $http syntax is:

```
$http(config)
```

The $http service takes a configuration object as a parameter and returns a promise. The config object contains a set of properties that affect the remote request behavior. These properties include arguments such as the HTTP action type (GET, POST, PUT,...), the remote server URL, query string parameters, headers to send, and a number of other such options.

The exact configuration option details are available in framework documentation for the $http service at https://code.angularjs.org/1.3.3/docs/api/ng/service/$http. As we work through the chapter, we will use some of these configurations in our implementation too.

A $http invocation returns a promise object. Other than the standard Promise API functions (such as then), this object contains two extra callback functions: success and error, that get invoked based on whether the HTTP request was completed successfully or not.

Here is a simple HTTP request using $http:

```
$http({method: 'GET', url: '/endpoint'}).
    success(function(data, status, headers, config) {
        // called when http call completes successfully
    }).
    error(function(error, status, headers, config) {
        // called when the http call fails.
    // The error parameter contains the failure reason.
    });
```

The preceding code issues an HTTP GET request to /endpoint and when the response is available either the success or error callback is invoked.

 HTTP responses in the - range 200-299 are considered successful. Responses in the range of 40x and 50x are treated as failure and result in the error callback function being invoked.

The callback functions (success or error) are invoked with four arguments:

- data or error: This is the response returned from the server. It can be the data returned or an error if the request fails.
- status: This is the HTTP status code for the response.
- headers: This is used for the HTTP response headers.
- config: This is the configuration object used during the original $http invocation.

The $http(config) syntax for making an AJAX request is very uncommon. The service has a number of shortcut methods to make a specific type of HTTP request. These include:

- $http.get(url, [config])
- $http.post(url, data, [config])
- $http.put(url, data, [config])
- $http.delete(url, [config])
- $http.head(url, [config])
- $http.jsonp(url, [config])

All these function take the same (optional) config object as the last parameter.

An interesting thing about the standard `$http` configuration is that these settings make JSON data handling easy. The end effect of this is:

- For standard `GET` operations, if the response is JSON, the framework automatically parses the JSON string and converts it into a JavaScript object. The end result is that the first argument of the `success` callback function (`data`) contains a JavaScript object, not a string value.

- For `POST` and `PUT`, objects are automatically serialized and the corresponding content type header is set (`Content-Type: application/json`) before the request is made.

Does that mean that `$http` cannot handle other formats? That is far from true. The `$http` service is the generic AJAX service exposed by the Angular framework and can handle any format of request/response. Every AJAX request that happens in AngularJS is done by the `$http` service directly or indirectly. For example, the remote views that we load for the `ng-view` or `ng-include` directives use the `$http` service under the hood.

> Checkout the jsFiddle web page at http://jsfiddle.net/cmyworld/doLhmgL6/ where we use the `$http` service to post data to a server in a more traditional format that is associated with the standard post form. (`'Content-Type': 'application/x-www-form-urlencoded'`).

It is just that Angular makes it easy to work with JSON data, helping us to avoid writing boilerplate serialization/deserialization logic, and setting HTTP headers, which we normally do when working with JSON data.

With this backgrounder on the `$http` service, we now are in a position to implement something useful using `$http`. Let's add some workout persistence.

Personal Trainer and server integration

As described in the previous section, client-server interaction is all about asynchronicity. As we alter our *Personal Trainer* app to load data from the server, this pattern becomes self-evident.

In the preceding chapter, the initial set of workouts and exercises was hardcoded in the `WorkoutService` implementation itself. Let's see how to load this data from the server first.

Loading exercise and workout data

Earlier in this chapter, we seeded our database with a data form, the `seed.js` file. We now need to render this data in our views. The MongoLab REST API is going to help us here.

 The MongoLab REST API uses an API key to authenticate access request. Every request made to the MongoLab endpoints needs to have a query string parameter `apikey=<key>` where `key` is the API key that we provisioned earlier in the chapter. Remember, the key is always provided to a user and associated with his/her account. Avoid sharing your API keys with others.

The API follows a predictable pattern to query and update data. For any MongoDB collection, the typical endpoint access pattern is one of the following (given here is the base URL: `https://api.mongolab.com/api/1/databases`):

- `/<dbname>/collections/<name>?apiKey=<key>`. This has the following requests:
    - ° GET: This action gets all objects in the given collection name.
    - ° POST: This action adds a new object to the collection `name`. MongoLab has an `_id` property that uniquely identifies the document (object). If not provided in the posted data, it is autogenerated.

- `/<dbname>/collections/<name>/<id>?apiKey=<key>`. This has the following requests:
    - ° GET: This gets a specific document/collection item with a specific ID (a match done on the `_id` property) from the collection name
    - ° PUT: This updates the specific item (`id`) in the collection name
    - ° DELETE: This deletes the item with a specific ID from the collection name

 For more details on the REST API interface, visit the MongoLab REST API documentation at `http://docs.mongolab.com/restapi/#insert-multidocuments`.

Now, we are in a position to start implementing exercise/workout list pages.

Before we start, please download the working copy of *Personal Trainer* from `chapter4/checkpoint7`. It contains the complete implementation for *Personal Trainer* including exercise building, which was left as a **Do-it-yourself (DIY)** assignment for everyone to try.

The code is also available on GitHub (`https://github.com/chandermani/angularjsbyexample`) for everyone to download. Checkpoints are implemented as branches in GitHub.

The branch to download is as follows:

GitHub branch: checkpoint4.7 (folder – trainer)

Loading exercise and workout lists from a server

To pull exercise and workout lists from the MongoLab database, we have to rewrite our `WorkoutService` service methods, `getExercises` and `getWorkouts`.

Open `services.js` from `app/js/shared` and change the `getExercises` function to this:

```
service.getExercises = function () {
   var collectionsUrl = "https://api.mongolab.com/api/1/
databases/<dbname>/collections";
   return $http.get(collectionsUrl + "/exercises", {
       params: { apiKey: '<key>'}
   });
};
```

Replace the tokens: `<dbname>` and `<key>` with the DB name and API key of the database that we provisioned earlier in the chapter.

Also remember to add the `$http` dependency in the `WorkoutService` declaration.

The new function created here just builds the MongoLab URL and then calls the `$http.get` function to get the list of exercises. The first parameter we have is the URL to connect to and the second parameter is the `config` object.

The `params` property of the `config` object allows us to add query string parameters to the URL. We add the API key (`?apiKey=98dkdd`) as a query string for API access.

Now that the `getExercises` function is updated, and the new implementation returns a promise, we need to fix the upstream callers.

Open `exercise.js` placed under `WorkoutBuilder` and fix the
`ExerciseListController` by replacing the existing `init` function implementation
(the code inside `init`) with these lines:

```
WorkoutService.getExercises().success(function (data) {
    $scope.exercises = data;
});
```

We use the HTTP promise success callback to bind the exercises list in a controller.
We can clearly observe the asynchronous behavior of `$http` and the promise-based
callback in action as we set the `exercises` data after receiving a server response in a
callback function.

Go ahead and load the exercise list page (`#/builder/exercises`) and make sure the
exercise list is loading from the server. The browser network logs should log requests
such as this:

Exercises are loading fine, but what about workouts? The workout list page can also
be fixed on similar lines.

Update the `getWorkouts` function of `WorkoutService` to load data from the
server. The `getWorkouts` implementation is similar to `getExercises` except
that the collection name now becomes `workouts`. Then fix the `init` function of
`WorkoutListController` along the same lines as the preceding `init` function and
we are done.

That was easy! We can fix all other `get` scenarios in a similar manner. But before we
do that, there is still scope to improve our implementation.

The first problem with `getExercises`/`getWorkouts` is that the DB name and API
key are hardcoded and will cause maintenance issues in the future. The best way is
to inject these values into `WorkoutService` through some kind of mechanism.

With our past experience and learnings, we know that, if we implement this service
using `provider`, we can pass configuration data required to set up the service at the
configuration stage of app bootstrapping. This allows us to configure the service
before use. Time to put this theory to practice!

Implementing the WorkoutService provider

Implementing `WorkoutService` as a provider will help us to configure the database name and API key for the service at the configuration stage.

Copy and replace the updated `WorkoutService` definition from the `services.js` file in `chapter5/checkpoint1/app/js/shared`. The service has now been converted into a provider implementation.

The service has a `configure` method that sets up the database name, the API key, and the collection URL address, as given here:

```
this.configure = function (dbName, key) {
database = database;
    apiKey = key;
    collectionsUrl = apiUrl + dbName + "/collections";
}
```

The functions: `setupInitialExercises`, `setupInitialWorkouts`, and `init` have also been removed as the data will now come from the MongoLab server.

The implementation of the `getExercise` and `getWorkouts` functions has been updated to use the configured parameters:

```
service.getExercises = function () {
  return $http.get(collectionsUrl + "/exercises",
                    { params: { apiKey: apiKey } });
};
```

And finally, the `service` object creation has been moved into the `$get` function of the provider. `$get` is the factory function responsible for creating the actual service.

Let's update the `config` function of the `app` module and inject the MongoLab configuration into `WorkoutService` (using `WorkoutServiceProvider`).

Open the `app.js` file, inject the new provider dependency `WorkoutServiceProvider` with the other provider dependencies, and call its configure method with your database name and API key:

```
WorkoutServiceProvider.configure("<mydb>", "<mykey>");
```

We now have a better `WorkoutService` implementation as it allows the calling code to configure the service before use.

The provider implementation may look overtly complex as this could be achieved by creating a constant service like this:

```
angular.module('app').constant('dbConfig', {
    database: "<dbname>",
    apiKey: "<apikey>"
});
```

And then inject the implementation into the existing WorkoutService implementation.

The advantage of the provider approach is that the configuration data is not globally exposed. Had we used a constant service such as dbConfig, any other service/controller could have got hold of the database name and API key by injecting the dbConfig service, which would be less than desirable.

The preceding provider refactoring is still not complete and we can verify this by refreshing the workout list page. There will be an unknown provider WorkoutServiceProvider error in the browser developer console.

We have just hit a bug with Angular that causes the config function module to execute before provider registration. This happened because the script registration for app.js precedes the service.js registration in index.html.

There is already a bug (https://github.com/angular/angular.js/issues/7139) logged against this issue and the current workaround is to call the config function at the end, after all provider/service registrations. This requires us to move the config function implementation to a new file.

 There was this issue while writing this chapter. The newer versions of Angular 1.3 and above have fixed this issue. We will still continue with the approach outline given next as it works irrespective of the version of Angular.

Copy the updated app.js and config.js (new file) files from chapter5/checkpoint1 and update your local copy. Once copied, update the configure function of WorkoutServiceProvider in the config.js file with your database name and API key. And finally, add a reference to config.js in the script declaration section of index.html at the end.

Refresh the workout/exercise list page and the workout and exercise data is loaded from the database server.

Look at the complete implementation in `chapter5/checkpoint1` if you are having difficulty in retrieving/showing data.

Also remember to replace the database name and API key before running the code from `checkpoint1`.

GitHub branch: checkpoint5.1 (folder: trainer)

This looks good and the lists are loading fine. Well, almost! There is a small glitch in the workout list page. We can easily spot it if we look carefully at any list item (in fact there is only one item):

The workout duration calculations are not working anymore! What could be the reason? We need to look back on how these calculations were implemented. The `WorkoutPlan` service (in `model.js`) defines a function `totalWorkoutDuration` that does the math for this.

The difference is in terms of the workout array that is bound to the view. In the previous chapter, we created the array with model objects that were created using the `WorkoutPlan` service. But now, since we are retrieving data from the server, we bind a simple array of JavaScript objects to the view, which for obvious reasons has no calculation logic.

We can fix this problem by mapping a server response into our model class objects and returning that to any upstream caller.

Mapping server data to application models

Mapping server data to our model and vice versa may be unnecessary if the model and server storage definition match. If we look at the `Exercise` model class and the seed data that we have added for the exercise in MongoLab, they do match and hence mapping becomes unnecessary.

Mapping server response to model data becomes imperative if:

- Our model defines any functions
- A stored model stored is different from its representation in code
- The same model class is used to represent data from different sources (this can happen for mashups where we pull data from disparate sources)

WorkoutPlan is a prime example of an impedance mismatch between a model representation and its storage. Look at the following screenshot to understand these differences:

The two major differences between a model and server data are as follows:

- The model defines the totalWorkoutDuration function.
- The exercises array representation also differs. The exercises array of a model contains the Exercise object (the details property) whereas the server data stores just the exercise identifier or name.

This clearly means loading and saving a workout requires model mapping. And for consistency, we plan to map data for both the exercise and the workout.

Change the `getExercises` implementation in `WorkoutService` to this:

```
service.getExercises = function () {
    return $http.get(collectionsUrl + "/exercises", {
        params: { apiKey: apiKey}
    }).then(function (response) {
        return response.data.map(function (exercise) {
            return new Exercise(exercise);
        })});
};
```

And since the return value for the `getExercises` function now is not a promise object returned by `$http` (see the following discussion) but a standard promise, we need to use the `then` function instead of the `success` function wherever we are calling `getExercises`.

Change the `init` implementation in both `ExercisesNavController` and `ExerciseListController` to this:

```
var init = function () {
WorkoutService.getExercises().then(function (data) {
    $scope.exercises = data;
});
};
```

Look back at the highlighted code for the updated `getExercises` implementation. There are a number of interesting things going on here that you should understand:

- Firstly, inside the `then` success callback function (the first parameter), we call the `Array.map` function to map the list of exercises received from a server to the `Exercise` object array. The `Array.map` function is generally used to map from one array to another array. Check out the MDN documentation for the `Array.map` (https://developer.mozilla.org/en-US/docs/Web/JavaScript/Reference/Global_Objects/Array/map) function to know more about how it works.

- Secondly, this is a good example of promise chaining in action. The `$http.get` function returns the first promise; we attach a `then` callback to it that itself returns a promise that is finally returned to the calling code. We can visualize this with the help of the following diagram:

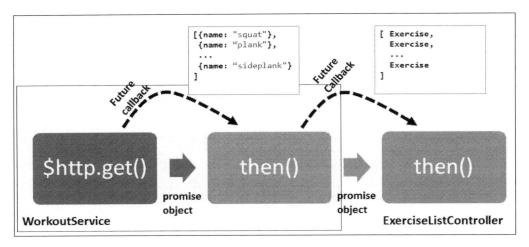

In future, when the first `$http.get` promise is resolved, the `then` callback is invoked with the exercise list from the server. The `then` callback processes the response and returns a new array of the `Exercise` objects. This return value feeds into the promise resolution for the next callback in the line defined in `ExerciseListController`.

> The promise returned by `then` is resolved by the return value of its `success` and `error` callback function.

The `then` function of `ExercisesController` finally assigns the `Exercise` objects received to the `exercises` variable. The promise resolution data has been highlighted in the preceding diagram above the dotted arrows.

Promise chaining acts like a pipeline for response flow; this is a very powerful pattern and can be used to do some nifty stuff as we have previously done.

- Lastly, we are using the promise function `then` instead of the `$http.get` `success` callback due to a subtle difference between what `success` and `then` returns. The `success` function returns the original promise (in this case, a promise is created on calling `$http.get`) whereas `then` returns a new promise that is resolved with the return value of the *success* or *error* functions that we attach to `then`.

Since we are using `then` instead of `success`, the callback function receives a single object with all four properties `config`, `data`, `header`, and `status`.

Before we continue any further, let's learn a bit more about *promise chaining* with some simpler examples. It's a very useful and powerful concept.

Understanding promise chaining

Promise chaining is about feeding the result of one promise resolution into another promise. Since promises wrap asynchronous operations, this chaining allows us to organize asynchronous code in a chained manner instead of nested callbacks. We saw an example of promise chaining earlier. The exercises were retrieved (the first asynchronous operation), transformed (the second asynchronous operation), and finally bound to the view (the third asynchronous operation), all using promise chaining. The previous diagram also highlights this.

Such chaining allows us to create chains of any length as long as the methods involved in the chain return a promise. In this case, both the `$http.get` and `then` functions return a promise.

Let's look at a much simpler example of chaining in action. The code for this example is as follows:

```
var promise = $q.when(1);
var result = promise
.then(function (i) { return i + 1;})
   .then(function (i) { return i + 1;})
   .then(function (i) { return i + 1;});
   .then(function (i) { console.log("Value of i:" + i);});
```

I have created a jsFiddle (`http://jsfiddle.net/cmyworld/9ak1gahe/`) too to demonstrate the working of promise chaining.

The preceding code uses promise chaining, and every chained function increments the value passed to it and passes it along to the next promise in the chain. The final value of `i` in the last `then` function is 4.

The `$q.when` function returns a promise that resolves to a value 1.

As described earlier, such chaining is possible due to the fact that the `then` function itself returns a promise. This promise is resolved to the return value of either the `success` or `error` callback. Look at the preceding code; there is a return statement in every success callback (except the last).

The behavior of promise chaining when it comes to the `error` callback may surprise us. An example will be the best way to illustrate that too. Consider this code:

```
var errorPromise = $q.reject("error");

var resultError = errorPromise.then(function (data) {
    return "success";
}, function (e) {
    return "error";
});
resultError.then(function (data) {
    console.log("In success with data:" + data);
}, function (e) {
    console.log("In error with error:" + e);
});
```

The `$q.reject` function creates a promise that is rejected with the value as error. Hence, the `resultError` promise is resolved with the return value error (return error).

The question now is, "What should the `resultError.then` callback print?" Well, it prints **In success with data: error**, since the `success` callback is invoked not `error`. This happened because we used a standard `return` call in both the `success` and `error` callbacks for `errorPromise.then` (or `resultError`).

If we want the promise chain to fail all along, we need to reject the promise in every `error` callback. Change the `resultError` promise to this:

```
var resultError = errorPromise.then(function (data) {
    return "success";
}, function (e) {
    return $q.reject(e);
});
```

The correct error callback in the next chained `then` is called, and the console logs `In error with error: error`.

By returning `$q.reject(e)` in the `error` callback, the resolved value of the `resultError` promise will be a rejected promise (`$q.reject` returns a promise that is always rejected).

Promise chaining is a very powerful concept, and mastering it will help us write more compact and well organized code. We will be extensively using promise chaining throughout this chapter to handle server response and to transform and load data.

Let's get back to where we left off, loading exercise and workout data from the server.

Loading exercise and workout data from the server

As we fixed the `getExercises` implementation in `WorkoutService` earlier, we can implement other get operations for exercise- and workout-related stuff. Copy the service implementation for the `getExercise`, `getWorkouts`, and `getWorkout` functions of `WorkoutService` from `chapter3/checkpoint2/app/js/shared/services.js`.

> The `getWorkout` and `getExercise` functions use the name of the workout/exercise to retrieve results. Every MongoLab collection item has an `_id` property that uniquely identifies the item/entity. In the case of our `Exercise` and `WorkoutPlan` object, we use the name of the exercise for unique identification, and hence the name and `_id` property always match.

Pay special attention to implementation for both the `getWorkouts` and `getWorkout` functions because there is a decent amount of data transformation happening in both the functions due to the model and data storage format mismatch.

The `getWorkouts` function is similar to `getExercises` except it creates the `WorkoutPlan` object and the `exercises` array is not mapped to the list of class objects of `Exercises`, instead server structure of `{name:'name', duration:value}` is used as it is.

The `getWorkout` function implementation involves a good amount of data mapping. This is how the `getWorkout` function now looks:

```
service.getWorkout = function (name) {
  return $q.all([service.getExercises(), $http.get(collectionsUrl
    + "/workouts/" + name, { params: { apiKey: apiKey } })])
    .then(function (response) {
        var allExercises = response[0];
        var workout = new WorkoutPlan(response[1].data);
        angular.forEach(response[1].data.exercises,
          function (exercise) {
            exercise.details = allExercises.filter(function (e) {
```

```
                    return e.name === exercise.name; })[0];
            });
         return workout;
      });
   };
```

There is a lot happening inside `getWorkout` that we need to understand.

The `getWorkout` function starts the execution by calling the `$q.all` function. This function is used to wait over multiple promise calls. It takes an array of promises and returns a promise. This aggregate promise is resolved or rejected (an error) when all promises within the array are either resolved or at least one of the promises is rejected. In the preceding case, we pass an array with two promises: the first is the promise returned by the `service.getExercises` function and the second is the `http.get` call (to get the workout with a specific identifier).

The `$q.all` function callback parameter response is also an array corresponding to the resolved values of the input promise array. In our case, `response[0]` contains the list of exercises and `response[1]` contains workout collection responses received from the server (`response[1].data` contains the data part of the HTTP response).

Once we have the workout details and the complete list of exercises, the code just after this updates the `exercises` array of the workout to the correct `Exercise` class object. It does this by searching the `allExercises` array for the name of the exercise as available in the `workout.exercises` array item returned from the server. The end result is that we have a complete `WorkoutPlan` object with the `exercises` array setup correctly.

These `WorkoutService` changes warrant fixes in upstream callers too. We have already fixed both `ExercisesNavController` and `ExerciseListController`. Fix the `WorkoutListController` object along similar lines. The `getWorkout` and `getExercise` functions are not directly used by the controller but by our builder services. Let's now fix the builder services together with the workout/exercise detail pages.

Fixing workout and exercise detail pages

We fix the workout detail page and I will leave it to you to fix the exercise detail page yourself as it follows a similar pattern.

`ExeriseNavController`, used in the workout detail page navigation rendering, is already fixed so let's jump onto fixing `WorkoutDetailsController`.

`WorkoutDetailController` does not load workout details directly but is dependent on the `resolve` route (see route configuration in `config.js`) invocation; when the route changes, this injects the selected workout (`selectedWorkout`) into the controller. The `resolve selectedWorkout` function in turn is dependent upon `WorkoutBuilderService` to load the workout, new or existing. Therefore the first fix should be `WorkoutBuilderService`.

The function that pulls workout details is `startBuilding`. Update the `startBuilding` implementation to the following code:

```
service.startBuilding = function (name) {
    var defer = $q.defer();
    if (name) {
        WorkoutService.getWorkout(name).then(function (workout) {
            buildingWorkout = workout;
            newWorkout = false;
            defer.resolve(buildingWorkout);
        });
    } else {
        buildingWorkout = new WorkoutPlan({});
        defer.resolve(buildingWorkout);
        newWorkout = true;
    }
    return defer.promise;
};
```

In the preceding implementation, we use the `$q` service of the Promise API to create and resolve our own promise. The preceding scenario required us to create our own promise because creating new workouts and returning is a synchronous process, whereas loading the existing workout is not. To make the return value consistent, we return promises in both the new workout and edit workout cases.

To test the implementation, just load any existing workout detail page such as `7minWorkout` under `#/builder/workouts/`. The workout data should load with some delay.

This is the first time we are actually creating our own promise and hence it's a good time to delve deeper into this topic.

Creating and resolving custom promises

Creating and resolving a standard promise involves the following steps:

1. Create a new `defer` object by calling the `$q.defer()` API function. The `defer` object is like an (conceptually) action that will complete some time in the future.

2. Return the promise object by calling `defer.promise` at the end of the function call.

3. Any time in the future, use a `defer.resolve(data)` function to resolve the promise with a specific `data` or `defer.reject(error)` object to reject the promise with the specific `error` function. The `resolve` and `reject` functions are part of the defer API. The `resolve` function implies work is complete whereas `reject` means there is an error.

The preceding `startBuilding` function follows the same pattern.

An interesting thing about the preceding `startBuilding` implementation is that, in the case of the `else` condition, we immediately resolve the promise by calling `defer.resolve` with a new workout object instance, even before we have returned a promise to the caller. The end result is that, in the case of a new workout, the promise is immediately resolved once the `startBuilding` function completes.

The ability to create and resolve our own custom promise is a powerful feature. Such an ability is very useful in scenarios that involve invocation and coordination of one or more asynchronous methods before a result can be delivered. Consider a hypothetical example of a service function that gets product quotes from multiple e-commerce platforms:

```
getProductPriceQuotes(productCode) {
    var defer = $q.defer()
    var promiseA = getQuotesAmazon(productCode);
    var promiseB = getQuotesBestBuy(productCode);
    var promiseE = getQuotesEbay(productCode);
    $q.all([promiseA, promiseB, promiseE])
      .then(function (response) {
         defer.resolve([buildModel(response[0]),
         buildModel(response[1]), buildModel(response[2])]);
         });
    defer.promise;
}
```

The get Product PriceQuotes service function needs to make asynchronous requests to multiple e-commerce sites, collate the date received, and return the data to the user. Such a coordinated effort can be managed by the Promise/defer API. In the preceding sample, we use the `$q.all` function that can wait on multiple promises to get resolved. Once all the remote calls are complete, the `then` success callback is invoked. The hypothetical `buildModel` function is used to build a common `Quote` model as the response can vary from one e-commerce platform to another. The `defer.resolve` function finally collates the new model data and returns it in an array. A well-coordinated effort!

When it comes to creating and using the defer/Promise API there are some rules/guidance that come in handy. These include:

- A promise once resolved cannot be changed. A promise is like a return statement that gets called in the future. But once a promise is resolved, the value cannot change.

- We can call `then` of the exiting promise object any number of times, irrespective of whether the promise has been resolved or not.

- Calling `then` on the existing resolved/rejected promise invokes the `then` callback immediately.

Other than creating our own promise and resolving it, there is another way to achieve the same behavior. We can use another Promise API function: `$q.when`.

The $q "when" function

We will be super greedy and try to shave some more lines from the `startBuilding` implementation by using the `$q.when` function. Creating custom promising just to support a uniform return type (a promise) maybe an overkill here. The `$q.when` function exists for this very purpose.

The `when` function takes an argument and returns a promise:

```
when(value);
```

The `value` can be a normal JavaScript object or a promise. The promise returned by `when` is resolved with the value if it is a simple JavaScript type or with the resolved promise value if `value` is a promise. Let's see how to use `when` in `startBuilding`.

Replace the existing `startBuilding` implementation with this one:

```
service.startBuilding = function (name) {
    if (name) {
        return WorkoutService.getWorkout(name)
          .then(function (workout) {
```

```
        buildingWorkout = workout;
        newWorkout = false;
        return buildingWorkout;
    });
} else {
    buildingWorkout = new WorkoutPlan({});
    newWorkout = true;
    return $q.when(buildingWorkout);
}
};
```

The changed code has been highlighted in the preceding code. And it is the `else` condition where we use `$q.when` to return a new `WorkoutPlan` object, through a promise.

We have reduced some lines of code from `startBuilding` and it still works fine. We now also have an understanding of `$q.when` and where can it be used. It's time to complete the workout detail page fixes.

Fixing workout and exercise detail pages continued...

Fixing `startBuilding` is enough to make the workout detail page load data. We can verify this and make sure the new workout and existing workout scenarios are loading data correctly.

We do not need to write a callback implementation in our `WorkoutDetailController`. Why? Because the route resolve configuration takes care of it. We touched upon the `resolve` route in the last chapter when we used it to inject the `selectedWorkout` object into `WorkoutDetailController`. Let's try to understand how this refactoring for asynchronous calls and promise implementation has affected the `resolve` function.

Route resolutions and promises

If we look at the new `$routeProvider.when` configurations for the *Workout Builder* page (in the edit case), the `selectedWorkout` function of `resolve` has just one line now:

```
return WorkoutBuilderService.startBuilding(
    $route.current.params.id);
```

As you learned in the previous chapter, the `resolve` configuration is used to inject dependencies into a controller before it is instantiated. In the preceding case, the return value now is a *promise* object, not a fully constructed `WorkoutPlan` object.

When a return value of a resolve function is promise, Angular routing infrastructure waits for this promise to resolve, before loading the corresponding route. Once the promise is resolved, the resolved data is injected into the controller as it happens with standard return values. In our implementation too, the selected workout is injected automatically into the `WorkoutDetailController` once the promise is resolved. We can verify this by double-clicking on the workout name tile on the list page; there is a visible delay before the *Workout Builder* page is loaded.

The clear advantage with the `$routeProvider.when resolve` property is that we do not have to write asynchronous (`then`) callbacks in the controller as we did to load the workout list in `WorkoutListController`.

The exercise detail page too needs fixing, but since the implementation that we have shared does not use `resolve` for the exercise detail page, we will have to implement the promise-based callback pattern to load the exercise in the `init` controller function. The `checkpoint2` folder under `chapter5` contains the fixes `ExerciseBuilderService` and `ExerciseDetailController` that you can copy to load exercise details, or you can do it yourself and compare the implementation.

 The `checkpoint2` folder under `chapter5` contains the working implementation for what we have covered thus far.
GitHub Branch: checkpoint5.2 (folder: trainer)

It is now time to fix, create, and update scenarios for the exercises and workouts.

Performing CRUD on exercises/workouts

When it comes to the **create**, **read**, **update**, and **delete** (**CRUD**) operations, all save, update, and delete functions need to be converted to the callback promise pattern.

Earlier in the chapter we detailed the endpoint access pattern for CRUD operations in a MongoLab collection. Head back to that section and revisit the access patterns. We need it now as we plan to create/update workouts.

Before we start the implementation, it is important to understand how MongoLab identified a collection item and what our ID generation strategy is . Each collection item in MongoDB is uniquely identified in the collection using the `_id` property. While creating a new item, either we supply an ID or the server generates one itself. Once `_id` is set, it cannot be changed. For our model, we will use the `name` property of the exercise/workout as the unique ID and copy the name into the `_id` field (hence, there is no autogeneration of `_id`). Also, remember our model classes do not contain this `_id` field, it has to be created before saving the record for the first time.

Let's fix the workout creation scenario first.

Fixing and creating a new workout

Taking the bottom-up approach, the first thing that needs to be fixed is `WorkoutService`. Update the `addWorkout` function as shown in the following code:

```
service.addWorkout = function (workout) {
  if (workout.name) {
    var workoutToSave = angular.copy(workout);
    workoutToSave.exercises =
    workoutToSave.exercises.map(function (exercise) {
        return {
                name: exercise.details.name,
                duration: exercise.duration
        }
      });
    workoutToSave._id = workoutToSave.name;
    return $http.post(collectionsUrl + "/workouts", workoutToSave,
{ params: { apiKey: apiKey }})
    .then(function (response) { return workout });
}}
```

In `getWorkout`, we had to map data from the server model to our client model; the reverse has to be done here. Since we do not want to alter the model that is bound to the view, the first thing we do is make a copy of the workout.

Next, we map the exercises array (`workoutToSave.exercises`) to a format that is more compact for server storage. We only want to store the exercise name and duration in the `exercises` array on the server.

We then set the `_id` property as the name of the workout to uniquely identify it in the database of the `Workouts` collection.

A word of caution

The simplistic approach of using the *name* of the workout/exercise as a record identifier (or `id`) in MongoDB will break for any decent-sized app. Remember that we are creating a web-based application that can be simultaneously accessed by many users. Since there is always the possibility of two users coming up with the same name for a workout/exercise, we need a strong mechanism to make sure names are not duplicated.

Another problem with the MongoLab REST API is that, if there is a duplicate `POST` request with the same `id` field, one will create a new document and the second will update it, instead of the second failing. This implies that any duplicate checks on the `id` field on the client side still cannot safeguard against data loss. In such a scenario, assigning autogeneration of the `id` value is preferable.

Lastly, we call the `post` function of the `$http` API, passing in the URL to connect to, data to send, and extra query string parameter (`apiKey`). The last `return` statement may look familiar as we again perform *promise chaining* to return the workout object as part of the promise resolution.

In standard create entity cases, unique ID generation is done on the server (mostly by the database). The response to the create entity then contains the generated ID. In such a case, we need to update the model object before we return data to the calling code.

Why not try to implement the update operation? The `updateWorkout` function can be fixed in the same manner, the only difference being that the `$http.put` function is required:

```
return $http.put(collectionsUrl + "/workouts/" + workout.name,
    workoutToSave, { params: { apiKey: apiKey } });
```

The preceding request URL now contains an extra fragment (`workout.name`) that denotes the identifier of the collection item that needs to be updated.

The MongoLab PUT API request creates the document passed in as the request body, if not found in the collection. While making the PUTrequest, make sure that the original record exists. We can do this by making a GET request for the same document first, and confirm that we get a document before updating it.

The last operation that needs to be fixed is deleting the workout. Here is a trivial implementation where we call the $http.delete API to delete the workout referenced by a specific URL:

```
service.deleteWorkout = function (workoutName) {
    return $http.delete(collectionsUrl + "/workouts/" +
    workoutName, { params: { apiKey: apiKey } });
};
```

With that it's time now to fix WorkoutBuilderService and WorkoutDetailController. The save function of WorkoutBuilderService now looks like this:

```
service.save = function () {
    var promise = newWorkout ?
      WorkoutService.addWorkout(buildingWorkout) :
      WorkoutService.updateWorkout(buildingWorkout);
    promise.then(function (workout) {
        newWorkout = false;
    });
    return promise;
};
```

Most of it looks the same as it was earlier except that newWorkout is flipped in the then success callback and this returns a promise.

Finally, WorkoutDetailController also needs to use the same callback pattern for handling save and delete, as shown here:

```
$scope.save = function () {
    $scope.submitted = true; // Will force validations
    if ($scope.formWorkout.$invalid) return;
    WorkoutBuilderService.save().then(function (workout) {
        $scope.workout = workout;
        $scope.formWorkout.$setPristine();
        $scope.submitted = false;
    });
}
service.delete = function () {
```

```
        if (newWorkout) return; // A new workout cannot be deleted.
        return WorkoutService.deleteWorkout(buildingWorkout.name);
    }
```

And that's it. We can now create new workouts, update existing workouts, and delete them too. That was not too difficult!

Let's try it out; open the new *Workout Builder* page, create a workout, and save it. Also try to edit an existing workout. Both scenarios should work seamlessly.

 Check `chapter5/checkpoint3` for an up-to-date implementation if you are having issues running your local copy.

GitHub branch: checkpoint5.3 (folder – trainer)

There is something interesting happening on the network side while we make POST and PUT requests to save data. Open the browsers network log console (*F12*) and see requests being made. The log looks something like this:

Pat		Text
workouts?apiKey=E16WgsIFduXHiMAdAg6qcG1KKYx7WNWg	OPTIONS	200
api.mongolab.com/api/1/databases/angularjsbyexample/collections		OK
workouts?apiKey=E16WgsIFduXHiMAdAg6qcG1KKYx7WNWg	POST	200
api.mongolab.com/api/1/databases/angularjsbyexample/collections		OK

There is an **OPTIONS** request made to the same endpoint before the actual POST is done. The behavior that we witness here is termed as a **prefight request**. And this happens because we are making a cross-domain request to `api.mongolab.com`.

It is important to understand the cross-domain behavior of the HTTP request and the constructs AngularJS provides to make cross-domain requests.

Cross-domain access and AngularJS

Cross-domain requests are requests made for resources in a different domain. Such requests when originated from JavaScript have some restrictions imposed by the browser; these are termed as *same-origin policy* restrictions. This restriction stops the browser from making AJAX requests to domains that are different from the script's original source. The source match is done strictly based on a combination of protocol, host, and port.

For our own app, the calls to `https://api.mongolab.com` are cross-domain invocations as our source code hosting is in a different domain (most probably something like `http://localhost/....`).

There are some workarounds and some standards that help relax/control cross-domain access. We will be exploring two of these techniques as they are the most commonly used ones. These are as follows:

- **JSON with Padding (JSONP)**
- **Cross-origin resource sharing** (CORS)

A common way to circumvent this same-origin policy is to use the JSONP technique.

Using JSONP to make cross-domain requests

The JSONP mechanism of remote invocation relies on the fact that browsers can execute JavaScript files from any domain irrespective of the source of origin, as long as the script is included via the `<script>` tag. In fact, a number of framework files that we are loading in *Personal Trainer* come from a CDN source (`ajax.googleapis.com`) and are referenced using the `script` tag.

In JSONP, instead of making a direct request to a server, a dynamic `script` tag is generated with the `src` attribute set to the server endpoint that needs to be invoked. This script tag, when appended to the browser's DOM, causes a request to be made to the target server.

The server then needs to send a response in a specific format wrapping the response content inside a function invocation code (this extra padding around response data gives this technique the name JSONP).

The `$http.jsonp` function of AngularJS hides this complexity and provides an easy API to make JSONP requests. The jsFiddle link at `http://jsfiddle.net/cmyworld/v9y4uby2/` highlights how JSONP requests are made. jsFiddle uses the *Yahoo Stock API* to get quotes for any stock symbol.

The `getQuote` method in the fiddle looks like this:

```
$scope.getQuote = function () {
  var url =
    "https://query.yahooapis.com/v1/public/yql?q=
    select%20*%20from%20yahoo.finance.
    quote%20where%20symbol%20in%20(%22" + $scope.symbol +
    "%22)&format=json&env=store%3A%2F%2Fdatatables.
    org%2Falltableswithkeys&callback=JSON_CALLBACK";

$http.jsonp(url).success(function (data) {
    $scope.quote = data;
});
};
```

To make a JSONP request using AngularJS, the `jsonp` function requires us to augment the original URL with an extra query string parameter `callback=JSON_CALLBACK` verbatim. Internally, the `jsonp` function generates a dynamic script tag and a function. It then substitutes the JSON_CALLBACK token with the function name generated and makes the remote request.

Open the preceding jsFiddle page and enter symbols such as GOOG, MSFT, or YHOO to see the stock quote service in action. The browser network log for requests looks like this:

```
https://query.yahooapis.com/... &callback=angular.callbacks._1
```

Here, `angular.callbacks._1` is the dynamically generated function. And the response looks like this:

```
angular.callbacks._1({"query": ...});
```

The response is wrapped in the callback function. Angular parses and evaluates this response, which results in the invocation of the `angular.callbacks._1` callback function. Then, this function internally routes the data to our `success` function callback.

Hope this explains how JSONP works and what the underlying mechanism of a JSONP request is. But JSONP has its limitations, as given here:

- Firstly, we can only make GET requests (which is obvious as these requests originate due to script tags)
- Secondly, the server also needs to implement part of the solution that involved wrapping the response in a function callback as seen before
- Then there is always a security risk involved as JSONP depends upon dynamic script generation and injection
- Error handling too is not reliable because it is not easy to determine whether a script load failed due to some reason

At the end, we must realize JSONP is more of a workaround that a solution. As we moved towards Web 2.0, where mashups became commonplace and more and more service providers decided to expose their API over the Web, a far better solution/standard emerged: CORS.

Cross-origin resource sharing

Cross-origin resource sharing (CORS) provides a mechanism for the web server to support cross-site access control, allowing browsers to make cross-domain requests from scripts. With this standard, the consumer application (such as *Personal Trainer*) is allowed to make some types of requests termed as simple requests without any special setup requirements. These simple requests are limited to GET, POST (with specific MIME types), and HEAD. All other types of requests are termed as complex requests.

For complex requests, CORS mandates that the request should be preceded with a HTTP OPTIONS request (also called a preflight request), that queries the server for HTTP methods allowed for cross-domain requests. And only on successful probing is the actual request made.

 You can learn more about CORS from the MDN documentation available at https://developer.mozilla.org/en-US/docs/ Web/HTTP/Access_control_CORS.

The best part about CORS is that the client does not have to make any adjustment as in the case of JSONP. The complete handshake mechanism is transparent to calling code and our AngularJS AJAX calls work without any hitch.

CORS requires configurations to be made on the server, and the MongoLab servers have already been configured to allow cross-domain requests. The preceding POST request to MongoLab caused the preflight OPTIONS request.

We have now covered the $http service and cross-domain invocation topics. The next topic that needs our attention is the $resource service.

Getting started with $resource

Our discussion on the $resource service should start with understanding why we require $resource. The $http service seems to be capable of performing all types of server interactions. Why is this abstraction required and against what type of system does the $resource service work?

To answer all these questions, we have to introduce a new breed of service (server side, not Angular services): *RESTful* services.

RESTful API services

"There is an API for that!"

Apple did not coin this, but this indeed is a reality now. There is an API for everything. Almost all of the public and private services (Google, Facebook, Twitter, and so on) out there have an API. And if the API works over HTTP, there is a pretty good chance that the API is RESTful in nature. We don't have to look far; MongoLab too has a RESTful API interface and we have used it!

Representational State Transfer (REST) is an architectural style that defines the components of a system as resources. Actions are defined at the resource level and the server controls how the process flows dynamically using the concept of hypermedia.

 We will not be cover details about RESTful services here, but will concentrate our efforts on how AngularJS helps us consume RESTful services. If you are interested in discovering how a true RESTful service behaves, go through this excellent InfoQ article at `http://www.infoq.com/articles/webber-rest-workflow`. A fascinating read!

Most of the API interfaces that set out to be RESTful may not be a true RESTful service but may satisfy only a few constraints of a RESTful service. The RESTful service over HTTP has at least these common traits:

- Resources are defined using URLs. These are some of the resources:
  - There is a collection resource with the URL format as `http://myserver.com/resources`
  - There is a collection item resource with the URL format `http://myserver.com/resources/id`, where `id` identifies a specific resource in the collection

- The HTTP verb `GET` is used to retrieve data for collection or the *collection item* resource
- HTTP `POST` is used to create a new resource
- HTTP `PUT` is used to update a resource
- HTTP DELETE is used to delete a resource

Go a few sections back to the *Loading exercise and workout data* section and look at the MongoLab service endpoint access patterns; they are consistent with what we have defined earlier.

AngularJS provides the $resource service that specifically targets server implementations that have RESTful HTTP endpoints. In coming sections, we explain how $resource works and implement part of our *Personal Trainer* app using the $resource service.

$resource basics

The $resource service is an abstraction built over the $http service, and makes consuming RESTful services (server-based) easy. A resource in AngularJS is defined as follows:

```
$resource(url, [paramDefaults], [actions]);
```

The parameters used are:

- url: This specifies the endpoint URL. This URL can be parameterized with parameterized arguments prefixed with :: For example, these are valid URLs:
  - /collection/:identifier: This indicates a URL with a parameterized identifier fragment
  - /:collection/:identifier: This indicates a URL with collection and identifier parameterized

  If the parameter value is not available during invocation, the parameter is removed from the URL. See the following examples to understand how this URL parameterization works.

- paramDefaults: This parameter serves a dual purpose. For parameterized URLs, paramDefaults provides a default replacement whereas any extra values in the paramDefaults object are added to a query string.

  Consider a resource url /users/:name. The following table details the resultant URL based on the paramDefaults passed:

The paramDefaults value	The Resultant URL
{}	/users
{name:'david'}	/users/david
{search:'david'}	/users?search=david
{name:'david', search:'out'}	/users/david?search=out

As we will learn later, these parameters can be overridden during actual action invocation.

- `actions`: This parameter is nothing but a JavaScript function attached to the `$resource` object to perform a specific task. The `$resource` object comes with a standard set of operations that are common to every resource such as `get`, `query`, `save`, and `delete`. This `actions` parameter is used to extend the default list of actions with our own custom action or alter any predefined action.

  The `actions` parameter takes an object hash, with the key being `action name` and the value being a `config` object. This is the same `config` object that is used with the `$http` service (passed in as the second parameter to `$http`).

Creating a resource with the preceding resource declaration statement actually creates a `Resource` class. This `Resource` class encapsulates the configuration that we have defined while creating it. To make HTTP requests using this class, we need to invoke the action methods that are available on the class, including the custom ones that we define.

Let's look at some concrete examples on how to invoke resource actions and also try to understand a bit more about the third parameter to resource creation, `actions`.

Understanding $resource actions

To understand how to invoke resource actions and the role the `actions` parameter plays while defining a resource, let's look at an example. Consider this resource usage:

```
var Exercises = $resource('https://api.mongolab.com/
  api/1/databases/angularjsbyexample/collections/
  exercises/:param,{},{update:{action:PUT'}});
```

This statement creates a `Resource` class named `Exercises` with a total of six class-level actions namely `get`, `save`, `update`, `query`, `remove`, and `delete`. Five of these actions are standard actions defined on any resource. The sixth one, `update`, has been added to this resource class by passing in the `actions` parameter (the third argument). The `actions` parameter declaration looks like this:

```
actions:{action1: config, action2 : config, action3 : config}
```

This line defines three actions and configurations for those actions. The `config` object is the same object passed as a parameter to `$http`.

In the preceding scenario, the `config` object passed in for the `update` action has only one property `action` (not to be confused with `$resource` actions parameter), which specifies the HTTP action verb to use on invocation of the action method: `update`.

For the five default actions on `$resource` the standard `config` is:

```
{    'get':     {method:'GET'},
     'save':    {method:'POST'},
     'query':   {method:'GET', isArray:true},
     'remove':  {method:'DELETE'},
     'delete':  {method:'DELETE'}
};
```

The HTTP verb on these actions makes perfect sense and complies with the RESTful URL access pattern. The surprising part is the omission of the `update` action or an action that does the HTTP `PUT` operation. Hence, when defining a RESTful endpoint, we may require to augment the action list with a `PUT` based `update` action. The first example described previously does this.

In the preceding configuration, the `isArray` attribute on the `query` action seems interesting. To understand the behavior of `isArray`, we need to see how resource actions are invoked.

$resource action invocation

The resource statement in the preceding section just creates a resource class named `Exercises`. To actually invoke a server operation, we need to invoke one of the six action methods defined in the `Exercises` class. Here are some sample invocations:

```
Exercises.query();// get all workouts
Exercises.get({id:'test'}); // get exercise with id 'test'
Exercises.save({},workout); // save the workout
```

For action methods based on `GET`, the general syntax is as follows:

```
Exercises.actionName([parameters],[successcallback],
   [errorcallback]);
```

And for `POST` actions (`save` and `update`), the general syntax is as follows:

```
Exercises.actionName([parameters], [postData], [successcallback],
   [errorcallback]);
```

For POST actions, there is an extra `postData` parameter to post the actual payload to the server.

The last two parameters: **successcallback** and **errorcallback** get called when the response is received based on the response status.

When a resource action is invoked, it returns either of these:

- A `Resource` class object (the resource object): This is returned when the `isArray` action configuration is `false`, for example, the `get` action
- An empty array: This is returned when the `isArray` action configuration is `true`, for example, the `query` action

This is in sharp contrast to the `$http` invocation that returns a promise.

And if we keep holding the returned value, then AngularJS fills this object or array with the response received from a server in future. This behavior results in code that is devoid of callback pattern implementation. For example, we can load exercises in `ExerciseListController` using this statement:

```
$scope.exercises = Exercises.query();
```

The preceding `query` invocation immediately returns an empty array. In future, when the response arrives, it is pushed into the array. And due to the super awesome data-binding infrastructure that Angular has, any view bindings for the `exercises` array get automatically refreshed.

Another interesting thing about the `isArray` action configuration is that a misconfigured `isArray` attribute can cause response parsing issues. The `isArray` attribute helps AngularJS decide whether to de-serialize the response as an array or object. If configured incorrectly, Angular throws errors such as this:

```
"Error in resource configuration. Expected response to contain an
  object but got an array"
```

Alternatively, it throws errors such as this:

```
"Error in resource configuration. Expected response to contain an
array but got an object"
```

It is very easy to reproduce these errors. Let's try these calls in this way:

```
Exercises.get(); // Returns an array
Exercises.query({params:'plank'}); //Returns exercise object
```

The first statement in the preceding code results in the first error, and the second statement in the second error. Look at the configurations for action methods: get and query, to know why there were errors.

Before we move forward, there is something that needs to be reiterated. There is a marked difference between the $resource and $http return values. The return value of $http invocation is always a *promise* whereas it can be a Resource class object or an array for $resource. Due to this reason, binding of the $resource response is possible to view without involving callbacks.

The resource object or collection returned as part of the action invocation contains some useful properties:

- $promise: This is the underlying promise for the request made. We can wait over it if desired, similar to the $http promise. Else, we can use the successcallback or errorcallback functions that we register when invoking the resource action.

- $resolved: This is True after the preceding promise has been resolved, false otherwise.

Let us change parts of our *Personal Trainer* app to use server access based on $resource and put what we have learned into practice.

Using $resource to access exercise data

Until now, we have used $http for exercise/workout data management. To elaborate on the $resource behavior, let's change the exercise data load and save this to use the $resource service.

Open the services.js file and add the following lines to the WorkoutService implementation above the service.getExercises function:

```
service.Exercises = $resource(collectionsUrl + "/exercises/:id",
  { apiKey: apiKey}, { update: { method: 'PUT' } });
```

The statement creates a Resource class configured with a specific URL and API key. The key is passed in to the default parameter collection.

Go ahead and delete all exercise-related functions from WorkoutService. These include the service.getExercises, service.getExercise, service.updateExercise, service.addExercise, and service.deleteExercise functions. Everything related to the exercise will be done using resources now.

The $resource function is part of the ngResource module; therefore, we need to include the module script in index.html. Add this line to the script section after other AngularJS module declarations:

```
<script src="http://ajax.googleapis.com/ajax/libs/angularjs/
    1.3.3/angular-resource.js"></script>
```

Include the ngResource module dependencies in app.js, as follows:

```
angular.module('app', [...,'ngResource']);
```

Finally, add $resource as a dependency to WorkoutService. Remember that the dependency needs to be added to the this.$get function.

These changes have also affected the service.getWorkout function as it has a dependency on the getExercises function. To fix it, replace the service.getExercise() call inside $q.all with this:

```
service.Exercises.query().$promise
```

The query action returns an empty array that has a predefined $promise property that $q.all can wait over.

Let's now fix the upstream caller as we have removed a number of service functions.

To start with, let's fix the exercise list implementation as it is the easiest to fix. Open exercise.js from the WorkoutBuilder folder and fix the init method for ExerciseNavController. Replace its implementation with this single line:

```
$scope.exercises = WorkoutService.Exercises.query();
```

Do the same with ExerciseListController, replacing the init function implementation with the preceding code.

The empty array returned by the query action in the preceding code is filled in the future when the response is available. Once the model exercises updates, the bound view is automatically updated. No callback is required!

Next, we fix the exercise builder page (#/builder/exercises/new), the corresponding ExerciseDetailController object, and downstream services. All $http calls need to be replaced with $resource calls. Open services.js from workoutbuilder and fix the startBuilding function in ExerciseBuilderService in this way:

```
service.startBuilding = function (name) {
  if (name) {
    buildingExercise = WorkoutService.Exercises.get({ id: name },
function (data) {
```

```
                            newExercise = false;
                    });
    }
      else {
         buildingExercise = new Exercise({});
         newExercise = true;
      }
      return buildingExercise;
};
```

We use the `get` action method of the `Exercise` resource to get the specific exercise, passing in the name of the exercise (`{id:name}`). Remember, the name of the exercise is the exercise identifier.

Before we turn the `newExercise` flag to false we need to wait for the response. We make use of the success callback for that. Interestingly, the `data` argument to a function and the `buildingExercise` variable point to the same resource object.

The else part has been reverted to the older pre-`$http` implementation as we do not use promises anymore.

To fix the `ExerciseDetailController` implementation, we just need to revert the `init` function to the non-callback pattern implementation:

```
$scope.exercise =
    ExerciseBuilderService.startBuilding($routeParams.id);
```

All the `get` scenarios on the exercises are fixed now. The code has indeed been simplified. The callbacks that were with the `$http` implementation have been eliminated to a large extent. The asynchronous nature of the calls is almost hidden, which is both good and bad. It is good because it simplifies code but it is bad because it hides the asynchronicity. This often leads to an incorrect understanding of behavior and bugs.

The hidden cost of hiding asynchronicity

The ultimate aim of `$resource` is to make consumption of RESTful services easier. It also helps reduce the callback implementation that we need to do otherwise. But this abstraction comes at a cost. For example, consider this piece of code:

```
$scope.exercises = WorkoutService.Exercises.query();
console.log($scope.exercises.length);
```

We may think `console.log` prints the length of the `exercises` array, but that is absolutely incorrect. In fact, `$scope.exercises` is an empty array so `log` will always show `0`. The array is filled in the future with the data returned from the server. The JavaScript engine does not wait on the first line for the response to arrive. Such code just gives us the illusion that everything runs sequentially, but it does not.

> UI data binding still works because the Angular digest cycles are executed when the `$resource` service receives a response from the server.
>
> As part of this digest cycle, dirty checks are performed to detect model changes across the app. All these model changes trigger watches that result in UI bindings and interpolation updates. Remember, we covered the topic of digest cycles in *Chapter 3, More AngularJS Goodness for 7 Minute Workout*.

If any of our operations depend upon when the data is available, we need to implement a callback pattern using promises. We did it with the `startBuilding` function where we waited for exercise details to load before setting the `newExercise` flag.

> I am not advocating that you don't use `$resource`; in fact it is a great service that can help eliminate a sizable amount of code otherwise required with the `$http` implementation. But everyone using `$resource` should be aware of the peculiarities involved.

We now need to fix CRUD operation for exercises.

Exercising CRUD with $resource

The `Exercise` resource defined in `WorkoutService` already has the `save` and `update` (custom actions that we added) action. It's now just a matter of invoking the correct action inside the `WorkoutBuilderService` functions.

The first `ExerciseBuilderService` function we fix is `save`. Update the `save` implementation with the following code:

```
service.save = function () {
    if (!buildingExercise._id)
    buildingExercise._id = buildingExercise.name;
    var promise = newExercise ?
        WorkoutService.Exercises.save({},buildingExercise).$promise
        : buildingExercise.$update({ id: buildingExercise.name });
```

```
        return promise.then(function (data) {
            newExercise = false;
            return buildingExercise;
    });
    };
```

In the previous implementation based on the `newExercise` state, we call the appropriate resource action. We then pull out the underlying promise and again perform promise chaining to return the same exercise in future using `then`.

The `save` operation not only uses a `Resource` (`Exercise`) class but also a `Resource` object (`buildingExercise`). The preceding code illustrates an important difference between the `Resource` class and the `resource` object. Remember `buildingExercise` is a resource object that we assigned during the invocation of the `startBuilding` function in `ExerciseDetailController`.

A resource object is typically created when we invoke `get` operations on the corresponding `Resource` class, such as this:

```
buildingExercise = WorkoutService.Exercises.get({ id: name });
```

This operation creates an exercise resource object. And the following operation creates an array:

```
$scope.exercises = WorkoutService.Exercises.query();
```

The array is filled with exercise resource objects when the response is received.

The actions defined on a resource object are the same as the `Resource` class except that all action names are prefixed with $. Also, resource object actions can derive data from the resource object itself. For example, in the preceding code, `buildingExercise.$update` does not take the payload as an argument whereas the payload is required when using the `Exercise.save` action (the second argument).

The following table contrasts the `Resource` class and resource object usage:

	Resource class	Resource object

Creation	This is created using `$resource(url, param, actions)`.	This is created as part of action execution. Here is an example:
		
		`exercise = WorkoutService`
		`.Exercises.get({ id: name`
		`});`

Actions (querying)	`Exercises.`
	`get({id:name});`
	`Exercise.query();`
		`exercise.$get({id:name});`
		`exercise.$query();`

Actions (CRUD)	`Exercise.save({},`
	`data);`
	`Exercise.`
	`update({id:name},`
	`data);`
	`Exercise.`
	`delete({id:name});`
		`exercise.$save({});`
		`exercise.$update({id:name});`
		`exercise.$delete({id:name});`

Action returns	This returns the `Resource` object or array, with the `$promise` and `$resolved` properties.	This returns a promise object.

Use resource objects when the operation performed is in the context of a single item, such as `update` and `delete` operations. Otherwise, stick to the `$resource` service.

Deleting is simple; we just call the `$delete` action on the resource object and return the underlying promise:

```
service.delete = function () {
    return buildingExercise.$delete({ id: buildingExercise.name });
};
```

`WorkoutDetailController` needs no fixes as the return value for `save` and `delete` functions on `WorkoutBuilderService` is still a promise.

The `$resource` function fixes are complete and we can now test our implementation. Try to load and edit exercises and verify that everything looks good.

If you are having issues, `chapter5/checkpoint4` contains the complete working implementation.

GitHub branch: checkpoint5.4 (folder: trainer)

The `$resource` function is a pretty useful service from AngularJS for targeting RESTful HTTP endpoints. But what about other endpoints that might be non-conformant? Well, for *non-RESTful* endpoints, we can always use the `$http` service. Still, if we want to use the `$resource` service for the *non-RESTful* resources, we need to be aware of access pattern differences.

The $resource service with non-RESTful endpoints

As long as the HTTP endpoint returns and consumes JSON data (or data that can be converted to JSON), we can consume that endpoint using the `$resource` service. In such cases, we may need to create multiple `Resource` classes to target querying and CRUD-based operations. For example, consider these resources declarations:

```
$resource('/users/active'); //for querying
$resource('/users/createnew'); // for creation
$resource('/users/update/:id'); // for update
```

In such a case, most of the action invocation is limited to the `Resource` class, and resource object-level actions may not work.

Such endpoints might not even conform to the standard HTTP action usage. An HTTP `POST` request may be used for both saving and updating data. The `DELETE` verb may not be supported. There might also be other similar issues.

That sums up all that we plan to discuss on `$resource`. Let's end our discussion by summarizing what you have learned thus far:

- `$resource` is pretty useful for targeting RESTful service interactions. But still it can be used for non-RESTful endpoints.

- `$resource` can reduce a lot of boilerplate code required for server interaction if an endpoint confirms to RESTful access patterns.

- `$resource` action invocation returns a resource object or array that is updated in the future. This is in contrast with `$http` invocation that always returns a promise object.

- Because $resource actions return resource objects, we can implement some scenarios without using callback. This still does not mean calls using the $resource service are synchronous.

We have now worked our way through using the $http and $resource services. These are more than capable services that can take care of all your server interaction needs. In upcoming sections, we will explore some general usage scenarios and some advance concepts related to the $http and $resource services. The first in line is the request/response interceptors.

Request/response interceptors

Request and response interceptors, as the names suggest, can intercept HTTP requests and responses to augment/alter them. The typical use cases for using such interceptors include authentication, global error handling, manipulating HTTP headers, altering endpoint URLs, global retry logic, and some other such scenarios.

Interceptors are implemented as pipeline functions that get called one after another just like the *parser* and *formatter* pipelines for NgModelController (see the previous chapter).

Interceptions can happen at four places and hence there are four interceptor pipelines. This happens:

- Before a request is sent.
- After there is a request error. A request error may sound strange but, in a pipeline mode when the request travels through the pipeline function and any one of them rejects the request (for reasons such as data validation), the request lands up on an error pipeline with the rejection reason.
- After receiving the response from the server.
- On receiving an error from the server, or from a response pipeline component that may still reject a successful response from the server due to some technicalities.

Interceptors in Angular are mostly implemented as a *service factory*. They are then added to a collection of interceptors defined over $httpProvider during the configuration module stage.

A typical interceptor service factory outline looks something like this:

```
myModule.factory('myHttpInterceptor', function ($q, dependency1,
dependency2) {
    return {
        'request': function (config) {},
        'requestError': function (rejection) {},
        'response': function (response) {},
        'responseError': function (rejection) {}
    };});
```

And this is how it is registered at the configuration stage:

```
$httpProvider.interceptors.push('myHttpInterceptor');
```

The `request` and `requestError` interceptors are invoked before a request is sent and the `response` and `responseError` interceptors are invoked after the response is received. It is not mandatory to implement all four interceptor functions. We can implement the ones that serve our purpose.

A skeleton implementation of interceptors is available in the framework documentation for `$http` (https://code.angularjs.org/1.3.3/docs/api/ng/service/$http) under the **Interceptors** section.

> The Angular `$httpProvider` function is something that we have used here for the first time. Like any *provider*, it too allows us to configure `$http` service behavior at the configuration stage.

To see an interceptor in action, let's implement one!

Using an interceptor to pass the API key

The `WorkoutService` implementation is littered with API key references within every `$http` or `$resource` call/declaration. There is code like this everywhere:

```
$http.get(collectionsUrl + "/workouts", { params: { apiKey: apiKey
    } })
```

Every API request to MongoLab requires an API key to be appended to the query string. And, it is quite obvious that if we implement a request interceptor that appends this API key to every request made to MongoLab, we can get rid of this `params` assignment performed in every API call.

Time to get in an interceptor! Open `services.js` under `shared` and add these lines of code at the end of the file:

```
angular.module('app').provider('ApiKeyAppenderInterceptor', function
() {
    var apiKey = null;
    this.setApiKey = function (key) {
        apiKey = key;
    }
    this.$get = ['$q', function ($q) {
        return {
            'request': function (config) {
                if (apiKey && config && config.url.toLowerCase()
                .indexOf("https://api.mongolab.com") >= 0) {
                    config.params = config.params || {};
                    config.params.apiKey = apiKey;
                }
                return config || $q.when(config);
            }
        }
    }];
});
```

We create a `'ApiKeyAppenderInterceptor'` provider service (not a factory). The provider function `setApiKey` is used to set up the API key before an interceptor is used.

For the factory function that we return as part of `$get`, we only implement a *request interceptor*. The `request` interceptor function takes a single argument: `config` and has to return the `config` object or a promise that resolves to the `config` object. The same `config` object is used with the `$http` service.

In our request interceptor implementation, we make sure that the `apiKey` has been set and the request is for `api.mongolab.com`. If `true`, we update the configuration's `param` object with `apiKey` and this results in the API key being appended to the query string.

The interceptor implementation is complete but the way we have implemented this interceptor requires some other refactoring.

The `WorkoutService` method now does not need the API key, therefore we need to fix the `configure` function. Update the `config.js` file and add a dependency of `ApiKeyAppenderInterceptorProvider` on the `config` module function.

Inside the `config` function, add the following lines at the start:

```
ApiKeyAppenderInterceptorProvider.setApiKey("<mykey>");
$httpProvider.interceptors.push('ApiKeyAppenderInterceptor');
```

Update the `configure` method of `WorkoutServiceProvider` to this:

```
WorkoutServiceProvider.configure("angularjsbyexample");
```

The `configure` function declaration in `WorkoutServiceProvider` itself needs to be fixed. Open the `services.js` file from `shared` and fix the configure function as shown here:

```
this.configure = function (dbName) {
database = database;
    collectionsUrl = apiUrl + dbName + "/collections";
}
```

The last part is now to actually remove references to the API key from all `$http` and `$resource` calls. The resource declaration now should look like this:

```
$resource(collectionsUrl + "/exercises/:id", {}, { update: {
  method: 'PUT' } });
```

And for all `$http` invocations, get rid of the `params` object.

Time to test out the implementation! Load any of the list or details pages and verify them. Also try to add breakpoints in the interceptor code and see how the process flows.

> The update code is available in `chapter5/checkpoint5` for reference.
> *GitHub branch: checkpoint5.5 (folder – trainer)*

Request/response interception is a powerful feature that can be used to implement any cross-cutting concern related to remote HTTP invocation. If used correctly, it can simplify implementation and reduce a lot of boilerplate code.

Interceptors work at a level where they can manipulate the complete request and response. These work from headers, to the endpoint, to the message itself! There is another related concept that is similar to interceptors but involves only request and response payload transformation and is aptly named **AngularJS transformers**.

AngularJS request/response transformers

The job of a transformer or a transformer function is to transform the input data from one format to another. These transformers plug into the HTTP request/response processing pipeline of Angular and can alter the message received or sent. A good example of the transformation function usage is AngularJS global transformers that are responsible for converting a JSON string response into a JavaScript object and vice versa.

Since data transformation can be done while making a request or processing a response, there are two transformer pipelines available, one for a request and another for a response.

Transformer functions can be registered:

- Globally for all requests/responses. The standard JSON string-object transformers are registered at a global level. To register global transformer function we need to push or shift a function either to the `$httpProvider.defaults.transformRequest` or `$httpProvider.defaults.transformResponse` array. As always with a pipeline, order of registration is important. Global transformer functions are invoked for every request made or response received using the `$http` service, depending upon the pipeline they are registered in.

> The `$http` service too contains `$http.defaults`, which is equivalent to `$httpProvider.defaults`. This allows us to change these configurations at any time during app execution.

- Locally on a specific `$http` or `$resource` action invocation. The `config` object has two properties: `transformRequest` and `transformResponse`, which can be used to register any transformer function. Such a transformer function overrides any global transformation functions for that action.

The $httpProvider.defaults or $http.defaults function also contains settings related to default HTTP headers that are sent with every HTTP request.

This configuration can come in handy in some scenarios. For example, if the backend requires some specific headers to be passed with every request, we can use the $http.defaults.headers.common collection to append this custom header:

```
$http.defaults.headers.common.Authorization = 'Basic
YmVlcDpib29w'
```

Coming back to transformers! From an implementation standpoint, a transformer function takes a single argument, data, and has to return the transformed data.

Next, we have an implementation for one such transformer that AngularJS uses to convert a JavaScript object to a JSON string. This is a part of the AngularJS framework code:

```
function(d) {
        return isObject(d) && !isFile(d) ? toJson(d) : d;
}
```

The function takes data and transforms it into a string by calling an internal method toJson and returning the string representation. This transformer is registered in the global request transformer pipeline by the framework.

Local transformation functions are useful if we do not want to use the global transformation pipeline and want to do something specific. The following example shows how to register a transformer at the action or HTTP request level:

```
service.Exercises = $resource(collectionsUrl + "/exercises/:id", {}, {
update: { method: 'PUT' },
        get: {
            transformResponse: function (data) {
                return JSON.parse(data); }
        }
});
```

In this Resource class declaration we register a response transformer for the get action. This function converts the string input (data) into an object, something similar to what the global response transformer does.

A word of caution

Using a local transform function with specific $resource or $http overrides any global transformation function.

In the preceding example, the data variable will contain the string value of a response received from a server instead of the deserialized object. By supplying our custom response transformer to tranformResponse, we have overridden the default transformer that deserializes JSON response.

If we need to run global transform functions too, we need to create an array of transformers, containing both the global and custom transformers, and assign it to transformRequest or transformResponse, something like this:

```
service.Exercises = $resource(collectionsUrl + "/exercises/:id", {}, {
update: { method: 'PUT' },
    get: {
       transformResponse:
       $http.defaults.transformResponse.concat(function (value) {
       return doTransform(value); })
    }
});
```

The next topic that we take up here is route resolution when promises are rejected.

Handling routing failure for rejected promises

The *Workout Builder* page in *Personal Trainer* depends upon the resolve route configuration to inject the selected workout into WorkoutDetailController.

The resolve configuration has an additional advantage if any of the resolve functions return a promise like the selectedWorkout function:

```
return WorkoutBuilderService.startBuilding(
  $route.current.params.id);
```

When the promise is resolved successfully, the data is injected into the controller, but what happens on promise rejection or error? The preceding promise can fail if we enter a random workout name in the URL such as /builder/workouts/dummy and try to navigate, or if there is a server error. With a failed promise, two things happen:

- Firstly, the app route does not change. If you refresh the page using the browser, the complete content is cleared.

- Secondly, a $routeChangeError event is broadcasted on $rootScope (remember Angular events $emit and $broadcast).

We can use this event to give visual clues to a user about the path/route not found. Let's try to do it for the Workout Builder route.

Handling workouts not found

We can an some error on the page if the user tries to navigate to a non-existing workout. The error has to be shown at the container level outside the ng-view directive.

Update index.html and add this line before the ng-view declaration:

```
<label ng-if="routeHasError" class="alert
  alert-danger">{{routeError}}</label>
```

Open root.js and update the event handler for the $routeChangeSuccess event with the highlighted code:

```
$scope.$on('$routeChangeSuccess', function (event, current,previous) {
    $scope.currentRoute = current;
    $scope.routeHasError = false;
});
```

Add another event handler for $routeChangeError:

```
$scope.$on('$routeChangeError', function (event, current, previous,
error) {
    if (error.status === 404
&& current.originalPath === "/builder/workouts/:id") {
            $scope.routeHasError = true;
            $scope.routeError = current.routeErrorMessage; }
});
```

Lastly, update `config.js` by adding the `routeErrorMessage` property on the route configuration to edit workouts:

```
$routeProvider.when('/builder/workouts/:id', {
  // existing configuration
  topNav: 'partials/workoutbuilder/top-nav.html',
  routeErrorMessage:"Could not load the specific workout!",
  //existing configuration
```

Now go ahead and try to load a workout route such as this: `/builder/workouts/dummy`; the page should show an error message.

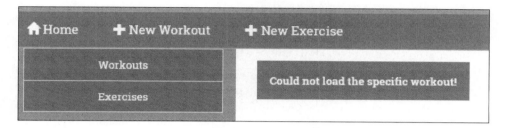

The implementation was simple. We declared model properties `routeError` to track the error message and `routeHasError` to determine whether the route has an error.

On the `$routeChangeSuccess` and `$routeChangeError` event handler, we manipulate these properties to produce the desired result. The implementation of `$routeChangeError` has extra checks to make sure that the error is only shown when the workout is not found. Take note of the `routeErrorMessage` property that we define on the route configuration. We did such route configuration customization in the last chapter for configuring navigation elements for the active view.

We have fixed routing failure for the *Workout Builder* page, but the exercise builder page is still pending. And again, I will leave it to you to fix it yourself and compare it with the implementation available in the companion codebase.

 Checkout the implementation done so far in `chapter5/checkpoint6`.

GitHub branch: checkpoint5.6 (folder: trainer)

Another major implementation that is pending is fixing of *7 Minute Workout* as currently it caters only to one workout routine.

Fixing the 7 Minute Workout app

As it stands now, the *7 Minute Workout* (or *Workout Runner*) app can only play one specific workout. It needs to be fixed to support execution of any workout plan built using *Personal Trainer*. There is an obvious need to integrate these two solutions. We already have the groundwork done to commence this integration. We have the shared model services and we have the `WorkoutService` to load data—enough to get us started.

Fixing *7 Minute Workout* and converting it into a generic *Workout Runner* roughly involves the following steps:

1. Removing the hardcoded workout and exercises used in *7 Minute Workout* from the controller.

2. Fixing the start page to show all available workouts and allowing users to select a workout to run.

3. Fixing the workout route configuration to pass the selected workout name as the route parameter to the workout page.

4. Loading the selected workout data using `WorkoutService` and starting the workout.

And, of course, we need to rename the *7 Minute Workout* part of the app; the name now is a misnomer. I think the complete app can now be called *Personal Trainer*. We can remove all references to *7 Minute Workout* from the view as well.

An excellent exercise to try out ourselves! And that is why I am not going to walk you through the solution. Instead, go ahead and implement the solution and compare your implementation with the one available in `chapter5/checkpoint7` (*GitHub branch: checkpoint5.7 (folder: trainer)*).

It's time now to end the chapter and summarize your learning.

Summary

We now have an app that can do a lot of stuff. It can run workouts, load workouts, save and update them, and track history. And if we look back, we have achieved this with minimal code. I can bet if we try this in standard jQuery or some other framework, it would require substantially more effort as compared to AngularJS.

We started the chapter by providing a *MongoDB* database on *MongoLab* servers. Since *MongoLab* provided a *RESTful* API to access the database, we saved some time by not setting up our own server infrastructure.

The first AngularJS construct that we touched upon was the `$http` service. `$http` is the primary service for connecting to any HTTP backend.

You learned about the `$http config` object and how it is used to configure any HTTP request. We also saw how the standard `$http` configuration helps us to readily consume server endpoints that consume and return JSON data.

You also learned how the complete `$http` infrastructure is based on *promises* and *callback* invocation and is totally asynchronous in nature.

For the first time, in this chapter we created our own promise and you learned how to create custom promises and resolve them.

We fixed our *Personal Trainer* app so it uses the `$http` service to load and save workout / exercise data. In the process, you also learned about issues surrounding cross-domain resource access. You learned about JSONP, a workaround to circumvent a browser's *same origin* restrictions and how to issue JSONP requests using Angular. We also touched upon CORS, which has emerged as a standard when it comes to cross-domain communication.

Next in line was the `$resource` service. This is a service that makes consuming *RESTful* endpoints easy. We replaced the exercise load and save implementation using `$http` with a `$resource` implementation. This refactoring resulted in more compact code that has a limited number of callbacks.

We then focused our attention on some common scenarios when dealing with remote server calls. We explored the concept of *Interceptors* used by AngularJS to manipulate a HTTP request/response at a global level. We created our own request interceptor to append the API key to every request made to the MongoLab server.

Then came Angular transformers that could intercept request/response message payloads and do some transformation. We saw how AngularJS uses these transformers to handle JSON data and automatically serializes and deserializes it.

Lastly, we touched upon routing failures when the route uses `resolve` configurations that return a promise.

We have now covered most of the building blocks of Angular, except the big one: AngularJS directives. We have used directives everywhere but have not created one. The next chapter is exclusively dedicated to AngularJS directives. We will be creating a number of small directives, such as a remote validator, AJAX button, and validation clues directive for the *Workout Builder* app. You will also learn how to integrate a jQuery plugin as a directive in Angular.

6
Working with Directives

One of the major reasons for AngularJS' popularity is **directives** and they are everywhere. We have used them throughout the book without putting much thought into how they actually function and how to create one. Directives, together with data-binding infrastructure, make true view-logic separation possible.

Consuming directives is easy, but creating one is a complex task and requires an understanding of the inner workings of the framework and directives itself. This chapter will give an insight into the world of directives and in the process you will build some useful directives for the *Personal Trainer* app.

The following topics will be covered in this chapter:

- **Understanding directive basics**: We learn about what directives are and build a rudimentary directive.

- **Understanding the phases of directive execution**: We look at the compile and link phases of directive execution and analyze the framework's ng-click directive in this context.

- **Implementing inter-directive communication**: You will build interdependent directives and learn the intricacies of inter-directive communication.

- **Working with the $compile and $parser services**. You will explore two important services: $compile and $parser, and learn to utilize them to build directives.

- **Using templates and transcludes directives**: When working with directive templates, transclusion is an important concept to understand and use. We build directives that utilize templates and transclude content.

- **Directives and scopes**: Explore and learn about the different scope models associated with directives, from the original parent scope and child scope to the isolated scope.

- **Building reusable directives with isolated scope**. Understanding and using isolated scopes to create reusable directive components, and creating multiple directives with isolated scopes.

- **Integrating jQuery and AngularJS**: They may seem orthogonal, but they can be made to co-exist. By creating a wrapper directive over a jQuery plugin, we will explore and understand the integration patterns.

Let's get started.

Directives – an introduction

We know what *directives* are and we have used them all along: `ng-click`, `ng-show`, `ng-style`, and `ng-repeat` are all directives. These are JavaScript objects defined using the `directive` function of the Module API. Once constructed, they are either attached to existing HTML elements or extend the existing HTML vocabulary with new elements/tags.

Directives have been conceptualized and incorporated into the framework in such a way that they allow the integration of controllers and views naturally and in a less verbose manner. It's the job of a directive to orchestrate the interaction between the controller and the view, keeping the separation of concerns intact.

From a functional standpoint, there are broadly two families of directives:

- Directives that extend the behavior of existing HTML element, such as `ng-click`, `ng-show`, and `ng-style`.

- Component directives come with their own view templates and behavior. The one place that we have used such a directive is with the `$modal` service. The `$modal` service used in show history and YouTube video sections internally injects directives: `modal-backdrop` and `modal-window` into the HTML. These two directives actually provide the dark backdrop and the basic window layout for modal dialog.

- There is also a special class of directives that may not come with their own template, but can take any HTML content as a template and add some behavior. The `ng-repeat`, `ng-if`, `ng-include`, and `ng-view` directives are some of the examples.

In the next section, we will build directives that showcase working of the preceding types. Let's start our discussion with understanding how directives are structured.

Anatomy of a directive

To create a directive, we use the `directive` function on the Module API. The signature looks like this:

```
directive(name, directiveFactory);
```

The `name` attribute signifies the name and the `directiveFactory` function is a factory function that returns an object containing the directive configuration. The **directive configuration object** is a complex beast and will require most of our attention. This is where we define the complete directive configuration and behavior.

This is how the complete directive definition object returned by the factory function looks:

```
function directiveFactory (injectables) {
    var directiveDefinitionObject = {
        priority: 0,
        template: 'html', //use either template or templateUrl
        templateUrl: 'directive.html',
        replace: false,
        transclude: false,
        restrict: 'A',
        scope: false,
        controller: function ($scope, $element, $attrs,
          $transclude) {},
        require: 'siblingDirectiveName',
        compile: function compile(tElement, tAttrs, transclude)
          {}, // use compile or link function
        link: function postLink() {}
    };
    return directiveDefinitionObject;
};
```

This is one big configuration object that may look intimidating at first, but don't worry as all the properties are not required. Once we understand the working of directives, we can easily manage the directive definition object.

Let's start with something really simple.

Creating a workout-tile directive

Just to get our hands dirty, let's build our first bare minimum directive— `workout-tile`—a simple exercise in directive building. Let's convert the workout list item tile to a directive.

Before we start, please download the working copy of *Personal Trainer* from the `checkpoint7` folder under `chapter5`, available as part of this book's companion code. It contains the complete implementation for the *Personal Trainer* app we have discussed so far.

The code is also available on GitHub (`https://github.com/chandermani/angularjsbyexample`) for everyone to download. Checkpoints are implemented as branches in GitHub. Download the GitHub branch `checkpoint5.7` from the `trainer` folder.

Add a new file `directives.js` to the `workoutbuilder` folder under `js` and add this directive definition:

```
angular.module('WorkoutBuilder')
  .directive('workoutTile', function () {
return {
      templateUrl:'/partials/workoutbuilder/workout-tile.html'
    }
});
```

Next add the reference for `directives.js` in `index.html` in the script declaration section. The directive definition object for `workoutTile` uses only one property `tempateUrl`. The `templateUrl` property points to the location of the file that stores the directive template. What goes into this file will be clear in the next few steps.

The `templateUrl` property points to a file that we need to build. Add another file `workout-tile.html` to the `workoutbuilder` folder under `partials` and copy the complete content defined inside `ng-repeat` from the `workouts.html` file under `partials/workoutbuilder` to `workout-tile.html`. This is the content outline that goes into `workout-tile.html`:

```
<div class="title">{{workout.title}}</div>
<div class="stats"><!--Existing content --></div>
```

In `workouts.html`, remove the tile HTML content from `ng-repeat` and replace it with the following line:

```
<span workout-tile=''></span>
```

Go ahead and load the workout list page (`#/builder/workouts`). Well... nothing changed! But the tiles are now rendered using `workoutDirective`. We can confirm this by inspecting the source HTML. Look for the string: `workout-tile`.

We could have done this using the inbuilt `ng-include` directive, as follows:

```
<span ng-include='/partials/workoutbuilder/
    workout-tile.html'></span>
```

Essentially, `workout-tile` is doing what `ng-include` does, but the template HTML is fixed.

Let's make a small change before we try to derive some learning from our new directive. Update the directive definition object and include a new property `restrict` before `templateUrl`:

```
restrict:'E',
templateUrl:'/partials/workoutbuilder/workout-tile.html'
```

Now, we can change the directive declaration in HTML to:

```
<workout-tile></workout-tile> //replace the span declaration
```

Refresh the workout list page again. It's the same workout list, but this time tile content is wrapped in a new tag `<workout-tile>`, as shown here:

```
▼<div ng-repeat="workout in workouts|orderBy:'title'"
  ▶ <workout-tile>…</workout-tile>
  </div>
  <!-- end ngRepeat: workout in workouts|orderBy:'title
▼<div ng-repeat="workout in workouts|orderBy:'title'"
  ▶ <workout-tile>…</workout-tile>
  </div>
```

Not very impressive but not bad either. What have we achieved with these few lines?

We now have a directive that encapsulated the view template for the HTML workout tile. Any reference to this directive in HTML now renders the tile content. The first version (without the `restrict` configuration) rendered the template HTML inside span, whereas in the second revision we created a custom HTML tag `workout-tile` to host the workout tile's content.

There are few observations from our first directive:

- Directives have a name, and it is normalized. We are defining a directive in JavaScript as `workoutTile`, but we refer to it in HTML as `workout-tile`. Directive naming follows camel case but the directives are referenced in HTML using the dash delimiter (-) as shown in the previous screenshot. In fact, directives can be referenced in HTML with extra prefixes such as `x-` or `data-`. For example, the `workoutTile` directive in HTML can be referred to as `x-workout-tile`, `data-workout-tile`, or the standard `workout-tile` pattern. This process of matching the HTML directive reference to the actual directive name is called **normalization**.

 All framework directives are prefixed with the letters ng. It's always good to prefix the custom directive we create with some initials to avoid naming conflicts.

- Directives can have `template` (an inline template) or `templateUrl` (reference to the template). The `template` and `templateUrl` properties in the directive definition object refer to the HTML template the directive uses, except the former is used to define the template inline whereas the second one uses external templates (remote or based on `ng-template`).

  This is not a required property in directive configuration. We only use it if the directive comes with its own template. As explained at the start of the chapter, there are directives that only extend the behavior; such directives do not use `template` or `templateUrl`.

- Directives can be applied as an *attribute, element, class, or comment*. Interestingly, with the second version of the `workoutTile` directive, we created a new HTML tag. In other words, we extended the standard HTML **domain-specific language** (DSL). That's pretty cool! This was possible because the updated directive definition had a new `restrict` property with the value E (element).

- A directive can be applied as follows:
  - **Attribute** (`workout-tile=""`): This is the most common way and signifies that the directive is extending the existing HTML tag (in most of the cases). This is a default value (represented as A) for the `restrict` configuration property.
  - **Element** (`<workout-tile></workout-tile>`): This implies the directive can be an HTML element as in the previous example. This is often used for directives that come with their own template and logic. This is represented as E.

- ○ **Class** (`class="workout-tile"`): This allows you to add the directive name inside a class attribute. This is represented as `C`. This is mostly used to support older browsers, specifically older versions of **Internet Explorer (IE)** that do not like custom attributes or elements.

- ○ **Comment** (`<!-- directive:workout-tile-->`): This allows us to add directives as comments! This is not very common, in fact I have never used or seen one. This is represented as `M` in `restrict`.

When creating directives, it's better to stick to `A` and `E` if we are using modern browsers. We can use more than one restriction too. `AE`, `EC`, `AEC`, or `AECM` are all valid combinations. If we use a combination such as `AE`, it implies a directive can be added as an attribute or element.

Supporting IE with the directives element is a challenge in itself. Look at the framework documentation to understand how to handle IE compatibility issues (`https://code.angularjs.org/1.3.3/docs/guide/ie`).

To conclude, the `workoutTile` directive may not be a terribly useful directive, as it just creates an encapsulation over the workout tile HTML. But this directive allows us to represent the complete view as an HTML tag (`<workout-tile></workout-tile>`), adding to the readability of HTML content.

If you are having trouble running this directive, a working implementation is available in the `checkpoint1` folder under `chapter6` in the companion codebase. The GitHub branch is `checkpoint6.1` and the folder is `trainer`.

Let's look at a different directive that instead extends the behavior of the existing HTML element: the `ng-click` directive.

Exploring the ng-click directive

The useful and well-defined `ng-click` directive allows us to attach behavior to an existing HTML element. It evaluates the expression defined on the `ng-click` attribute when the element is clicked. If we look at the Angular source code, here is how the directive is defined:

```
ngModule.directive('ngClick', ['$parse', function ($parse) {
  return {
    compile: function (element, attr) {
```

```
          var fn = $parse(attr['ngClick']);
          return function (scope, element, attr) {
              element.on('click', function (event) {
              scope.$apply(function () {
  fn(scope, { $event: event });
    });
              });
        };
}};}]);
```

 The preceding directive has been simplified a bit, but the implementation is intact.

These few lines of code touch every aspect of directive building, and we are going to dissect this code bit by bit to understand what is happening.

A directive setup is all about creating a directive definition object and returning it. The directive definition object for ng-click only defines one property, the compile function with arguments such as these:

- element: This is the DOM element on which the directive has been defined. The element can be a jQuery element wrapper (if the jQuery library has been included) or a jqLite wrapper, which is the lite version of jQuery included as part of the Angular framework itself.

 Reference to jQuery has to be included in the script references before AngularJS libraries. Then, Angular will use the jQuery wrapper element. Otherwise, Angular falls back to the jqLite wrapper element.

The capabilities of the jqLite element have been detailed in the framework documentation at https://code.angularjs.org/1.3.3/docs/api/ng/function/angular.element.

- attr: This is an object that contains values for all the attributes defined on the directive element. The attributes available on this object are already normalized. Consider this example:

```
<button ng-click='doWork()' class='one two three'>
Click Me</button>
```

The attr object will have the properties: attr.ngClick and attr.class with the values doWork() and one two three, respectively.

Remember `attr` contains all attributes defined on the directive element not just the directive attribute.

The `compile` function should always return a function commonly referred to as the *link* function. Angular invokes these `compile` and `link` functions as part of the directive's compilation process. We will cover the directive life cycle later in the chapter, where we look at the *compile* and *link* phases of a directive execution and their significance.

For now, the things to remember are:

- Directive compilation has two phases: compile and link
- The `compile` function mentioned earlier is invoked during the directive's compile phase
- The function that `compile` returns (also referred to as the `link` function) is invoked during the link phase

The very first line in the compile function uses an injected dependency, `$parse`. The job of the `$parse` service is to translate an AngularJS expression string into a function. For the `ng-click` directive, the expression string points to value of the HTML attribute `ng-click`.

Ever wondered how the `ng-click="showWorkoutHistory()"` declaration on the view translates into a function call to `showWorkoutHistory()` on the controller scope? Well, `$parse` has a role to play here, it converts the expression string to a function.

This function is then used to evaluate the expression in context of a specific object (mostly a scope object). These two lines in the preceding directive do exactly what we just described:

```
var fn = $parse(attr['ngClick']);  // generate expression function
...
fn(scope, { $event: event }); //evaluates in scope object context
```

Check the AngularJS documentation for the `$parse` service (https://code.angularjs.org/1.3.3/docs/api/ng/service/$parse) for more details, including examples.

Use the $parse service to parse string expressions when building directives that rely on such expressions. Framework directives such as ng-click, ng-show, ng-if, and many others are good examples of such directives.

After setting up the expression function at the start, the compile implementation returns the link function.

When the link function for ng-click is executed, it sets up an event listener for the DOM event click by calling the element.on function on the directive element. This completes the directive setup process, and the event handler now waits for the click event.

When the actual DOM click event occurs on the element, the event handler executes the expression function (fn(scope, { $event: event });).

It's the same function created by parsing the ng-click attribute value (such as ng-click='doWork()').

By wrapping the expression execution inside scope.$apply, we allow Angular to detect model changes that may occur when the expression function is executed and update the appropriate view bindings.

Consider the following example where we have an ng-click setup:

```
<button ng-click="doWork()">Do Work</button>
```

Here is the doWork implementation:

```
$scope.doWork= function() {
    $scope.someVal="Work done";
}
```

The expression function execution for the preceding example executes doWork and updates the scope variable: someVal. By wrapping the expression execution in $scope.$apply, Angular is able to detect whether the someVal property has changed and hence can update any view bindings for someVal.

 If you are still confused, it would be a good time to look at *Chapter 3, More AngularJS Goodness for 7-Minute Workout* and read the *AngularJS dirty checking and digest cycles* section.

The bottom line is that any expression evaluation that is triggered from outside the AngularJS execution context needs to be wrapped in scope.$apply.

This completes the execution flow for the `ng-click` directive. It's time to build something useful ourselves: a directive that can do remote validation!

Building a remote validation directive to validate the workout name

Each exercise/workout is uniquely identified by its `name` property. Thus, before persisting for the first time, we need to make sure that the user has entered a unique name for the workout/exercise. If the exercise/workout already exists with this name, we need to inform the user with the appropriate validation message.

This can be achieved by performing some custom validation logic in the controller's `save` function and binding the result to some validation label in the view. Instead, a better approach will be to create a validation directive, which can be integrated with the form validation infrastructure for consistent user experience.

 In *Chapter 4, Building Personal Trainer*, we touched upon *Angular form validations* and how it works, but did not create a true custom validator. We are going to build one now using a directive.

We can either create a directive specifically for unique name validation or a generic directive that can perform any remote validation. At first, the requirement of checking a duplicate name against a datasource (the MongLab database) seems to be too specific a requirement which cannot be handled by a generic validator. But with some sensible assumptions and design choices, we can still implement a validator that can handle all types of remote validation, including workout name validation, using the MongoLab REST API.

The plan is to create a validator that externalizes the actual validation logic. The directive will take the validation function as input from the controller scope. This implies that the actual validation logic is not part of the validator but is part of the controller that actually needs to validate input data. The job of the directive is just to call the scope function and set error keys on input element's `ngModelController.$error` object. We have already seen how the `$error` object is used to show validation messages for `input` in *Chapter 4, Building Personal Trainer*.

Remote calls add another layer of complexity due to asynchronous nature of these calls. The validator cannot get the validation results immediately; it has to wait. AngularJS *promises* can be of great help here. The remote validation function defined on the controller needs to return a promise instead of validating results and the remote validation directive needs to wait over it before setting the validation key.

Let's put this theory to practice and build our remote validation directive, aptly named `remote-validator`.

> This is the first time we are building a form validation directive in Angular. We will be building two implementation `remote-validator` directives, one for Angular 1.3 or less and one for Angular 1.3. Form validations, especially model validators in Angular 1.3 have gone through some major changes, as we saw in *Chapter 4, Building Personal Trainer*. The model validators are no longer part of parser/formatter pipeline in Angular 1.3, hence the two directives.
>
> We could still have built the directive using an older version of Angular and it would have worked fine with Angular 1.3 as well. However, building two separate directives allows us to highlight the new features of Angular 1.3 and how to utilize them.
>
> Please read how `remote-validator` is implemented for Angular 1.3 or less before proceeding to Angular 1.3. We will cover some important concepts in the first implementation that are common for both versions.

The remote-validator directive (for v1.3 or less)

The `remote-validator` directive does validation against remote data source via a function defined on the inherited scope. This function should return a promise. If the promise is resolved successfully, validation succeeds, else the validation fails (on promise rejection).

Let's integrate it with the workout builder view. Open `workout.html` from the `workoutbuilder` folder and update the `workoutName` input by adding two new attributes:

```
<input type="text" name="workoutName" ...
    remote-validator="uniqueName" remote-validator-function=
    "uniqueUserName(value)">
```

Then, add the validation label after other validation labels for the `workoutName` input:

```
<label ng-show = "hasError(formWorkout.workoutName,
    formWorkout.workoutName.$error.uniqueName)" ng-class = "{
    'text-danger': formWorkout.workoutName.$error.uniqueName}">
    Workout with this name exists.</label>
```

The `remote-validator` attribute has the value `uniqueName` and is used as the error key for the validation (`$error.uniqueName`). See the preceding validation label to know how the key is utilized. The other attribute `remote-validator-function` is not a directive but still has an expression assigned to it (`uniqueUserName(value)`) and a function defined on `WorkoutDetailController`. This function validates whether the workout name is uniquely passed in the workout name (`value`) as parameter.

Our next job now is to implement the controller method `uniqueUserName`. Copy this piece of code to the `WorkoutDetailController` implementation:

```
$scope.uniqueUserName = function (value) {
if (!value || value === $routeParams.id) return $q.when(true);
    return WorkoutService
      .getWorkout(value.toLowerCase())
    .then(function (data) { return $q.reject(); },
            function (error) { return true; });
};
```

This function uses two new services: `$q` and `WorkoutService`. Add these dependencies to `WorkoutDetailController` before proceeding further

The `uniqueUserName` method checks whether a workout exists with the same name by calling the `getWorkout` function on `WorkoutService`. We use promise chaining (see *Chapter 5, Adding Data Persistence to Personal Trainer*) here and return the promise object received as part of the `then` function invocation.

The promise returned as part of the `then` invocation is rejected if success callback is invoked (using `return $q.reject()`), else it is successfully resolved with the `true` value.

> Remember the promise returned by `then` is resolved with the return values of its success or error callback.

The very first line uses `$q.when` to return a promise object that always resolves to true. If the value parameter is `null/undefined` or the workout name is the same as the original name (happens in edit cases), we want the validation to pass.

The last part of this puzzle is the `remote-validator` directive implementation itself. Open `directives.js` under `shared` and add the following directive code:

```
angular.module('app').directive('remoteValidator', ['$parse', function
($parse) {
  return {
    require: 'ngModel',
    link: function (scope, elm, attr, ngModelCtrl) {
    var expfn = $parse(attr["remoteValidatorFunction"]);
      var validatorName = attr["remoteValidator"];
      ngModelCtrl.$parsers.push(function (value) {
       var result = expfn(scope, { 'value': value });
       if (result.then) {
          result.then(function (data) {
              ngModelCtrl.$setValidity(validatorName, true);
              }, function (error) {
              ngModelCtrl.$setValidity(validatorName, false); });
        }
        return value;
      });
    }
  }
}]);
```

Let's first verify remote validation is working fine. Open the workout builder page by clicking on the new workout button on the top menu. Enter a workout name that already exists (such as `7minworkout`) and wait for a few seconds. If the workout name matches an existing workout name, validation will trigger with this validation message:

Name:
7minworkout
Workout with this name exists.

 A working implementation for this directive is available in `chapter6/checkpoint2`. The GitHub branch is `checkpoint6.2` and the folder is `trainer`.

Let's dissect the directive code as there are some new concepts implemented. The first one is the `require` property with the value is `ngModel`. Let's first try to understand the role of require.

The require directive definition

Directives in Angular are not standalone components. The framework does provide a mechanism where a directive can take a dependency on one or more directives. The `require` property is used to denote this dependency. The `remote-validator` directive requires an `ng-model` directive to be available on the same HTML element.

When Angular encounters such a dependency during directive execution (during the link phase), it injects the required directive controller into the last argument of the `link` function as seen in the preceding section (the `ngModelCtrl` parameter).

 A directive dependency is actually a dependency on the directive's controller function.

The `require` parameter can take a single or array of dependency. For an array of dependency, the dependencies are injected as an array (of directive controllers) into the last argument of the `link` function.

Such a directive dependency setup has a limitation. A directive can take dependency on a directive that is defined on the same element or its parent tree. By default, it searches for the dependent directive on the same element. We can add a prefix to affect the behavior of this search. The following descriptions were taken from the Angular `compile` documentation (`https://code.angularjs.org/1.2.14/docs/api/ng/service/$compile`):

? - Attempt to locate the required controller or pass null to the link fn if not found. The standard behavior otherwise is to throw exception if dependency is not found.

^ - Locate the required controller by searching the element's parents. Throw an error if not found.

?^ - Attempt to locate the required controller by searching the element's parents or pass null to the link fn if not found.

To reiterate, the dependency that we add using `require` is a directive (`require: 'ngModel'`), what gets injected is a directive controller (in this case, `NgModelController`).

Other than the `restrict` property, we use the `link` function where most of the action is happening.

The link function

The `link` function of the directive gets called during the link phase of directive execution. Most of the Angular directives use the `link` function to implement their core functionality.

 The `compile` and `controller` functions are some other extension points to attach behaviors to a directive.

Here is the signature of the `link` function:

```
link: function (scope, element, attr, ctrls) {
```

The parameters are as follows:

- `scope`: This is the scope against which the directive has been set up. It can be the original parent scope, a new child scope or an isolated scope. We will look at directive scopes later in this chapter.

- `element`: Like the compile function's element property, this is the DOM element on which the directive is defined.

 Angular extends the `element` property and adds some handy functions to it, for example, functions such as `controller(name)` to extract the controller linked to element, `scope()` to get the scope object associated with the element, and others such functions.

Check the documentation on `angular.element` (`https://code.angularjs.org/1.3.3/docs/api/ng/function/angular.element`) to understand the complete API.

- `attr`: This is a normalized list of attributes defined on elements.
- `ctrls`: This is a single controller or an array of controllers passed into the `link` function.

The `compile` and `link` function parameters are assigned based on position; there is no dependency injection involved in the `link` function's invocation.

The `remote-validator` directive uses the `link` function to set up the remote validation logic. Let's look at how the actual validation is done:

- First, we extract the error key name from the HTML attribute `remote-validator` (`uniqueName`) and the validation function (`uniqueUserName(value)`) from the `remote-validator-function` attribute.

- Then, the `$parse` service is used to create an expression function. This is similar to the `ng-click` directive implementation earlier.

- We then register our custom validation function with the input model controller's (`ngModelCtrl`) parser pipeline. The `ngModelCtrl` controller is injected into the `link` function due to our dependency on `ngModel` defined on the `restrict` property.

- This validation function is called on every user input. The function invokes the expression function setup earlier in the context of the current scope and also passes the input value in `value` (second argument).

  ```
  var result = expfn(scope, { 'value': value });
  ```

- This results in invocation of the `$scope` function's `uniqueUserName` value defined on `workoutDetailController`. The `uniqueUserName` function should returns a promise and it does.

- We attach callbacks to the promise API's `then` function.

  - The success callback marks that the validation is successful.

    ```
    ngModelCtrl.$setValidity(validatorName, true);
    ```

  - The error callback sets the key to `false` and hence the validation fails.

- Finally the parser function returns the original `value` at the end of parser execution without modification.

 Remember the `then` callback occurs sometime in future after the parser function execution completes. Therefore, the parser function just returns the original `value`.

This is what makes the remote validation work. By offloading some of the work that a validator does to a controller function, we get an ability to use this validator anywhere and in any scenario where a remote check is required.

 A similar validator can be implemented for standard nonasynchronous validations too. Such validators can do validations by referencing a validation function defined on the parent controller. The validation function instead of returning a promise, returns `true` or `false`.

An interesting thing with this directive is that the `link` function uses all the parameters passed to it, which gives us a fair idea of how to utilize `scope`, `element`, `attributes`, and `controller` in directives.

The remote-validator directive in Angular 1.3

I hope you have read the last few sections/subsections on `remote-validator`, as this section will only cover the parts that have changed post Angular 1.3.

As we saw in *Chapter 4, Building Personal Trainer,* form validation has gone through some changes post Angular 1.3. Validators in v1.3 are registered with the `$validators` and `$asyncValidators` properties of `NgModelController`. As the name of the properties suggest, standard validators are registered with `$validators` and validators that perform asynchronous operations with `$asyncValidators`.

```
Since we too are doing remote validations, we need to use the
$asyncValidators object to register our validator. Let's create
a new definition of the remote-validator directive that uses
$asyncValidators. Add this directive definition to directives.js
file under shared:
angular.module('app').directive('remoteValidator', ['$parse',
    function ($parse) {
        return {
            require: 'ngModel',
            link: function (scope, elm, attr, ngModelCtrl) {
                var expfn = $parse(attr["remoteValidatorFunction"]);
                var validatorName = attr["remoteValidator"];
                ngModelCtrl.$asyncValidators[validatorName] =
function (value) {
                    return expfn(scope, { 'value': value });
                }
            }
        }
    }]);
```

We register a function with `$asyncValidators`, with a name derived from the `remote-validator` attribute value (such as `remote-validator="uniquename"`).

> The `function` property name registered with `$asyncValidators` is used as the error key when the validation fails. In the preceding case, the error key will be `uniquename` (check the HTML declaration for the directive).

The asynchronous validation function should take an input (`value`) and should return a promise. If the promise is resolved to success, then the validation passes, else it is considered failed.

One important difference between the v1.3 (or lesser) and this one is that in the earlier version, we need to explicitly call `ngModelCtrl.$setValidity` to set the validity of the model controller. In Angular 1.3, this is automatically done based on the resolved state of the promise.

> Standard validators (nonasynchronous ones) in Angular 1.3 also work in a similar fashion. For standard validators, the validation function is registered with the `$validators` object, and the function should return a Boolean value instead of a promise.

That's how we implement the same validation in Angular 1.3 and upwards.

The `remote-validator` directive seems to be working now, but it still has some flaws that need to be addressed. The first being remote validation being called on every input update. We can verify this by looking at the browser network log as we type something into the workout name input:

> Angular 1.3 version of the directive is available in the `checkpoint2` folder of `chapter6`. The GitHub branch is `checkpoint6.2` and the folder is `trainer`.

Well, this is how two-way binding works. The view changes are immediately synced with the model and the other way around too. For remote validation, this is a nonperformant approach as we should avoid triggering remote validation so frequently. The better way will be to validate once the input loses focus (*blur*).

There is a directive for that! Let's add a directive for that, `update-on-blur`.

Angular 1.3 already supports model update on blur using the `ng-model` and `ng-model-options` directives. We have already covered these directives in *Chapter 4, Building Personal Trainer*. The `update-on-blur` equivalent in Angular 1.3 would be as follows:

```
<input type="text" name="workoutName"
...
   ng-model-options="{ updateOn: 'blur' }">
```

If you are using Angular 1.3, using the `ng-model-option` directive would be more appropriate.

Do read the next section to understand how `update-on-blur` is implemented, and how it uses the `priority` property to alter the behavior of other directives applied to same element.

Model update on blur

We want a directive that updates the underlying model only when the input loses focus. Not my original idea but derived from the SO post at http://stackoverflow.com/questions/11868393/angularjs-inputtext-ngchange-fires-while-the-value-is-changing.

Add this directive to `directives.js` under `shared`:

```
angular.module('app').directive('updateOnBlur', function () {
    return {
        restrict: 'A',
        require: 'ngModel',
        link: function (scope, elm, attr, ngModelCtrl) {
            if (attr.type === 'radio' || attr.type === 'checkbox')
return;
            elm.unbind('input').unbind('keydown').unbind(
              'change');
            elm.bind('blur', function () {
               scope.$apply(function () {
                  ngModelCtrl.$setViewValue(elm.val());
               });
```

```
                });
            }
        };
    });
```

This directive definition object structure looks similar to the `remote-validator` directive. Like `remote-validator`, the implementation here has been done in the `link` function.

The `link` function basically unbinds all existing event handlers on the target input and rebinds only the `blur` event. The `blur` event handler updates the model by calling `ngModelCtrl.$setViewValue`, retrieving the actual view content from view using the `elm.val()` DOM function.

Go ahead and refresh the new workout page and enter some data in the workout name field. This time validation only triggers on *blur*, and hence the remote calls are made once the focus is lost.

> This directive has affected the overall model and view synchronization behavior for the workout name input element. Model updates now only happened when focus on input is lost. This implies other validations also happen on lost focus.
>
> To reiterate, we don't need this directive in Angular 1.3. The `ng-model-options="{ updateOn: 'blur' }"` statement does the same job.

The `update-on-blur` function fixes the performance issue with remote validation, but there is one more optimization we can do.

Using priority to affect the order of execution of the compile and link functions

Remote validation is a costly operation and we want to make sure remote validation only happens when deemed necessary. Since the workout name input has other validations too, remote validation should only trigger if there is no other validation error, but that is not the case at present.

Remote validation is fired irrespective of whether other validations on `input` fail or not. Enter a workout name bigger than 15 characters and tab out. The `remote-validator` directive still fires the remote call (see the browser network log) in spite of the failure of regex pattern validation, as shown here:

Name:

greaterthan15characters

Only alpha numberic values are allowed in workout name with max length 15.

greaterthan15characters?apiKey=E16WgsIFduXHiMAdAg6qcG1KKYx7WNWg
api.mongolab.com/api/1/databases/angularjsbyexample/collections/workouts

Theoretically, for the `remote-validator` directive, if we register the remote validator parser function as the last function in the parser pipeline, these issues should get resolved automatically. By registering our validators at the end of the parser pipeline, we allow other validators to clear the value before it reaches our parser function. It seems we are already doing that in the `remote-validator` directive of the `link` function:

```
ngModelCtrl.$parsers.push(function (value) {
```

Still it does not work! Remote requests are still made.

This is because we are missing a small but relevant detail. There are other directives defined on the same element as well. Specifically for this `input` function, there are validation directives `required` and `ng-pattern`, both having their own link function that registers validators in the parser and formatter pipelines. This implies the order of registration of parser functions becomes important. To register our parser function at last, the `remote-validator` link function should be executed at the end. However, how do we affect the order of execution of link function? The answer is the property `priority`.

The Angular 1.3 implementation of `remote-validator` does not suffer from this issue as validators are not part of parser/formatter pipelines in v1.3. Add to that, asynchronous validators in v1.3 always run after the synchronous validators. Hence v1.3 of the validator does not require the `priority` fix. The following content is a good read to understand the role of `priority` in directive execution.

Go ahead and add the property `priority` on the `remote-validator` directive definition object, and set it any non-zero positive number (for example, `priority: 5`). Refresh the page and again enter a workout name bigger than 15 characters and tab out. This time the remote call is not fired, and we can confirm this in the network tab of the browser.

Great! This fixed the issue, now we just need to understand what happened when we set the `priority` fix to a positive number.

Time to dig deeper into the directive life cycle events and their effect on directive execution!

Life cycle of a directive

Directive setup starts when Angular compiles a view. View compilation can happen at different times during application execution. It can happen due to the following reasons:

- When the application bootstraps (setting up `ng-app`) while loading the app for the first time

- When a view template is loaded dynamically for the first time using directives such as `ng-view` and `ng-include`

- When we use the `$compile` service to explicitly compile a view fragment (we will discuss more about the `$compile` service later in the chapter).

This compilation process for a directive is broken down into two phases: the *compile* and the *link* phases. Since there are always multiple directives on the view, this phased execution is repeated for each of the directives. Let's understand how

During the view compilation, Angular searches for directives defined on the view by traversing the DOM tree top down from parent to child. The matching happens based on the `restrict` property of directive definition object and directive name (normalized).

 A directive can be referenced in the view via an attribute, element, class, or comment.

Once Angular is able to determine the directive reference by a view fragment, it invokes the compile function for each of the matching directive. The `compile` function invocation in turns returns a `link` function. This is called the compile phase of the directive setup. At this time, view bindings are not set up; hence, we have a raw view template. Any template manipulation can be safely done at this stage.

 This is the same `link` function that we add to directive definition object, through the `link` property or as a return value of the `compile` function if the directive implements one.

The resultant link function is used to set up the bindings between the view and a scope object. When traversing down the DOM tree, Angular keeps invoking the compile functions on the directives and keeps collecting the link functions.

Once compilation is complete, it then invokes the link function in the reverse order with the child link function called before the parent link function (from children to parent DOM elements) to set up the scope and view binding. This phase is termed as the link phase.

During the link phase Angular may have to create a new scope for some directives (for example, ng-view, ng-repeat, and ng-include), or bind an existing scope to the view (for example ng-click, ng-class, and ng-show). Then, Angular invokes the controller function, followed by the link function on the directive definition object passing in the appropriate scope and some other relevant parameters.

 Since the scope linking only happens at the link phase, we cannot access the scope in the directive compile function, which is evident even from the parameters passed to compile; there is no parameter scope there.

The role of the controller function will be discussed in the following sections, but most directives use the link function to implement the core directive behavior. This stands true for each of the directives we have discussed. This is where we register DOM event handlers, alter directive scope, or set up any required Angular watch.

The reason to break the overall process into compile and link phase is due to performance optimization. For directives such as ng-repeat, the inner HTML of the directive is compiled once. Linking happens for each ng-repeat iteration, where Angular clones the compiled view and attaches a new scope to it before injecting it into DOM.

While defining a directive, we can use only one of the compile or link functions. If the compile function is used, it should return a function or object:

```
compile: function compile(tElement, tAttrs) {
  return {
    pre: function(scope, elmement, attr, ctrl) { ... },
    post: function (scope, elmement, attr, ctrl) { ... }
  };}
```

Or it should return this:

```
compile: function compile(tElement, tAttrs) {
    return function(scope, elmement, attr, ctrl) { ... }; //post link
        function
}
```

The bottom line is that the compile function should return a `link` function. This function is invoked during the compile phase of directive execution.

Instead of implementing the `compile` function and returning a `link` function, we can directly implement the `link` function (or the `link` object) of the directive configuration object, as shown here:

```
link:function(scope, elmement, attr, ctrl)   //post link function
```

Or we can implement this:

```
link: {
    pre: function preLink(scope, elmement, attr, ctrl) { ... },
    post: function postLink(scope, elmement, attr, ctrl) { ... }
}
```

The signature is the same as the return value of the `compile` function. This function is invoked during the link phase of directive execution.

The `pre` and `post` link functions that we see on the preceding `compile` and `link` objects allow fine-grain control over the link phase. Angular divides the link phase execution again into the *prelink* and *postlink* phases. It invokes `pre` during the *prelinking* and `post` during the *postlinking* phase.

> If the return value of `compile` is a function, it is actually a postlink function. Similarly, if the `link` property is a function, it is actually a postlink function.
>
> Stick to the *postlink* phase and use the `link` function. There is seldom a need to use the *prelink* phase.

This completes our discussion on directive life cycle. The original intent of this discussion was to understand how the `priority` property helped us fix the order of execution of the `link` function of `remote-validator`. Let's continue that pursuit.

The priority and multiple directives on a single element

We now understand that directive setup goes through two phases. The *compile phase* where Angular calls the `compile` function *top-down*, and the *link phase* where the `link` function is invoked *bottom-up*. Wondering what happens when there are multiple directives defined on a single element?

When multiple directives are defined on a single element, `priority` decides the execution order. *The directives with higher priority are compiled first and linked last.*

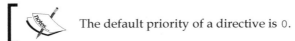 The default priority of a directive is 0.

By setting the directive priority for `remote-validator` to a positive number, we force Angular to run the directive's `link` function at the last. This allows us to push our remote validator function at the end of *parser pipeline*, and it runs last during validation.

 The `priority` property is a seldom used property and for most of our directive implementation we do not need or want to tinker with the default order of the `compile` or `link` function execution.

Let's add some more goodness to our remote validation, improving the overall user experience. The plan is to implement a new directive that gives a visual clue when remote validation happens and when it completes.

Implementing a remote validation clues directive

The workout name's remote validation works well now, but the user does not realize that the workout name is being validated remotely, and may be surprised when all of a sudden a validation message appears.

We can improve the overall user experience if we can show a busy/progress indicator every time remote validation happens. Let's build a **busy-indicator** directive. We plan to build three versions of the same validator with a slightly different approach and work our way through some new concepts in directive building.

Here is what the first version `busy-indicator` implementation looks like:

```
angular.module('app').directive('busyIndicator', ['$compile', function
($compile) {
  return {
    scope: true,
    link: function (scope, element, attr) {
      var linkfn = $compile('<div><label ng-show="busy"
  class="text-info glyphicon glyphicon-refresh
    spin"></label></div>');
          element.append(linkfn(scope));
    },
    controller: ['$scope', function ($scope) {
      this.show = function () { $scope.busy = true; }
      this.hide = function () { $scope.busy = false; }
    }]
  }
}]);
```

Add this code to the `shared/directive.js` file at the end of the file. Also, copy the updated CSS (`app.css`) from the folder `checkpoint3` under `chapter6` in the codebase.

A simple directive shows an animation when the `busy` property is `true`, and hides it otherwise.

Setting `scope:true` on directive definition causes a new scope to be created when the directive is executed and link function is called. This scope inherits from its parent scope (*prototypal inheritance*).

The `scope` property can also take an object, in which case an *isolated scope* is created. We will cover *isolated scopes* later in the chapter.

The reason we create a new scope for `busy-indicator` is because we want to support any number of busy indicators on the page. Look at the directive definition; it manipulates a `busy` flag in its `controller` function. If we do not create a new scope, the `busy` flag gets added to the parent scope (or container scope) of the directive. This limits our ability to add more than one busy variable as there is only one scope. With scope set to `true`, every directive reference in HTML creates a new scope and the `busy` flag is set on this child scope, hence avoiding any conflict.

The link function here does some DOM manipulation and appends an HTML fragment (a spinner HTML) to the element using element.append.

Any type of DOM manipulation belongs to directives. As highlighted earlier, never reference the DOM inside controller.

The busy-indicator function of link uses the $compile service to compile the HTML fragment before it injects the HTML fragment into the DOM. Let's look at how the $compile service works to comprehend the link function implementation.

Angular $compile service

The AngularJS $compile service is responsible for compiling the view and linking it to the appropriate scope. The *compiling* and *link phase* of a directive are supported using this very service. By exposing it as a service, the framework allows us to leverage the compile and link infrastructure as and when required.

Why would one require the $compile service?

If we want to inject dynamic HTML into the view and expect *interpolations* and *directives* bindings for the injected HTML to work, we need to use $compile.

The busy-indicator function of link does not append the busy indicator HTML directly to the directive element. Instead, it uses the $compile service first to compile the HTML fragment. This results in the creation of a link function (linkFn) for the HTML fragment (the compile phase). The link function is then linked to the directive scope by calling linkFn(scope) (the link phase).

In this case, the directive scope is a new child scope as we have set scope:true. The linkFn function invocation returns a compiled + linked element that is finally appended to the directive element.

We have manually *compiled*, *linked*, and *injected* a custom HTML fragment into DOM. Without *compiling* and *linking*, the ng-show binding will not work and we will end up with a busy indicator that is permanent visible.

When injecting dynamic HTML into DOM, use the $compile service if the HTML contains Angular directives and interpolations.

Content without Angular *directives* and *interpolation* can always be injected using the ng-bind-html directive.

The `$compile` service function can take an HTML fragment string (as shown earlier) or a DOM element as input. We can convert the HTML fragment into DOM element using the `angular.element` helper function:

```
var content = '<div ng-show="exp"></div>';
var template = angular.element(content);
var linkFn=$compile(template);
```

This covers the `$compile` service and how we use it to dynamically add the template HTML inside the directive element. Things will be clearer once we integrate this directive with the `remote-validator` directive. But before we start the integration, we need to learn about the new **controller** function defined on the `busy-indicator` definition and the role it plays in in integrating the two directives.

Directive controller function

The primary role of a directive controller function defined on a *directive definition object* is to support **inter-directive communication** and expose an API that can be used to control the directive from outside.

The `ng-model` directive is an excellent example of a directive that exposes its controller (`NgModelController`). This controller has functions and properties to manage two-way data binding behavior. The directives: `remote-validator` and `update-on-blur`, make use of the `NgModelController` API too.

The controller API for busy-indicator is pretty simple. A function `show` is used to start the indicator and `hide` is used to stop it.

Now let's integrate both these directives.

Inter-directive communication – integrating busy-indicator and remote-validator

The integration approach here is to add the dependency of `busy-indicator` in the `remote-validator` directive. In the `link` function, use the `busy-indicator` controller to show or hide the indicator when remote validation happens.

> Earlier in this chapter, we created two versions of the `remote-validator` directive, that of pre-*Angular 1.3* and *Angular 1.3* versions. Both directives need to be fixed now.
>
> Read the next section even if you are on Angular 1.3 and above. We cover the common concepts related to both directive implementations in the next section.

Fixing remote-validator – pre-Angular 1.3

Update the `remote-validator` directive definition by adding another dependency
in the `require` property:

```
require: ['ngModel', '?^busyIndicator'],
```

The `?^` symbol implies AngularJS should search for dependency on the parent
HTML tree. If it is not found, Angular injects a `null` value in the `link` function for
the `busy-indicator` controller. For this dependency to work, the `busy-indicator`
directive should apply to the parent HTML of `remote-validator`.

The `link` function of `remote-validator` needs to be updated as dependencies have
changes. Update the `link` function implementation with the highlighted code:

```
link: function (scope, elm, attr, ctrls) {
    var expfn = $parse(attr["remoteValidatorFunction"]);
    var validatorName = attr["remoteValidator"];
    var modelCtrl = ctrls[0];
    var busyIndicator = ctrls[1];
    modelCtrl.$parsers.push(function (value) {
      var result = expfn(scope, { 'value': value });
      if (result.then) {
          if (busyIndicator) busyIndicator.show();
          result.then(function (data) {
              if (busyIndicator) busyIndicator.hide();
              modelCtrl.$setValidity(validatorName, true);
          }, function (error) {
              if (busyIndicator) busyIndicator.hide();
              modelCtrl.$setValidity(validatorName, false);
          });
      }
      return value;
    });
```

 The last parameter to the directive `link` function is an array
of controllers, if the `require` property takes dependency on
multiple directives.

The `link` function extracts the `busy-indicator` controller from the `ctrls` array.
It then calls the `show` function before a remote request is made, and it calls the
`hide` function when the promise is resolved either to success or error. Since the
dependency is optional, we need to check for *nullability* of `busyIndicator` every
time before invocation.

The last part before we can test our implementation is to add the directive to HTML. Since the directive needs to be added to the parent of the workout name `input` (as `remote-validator` is defined on this input), add it to the parent `form-group` attribute of `div`:

```
<div class="form-group row" ng-class="{'
  has-error':formWorkout.workoutName.$invalid}" busy-indicator="">
```

We can now test our implementation. Open the new workout page and enter some text in workout name input and tab out. A nice busy indicator shows on screen that gets cleared when the AJAX call completes! This is shown here:

Let's look at the *Angular 1.3* version of the validator.

Fixing remote-validator (Angular 1.3)

As we did in the previous section, add the `require` property to the `remote-validator` definition:

```
require: ['ngModel', '?^busyIndicator'],
```

Check the previous section to know how `require` works.

Update the `link` function implementation with the highlighted code:

```
link: function (scope, elm, attr, ctrls) {
  var expfn = $parse(attr["remoteValidatorFunction"]);
  var validatorName = attr["remoteValidator"];
  var ngModelCtrl = ctrls[0];
  var busyIndicator = ctrls[1];

  ngModelCtrl.$asyncValidators[validatorName] = function (value) {
      return expfn(scope, { 'value': value });
  }

    if (busyIndicator) {
      scope.$watch(function () { return ngModelCtrl.$pending; },
```

```
        function (newValue) {
        if (newValue && newValue[validatorName])
        busyIndicator.show();
        else busyIndicator.hide();});
        }
    }
```

With v1.3, we use a new ngModelController property $pending. This property reflects the state of asynchronous validators registered with $asyncValidators.

 In the preceding code, newValue is actually the ngModelCtrl.$pending property (return value of the watched function).

The $pending property on ngModelController is an object hash having keys of all asynchronous validators that have a pending remote request. In the preceding implementation, when the $pending property has the validator function key (the same key that is used to register the validator function with the $asyncValidators object earlier), we show the busy indicator or we hide it. Remember Angular automatically adds this key when the asynchronous validation function is called, and removes it once the validation promise is resolved. To verify this, just add a break point inside the watch and look at the value of newValue.

Awesome! We now have a nice-looking textbox that does remote validation, shows a busy indicator, updates on blur, and binds to the model all using some small and well-defined directives. We can see how four directives: busy-indicator, remote-validator, update-on-blur, and ng-model work together to achieve the desired functionality. Directives are a powerful concept that applied judiciously can produce some great results.

Another interesting thing that needs to be highlighted here is the scope setup. Remember busy-indicator had set scope:true in its definition. This implies busy-indicator creates a new scope, and the view scope hierarchy for the preceding setup looks like this:

```
<form name="formWorkout" ...>
    <!--Other html-->
    <div id="workout-data" class="col-sm-3">
        <div class="form-group" ... busy-indicator="">
            <label for="workout-name" class="ng-scope">...
            <input type="text" name="workoutName" ...>
            <!--Other html-->
            <div>
                <label ng-show="busy" ...></label>  Scope (005)
            </div>
        </div>
        <!--Other html-->
    </div>
</form>
```

Scope (004)

Scope (004)

child

Scope (005)

Execution of `busy-indicator` creates a scope (`005`) and all the child elements of `busy-indicator` use this scope. Since scope (`005`) inherits from the parent scope, the children can still refer to parent scope properties for the `ng-model` bindings and validation.

> When a directive creates a new scope by setting `scope:true`, all its child elements are now bound to the new scope. Since this scope inherits from its parent, all existing bindings work as before.

We can run some more experiments with `busy-indicator` and, as described earlier, implement the other two variations of the directive, each being better than the last one.

Injecting HTML in the directive compile function

The first version of directive used the `link` function to add an HTML fragment to directive element. The `link` function first had to compile the HTML fragment before inserting it.

We can avoid this extra compilation if we add the DOM during the compile phase, when the `compile` function is called. Let's confirm it by implementing the directive compile function for `busy-indicator`.

Comment the `link` function implementation and add this `compile` function instead.

```
compile: function (element, attr) {
var busyHtml = '<div><label ng-show="busy" class = "text-info
glyphicon glyphicon-refresh spin"></label></div>';
element.append(busyHtml);
},
```

Refresh the new workout page and verify that the busy indicator implementation is still intact. The busy indicator should work as it did earlier.

By moving the DOM manipulation code into the `compile` function, we have got rid of the manual compilation process. Angular will now take care of compiling and linking the dynamically injected content.

This version of `busy-indicator` looks better, but a one up version would be the one that does not require any DOM manipulation. We can actually get rid of the `compile/link` function for `busy-indicator`.

 The scope hierarchy for this setup is similar to the one defined previously.

Let's work on the third version of this directive.

Understanding directive templates and transclude

Directive templates allow directives to embed their own markup as part of directive execution. Our first directive `workout-tile` used such a template. A template can either be provided in-line using property `template` or can come from a remote server/script block using the `templateUrl` configuration. Interestingly, `busy-indicator` too has a template. In the previous implementations, we have injected the template HTML manually inside the `compile/link` functions.

Let's update the `busy-indicator` directive with its own template. Update the directive definition and add the property `template` to it definition:

```
template: '<div><label ng-show="busy" class="text-info glyphicon
   glyphicon-refresh spin"></label></div>',
```

Now go ahead and remove the `link` or `compile` function from the directive. Refresh the workout builder page. Surprise, surprise... the label `name` and workout name `input` disappear! We can view the source and verify that the directive template has replaced the complete the *inner HTML* of `div` on which it was declared.

If we think about this behavior it makes sense, the directive had a template and it applied the template on the HTML element it was declared. But in this case, that element had child elements that we did not take into account.

How can we fix this? Well, we need to introduce a new concept: transclusion. Trasclusion is the process of extracting a part of DOM and making it available to a directive so that it can be inserted at some location within the directive template. Add a `transclude` property and update the property `template` on the directive definition object:

```
transclude:true,
template: '<div><div ng-transclude=""></div><label ng-show="busy"
   class="text-info glyphicon glyphicon-refresh
   spin"></label></div>',
```

Refresh the page again, but this time the workout input appears and the directives seem to be working as they were earlier. We can now also remove the dependency on the `$compile` service as we are not using it any more. Angular is doing the compilation for us.

Run the app and open the workout detail page. The busy indicator is showing up fine during workout name validation. To understand what is happening during transclusion, check out the following screenshot:

```
<div class="form-group row" busy-indicator="">
    ⌐ <label for="workout-name">Name:</label>
    │ <input type="text" name="workoutName" class=
  ──┤ <label ng-show="  Inner HTML  Workout.workout
    │ <label ng-show="hasError(formWorkout.workout
    └ <label ng-show="hasError(formWorkout.workout
</div>                                    Directive Declaration

<div>
    <div ng-transclude=""></div>
    <label ng-show="busy" class="text-info g!
</div>                        Directive Template

<div class="form-group row ng-scope" busy-indicator="">
    <div>
        <div ng-transclude="">
            ⌐ <label for="workout-name" class="ng-scope">Na
            │ <input type="text" name="workoutName" class="
          ──┤ <label ng-  Inner HTML  r(formWorkout.workoutN
            │ <label ng-  Transcluded  r(formWorkout.workoutN
            └ <label ng-show="hasError(formWorkout.workoutN
        </div>
        <label ng-show="busy" class="text-info glyphicon
    </div>
</div>                                    Rendered HTML
```

The `transclude:true` property tells Angular to extract the inner HTML of a directive declaration and make it available for injection. The injection location is decided by the `ng-transclude` directive (also show in preceding screenshot). When the `busy-indicator` directive executes, Angular pulls the inner HTML of the directive declaration and injects it into directive template HTML wherever `ng-transclude` is declared.

This injection is like creating a hole in the directive template and injecting the HTML content from the main view into the hole. The `ng-transclude` directive allows us to control where the content is injected/transcluded.

Other than a Boolean value, `transclude` can be an element, in which case the complete HTML fragment on which the directive is defined is *transcluded* and not just the inner HTML.

An important question that we need to ask with respect to transclusive behavior is about the scope of the transcluded element. *Transcluded HTML creates a new scope that always inherits the original parent scope instead of a directive scope.* Irrespective of whether the directive creates a new scope or not, this allows the directive template to define new properties on its scope but lets the transcluded content still refer the parent scope without possibility of conflicts.

This is what the HTML and scope hierarchy looks like now:

```
<form name="formWorkout" ...>
    <div id="workout-data" class="col-sm-3">
        <div class="form-group" ... busy-indicator="">
Scope (004)    <div>
                <div ng-transclude="">
                    <label for="workout-name" class="ng-scope">...
                    <input type="text" name="workoutName" ...>
    Scope (006)     <!--Other html-->
                </div>
                <label ng-show="busy" ...></label>
            </div>                              Scope (005)
        </div>
        <!--Other html-->
    </div>                    Transcluded content
</form>
```

Scope (004)
child — child
Scope (005) — Scope (006)

The preceding screenshot highlights the resultant scope hierarchy once transcluded content is inserted. The form has scope ID 004. The busy-indicator HTML has scope ID 005 as we have configured scope:true. Finally, the scope for transcluded content is 006. In terms of hierarchy, the busy-indicator and its transcluded content are **sibling scopes**, inheriting from parent scope (004).

Transclusion and the resultant scope setup are important concepts to understand when creating or dealing with directives that create transclusions.

To reiterate, directive and transclusion scopes are sibling scopes and the transclusion scope always inherits from parent scope.

 Check chapter6/checkpoint3 for working implementation of all directives implemented thus far. The *GitHub* branch is checkpoint6.3 and the folder is trainer).

That's enough on templates and transcludes. Time to start exploring a new concept, **isolated scopes**. Isolated scopes let us create truly reusable directives.

Understanding directive-isolated scopes

If we consider any directive as software components, such a component needs some input to work on, it produces some output and it may provide an API to manipulate its state.

Inputs to directives are provided in one or more forms using *directive templates*, *parent scope*, and *dependencies on other directives*.

Directive output could be behavior extension of an existing HTML element or the generation of new HTML content. The directive API is supported through directive controllers.

For a truly reusable component, all dependencies of a component should be externalized and explicitly stated. When a directive is dependent upon the parent scope for input (even when it creates a child scope), the dependency is implicit and hard to change/replace. Another side effect of an inherited scope is that a directive has access to the parent scope model and can manipulate it. This can lead to unintended bugs that are difficult to debug and fix.

Directive-isolated scopes can solve this problem. As the name suggests, if a directive is created with an isolated scope, it does not inherit from its parent scope but creates its own isolated scope. This may not seem to be a big thing, but the consequences are far reaching. This mechanism lets us create directives that do not have any implicit dependency on the parent scope, hence resulting in a truly reusable component.

To create a directive with an isolated scope, we just need to set the `scope` property on the directive definition object to this:

```
scope:{}
```

This statement creates a new isolated scope. Now, the scope injected into the `link` or `controller` function is the isolated scope and can be manipulated without affecting the directives parent scope.

> The parent scope of an isolated scope is still accessible through the `$parent` property defined on scope object. It's just that an isolated scope does not inherit from its parent scope.

Rarely do we create directives that are not dependent on their parent scope for some model data. The purpose of an isolated scope is to make this dependency explicit. The `scope` object notation is there for passing data to directives from the parent scope. The directive `scope` object can take dependency through three mechanisms. Consider a directive `directive-one` with this scope declaration:

```
scope: {
    prop: '@'
    data: '=',
    action: '&',
},
```

This declaration defines three properties on the directive-isolated scope: `prop`, `data`, and `action`; each one deriving its content from the parent scope, but in a different manner. The symbols @, =, and & defined how the linking is set up with the parent scope:

- @ or @attr: This binds the isolated scope property(`prop`) to a DOM attribute(`attr`) value. If the attribute name (`attr`) is not provided with the @ symbol, the compiler looks for the HTML attribute with the same name as the directive scope property (`prop` in the preceding case).

 Just like directives, attribute names too are normalization. A scope property `testAttribute` should be declared on HTML as `test-attribute="value"`.

Since HTML attributes have string values, we can define *interpolation* on the attribute value and the linked isolated scope property can detect and synchronize the changes. Consider this:

```
<div directive-one prop="Hi {{userName}}"></div>
```

The following table highlights the state of HTML and isolated scope property `prop`:

Parent scope	HTML attribute value	Isolated scope
`$scope.userName="Sid";`	`<div prop='Hi Sid'>`	`prop -> 'Hi Sid'`
`$scope. userName="Tim"`	`<div prop='Hi Tim'>`	`prop -> 'Hi Tim'`

- = or =attr: This creates a bidirectional binding between the isolated scope property and the parent attribute value. Similar to @, if attr is not suffixed after =, the compiler looks for the HTML attribute with the same name as the directive scope property (data in the preceding case). The HTML attribute value should be a property on the parent scope. Consider this:

```
<div directive-one data="user"></div>
```

This exposes the parent scope property user on isolated scope property data. Changes to user are reflected in data, and changes done to data are reflected back to user.

 Bidirectional bindings do not use the interpolation symbols ({ { } }) in declaration.

If the attribute value is not available on the parent scope, Angular throws an NON_ASSIGNABLE_MODEL_EXPRESSION exception. If we want the dependency to be optional we should use =? or =?attr.

- & or &attr: This allows us to execute an expression in the context of the parent scope. The expression is defined as part of the HTML attribute value. The behavior of & without the attr suffix is similar to that described earlier. The attribute value is wrapped inside a function and assigned to an isolated scope property (action is the preceding case). Consider this:

```
<div directive-one action="findUser(name)"></div>
```

The action property on the directive scope can invoke the parent scope function (expression) by calling $scope.action({name:'sid'}).

See how the parameter name is passed on the action function invocation. Instead of directly passing name, it is wrapped inside an object.

Each of the techniques to link the parent scope and isolated scope has its relevance. Let's create another directive for *Personal Trainer* and utilize isolated scopes.

Creating the AJAX button directive

When we save/update exercise, there is always a possibility of duplicate submission (duplicate POST requests). The current implementation does not provide any feedback as to when the save/update operations started and when they completed. The user of an app can knowingly or unknowingly click the save button multiple times due to a lack of visual clues.

Let's create an AJAX button that gives some visual clues when clicked and also stops duplicate AJAX submissions.

This `ajax-button` directive will create an isolated scope, with parameters `onClick` and `submitting`. Here we have it expounded:

- `onClick`: Like ng-click, this allows the user to specify the function to call for on AJAX submit. If the function returns a promise, we use the promise to show/hide the busy indicator as we did while integrating the `busy-indicator` and `remote-validator` directives.

- `submitting`: This property gives the parent scope control over when to show/hide the busy indicator. The parent scope should set `submitting = true` before AJAX request is made and set it to `false` once the request completes.

 The `submitting` property is an optional property. In case, the `onClick` function does not return a promise, `submitting` should be used to signal completion of the AJAX request.

During the busy state, the `ajax-button` object appears disabled to avoid duplicate submission.

Let's now look at some code. Add the following `ajax-button` directive definition to `shared/directives.js`:

```
angular.module('app').directive('ajaxButton', ['$compile', '$animate',
function ($compile, $animate) {
    return {
        transclude: true,
        restrict: 'E',
         scope: { onClick: '&', submitting: '@' },
        replace: true,
        template: '<button ng-disabled="busy"><span class="glyphicon
glyphicon-refresh spin" ng-show="busy"></span><span ng-
transclude=""></span></button>',
        link: function (scope, element, attr) {
            if (attr.submitting !== undefined &&
attr.submitting != null) {
                attr.$observe("submitting", function (value) {
                    if (value) scope.busy = JSON.parse(value); });
            }
            if (attr.onClick) {
                element.on('click', function (event) {
                    scope.$apply(function () {
                        var result = scope.onClick();
```

```
                                  if (attr.submitting !== undefined &&
                                  attr.submitting != null) return;
                                  if (result.finally) {
                                      scope.busy = true;
                                      result.finally(function () {
                                          scope.busy = false });
                                  }
                              });
                          });
                      }
                  }
              }
      }]);
```

The directive implementation creates an isolated scope with a function binding using the `onClick` property and an attribute binding with `submitting`. It also sets the directive property `replace:true`.

> For directives that have their own template, the standard behavior is to insert the template as inner HTML on the element where a directive is declared. To change this behavior, use the directive property `replace`. If set to `true`, it replaces the directive DOM element with template content instead of replacing the inner HTML. All the attributes of the original directive element are copied onto the template HTML.
>
> An important note here: `replace` has been deprecated in recent versions of Angular. To implement the directive without `replace` will require us to manually implement the attribute copying behavior of `replace` and handle the original button styles.

Before we look at how the directive works and understands its `link` function implementation, let's try to apply the directive to workout builder HTML. Open the `workout.html` file under `workoutbuilder`, and update the existing `Save` button HTML by changing the `button` tag to `ajax-button` and rename `ng-click` to `on-click`:

```
<ajax-button ... on-click="save()" ... >Save</ajax-button>
```

Open the workout edit page by double-clicking on any existing the workout in workout list page. If your `ajax-button` HTML references popover directive too, the workout builder page fails to load. The browser console log clearly states this error:

```
Error: [$compile:multidir] Multiple directives [ajaxButton,
    popover] asking for new/isolated scope on: <button ...
```

One of the oddities of isolated scopes is that two directives declared on the same element cannot both ask for an isolated scope. Isolated scopes are there to support truly reusable components, which mostly come with their own template and scope and can be use anywhere, hence it makes sense that they control the DOM element that they are applied to.

To break this stalemate, we can move the popover directive inside the `ajax-button` directive; with transclusion enabled, the popover works inside the `ajax-button` directive. Change the `ajax-button` html to make popover directive a child of `ajax-button`:

```html
<ajax-button class="btn pull-right has-spinner active"
ng-class= "{'btn-default':formWorkout.$valid,'btn-warning':!
  formWorkout.$valid}" on-click="save()">
  <span popover="{{formWorkout.$invalid ? 'The form has errors.'
: null}}" popover-trigger="mouseenter">Save</span>
</ajax-button>
```

 Since the transcluded content is always bound to the original parent scope, the popover directive above can still can access the `formWorkout.$valid` property defined on the parent scope.

The directive integration is still incomplete. Linking the `ajax-button` scope with the parent scope using either the `on-click` or `submitting` properties is pending. Let's see the current implementation of save in `WorkoutDetailController`:

```
$scope.save = function () {
    $scope.submitted = true; // Will force validations
    if ($scope.formWorkout.$invalid) return;
    WorkoutBuilderService.save().then(function (workout) {
    ...
        $scope.submitted = false;
```

For `ajax-button`, we can depend either on the `$scope.submitted` property as it is set to `true` before the AJAX call or `false` when the call is complete. Alternatively, we can do a return on the line that calls the `WorkoutService` save function, as the `then` function returns a promise, something like this:

```
return WorkoutBuilderService.save().then(function (workout) {
```

Both the approaches work as we have designed the directive to support these scenarios.

To use the `submitting` attribute-based linking, just add this attribute to the `ajax-button` HTML tag:

```
submitting = "{{submitted}}"
```

Now create a new workout or open an existing workout and click on **Save**. There should be a busy indicator and the button remains disabled until the AJAX call completes:

This is how attribute (@) based linking works. When we change the value of `submitted` in the `save` function, the `submitting` attribute value is updated and so is the isolated scope property `submitting`. The link function implementation is as follows:

```
attr.$observe("submitting", function (value) {
    if (value) scope.busy = JSON.parse(value); });
```

It registers an attribute watch over a scope property `submitting` using the `attr.$observe` function. This function looks similar to `scope.$watch` that we have used already.

Whenever the `submitting` attribute changes, this watch is triggered with the new value. The watch callback implementation requires `JSON.parse` because `value` is always string and we need to convert it to Boolean for the `busy` flag.

The job of the `busy` flag is to control when the button is disabled and when the busy spinner is shown.

The ajax-button template binds the busy flag to both the ng-disabled and ng-show directives. Strangely enough, ng-show can correctly parse true and false values but ng-disabled treats both as strings, equivalent to Boolean true. Because of this behavior we need to introduce the busy flag in the directive scope instead of using the submitting flag directly.

Since most of the action is happening on the link function, let's quickly go through how the function works.

The first part of the function sets up a watch on the submitting attribute, if it is defined. Then an event handler for click event is attached to the button element.

When the button is clicked, the event handler code invokes the onClick function, which internally executes the function save() in context of parent scope.

If the submitting attribute is defined on the directive, the code returns. In such a case, showing/hiding the busy indicator is taken care of by the submitting interpolation and the attr.observe watch setup earlier in the function.

If submitting is not defined and the onClick invocation returns a *promise*, the directive set the busy flag and wait for the response using the Promise API finally function, where it resets the busy flag.

The complete event handler code is wrapped inside scope.$apply, as the context in which the click event is fired is outside of Angular.

This is how we implement a fully functional ajax-button directive that can show a progress indicator and stop duplicate submission.

A working implementation for the directives covered so far is available in chapter6/checkpoint4. The *GitHub branch* is checkpoint6.4 and the folder is trainer.

With this, we have covered almost all facets of directive development. Before we conclude the chapter, there is one more big ticket item that needs our attention. Integration between AngularJS and jQuery!

AngularJS jQuery integration

If you are a web stack developer, you know jQuery is omnipresent. jQuery has a vibrant community and plethora of plugins that can be readily used in any JavaScript-based implementation.

Angular is in a different league! In AngularJS, we don't directly work on DOM. The only place DOM manipulations are acceptable is within directives. In fact, as we saw earlier, the parameter element to the directive compile and link function is a jQuery/ jqLite object that can be manipulated as the standard jQuery element.

Anyone from a jQuery background will have two major challenges when trying to adopt AngularJS:

- How to think and design the Angular way?
- How to integrate something written in jQuery into Angular?

The first challenge is a mindset change, a paradigm shift. With frameworks such as jQuery, we work at DOM level whereas with AngularJS we work with models and controllers that require no DOM manipulation.

Here are some pointers that can help us think the Angular way if we have a jQuery background:

- **AngularJS is a framework, jQuery is a library**: Angular is just not a DOM manipulation library nor is it a templating / data-binding engine. It's is a full-fledged **single-page application (SPA)** framework that comes with its own set of constructs and requires us to design and layout components in a specific way. It is not a generic utility belt like jQuery.

- **Model drives the view**: Another stark contrast to jQuery development is that it is the model and controller that drive the view. We don't write code to create/update DOM, we write code to mutate model and let the view react to it. The app design and implementation revolves around designing the model and controller to support a view.

- **Stop thinking in terms of the selector**: Most of the jQuery implementation involves CSS selector-based operation. Select an element or collection of elements and perform operation. Adding an item to a collection, removing an item from a collection, and manipulating the collection item are all we do in jQuery. Our mind is tuned to think in terms of selectors when working with jQuery. Whereas if we look back at the sample apps that we have built over the last few chapters, we have never thought of DOM elements, selectors, or things like that—at least not in a direct manner.

- **It's not about DOM manipulation**: With jQuery, the focus is on the view and how to manipulate it to achieve the desired results. It's all about DOM manipulations using CSS selectors. With Angular, the focus shifts to model, controller, and the desired behavior. The thought process is never like "Let me add/remove this div to HTML when a user clicks this button".

- **Views are declarative**: With jQuery development, the concept of unobtrusive JavaScript became popular. The unobtrusive way dictates that view and view behavior should be separated. The HTML should not have any JavaScript code references keeping the separation intact. This was easily achievable with jQuery and everyone embraced this separation.

  But Angular took a step back. Angular views do seem to have expressions (JavaScript code). Since AngularJS uses the declarative approach, views contain *directives expression* and *interpolations*. This helps us to easily predict the view behavior without constantly checking the implementation. Also, AngularJS expressions unlike JavaScript expressions are evaluated always in the context of a scope. As long as we can keep our expression small and move anything complex into a controller function, the AngularJS views are always manageable.

- **Data-binding is awesome, embrace it**: The *templating* and *live data-binding* feature of Angular alone makes it worth using. We have already seen how data-binding infrastructure can reduce the amount of boilerplate code we write. This reduction is substantial if we have a large jQuery codebase.

- **Directives replace plugins**: Both plugins and directives extend the underlying library/framework. Their mechanism for doing this may differ. Directives are the only place where DOM manipulations are done.

- **Avoid mixing both worlds**: The best advice that I can give to a jQuery developer is to drop jQuery altogether when developing with Angular. Don't even include it in the script reference! The only reason for the existence of jQuery script reference could be to support some jQuery plugin.

Hope these pointers together with the apps we have built using Angular provide enough guidance for anyone from a jQuery background to build apps the Angular way.

> There is a truck load of information available on this topic on this SO post `http://stackoverflow.com/questions/14994391/how-do-i-think-in-angularjs-if-i-have-a-jquery-background`. It is highly recommended!

When compared to jQuery, Angular is a new entry and hence there are still a number of popular jQuery plugins that may not have their Angular counterpart. We may face situations many times where we want to utilize a jQuery plugin in an Angular solution. We then have two options:

- **Either rewrite the plugin using AngularJS directives**: A time consuming and hard option but a cleaner approach. **angular-ui** (`http://angular-ui.github.io/`) is a great example of this. The *angular-ui* ports all the Bootstrap JavaScript components (`http://getbootstrap.com/javascript/`) to a native Angular implementation.
- **Create a wrapper directive over the jQuery plugin**: This can be a viable solution depending on the complexity of the plugin and nature of DOM manipulation the plugin does. Remember the underlying infrastructure of Angular too does some DOM trickery while compiling, linking, during template generation, and event binding. There can always be issues with jQuery and Angular conflicting with each other.

Let's take up an exercise to integrate a jQuery plugin into Angular and understand how it is done.

Integrating the Carousel jQuery plugin with Workout Runner

In the *Workout Runner* page when a workout is in progress, the current exercise image is displayed in the center of the page, and it updates as *Workout Runner* cycles through the exercises in the workout. Imagine you saw the *Owl Carousel* jQuery plugin (`http://owlgraphic.com/owlcarousel/`) and fell in love with it and want to integrate this carousel for image transition in workout runner app. Well, that is what we are going to do.

To integrate Owl Carousel, we first need to understand how the plugin works. The Owl carousel works on any DOM element with a single parent and multiple children. When the carousel is applied on a parent DOM element, it cycles through its child elements and show them one or more at a time.

Clearly, the current approach of swapping the image URL for the single img tag will not work. The carousel requires all the child elements to be available before cycling begins.

This is true at least for basic usage. I have not explored advance usage of Owl Carousel, which may provide a mechanism to keep a single child DOM element and still support transitions.

With this understanding in place, our action plan is as follows:

1. Create a model array of image URLs.

2. Update the workout runner view, replacing the single `image` tag with multiple `img` tags generated using `ng-repeat` on the previous model array.

3. Apply the `owl-carousal` directive on the parent element of `ng-repeat`.

4. Implement the directive `owl-carousal` and in the `link` function, apply the jQuery plugin on the html element.

5. On exercise transition, swap images using the *Owl Carousal API*.

The first thing that we need to do is to update `7minworkout/workout.js` with the implementation to generate an array of image path.

Add the function `fillImages` to the `WorkoutController` implementation:

```
var fillImages = function () {
  $scope.exerciseImages = [];
  angular.forEach($scope.workoutPlan.exercises,
   function (exercise, index)
   {
      $scope.exerciseImages.push(exercise.details.image);
      if (index < $scope.workoutPlan.exercises.length - 1)
$scope.exerciseImages.push("img/rest.png");
   });
}
```

Add the `fillImages` invocation to the `startWorkout` function just before the `startExercise` call:

```
fillImages();
startExercise($scope.workoutPlan.exercises[0]);
```

The `fillImages` implementation fills the scope variable `exerciseImages` with the workout exercise images and interleaves the `rest` image between two consecutive exercises.

Next, update the `index.html` file with the Owl script and style references. Since *Owl* is dependent on jQuery, it also needs to be added.

Instead of doing this manually, copy index.html from the companion codebase
checkpoint5/app/index.html and update your local copy.

 By adding jQuery before Angular, we are forcing AngularJS to
use jQuery as its primary DOM manipulation library instead
of using jqLite. If Angular loads before jQuery, it will load and
use jqLite.

Once we have the owl reference added to index.html, we can implement our
directive. Add this directive to the directives.js file under shared:

```
angular.module('app').directive('owlCarousel', ['$compile',
'$timeout', function ($compile, $timeout) {
    var owl = null;
    return {
      scope: { options: '=', source: '='},
      link: function (scope, element, attr) {
            var defaultOptions =
      { singleItem: true, pagination: false };
            if (scope.options)
      angular.extend(defaultOptions, scope.options);
            scope.$watch("source", function (newValue) {
              if (newValue) {
                $timeout(function () {
                  owl = element.owlCarousel(defaultOptions);
                }, 0);
              }
            });
      },
      controller: ['$scope', '$attrs', function ($scope, $attrs) {
  if ($attrs.owlCarousel)
$scope.$parent[$attrs.owlCarousel] = this;
 this.next = function () { owl.trigger('owl.next'); };
        this.previous = function () { owl.trigger('owl.prev'); };
      }]
    };
}]);
```

Update the `workout.html` file under `workout` to integrate the directive.
Replace the line:

```
<img class="img-responsive"
  src="{{currentExercise.details.image}}" />
```

With the following lines:

```
<div owl-carousel="carousel" options="carouselOptions"
  source="exerciseImages">
    <img class="img-responsive" ng-src="{{image}}"
      ng-repeat="image in exerciseImages track by $index" />
</div>
```

Since we will not use auto transition functionality of Owl Carousel, we need to
manually cycle these images. The `WorkoutController` function will cycle the images
when the exercise changes (using the `owl-carousel` directive controller). Update the
promise callback inside the `startExerciseTimeTracking` function by calling the
`carousel.next` function just before the `startExercise` call:

```
if (next) {

$scope.carousel.next();

    startExercise(next);

}
```

We can now verify our implementation by starting a workout. If things are set up
correctly, the image transition will now be done by the Owl plugin and controlled by
the `WorkoutController` controller (using the `owl-carousel` directive controller).

We have built enough directives now to easily comprehend what is happening in
the `owl-carousel` directive. But let's still go through some important parts of the
directive and understand how the directive works.

Similar to the `ajax-button` directive, this directive too uses an isolated scope. This is
what the HTML declaration specific to Owl Carousel looks like:

```
<div owl-carousel="carousel" options="carouselOptions"
  source="exerciseImages">
```

This time we use the = based attribute bindings. This allows us to support two-way binding between the *parent scope object* and the *directive isolated scope*. The following screenshot highlights this linkage:

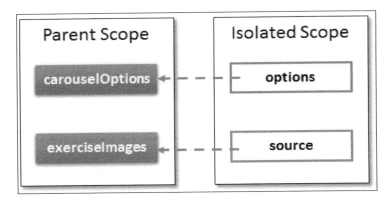

Let's now look at how this directive works. The directive `link` function firstly uses the `options` scope variable (bound to the parent scope `carouselOptions`) to set up the Owl plugin. It initializes some default value for the Owl plugin (`{ singleItem: true, pagination: false };`) and then extends it with the values that are passed through the `options` property.

Then a watch over source (bound to `exerciseImages`) is created to observe when the images data is available. Remember that the exercise details are retrieved from the server; therefore, the directive need to make sure that image data is available before the Owl carousel is executed on the HTML element.

The call to the Owl plugin is wrapped inside a `$timeout` callback because, not only do we want to make sure that the data is available but also that the `ng-repeat` has done its job before we run the plugin. By using `$timeout`, we delay the plugin execution to the next digest cycle by the time the `ng-repeat` has generated the required html.

The directive controller implementation exposes the directive API using two functions, namely `next` and `previous`. Internally, these functions invoke the Owl plugin and transition the element forward or backward. We also expose the directive controller on the parent scope by calling:

```
$scope.$parent[$attrs.owlCarousel] = this;
```

This allows `WorkoutController` to manipulate the carousel and move it forward when an exercise is complete (`$scope.carousel.next();`).

When working with jQuery plugins, another common requirement is to wrap plugin events and make them available as directive function binding (the `scope` property with `&`). Owl Carousel too has some events that we can bind in Angular. Let's try to integrate one such event in the existing `owl-Carousel` directive.

Tunneling jQuery events with directives

Tunneling jQuery events into the Angular world is translating any JavaScript/ jQuery based event into an AngularJS expression invocation, mostly a function call. Event `ng-click` implementation is a tunneling of the DOM `click` event.

The Owl Carousel plugin has an event/callback `afterAction` that is invoked when the plugin initializes or transitions elements forward or backward. If our directive can subscribe to this event, we can translate/tunnel the call to an expression invocation in Angular world. We can use the `&` attribute based binding to achieve this.

To start with, update the *directive definition object* for `owl-carousel` and add a new property `opUpdate` on scope declaration:

```
onUpdate:'&'
```

Also, update the `defaultOptions` object by adding another property `afterAction`:

```
afterAction: function () {
var itemIndex = this.currentItem;
scope.$evalAsync(function () {
scope.onUpdate({ currentItemIndex: itemIndex });
})

}
```

The `afterAction` function is an Owl plugin callback function. When the function is invoked, `this` refers to the Owl plugin. `currentItem` is the index of current item in the Owl element array. The `scope.$evalAsync` service wraps the call to the linked scope function.

The invocation of an Angular expression `onUpdate` requires a `scope.$apply` wrapper callback if invoked directly by the jQuery plugin, else Angular will not be able to detect model changes done in the invoked controller function.

In the case of `owl-carousal`, the callback is fire when the plugin is initialized and when `$scope.carousel.next();` is called in `WorkoutController`. The second type of invocation does not require the `scope.$apply` wrapper but first one does. Due to this conflicting requirement, we wrap the call inside `scope.$evalAsync`. `$evalAsync` makes sure that the expression is executed correctly in the next Angular digest cycle.

We can now update the directive declaration on html to use the `onUpdate` linking:

```
<div owl-carousel= ... on-update="imageUpdated(currentItemIndex)">
```

Finally, the bound function `imageUpdated` needs to be implemented. Since there is not specific need to track this event for workout runner we do some basic `console.log` and print the current image. Add this to `WorkoutController`:

```
$scope.imageUpdated = function (imageIndex) {
  console.log($scope.exerciseImages[imageIndex]);
};
```

With this, we have successfully tunnelled the `afterAction` event of *Owl Carousel* to directive's `onUpdate` — a translation from the jQuery plugin world to the AngularJS world.

Any jQuery — Angular integration boils down to tunneling events from jQuery to Angular and wrapping jQuery plugins access into AngularJS directives.

The `owl-carousel` directive implementation is a very thin wrapper over the actual plugin. It has been designed specifically to support our workout scenario. It neither has been tested nor supports all carousel scenarios. Creating a complete wrapper is a lengthy and tedious exercise where we need to test all the carousel options, expose its API using directive controller, decide what happens when the user changes the options or underlying data is updated and make sure directive execution (hence plugin execution) happens at the correct time.

This also concludes the implementation for our last directive in this chapter. We should now have a better understanding of how directives work and how to create our own directives.

`Chapter6/checkpoint5` contains a working implementation for all the directive we have covered in this chapter. The *GitHub branch* is `checkpoint6.5` and the folder is `trainer`)

Building a directive is not a simple exercise, unless we are building something very simple. It not only requires us to understand the multitude of options that *directive definition object* provides but also other facets of the AngularJS framework such as *compile and link phase, scopes, watches*, and some others. The more directives we build more we get comfortable with the overall concept and its implementations.

Since directives are components that can be used across all views they need to be designed and implemented with reusability in mind. Before we close the chapter, here are some guidelines that will help us in building our own directives with the above goal:

- **Keep it small**: Small is beautiful and small is easy to reuse. Keep your directive implementation small. All the framework directives are small with well-defined functionality. The directives that we have created too are small and implementation simple.

- **Implement one behavior and implement it well**: The directive should do one thing and should do it well. Again the framework directives are small and serve a specific purpose. Small and well-defined directives are far more easy to consume compared to a directive that provides a diverse range of features, not all useful in every scenario.

- **Directive composition is a powerful concept**: We have seen this already, when we integrated `remote-validator`, `busy-indicator`, `ng-model` and `update-on-blur` together while building remote validation for a workout name. Small and well defined directives can be combined to achieve some great results.

- **Prefer isolated scope when creating a component directive**: To create a true component, we need to use an isolated scope and make dependencies explicit. Anyone integrating a directive can just look at the isolated scope definition and know what parent scope properties/functions are required by the directive.

- **Minimize dependency on a parent scope**: One way to do this is to create an isolated scope. Using a parent scope or inheriting a parent scope in directives can have unintended consequences. Such directives may access and manipulate any parent scope data; hence, creating a dependency that is hard to alter. This also reduces the overall reusability of the directive as we always need to make sure the same model properties are present on the parent scope wherever the directive is utilized, which may not always be possible.

- **Directives with an isolated scope have limitations**: In Angular, two directives cannot create an isolated scope on the same element. Keep this in mind while designing directives with isolated scope.

- **DOM manipulation belongs to a directive**: The only place we should interact with DOM is inside a directive. Our model and controllers should be devoid of any DOM access for read or for write.

It's time now to conclude the chapter and list out our learning in the summary section.

Summary

In this chapter, we covered almost all aspects of directive building. We built all sorts of directives, from the trivial ones to the seemingly more complex ones. We created directives that just extended behavior and ones that came with their own template and behavior.

You learned how the complete directive configuration can be controlled by a *directive definition object*.

When building directives, we explored the *compile* and *link phase* of directive execution. Together with `controller` function, the `compile` and `link` function provide extension points to implement directive behavior.

We also covered two interesting services the `$compile` and `$parse` service. We utilized `$compile` to compile dynamic html fragments and the `$parse` service to evaluate *AngularJS expression*.

You learned how a directive can control scope creation using the `scope` property. We also created directives with *isolated scope* that allow us create really reusable components in AngularJS.

Finally, we looked at some integration techniques to integrate jQuery plugins with AngularJS.

We now have a good understanding of how directives work and how to build our own directives. The next chapter focusses on testing AngularJS code. AngularJS was created with testability in mind and we employ this framework characteristic to build some test suites for our *Personal Trainer* and *Workout Runner* apps.

7
Testing the AngularJS App

Unless you are a superhero who codes, you need to test what you build. Also, unless you have loads of free time to test your application again and again, you need some test automation.

When we say Angular was built with testability in mind, we really mean it. It has a strong **dependency injection (DI)** framework, some good mock constructs, and awesome tools that make testing in an Angular app a fruitful endeavor.

This chapter is all about testing and is dedicated to testing what we have built over the course of this book. We test everything from controllers to filters, services, and our app directives.

The topics we cover in this chapter include:

- **Understanding the big picture**: We will try to understand how testing fits in the overall context of Angular app development. We will also discuss types of testing Angular supports, including unit and **end-to-end (E2E)** testing.

- **Overview of tools and framework**: We cover the tools and frameworks that help in both unit and end-to-end testing with Angular. These include **Karma** and **Protractor**.

- **Writing unit tests**: You will learn how to do unit testing with Angular using Jasmine and Karma inside a browser. We will unit test what we have built in the last few chapters. This section also teaches us how to unit test various Angular constructs, including filters, controllers, services, and directives.

- **Creating end-to-end tests**: Automated end-to-end tests work by mimicking the behavior of the actual user through browser automation. You will learn how to use Protractor combined with WebDriver to perform end-to-end testing.

Let the testing begin.

The need for automation

The size and complexity of apps being built for the Web are growing with each passing day. The plethora of options that we have now to build web apps is just mind-boggling. Add to that the fact the release cycles for products/apps have shrunk drastically from months to days or even multiple releases per day! This puts a lot of burden on software testing. There is too much to be tested. Multiple browsers, multiple clients and screen sizes (desktop and mobile), multiple resolution, and things like that.

To be effective in such a diverse landscape, automation is the key. *Automate everything that can be automated* should be our mantra.

Testing in AngularJS

The Angular team realized the importance of testability and hence created a framework that allowed easy testing (automated) for apps built on it. The design choice of using DI construct to inject dependencies everywhere helped. This will become clear as the chapter progresses and we build a number of tests for our apps. However, before that, let's understand the types of testing that we target when building apps on this platform.

Types of testing

There are broadly two forms of testing that we do for a typical AngularJS app:

- **Unit testing**: Unit testing is all about testing a component in isolation to verify the correctness of its behavior. Most of the dependencies of the component under test need to be replaced with mock implementations to make sure the unit tests do not fail due to failure in a dependent component.

- **End-to-end testing**: This type of testing is all about executing the application like a real end user and verifying the behavior of the application. Unlike unit testing, components are not tested in isolation. Tests are done against a running system in real browsers and assertions are done based on the state of the user interface and the content displayed.

Unit testing is the first line of defense against bugs and we should be able to iron out most of the issues with code while unit testing. But unless E2E is done, we cannot confirm whether the software is working correctly. Only when all the components within a system interact in the desired manner can we confirm that the software works — hence, E2E testing becomes a necessity.

Who writes unit and E2E tests and when are they written are important questions to answer.

Testing who and when

Traditionally, E2E testing was done by the **Quality Assurance (QA)** team and developers were responsible for unit testing their code before submitting. The developers too did some amount of E2E testing but the overall E2E testing process was manual.

With the changing landscape, modern testing tools especially on the web front have allowed developers to write automated E2E tests themselves and execute them against any deployment setup (such as development/stage/production). Tools such as Selenium together with WebDrivers allow easy browser automation, thus making it easy to write and execute E2E tests against real web browsers.

A good time to write E2E scenario tests is when the development is complete and ready to be deployed.

When it comes to unit testing, there are different schools of thought around when a test should be written. *TDDer* writes tests before the functionality is implemented. Others write tests when the implementation is complete to confirm the behavior. Some write while developing the component itself. Choose a style that suits you, keeping in mind that the earlier you write your tests, the better.

> I am not going to give any recommendation, nor am I going to get into an argument over which one is better. Any amount of unit tests is better than nothing.
>
> My personal preference is to use the *middle approach*. With TDD, I feel test creation effort at times is lost as the specification/requirements change. Tests written at the start are prone to constant fixes as the requirement changes.
>
> The problem with writing unit tests at the end is that our target is to create tests that pass according to the current implementation. The tests that are written are retrofitted to test the implementation whereas they should test the specifications.
>
> Adding tests somewhere in the middle works best for me.

Let's now try to understand the tooling and technology landscape available for AngularJS testing.

The AngularJS testing ecosystem

Look at the following diagram to understand the tools and frameworks that are there to support AngularJS testing:

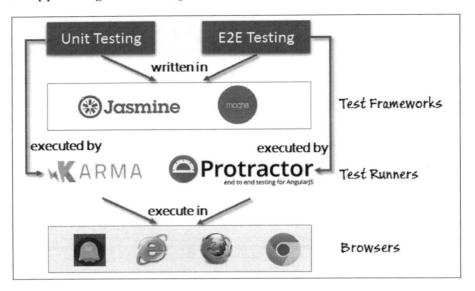

As we can see, we write our tests using unit testing libraries such as Jasmine or Mocha. These tests are either executed by Karma or Protractor, depending upon whether we are writing unit or integration tests. These test runners in turn run these tests in a browser such as Chrome, Firefox, IE, or headless browsers such as PhantomJS. It is important to highlight that not only E2E but unit tests too are executed in a real browser.

 Except for browsers, the complete AngularJS testing setup is supported by the awesome libraries and framework made available through the **Node.js** ecosystem. Some libraries such as Jasmine have standalone versions too but we will stick to Node.js packages.

All the tests in this chapter are written using Jasmine (both unit and integration tests). Karma will be our test runner for unit tests and Protractor for E2E tests.

Getting started with unit testing

The ultimate aim of unit testing is to test a specific piece of code/component in isolation to make sure that components work according to specification. This reduces the chances of failures/bugs in the component when integrated with other parts of the software. Before we start writing tests, there are some guidelines that can help us write good and maintainable tests:

- One unit should test one behavior. For obvious reasons, testing one behavior per unit test makes sense. A failing unit test should clearly highlight the problem area. If multiple behaviors are tested together, a failed test requires more probing to assert what behavior was violated.

- Dependencies in a unit test should be mocked away. Unit testing, as the name suggests, should test the unit and not its dependencies.

- Unit tests should not change the state of the component being tested permanently. If it does, the other tests may get affected.

- The order of execution of unit tests should be immaterial. One unit test should not be dependent on another unit test to execute before it. This is a sign of a brittle unit test. It may also mean that the dependencies are not mocked.

- Unit tests should be fast. If unit tests are not fast enough, developers will not run them. This is a good reason to mock all dependencies such as database access, remote web service call, and others in a unit tests.

- Unit tests should try to cover all code paths. Code coverage is a metric that can help us assess the effectiveness of unit tests. If we have covered all positive and negative scenarios during testing, the coverage will indeed be higher. A word of caution here: with code coverage, high code coverage does not imply code is bug-free, but a low coverage clearly highlights lack of areas covered in unit tests.

- Unit tests should test positive and negative scenarios. Just don't concentrate on positive test cases; all software can fail and hence unit testing failure scenarios are as important to test as success scenarios.

These guidelines are not framework-specific but give us enough ammunition for writing good tests. Let's begin the process of unit testing by setting up the required components for unit testing.

Setting up Karma for unit testing

Since the complete test automation infrastructure is supported using Node, this needs to be installed first. Follow the instructions on the Node website (`https://nodejs.org`) and get Node installed locally.

Node comes with a package manager **Node Package Manager** (**NPM**) that is used to install all other components (**packages** in the Node world) required for testing.

Start by installing Karma from the command line. Navigate to the root of your application codebase (in the same folder where the app folder is located) and install Karma using this command:

```
npm install karma --save-dev
```

To use Karma from the command line, we need to install its command-line interface:

```
npm install -g karma-cli
```

> The Karma version against which the code was tested is 0.12.31. The `karma-cli` version was 0.0.4.
>
> To install a specific version of a package, suffix the package name with `@` version, for example, `npm install karma@0.12.31 --save-dev`.

This completes Karma installation and it's time to configure the test runner. Configuring Karma is all about setting up its configuration file that contains enough details for it to run our scripts and test them. Create a `tests` folder in the root (next to the `app` folder), navigate to it, and start the Karma configuration setup with the following command:

```
karma init
```

This starts a command-line wizard that guides us through the options available, including the test framework, folders to watch, and other such settings. Once the wizard is complete, it generates a `karma.config.js` file. Instead of using the generated configuration file, copy the `karma.config.js` file from the companion codebase at `chapter7/checkpoint1/tests` to your local `tests` folder.

> The `karma init` wizard installs some packages based on our selection. If we skip the wizard, the packages `karma-chrome-launcher` and `karma-jasmine` need to be installed manually for unit testing.

The Karma test runner by default uses Jasmine 1.3.x as the testing framework. We need to update it to v2.0, as we are going to use some features from v2.0. To update the Jasmine version used by Karma, update this package:

```
npm install karma-jasmine@2_0 --save-dev
```

The Karma configuration files contain settings that affect the tests we run. We will not be covering each and every configuration supported by Karma here, but will focus on configurations that are unique and/or required for our test setup. Refer to the Karma documentation (`http://karma-runner.github.io/0.8/config/configuration-file.html`) to understand more about the various Karma configuration options.

One of the Karma configurations is the `files` array that references the files that Karma will load in the browser for testing. This list contains a path to our application script files (code that we have been building throughout the earlier chapters), as well as a path to the test scripts we will create.

To unit test our app, the plan is to create one test (such as `directives.spec.js`) file for each JavaScript file that we have in our project. This test file will contain the unit test specification for the corresponding JavaScript component, as shown in the following screenshot:

Karma test runner will load these test scripts together with the standard app scripts. The `files` array configuration also contains a reference to the `bower_components` folder for all script files that were referenced through CDN, such as `app/bower_components/angular/angular.js`.

To unit test our app implementation, Karma needs to load all script files referenced/ used by the app. It can load these scripts from local filesystem, or we can specify remote URLs. However, referencing remote scripts in a unit test is never a good idea. It just slows the overall process of unit testing as the remote scripts are downloaded every time a test is run. We need to have a local copy of all the referenced libraries for our tests. We use Bower for that.

Managing script dependencies with Bower

Since we are using the Node infrastructure, we do have a package (dependency) manager for web apps: **Bower**. Instead of downloading every CDN dependency manually and copying it to our app folder, we use Bower.

Install Bower from the command line using this:

```
npm install -g bower
```

> Bower prerequisites are Node and Git. Git is a distributed source control system for managing code. Check the site, `http://git-scm.com/` for instructions on how to install and configure Git for local usage.

Copy the `bower.json` and `.bowerrc` files from `chapter7/checkpoint1` into the parent of your `app` folder. The `bower.json` file references all the CDN dependencies used by our app. To actually download these dependencies, use the following command:

```
bower update
```

Bower will download all the dependencies and add them to the `bower_components` folder inside the `app` folder. The download location (`bower_components`) has been configured in the `.bowerrc` file.

> The app folder is the root of our application. Some servers do not allow referencing files outside the root folder and hence the Bower components (third-party scripts) should be installed inside the app folder.

With Karma installed and remote script files included using Bower, it is time to start writing some unit tests. Before we start, just make sure that the overall folder hierarchy setup looks something like this:

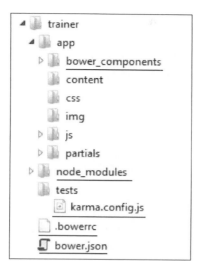

We are now all set to write unit tests for our apps.

Unit testing AngularJS components

Over the course of this book, we have built components that cover every construct available in Angular. We have built controllers, a filter, a few services, and finally some directives too. All of these are testable components that we will test.

Just to get the hang of unit testing with Jasmine, let's test the smallest and easiest component first: the filters.

Unit testing filters

Filters are easiest to test as they have minimum or zero dependencies on other constructs. The secondsToTime filter that we created for *Workout Runner* (the *7 Minute Workout* app) has no dependency and can be easily unit tested.

Look at the Jasmine framework documentation to understand how to write unit tests using Jasmine. We use Jasmine 2.0 for our unit tests (`http://jasmine.github.io/2.0/introduction.html`). Jasmine has one of the best documentations available and the overall framework is very intuitive to use. I strongly recommend you head over to the Jasmine site and get yourself familiar with the framework before you proceed.

Add a `filters.spec.js` file to the `7minworkout` folder under `js` and add this setup code and unit test to it:

```
describe("Filters", function () {
    beforeEach(module('7minWorkout'));
    describe("secondsToTime filter", function () {
        it('should convert integer to time format',
        inject(function ($filter) {
            expect($filter("secondsToTime")(5)).toBe("00:00:05");
            expect($filter("secondsToTime")(65)).toBe("00:01:05");
    expect($filter("secondsToTime")(3610))
    .toBe("01:00:10");
        }));
    });
});
```

This is a simple unit test that verified whether the input integer values are correctly converted into the hh:mm:ss format using the Jasmine assert statement, `expect`.

To run this test, start Karma from the command line with the following command:

```
karma start tests/karma.config.js
```

Make sure the path to the `karma.config.js` file is correct. If Karma is set up correctly, this should start the test runner and automatically open one or more browser windows to execute the tests. Karma then executes the test and logs the results in the console. The preceding filter test should pass and the logs should confirm this:

```
INFO [watcher]: Changed file "F:/bookcode/trainer/app/js/7MinWorkout/filters.spec.js".
Chrome 38.0.2125 (Windows 8.1): Executed 1 of 1 SUCCESS (0.021 secs / 0.011 secs)
```

While this unit test is simple, we need to understand how it has been set up in the context of Angular. Other than the vocabulary that is part of the Jasmine framework (beforeEach, it, and expect), there are two new keywords used in this test: **module** and **inject**.

- Module: This is an Angular library function exposed on the global level that allows us to create or load a module for unit tests. Since we are testing the secondsToTime filter defined in the 7minWorkout module, we load this module using the module function in beforeEach.

 As the name implies, the beforeEach function is called once before each test in the describe block is run.

- Inject: This complements module and is used to inject dependencies into a unit test. Since no views are involved in unit testing, the standard app bootstrapping process that allows module initialization and automatic dependency injection does not take place. We always need to use the inject function to inject dependencies.

  In the preceding implementation, we inject the $filter service into the it block, which in turn loads the secondsToTime filter for testing.

 Module registration should happen before any inject call takes place. If Karma console throws this error:

```
Error: Injector already created, can not register a
module!
```

It simply means the module function was invoked after an inject call.

The module and inject functions are actually part of the ngMock module that is exclusively there to support unit testing. Let's try to understand what services this module provides to help us with unit testing.

Unit testing using the ngMock module

The ngMock module has been created specifically to support unit testing and it provides strong mocking capabilities. But what exactly is a **mock** or what is this process of mocking?

The general idea of mocking is to create a dummy implementation for a real service/component that can be substituted for original service during unit testing components that depend upon the original service/component. The reason behind creating mocks or mocking dependencies is to make sure that the component under the test does not fail due to the failure of any dependent component.

> The complexity of mock implementation varies and depending upon this complexity, a mock implementation may also be referred to as *dummy*, *fake*, or *stub*. The article by Martin Fowler at http://martinfowler.com/articles/mocksArentStubs.html is a great read if you are interested in exploring the differences between the mock types.

As described earlier, the `module` function allows us to load as well as create our own modules on the fly. It also allows us to override any service implementation in any module with our own custom (mock) implementation.

> The ngMock module is not part of the standard framework and hence needs to be included when we perform unit testing. Look at the `karma.config.js` files property; you will see that the `angular-mock.js` file has been included as a Bower package.

Interestingly, the ngMock module itself comes with mock implementations for some of the standard AngularJS services such as `$interval`, `$timeout`, `$httpBackend`, and others.

> This implies that if our implementation uses any of these services, then a mock implementation of the service is injected during unit testing. How it helps us during unit testing will be clear as we write more tests.

After testing the easiest part, let's unit test a component that is difficult to test: the controller.

Unit testing controllers

Controllers in Angular integrate the view with everything else. Due to this, controllers normally have more dependencies as compared to any of the services, filters, or directives. Since unit testing is all about setting up the dependencies and then performing the actual tests, there is a decent amount of effort required to set up dependencies for controllers. We skipped the dependency setup for filter testing as it did not have external dependencies.

The controller that we plan to test in this section is `WorkoutController`. Located inside `js/7MinWorkout/workout.js`, this is the controller that runs a specific workout. Before we can actually test the controller implementation, its dependencies need to be set up.

Setting up controller dependencies

`WorkoutController` has a total of eight dependencies:

```
'$scope', '$interval', '$location', 'workoutHistoryTracker',
  'appEvents', 'WorkoutService', '$routeParams', 'Exercise'
```

Therefore, we need to manage these eight dependencies to test `WorkoutController`. Add the `workout.spec.js` file to the `7minworkout` folder under `js` and now let's first set up these dependencies. Add the following code to `workout.spec.js` (you have an option to copy it from the `workout.spec.js` file under `checkpoint1/app/js/7minworkout/` too):

```
describe("Controllers", function () {
    beforeEach(module('app'));

    describe("WorkoutController", function () {
        var ctrl, $scope;
        beforeEach(inject(function ($rootScope, $controller, $interval,
    $location, workoutHistoryTracker, WorkoutService, appEvents, Exercise)
    {
            $scope = $rootScope.$new();
            $scope.carousel = {
                next: function () {}
            };
            ctrl = $controller('WorkoutController', {
                $scope: $scope,
                $interval: $interval,
                $location: $location,
                workoutHistoryTracker: workoutHistoryTracker,
                appEvents: appEvents,
                WorkoutService: WorkoutService,
                $routeParams: { id: "DummyWorkout" },
                Exercise: Exercise
            });
        }));
    });
});
```

As we can see, there is good amount of initial setup required here, but this setup is still incomplete. To know what is pending, we need to understand what has been set up in the preceding code.

The test setup has been organized into a nested `describe` block as Jasmine allows us to group multiple tests/specifications using such nested blocks. Things common to every block can be hosted in the parent block.

In the preceding test, the parent `describe` block (`Controllers`) sets up the module `app` that is required for all of the tests. The `app` module initialization code, `beforeEach(module('app'));`, automatically initializes all dependent modules and hence does not require us to load dependent modules explicitly.

The nested `describe` block (`WorkoutController`) is dedicated exclusively to test `WorkoutController`. The first `beforeEach` function inside this block is there to set up the controller dependencies.

The `beforeEach` method takes the `inject` function that is used to inject a number of dependencies required to instantiate a controller. The first thing that the function does is to set up a new scope required for the controller by calling `$rootScope.$new`. This creates a new child scope. We keep the reference of this scope (in `$scope`) as we require it later.

Since `WorkoutController` uses the `next` function of the carousel directive controller, we mock the controller and the function. We do not use `inject` here as the carousel controller is injected as part of directive execution and not through DI. This is our first mock implementation.

The next step creates the `WorkoutController` instance. We use `$controller` to create a controller object during unit testing. The `$controller` service accepts the controller name and the required dependencies.

Most of the dependencies used in controller creation have been injected using the `inject` function earlier. While we can use some of these dependencies in their original form, we need to mock away some of them. Let's evaluate each of these dependencies to understand what to mock:

- `$scope`: This will be created and injected manually, so in a way we are already mocking it.
- `$interval`: This service needs mocking, and the ngMock module provides one by default. Hence, we don't have to worry.
- `$location`: This can be mocked but let's ignore it for the time being.
- `WorkoutHistoryTracker`: This has some behavior attached, hence we should mock it.

- **appEvents**: This is a plain JavaScript object that we can use as it is.

- **WorkoutService**: This definitely needs mocking, and it loads workout data required by **WorkoutController**.

- **$routeParams**: This already has a mock implementation (**$routeParams: { id: "DummyWorkout" }**).

- **Exercise**: This is a model service that we can use as it is.

As it turns out, we just need to mock two services: **WorkoutHistoryTracker** and **WorkoutService**. How? The answer is, using the **module** function.

Add the **beforeEach** block containing the mock implementation for **WorkoutHistoryTracker** inside the **describe** block for **WorkoutController**, after the variable declaration:

```
beforeEach(function () {
  module(function ($provide) {
    $provide.value("workoutHistoryTracker", {
      startTracking: function () {}, endTracking: function () {}
    });
  });
});
```

Since the mock **WorkoutService** definition is lengthy, copy the complete definition from the **workout.spec.js** file under **chapter7/checkpoint1**, and add it after the preceding **beforeEach** block. The following code outlines the mock implementation:

```
beforeEach(module(function ($provide) {
  $provide.factory("WorkoutService", function ($q, WorkoutPlan,
  ... Exercise) {
    var mock = {};
    mock.sampleWorkout = new WorkoutPlan({
        name: "testworkout",
        title: "Test Workout",
        description: "This is a test workout",
        restBetweenExercise: "40",
        exercises: [ dummy exercise data]
    });
    mock.getWorkout = function (name) {
        return $q.when(mock.sampleWorkout);
    }
    mock.totalWorkoutDuration = 180;
    return mock;
  });
}));
```

The preceding mock implementations are created using the Angular `$provide` service.

The `$provide` service allows us to define services with the familiar service creation syntax that we have already seen in the Module API (such as `module.factory` and `module.service`). The `$provide` service supports all the service creation recipes, including `constant`, `value`, `service`, `factory`, and `provider`.

As we can see, by registering the mock service implementation with the same name as the original services, we allow `$provide` to override/hide the original implementation from the two services.

The `WorkoutHistoryTracker` service mock is registered using the `value` recipe and the implementation has only two empty methods: `startTracking` and `endTracking`. Note that we have only mocked implementation for functions that we use in `WorkoutController` and not the complete service. Whenever the `inject` function asks for `WorkoutHistoryTracker`, this dummy implementation is returned.

The mock implementation for `WorkoutService` is simple too. The only function that needs to be mocked is `getWorkout`, which returns a predefined workout. The `$q.when` function helps us to return the workout data as a promise.

> `$q.when` is a very handy function, which returns a promise. The returned promise is resolved with the input value passed to `$q.when`. This is a very handy function that allows us to create promises that always resolve to a fixed value. Look at the `$q` documentation at `https://docs.angularjs.org/api/ng/service/$q` to know more about how `when` works.

The `WorkoutService` mock is implemented using the `factory` recipe and other than the `getWorkout`, has some other properties such as `totalWorkoutDuration` and `sampleWorkout` that will come handy during unit testing.

The `$provide` service provides a convenient mechanism to create mock and override dependencies. To know more about the `$provide` service, refer to the API documentation at `https://code.angularjs.org/1.3.3/docs/api/auto/object/$provide`.

Now that we have addressed all the `WorkoutController` dependencies, we can actually begin unit testing it.

Unit testing WorkoutController

Starting from the loading of workout data to transitioning of exercises, pausing workouts, and running exercise videos, there are number of aspects of `WorkoutController` that we can test. The `workout.spec.js` file available in `chapter7/checkpoint1/js/7MinWorkout` contains a number of unit tests that cover the preceding scenarios. We will pick up some of those tests and work through them.

To start with, let's add a test case that verifies that the workout starts running once the controller is loaded:

```
it("should start the workout", inject(function (WorkoutService) {
expect($scope.workoutPlan)
    .toEqual(WorkoutService.sampleWorkout);
    expect($scope.workoutTimeRemaining)
    .toEqual(WorkoutService.totalWorkoutDuration);
expect($scope.workoutPaused).toBeFalsy();
}));
```

This test asserts that if the correct workout plan is loaded in the scope, the total duration of the workout is correct, and the workout is in the running state. Note how we use the mock properties: `sampleWorkout` and `totalWorkoutDuration` of `WorkoutService` to test the expectations.

Assuming that the `autoWatch` property of `karma.config.js` is true, saving this test automatically triggers the test execution. But this test fails (check the Karma console). Strange! All dependencies have been set up correctly but still the `expect` function of the first `it` block fails as `$scope.workoutPlan` is undefined.

We need to debug this test.

Debugging unit tests in Karma

Debugging unit tests in Karma is easy as the tests are run in the browser. We debug tests as we debug the standard JavaScript code.

When Karma starts, it opens the specific browser window to run the tests. To debug any test in Karma, we just need to click on the **Debug** button available on the top navigation in the browser window.

There is one window opened by Karma and one when we click on **Debug**; we can use the original window too for testing but the original window is connected to Karma and does live reload. Also, the script files in the original window are time-stamped, which changes any time we update the test, and hence requires us to put in a breakpoint again to test.

Once we click on **Debug,** a new tab/window opens that has all the tests and other app scripts loaded for testing. These are scripts that were defined during Karma configuration setup in the `karma.config.js files` section.

To debug the preceding failure, we need to add breakpoints at two locations. One should be added inside the test itself, and the second one inside `WorkoutController` where it loads the workout and assigns the data to appropriate scope variables.

Perform the following steps to add a breakpoint in Google Chrome:

1. Open the Karma debug window/tab by clicking on the **Debug** button on the window loaded by Karma when it started.

2. Press the *F12* key to open the developer console.

3. Go to the **Source** tab and the files will be located in the **app** folder.

4. We can now put breakpoints at the required locations just by clicking on the line number. This is the standard mechanism to debug any script. Add breakpoints at the locations highlighted here:

```
▼ base
  ▼ app
    ► bower_components
    ▼ js
      ▼ 7MinWorkout
        Other files...
        workout.js
        workout.spec.js
```

```
59    it("should load the workoutController", function () {
60        expect(ctrl).toBeDefined();
61    });                          workout.spec.js
62
63    iit("should start the workout", inject(function (Workou
64        expect($scope.workoutPlan).toEqual(WorkoutService.s
65        expect($scope.workoutTimeRemaining).toEqual(Workout
66        expect($scope.workoutPaused).toBeFalsy();
67    }));
68
69    it("should start the first exercise", inject(function (
70        expect($scope.currentExercise).toEqual(WorkoutServi
```

```
    directives.js
    filters.js
    filters.spec.js
    services.js
    services.spec.js
```

```
9     var startWorkout = function () { workout.js
10        WorkoutService
11          .getWorkout($routeParams.id)
12          .then(function (workout) {
13              $scope.workoutPlan = workout;
14              $scope.workoutTimeRemaining = $scope.workoutP
15              restExercise = {
```

Refresh the **Debug** page (the one we opened when we clicked on the **Debug** button). The breakpoint in workout.js is never hit, causing the test to fail.

The reason for the failure is easy to guess. Workout data is attached to the scope only after the promise callback from getWorkout is resolved, an asynchronous process. By that time, the test execution is complete.

To fix this issue, we need to execute the AngularJS digest cycle explicitly before doing any assertions (expect). We can do this by calling either $scope.$digest() or the $scope.$apply() function. Add the $scope.$digest(); statement to the beforeEach block containing the controller declaration at the end. By adding $scope.$digest in beforeEach, we make sure the digest cycle is invoked after WorkoutController is created and before the test starts.

If you are working with asynchronous code, remember to call $scope.$digest or $scope.$apply() before any expect statement.

The new test should pass now.

As the number of tests grows, unit testing may require us to concentrate on a specific test or a specific suite of tests. Karma allows us to target one or more tests by prepending i to existing it block, that is, it become iit. If Karma finds tests with iit, it only executes those tests. Similarly, a specific test suite can be targeted by prepending d to the existing describe block, ddescribe.

Another handy tip that can help us with debugging is the $log service (https://code.angularjs.org/1.3.3/docs/api/ng/service/$log) or the console.log function. Any datum logged using these two functions shows up in the Karma console.

Let's continue unit testing the controller!

Unit testing WorkoutController continued...

What other interesting thing can we test? We can test whether the first exercise started. Add this test to workout.spec.js after the one we just added:

```
it("should start the first exercise", inject(function
    (WorkoutService, appEvents) {
expect($scope.currentExercise)
.toEqual(WorkoutService.sampleWorkout.exercises[0]);
expect($scope.currentExerciseIndex).toEqual(0);
            expect($scope.$emit).toHaveBeenCalledWith(
            appEvents.workout.exerciseStarted,
            WorkoutService.sampleWorkout.exercises[0].details);
}));
```

The last `expect` function in this test is interesting. It uses a Jasmine feature: **spies**. Spies are there to help us verify dependency invocations.

Using Jasmine spies to verify dependencies

We mock a dependency to make sure that the dependency does not adversely affect the component under test. But from a unit testing perspective, we still need to make sure these dependencies are called by the component being tested at the right time with the correct input. In the Jasmine world, spies help us assert whether dependencies were invoked.

A spy is an object that intercepts every call to the function it is spying on. Once the call is intercepted, it can either return fixed data or pass the call to the actual function being invoked. It also records the call invocation details that can be used later in `expect` as we did in the preceding test.

 Spies are very powerful and can be used in a number of ways during unit testing. Look at the documentation on spies at `http://jasmine.github.io/2.0/introduction.html#section-Spies` to learn more about them.

If we look at the `WorkoutController` implementation, we emit a message with the details of the workout whenever the workout starts. `WorkoutHistoryTracker` subscribes to this message/event. The last `expect` function verifies that the `$scope.$emit` function was called when the workout started (`toHaveBeenCalledWith`). It is also asserting the correctness of the parameters passed to the `$emit` function.

 Look at the Jasmine documentation for functions: `toHaveBeenCalled` and `toHaveBeenCalledWith`, to learn more about these assert functions.

The last `expect` statement asserts the behavior on the spy, but we first need to set up the spy to make this assert work. Before the `$scope.$digest();` statement, add the following line to the `beforeEach` block that has the controller creation code:

```
spyOn($scope, "$emit");
```

The `spyOn` function sets up the functions that Jasmine will spy on. It takes the object to target and the function to spy on as the first and second argument, respectively. With the preceding statement, every time we call `$scope.$emit`, the spy intercepts the call and records it. Run the test and it should pass.

On similar lines, we can create spy and confirm that `WorkoutHistoryTracker` started when the workout started. Add this spy after the preceding spy declaration:

```
spyOn(workoutHistoryTracker, 'startTracking');
```

Then, add the following test:

```
it("should start history tracking", inject(function
  (workoutHistoryTracker) {
  expect(workoutHistoryTracker.startTracking)
  .toHaveBeenCalled();
}));
```

Simple and expressive!

One of the interesting challenges for us is to verify that the workout progresses as the time elapses. The `WorkoutController` object uses the `$interval` service to move things forward with time. How can we simulate time without actually waiting?

We do have a mock `$interval` service.

Testing the $interval and $timeout implementations

Unit testing code that uses `$interval` or `$timeout` is difficult. This is due to the asynchronous nature of the code and the actual time delay that is required. The Angular team realized this and created mocks for both `$timeout` and `$interval`. If we inject the `ngMock` module, then the original `$timeout` and `$interval` services are replaced by the mock ones.

How do these mocks differ from the original `$timeout` and `$interval` services? These mocks do not automatically move forward as the time elapses. We can control the progress. How? The answer is to use the `$interval flush` function. Here is how we use it:

```
$interval.flush(5000);   // flushes 5 second
```

Therefore, the following code outputs with intervals firing five times:

```
$interval(function () { console.log("interval fired");}, 2000);
$interval.flush(10000); // flushes 10 second
```

`$interval.flush` takes a single argument: the amount of time to flush (in milliseconds).

 Remember that all interval callbacks attached to the `$interval` service will be fired when the time is flushed.

Let's see how we can test the `WorkoutController` implementation that uses `$interval`. We are testing the following exercise progress code:

```
var startExerciseTimeTracking = function () {
var promise = $interval(function () {
    ++$scope.currentExerciseDuration;
    --$scope.workoutTimeRemaining;}, 1000,
$scope.currentExercise.duration - $scope.currentExerciseDuration);
```

Add this test to the exiting `WorkoutController` test suite:

```
it("should increase current exercise duration with time",
   inject(function ($interval) {
expect($scope.currentExerciseDuration).toBe(0);
    $interval.flush(1000);
    expect($scope.currentExerciseDuration).toBe(1);
    $interval.flush(1000);
    expect($scope.currentExerciseDuration).toBe(2);
    $interval.flush(8000);
    expect($scope.currentExerciseDuration).toBe(10);
}));
```

The magic is done by the **flush** function. The preceding test flushes 1 second twice and then flushes 8 seconds. Multiple `expect` verify that the `currentExerciseDuration` counter moves as the `$interval` callbacks are fired.

 `$timeout` too uses the same mechanism for moving time forward. Use `flush` to unit test functionalities related to `$timeout` too.

On similar lines, we can check everything that is moving with time. In the case of `WorkoutController`, virtually everything is time-bound.

Let's now check whether exercise transitioning is happening.

Add another test, as follows:

```
it("should transition to next exercise on one exercise complete",
inject(function (WorkoutService, $interval) {
  $interval.
    flush(WorkoutService.sampleWorkout.exercises[0].duration
    * 1000);
expect($scope.currentExercise.details.name).toBe('rest');
  expect($scope.currentExercise.duration).
    toBe(WorkoutService.sampleWorkout.restBetweenExercise);
}));
```

This time, we flush time duration equal to the total exercise duration in the first line. Since the next exercise is a rest exercise, we check it by its name and also check whether the rest duration is consistent with the one defined at the workout level.

Now that we understand how to test implementations related to `$interval/$timeout`, let's check the pause and resume workout functionality.

Testing workout pause/resume

When we pause a workout, it should stop/cancel the running `$interval` service and the time counter should not lapse. To check this, add the following time test:

```
it("should not update workoutTimeRemaining for paused workout on
interval lapse", inject(function (WorkoutService, $interval) {
  expect($scope.workoutPaused).toBeFalsy();
  $interval.flush(1000);
  expect($scope.workoutTimeRemaining).
  toBe(WorkoutService.totalWorkoutDuration - 1);
  $scope.pauseWorkout();
  expect($scope.workoutPaused).toBe(true);
  $interval.flush(5000);
  expect($scope.workoutTimeRemaining).
    toBe(WorkoutService.totalWorkoutDuration - 1);
}));
```

The test starts with verifying the state of the workout, then pauses it, and again tries to flush a time to verify that the time of `workoutTimeRemaining` does not change after pause.

The `workout.spec.js` file in `chapter7/checkpoint1` has a number of tests other than the ones that we have covered so far. It is a good time to look at those test cases. For now, we plan to move to the next section of this chapter that is dedicated to testing services.

Unit testing services

Unit testing services is not much different from unit testing controllers. Once we get the hang of how to set up a component and its dependencies (mostly using mocks), it becomes a routine affair to test any Angular component. More often than not, the challenge is to set up the dependencies for the component so that testing can be done effectively.

Things are a little different for services that make remote requests (using either `$http` or `$resource`). There is some amount of setup required before we can test such services in isolation.

We will target `WorkoutService` and write some unit tests for it. Since this service makes remote requests to load workout data, we will explore how to test such a service with a mock HTTP backend.

AngularJS has a service for that: `$httpBackend`, which is again part of the `ngMock` module. Let's see how `$httpBackend` works.

Mocking HTTP request/response with $httpBackend

When testing services (or as a matter of fact any other Angular construct) that make remote requests, we obviously do not want to make actual requests to a backend to check the behavior. That does not even qualify for a unit test. The backend interaction just needs to be mocked away. Angular provides a service for precisely that: the `$httpBackend` service!

> There is a standard `$httpBackend` service in the core module that is used by the `$http` and `$resource` services. The `$httpBackend` service in the `ngMock` module is specifically targeted towards unit testing.

Using `$httpBackend`, we intercept HTTP requests, mock actual responses from the server, and assert endpoints invocation too. In fact, the framework throws an error if a unit test tries to connect to a remote location, for example:

Error: Unexpected request: GET https://api.mongolab.com/api/1/databases/testdb/ collections/workouts?apiKey=testK

> The bottom line is that remote requests of any kind during unit testing are forbidden.

The `$httpBackend` service has two sets of methods to mock the backend:

- **Functions for Request Expectations**: These methods start with the word `expect`, for example, `expect`, `expectGET`, `expectPOST`, `expectHEAD`, `expectDELETE`, `expectPUT`, and `expectPATCH`. The salient feature of these functions is that these methods not only set up a mock backend, but also set up assertions that fail if the request is not performed according to the setup specified in mock. For example, look at this test:

```
it("it should get google home",function() {
  $httpBackend.expectGET("http://www.google.com")
  service.getData();
  $httpBackend.flush();
});
```

The test fails if `getData` does not make a request to www.google.com. We do not need to set up any Jasmine spy or explicitly assert using `expect`. Such a setup is useful if we want to assert whether an HTTP request was actually made.

- **Functions for backend definitions**: These methods start with the word `when`, for example, when, whenGET, whenPOST, whenHEAD, whenDELETE, whenPUT, and whenPATCH. Their primary aim is to provide a mock backend that responds with data when a request is made. These functions do not assert whether invocation actually happened or not. This setup helps when we want to just mock remote calls, but are not interested in whether a call was made or not.

To provide a mock return value for an HTTP invocation, we need to call the `respond` function on the object returned by the `expect*` or `when*` function, such as:

```
$httpBackend.whenGET("http://api.endpoint.com").respond(200,
    {data:'data'});
```

Since HTTP requests are asynchronous, `$httpBackend` too has a `flush` function similar to `$interval`/`$timeout`. This function needs to be called explicitly to complete the request.

Let's add some tests for `WorkoutService`.

Testing WorkoutService

The original `WorkoutService` implementation requires some initial setup (during the configuration stage) before it can be used. This includes setting up the MongoLab database name and the API key. Hence, the same setup needs to be done for the unit test `WorkoutService`. This can be done with the `module` function.

Start by creating a `services.spec.js` file in the `shared` folder under `js` and add the following setup code:

```
describe("Shared Services", function () {
    beforeEach(module('app'));
    describe("Workout Service", function () {
        var WorkoutService, $httpBackend,
        collectionUrl = "https://api.mongolab.com/api/1/
          databases/testdb/collections",
        apiKey = "testKey";
        beforeEach(module(function (WorkoutServiceProvider,
        ApiKeyAppenderInterceptorProvider) {
            WorkoutServiceProvider.configure("testdb");
            ApiKeyAppenderInterceptorProvider.setApiKey("testKey")
```

```
      }));

  beforeEach(inject(function (_WorkoutService_, _$httpBackend_) {
    WorkoutService = _WorkoutService_;
    $httpBackend = _$httpBackend_;
  }));
  });
});
```

Two `beforeEach` blocks have been set up inside the `describe` block of `Workout Service`. The first block sets up `WorkoutService` and `ApiKeyAppenderInterceptor` using the `module` function. We configure the database name and a dummy API key for the interceptor. The `module` function call is different this time; we are passing in a function instead of passing in a module name to load. We are passing in an anonymous module initialization function. The function gets called during the configuration stage of app bootstrapping (evident from the providers passed to it) and sets up the necessary dependencies.

The second block also has something interesting: the prefix and suffix _ character in the `inject` function. They still represent the same `WorkoutService` and `$httpBackend` dependencies. Angular strips the _ character before searching for the actual dependency and injects the correct one. This syntax of dependency injection is useful when we want to use the same variable names as the dependency names, such as `WorkoutService` and `$httpBackend` that we declare at the top of the describe block.

With this setup, we are ready to write our first test. Add this code to the `services.spec.js` file after the `beforeEach` block:

```
it("should request all workouts endpoints", function () {
    $httpBackend.expectGET(collectionUrl + "/workouts?apiKey=" +
      "testKey").respond([]);
    WorkoutService.getWorkouts();
    $httpBackend.flush();
});
```

This is a simple test to make sure that the correct endpoint is hit when `getWorkouts` is invoked. There is no `expect` function defined in the test as `expectGET` automatically asserts if the correct endpoint is hit or not. The final `flush()` function call actually simulates the request.

Next, let's write a test for the service function `getWorkout` that loads workouts with a specific name. We plan to check whether the data is being returned correctly and mapped to the correct `WorkoutPlan` model. Add the following test:

```
it("should return a workout plan with specific name", inject(function
(WorkoutPlan, $q) {
    spyOn(WorkoutService.Exercises, "query").and.returnValue({
        $promise: $q.when([{ name: "exercise1",title: "exercise 1"
}])
    });
    $httpBackend.expectGET(collectionUrl +
        "/workouts/testplan?apiKey=" + "testKey")
    .respond({
        name: "Workout1", title: "Workout 1",
        restBetweenExercise: 30
        });
    var result = null;
    WorkoutService.getWorkout("testplan")
        .then(function (workout) { result = workout;});

    $httpBackend.flush();
    expect(result.name).toBe("Workout1");
    expect(result instanceof WorkoutPlan).toBe(true);
    expect(WorkoutService.Exercises.query).toHaveBeenCalled();
}));
```

The first thing that we do in this is to set up a spy that spies on the `resource query` function of `Exercises`. The spy is set up to return a promise with some exercise data. This setup is required, as the service `getWorkout` function uses the `Exercises` resource (the `$resource` class) to load all exercises for the mapping purpose.

Then, it is all about setting up the expectation for a query and responding with some dummy data. But this time, we store the result of the execution in the `result` variable. Before we can assert on result data, we first need to simulate a call by calling `flush`. The `flush` function simulates the HTTP call, triggers the promise success callback, and `result` has some value. The statements after that are just asserting on the data returned by the service call.

One last thing that we should add when testing services that use `$http` or `$resource` service is the following code block:

```
afterEach(function () {
  $httpBackend.verifyNoOutstandingExpectation();
    $httpBackend.verifyNoOutstandingRequest();
});
```

Add this to the test suite for `WorkoutService`. These statements will make sure that there are no outstanding expectations and all requests have been made. Since invoking a mock HTTP request requires a call to `flush`, these statements act as a safeguard against the scenario where we may forget to call `flush` after making an HTTP request using either `$http` or `$resource`.

With this, we have covered testing services. There are many more tests available in `chapter7/checkpoint1/app/js/shared/services.spec.js` that we can check to understand how other scenarios were tested.

Next we need to learn how to test directives. The next section is dedicated to understanding the challenges in directive testing and how to overcome them.

Unit testing directives

All other Angular constructs that we have tested so far do not involve any UI interaction. But directives—as we know—are a different beast. Directives are all about linking the view with models/controllers and extending the behavior of HTML elements. While testing directives, we cannot ignore the UI connections and hence directive testing may not strictly qualify as unit testing.

The good thing about directive testing is that its setup process is not as elaborate as services or controllers. The pattern to follow while unit testing directives is as follows:

1. Take an HTML fragment with the directive markup.
2. Compile and link it to a specific scope.
3. Verify that the generated HTML has the required attributes. This can be done using jQlite or jQuery library functions.
4. If the directive creates scope and/or changes the state of the scope, verify the changes.

In this section, we are going to test `remote-validator`, a combination of `remote-validator`, `busy-indicator`, and `workout-tile`, which seems to be the simplest directive but requires good amount of setup to test.

This will be a good time to revisit the directives that we built in the previous chapter. Also, keep the code handy for the tests we will create in the following sections.

Let's get started and add the `directives.spec.js` file to the `shared` folder under `app/js` where most of our directives are. Then, add this test setup code:

```
describe("Directives", function () {
    var $compile, $rootScope, $scope;
    beforeEach(module('app'));

    beforeEach(inject(function (_$compile_, _$rootScope_) {
        $compile = _$compile_;
        $rootScope = _$rootScope_;
        $scope = $rootScope.$new();
    }));
});
```

We just declared global services: `$compile`, `$scope`, and `$rootScope`, and set them up in `beforeEach` for our tests to follow.

Testing remote-validator

Let's start with unit testing `remote-validator`. Just to refresh our memory, `remote-validator` validates an input against remote rules. It does so by calling a function on the scope that returns a promise. If the promise is resolved with success, validation passes; otherwise, validation fails. The `scope` function invoked is linked to the directive through the `remote-validator-function` directive attribute.

Add the following code inside the `describe` block of `Directives` after the second `beforeEach` block:

```
describe("remote validator", function () {
var inputElement;
beforeEach(inject(function () {
  $scope.validate = function (value) {};
    inputElement = "<form name='testForm'><input type='text'
      name='unique' ng-model='name' remote-validator='unique'
      remote-validator-function='validate(value)' /></form>";
  }));

it("should verify unique value when use input changes",
  inject(function ($q) {
    spyOn($scope, "validate").and.returnValue($q.when(true));
```

```
        $compile(inputElement)($scope);
        $scope.testForm.unique.$setViewValue("dummy");
        expect($scope.validate).toHaveBeenCalled();
    }));
  });
});
```

The `remote-validator` test suite (the `describe` block) first sets up the scope with a dummy validation function (`validate`) and the input markup that contains the directive declaration, as highlighted in the preceding code. The reason we have wrapped the `input` in the `form` tag is due to the fact we want to access `NgModelController` for `input` to perform our assertions.

The unit first sets a spy on the `validate` function as the function is linked to `remote-validator`. The test then compiles the input element and links it to a scope. This results in the creation of a *form* (`testForm`) and a *model* (`unique`) controller on the scope.

To simulate an actual input and verify whether the validation function is being invoked, the test uses `$setViewValue` available on the *model* controller (`NgModelController`). This internally triggers the parser pipeline, and hence our `remote-validator` parser function.

 For directives of Angular 1.3, `$setViewValue` triggers both the parser pipeline and all the validators attached to `NgModelController`. The validators are not part of the parser pipeline but do get evaluated.

We are not bothered with the results of validation, hence the test just asserts whether the validation function on the scope was invoked.

Let's verify some behavior of `remote-validator` when validation fails. Add this test after the preceding `it` block:

```
it("verify failed 'unique' validation should set model controller
invalid.", inject(function ($q) {
    spyOn($scope, "validate").and.returnValue($q.reject());
    $compile(inputElement)($scope);
    $scope.testForm.unique.$setViewValue("dummy");
  expect($scope.validate).toHaveBeenCalled();
    $scope.$digest();

    expect($scope.testForm.$valid).toBe(false);
    expect($scope.testForm.unique.$valid).toBe(false);
    expect($scope.testForm.unique.$error.unique).toBe(true);
}));
```

The first four steps of this test are the same as the previous test; the only difference is that the promise is rejected ($q.reject()). This results in failed validation.

The next call to $scope.$digest() is required to sync the model as the validate call is asynchronous. Once the digest cycle is done, we can assert for the state of the *form* and *model* controllers and even confirm that the error object hash has the necessary failed validation.

On similar lines, we can also test successful remote validation and the state of the controller after validation.

Testing remote-validator and busy-indicator together

The remote-validator directive can work in tandem with busy-indicator. Let's see how well they work together. Add the following describe block after the existing describe block for remote validator:

```
describe("remote validator with busy indicator", function () {
  var inputElement;
  beforeEach(inject(function ($q) {
$scope.validate = function (value) {};
inputElement = "<form name='testForm'><div busy-
  indicator=''><input type='text' name='unique' ng-model='name'
  remote-validator='unique' remote-validator-function=
  'validate(value)' /></div></form>";
  }));

  it("should show busy indicator when remote request is made
  and hide later", function () {
   var defer = $q.defer(),
       html = $compile(inputElement)($scope),
       childElementScope = html.children().scope();

   spyOn($scope, "validate").and.returnValue(defer.promise);

   expect(childElementScope.busy).toBeUndefined();

   $scope.testForm.unique.$setViewValue("dummy");
   expect(childElementScope.busy).toBe(true);

   defer.resolve(true);
   $scope.$digest();

   expect(childElementScope.busy).toBe(false);

  }));
});
```

As with any component under test, there is some amount of code setup required. This time, we create `inputElement` with `input` and a `div` tag with the `busy-indicator` directive applied.

At the start of the test, we create a custom promise using the defer API. This is the promise that the validate function returns in the spy setup.

We compile and link the HTML file against the current `$scope` service. Since the busy indicator creates a child scope (as you can see in the definition, it has `scope:true`), we need to get hold of it for future asserting. The statement `html.children().scope()` does the magic and assigns it to `childElementScope`.

> The `scope()` function is an extension function for the jqLite/jQuery element class available in Angular. There is a similar function to retrieve an isolated scope too, aptly named `isolateScope()`. Check the Angular documentation at `https://code.angularjs.org/1.3.3/docs/api/ng/function/angular.element`.

Once everything is set up, we assert the state of the `busy` flag after firing `$setViewValue`. Calling `$setViewValue` triggers a call to the `validate` function. We immediately assert if the `busy` flag is set to `true`, as remote validation is in progress.

We then resolve the custom promise (marking remote validation complete), run a digest cycle, and assert whether the busy indicator flipped back to `false`. All these assertions are done on the child scope (`childElementScope`).

Observe carefully how we create a custom promise, return it as part of the `validate` function call, and resolve it manually to assert the behavior of `busy-indicator`. Also, this test does not validate the HTML content when remote validation is done. Instead, it only asserts the state of the `busy` flag.

That's it on testing `busy-indicator` and `remote-validator` together. We created some tests for the `ajax-button` directive too, but we will not be covering them in this chapter. Look at `chapter7/checkpoint1/app/js/shared/directives.spec.js` for tests that have been created for `ajax-button`. Since `ajax-button` uses an isolated scope, the mechanism to get the isolated scope for assertion involves calling `isolateScope()` on the directive HTML element.

> The `directives.spec.js` file also contains a number of new tests for directives that we have covered thus far.

The last directive that we plan to test here is the `workout-tile` directive. This trivial directive that just renders a remote HTML partial is difficult to set up.

Testing directives with templateUrl

The `workout-tile` directive uses `templateUrl` to load the partial and render it in HTML. The challenge is to make the template available for unit testing without making any remote request. Remember, Angular does not like server invocation during unit testing. So what options do we have?

We can manually prep the `$templateCache` service. For this, we need to copy the HTML content from each template file, create a string representation, and then add it to `$templateCache` manually.

> `$templateCache` is a service exposed by Angular to cache HTML fragments. Every view that we load in our app comes from the template cache.
>
> When a view is requested for the first time through either `ng-include`, a directive template (`templateUrl`), or `ng-view`, Angular retrieves the view and adds it to `$templateCache` before actually serving it.
>
> This performance optimization helps Angular serve all future requests for the same view from `$templateCache`, instead of making the same remote request again and again.

Something like this can be used:

```
$templateCache.put('/partials/workoutbuilder/workout-tile.html',
    '<div>templatehtml</div>');
```

> If we manually prep `$templateCache`, the cache key should be the path to the partial that is the same as that defined in the directive definition's `templateUrl` property.

While this approach works, it has some serious drawbacks. Firstly, we manually need to duplicate and format the HTML content as a string. Secondly, any change to the original partial view needs to be kept in sync with the HTML string we create for the unit test. That seems to be too much effort to set up a template. There should be something better.

Karma has the concept of **preprocessors**. Preprocessors allow us to manipulate files before they are loaded in a browser for testing. There is a preprocessor that can help us here. The `karma-ng-html2js-preprocessor` plugin (https://github.com/karma-runner/karma-ng-html2js-preprocessor) converts HTML files into the JavaScript template and makes them available for testing.

Let's integrate this preprocessor and see how it works and how can it help with unit testing our `workout-tile` directive.

Install the npm module from the command line using the following command:

```
npm install karma-ng-html2js-preprocessor --save-dev
```

 The version of `karma-ng-html2js-preprocessor` used is 0.1.2.

Then, update the `karma.cofig.js` file under `tests` with some configuration specific to this preprocessor. This is how sections of the configuration files should now look:

```
files: [
  //existing file references
  'app/partials/**/*.html', // Add this path reference.
],
  preprocessors: {
  'app/partials/**/*.html': ['ng-html2js'] //add this
},

  // Add this new property
  ngHtml2JsPreprocessor: {
  // strip this from the file path
  stripPrefix: 'app',
},
```

By adding the folder reference for HTML partials in the Karma `files` section (**'app/ partials/**/*.html'**), we instruct Karma to load these partials before testing starts. This allows preprocessors to work on them.

The `karma-ng-html2js-preprocessor` preprocessor is registered within the `preprocessors` section of the Karma configuration.

The `ngHtml2JsPreprocessor` property added later contains configurations specific to the preprocessor. The only configuration it has is `stripPrefix`. This setting strips away the `app` string from the template name (which is also the template path) before adding it to `$templateCache`. Without this, the `templateUrl` directive will not match the name in the `$templateCache` key, and the view will not load from cache.

Internally, the preceding preprocessor creates a script file for each HTML template. Each script file has one Angular module. The only thing the module does is to add the string representation of HTML to `$templateCache`. It is easy to understand what is happening if we look at the actual generated code.

If the Karma window is open, click on the **Debug** button. On the new debug window, open the browser's developer console and look at the **Source** tab. The generated code for `workout-tile.html` looks like this:

```
localhost:9876          angular
  base                  |.module('/partials/workoutbuilder/workout-tile.html', [])
  app                     .run(function($templateCache) {
    ▶ bower_components        $templateCache.put('/partials/workoutbuilder/workout-tile.html',
    ▶ js                        '*<div class="title">{{workout.title}}</div>\n' +
    ▼ partials                  '<div class="stats">\n' +
      ▶ workout                 '    <span class="duration" title="Duration"><span class="glyph
      ▼ workoutbuilder          '        <span class="length pull-right" title="Exercise Count"><sp
          exercise.html.js      '</div>');
          exercises.html.js   });
          *workout-tile.html.js
```

Now that the preprocessor setup is complete, let's add the test for the workout tile. Add a new file `directives.spec.js` under `js/workoutbuilder/` with the following code:

```javascript
describe("Directives", function () {
    var $compile, $rootScope, $scope;

    beforeEach(module('app'));
    beforeEach(module('/partials/workoutbuilder/
    workout-tile.html'));

    beforeEach(inject(function (_$compile_, _$rootScope_) {
        $compile = _$compile_;
        $rootScope = _$rootScope_;
        $scope = $rootScope.$new();
    }));

    describe("Workout tile", function () {
      it("should load workout tile directive",
        inject(function ($templateCache) {
         var e = $compile("<workout-tile></workout-tile")($scope);
         $scope.$digest();
         expect(e.html().indexOf('class="duration"') > 0);
      }));
    });

});
```

Since the preprocessor creates one module per partial, by using the following command we include the module that contains the template definition:

```
beforeEach(module('/partials/workoutbuilder/workout-tile.html'));
```

Testing the directive then becomes a simple affair. We compile and link the directive and assert whether the directive is loaded correctly, this time by verifying the HTML content. That is pretty much it.

We are done with directive testing. Let's test our app routes.

Unit testing routes and resolve

If we look at the route setup in `config.js`, there are some standard route definitions and a few routes use the `resolve` configuration to inject data into the controller. This is something that can be tested.

We can test the route configuration and make sure the correct path, route, and controller are set when the route changes. For routes with `resolve`, we can check if the associated resolve functions were actually invoked.

Create a `config.spec.js` file in the same folder as `config.js` and add the first route test:

```
describe("Trainer routes", function () {
    beforeEach(module('app'));

    it("should default to start workout route",
    inject(function($rootScope, $location, $route, $httpBackend) {
      $httpBackend.whenGET("partials/workout/start.html")
      .respond("<div/>");
            $location.path("/");
            $rootScope.$digest();
            expect($location.path()).toBe("/start");
            expect($route.current.templateUrl)
            .toBe("partials/workout/start.html");
             expect($route.current.controller).toBeUndefined();
    }));
});
```

The first thing we do is to set up the mock HTTP backend to respond to partial view requests—requests that are made when we do navigation. `$httpBackend.whenGET` makes sure that requests to get the start page HTML is responded to with mock HTML.

The previous test highlights the usefulness of the $httpBackend. whenGET function. Here, we just want to mock the request, and we are not interested in asserting whether the call was actually made.

The next step uses location.path to navigate to the root. The expectation here is that, due to the following route setup, the route is automatically set to start route and we assert this behavior:

```
$routeProvider.otherwise({ redirectTo: '/start' });
```

The next line $rootScope.$digest is required. Without this call, the transition does not happen. Once the digest cycle is complete, we assert the correctness of the new path.

Note the $route injection that we have used in the test. Without injecting $route, the actual transition does not happen. The $location service just triggers route transition. After the transition, we check location and the current route properties to confirm that the route change worked.

Let's now try to test a route that has parameters. Add the following test to the config.spec.js file

```
it("should load the workout.", inject(function ($rootScope,
  $location, $route, $httpBackend) {
  $httpBackend.whenGET("partials/workout/workout.html")
  .respond("<div/>");
  $location.path("/workout/dummyWorkout");
    $rootScope.$digest();
    expect($location.path()).toBe("/workout/dummyWorkout");
    expect($route.current.params.id).toBe('dummyWorkout');
}));
```

This is the *Workout Runner* route and we assert that the location path is set correctly and the route parameters have been set correctly ($route.current.params.id).

Next, let's test whether the resolved route is firing correctly and on the correct path. Add the following test to config.spec.js:

```
it("should start workout building when navigating to workout
  builder route.", inject(function ($rootScope, $location, $route,
  $httpBackend,WorkoutBuilderService) {
    spyOn(WorkoutBuilderService, "startBuilding");
    $httpBackend.whenGET("partials/workoutbuilder/workout.html")
    .respond("<div/>");
```

```
        $location.path("/builder/workouts/new");
        $rootScope.$digest();
        expect($location.path()).toBe("/builder/workouts/new");
        expect(WorkoutBuilderService.startBuilding)
        .toHaveBeenCalled();
        expect(WorkoutBuilderService.startBuilding.calls.count())
        .toBe(1);
    }));
```

This is the *Workout Builder* endpoint/route. To verify that the route resolve was called, instead of creating a mock for `WorkoutBuilderService`, we inject the real service but set up a spy on it to make sure the `startBuilding` function is called inside `resolve`. After that, it is all standard stuff where we verify the route path and whether spy was called or not.

This is really good as we aren't limited to testing all standard constructs of Angular; we can also test items such as the route setup. This gives us excellent unit test coverage.

With this, we have covered almost all aspects of unit testing, and it's time to turn our focus toward learning how to perform E2E testing in Angular.

Other than the unit tests we have covered in this chapter, there are a number of other tests that have been added for the app. Download the specification files from the `chapter7/checkpoint1` codebase and see what else has been unit tested.

The code is also available on GitHub (`https://github.com/chandermani/angularjsbyexample`) for everyone to download. *Checkpoints* are implemented as *branches* in GitHub. The branch to download is `checkpoint7.1` and the folder is `trainer`.

Getting started with E2E testing

Automated **E2E** testing is an invaluable asset if the underlying framework supports it. As the size of an app grows, automated E2E testing can save a lot of manual effort. Without automation it's just a never-ending battle to make sure the app is functional. However, remember that in an E2E setup, not everything is automatable; it may require a lot of effort to automate. With due diligence, we can offload a good amount of manual effort but not everything.

The process of E2E testing a web-based application is about running the application in a real browser and asserting the behavior of the application based on the user interface state. This is how an actual user does testing.

Browser automation holds the key here and modern browsers have become smarter and more capable in terms of supporting automation. Selenium tools for browser automation are the most popular option out there. Selenium has the WebDriver (`http://www.w3.org/TR/2013/WD-webdriver-20130117/`) API that allows us to control the browser through automation API that modern browsers natively support.

The reason behind bringing up Selenium WebDriver is due to the fact that the Angular E2E testing framework/runner **Protractor** also uses *WebDriverJS*, which is a JavaScript binding of WebDriver on Node. These language bindings (like the preceding JavaScript binding) allow us to use the automation API in the language of our choice.

Let's discuss Protractor before we start writing some integration tests for our app.

Introduction to Protractor

Protractor is the de facto test runner for E2E testing in Angular. Protractor uses Selenium WebDriver to control a browser and simulate user actions.

 Protractor supersedes an earlier E2E framework known as *AngularJS Scenario Runner*. Karma had a plugin that allowed Karma to execute E2E tests.

A typical Protractor setup has the following components:

- A test runner (Protractor)
- A Selenium Server
- A browser

We write our test in Jasmine and use some objects exposed by Protractors (which is a wrapper over WebDriverJS) to control the browser.

When these tests run, Protractor sends commands to the Selenium server. This interaction happens mostly over HTTP.

The Selenium server, in turn, communicates with the browser using the *WebDriver Wire Protocol* and internally the browser interprets the action commands using the browser driver (such as ChromeDriver in the case of Chrome).

It is not that important to understand the technicalities of this communication, but we should be aware of the E2E testing setup. Check the article from Protractor documentation at http://angular.github.io/protractor/#/infrastructure to learn more about this flow.

Another important thing to realize when using Protractor is that the overall interaction with the browser or the browser control flow is asynchronous in nature and promise-based. Any HTML element action, be it sendKeys, getText, click, submit, or any other, does not execute at the time of invocation; instead the action is queued up in a control flow queue. For this precise reason, the return value of every action statement is a promise that gets resolved when the action completes.

To handle this *asynchronicity* in Jasmine tests, Protractor patches Jasmine and therefore assertions like these work:

```
expect(element(by.id("start")).getText()).toBe("Select Workout");
```

They work despite the getText function returning a promise and not the element content.

 At the time of writing, Protractor supports Jasmine Version 1.3.

With this basic understanding of how Protractor works, let's set up Protractor for E2E tests.

Setting up Protractor for E2E testing

To install Protractor globally, run this command in the console:

```
npm install -g protractor
```

This installs two command-line tools: Protractor and webdriver-manager. Run the following command to make sure Protractor is set up correctly:

```
protractor --version
```

 All E2E tests have been verified against Protractor 1.6.1.

Webdriver-manager is a helper tool to easily get an instance of a running Selenium server. Before we start the Selenium server, we need to update the driver binaries with the following call:

```
webdriver-manager update
```

Finally, run this command to start the Selenium server:

```
webdriver-manager start
```

Protractor tests send requests to this server to control a local browser.

 Make sure that the Selenium server is running at all times during E2E testing. This can be verified by checking the status of the server at `http://localhost:4444/wd/hub` (default location).

Protractor also needs to be configured like Karma and has a configuration file. Copy the `protractor.config.js` file from the `tests` folder under `chapter7/checkpoint2/` to our local `tests` folder. The Protractor configuration file we just added contains three settings that we want to make sure are configured according to our local app setup, and these include the following:

Key	Description
`specs`	Location of the specification files (the E2E test files). The current assigned value `['e2e/*.js']` should work.
`baseUrl`	The base URL where the app is running. *Change the server name and port to match your local setup.* Navigate to the URL to make sure the app is running.
`seleniumAddress`	The base URL where the Selenium server is running. Unless you have reconfigured the selenium server settings, the default value should work.

 The configuration file documentation on the Protractor website (`https://github.com/angular/protractor/blob/master/docs/referenceConf.js`) contains details on the other supported configurations.

That is enough to start testing with Protractor. Let's begin writing and executing some tests.

Writing E2E tests for the app

Let's start in a simple manner and test our app start page (#/start). This page has some static content, a workout listing section with search capabilities, and the ability to start a workout by clicking any workout tile.

 All our E2E tests will be added to the e2e folder under tests.

Add a new file workout-runner.spec.js to the e2e folder under tests with the following code:

```
describe("Workout Runner", function () {
    describe("Start Page", function () {
        beforeEach(function () {
            browser.get("");
        });
        it("should load the start page.", function () {
            expect(browser.getTitle()).toBe("Personal Trainer");
            expect(element(by.id("start")).getText())
    .toBe("Select Workout");
        });
    });
});
```

Before we execute our first test, make sure the Selenium server is running (webdriver-manager start) and the app is running.

Now from the command line run the following command and see the browser dance to our tunes:

```
protractor tests/protractor.conf.js
```

Protractor will open the browser; navigate to the start page; wait for the page, the scripts, and the framework to load; and then perform the test. It finally logs the results of the test in the console. That is pretty awesome!

Let's walk through this simple test.

The first interesting piece is inside the beforeEach block. The browser object is a global object exposed by Protractor and is used to control the browser-level actions. Underneath, it is just a wrapper around *WebDriver*. The browser.get("") function navigates the browser to start the app page every time before the start of the test.

The actual test verifies whether the title of the page is correct. It also checks whether some random content is present on the page.

The preceding test employs two new globals: `element` and `by`, that are made available by Protractor:

- `element`: This function returns an `ElementFinder` object. The primary job of `ElementFinder` is to interact with the selected element. We will be using the `element` function to select `ElementFinder` extensively in our tests.

 Refer to the documentation for `ElementFinder` (`http://angular.github.io/protractor/#/api?view=ElementFinder`) and `webdriver.WebElement` (`http://angular.github.io/protractor/#/api?view=webdriver.WebElement`) to know more about element manipulation API support. Functions such as `getText()` are actually defined on `WebElement`, but are always accessed using `ElementFinder`. As the documentation for `ElementFinder` suggests, `ElementFinder` can be treated as `WebElement` for most purposes.

- `by`: This object is there to locate elements. It has functions that create **locators**. In the preceding test, a locator is created to search for elements with `id=start`. There are a number of locators that can be used to search for a specific element. These include by class, by ID, by model (`ng-model`), by binding, and many more. Refer to the Protractor documentation on locators at `http://angular.github.io/protractor/#/locators` to learn about the supported locators.

 Just to reiterate what we discussed earlier, `getTitle()` and `getText()` in the preceding test do not return the actual text, but a *promise* — we can still assert on the text value.

This simple test highlights another salient feature of Protractor. It automatically detects when the Angular app is loaded and when data is available for testing. There are no ugly hacks to delay testing (using *timeouts*) that may otherwise be required in standard E2E testing scenarios.

Remember, this is a *SPA*; full-page browser refresh does not happen, so it is not that simple to determine when the page is loaded and when data that is rendered for AJAX calls is available. Protractor makes it all possible.

Protractor may still timeout while trying to assess whether the page is available for testing. If you are hitting timeout errors with Protractor, this article in the Protractor documentation can be really helpful (`http://angular.github.io/protractor/#/timeouts`) in debugging such issues.

Let's do something more interesting. Why don't we test whether the search box in the start page is working fine?

Testing the search functionality is going to be a tricky affair. Since this is E2E testing, we need some data to test searches. Therein lies the challenge: not only do we need some data to test searches, but we need a fixed data set. This implies that the backend should always return a constant data set. From an E2E test perspective, the workouts returned by a MongoLab instance should always be the same.

What options do we have to handle E2E tests that involve some initial data setup?

Setting up backend data for E2E testing

Setting up backend data for E2E testing is a challenge, irrespective of the E2E framework we employ for testing. The ultimate aim is to assert the behavior of an application against some data and unless the data is fixed, we cannot verify behavior that involves getting or setting data.

One approach to set up data for E2E tests is to create a test data store specifically for E2E tests with some seed data. Once the E2E tests are over, the data store can be reset to its original state for future testing. For *Personal Trainer*, we can create a new database in MongoLab dedicated exclusively to E2E testing.

This may seem a lot of effort, but it is necessary. Who said E2E testing is easy! In fact, this challenge is there even if we do manual testing. For a real app, we always have to set up data stores/databases for every environment—be it *dev*, *test*, or *production*.

Having said that, we plan to do something different! We will again mock the backend!

Mocking the server backend in E2E testing

Before your hands go up in protest, let me remind you that this too is a viable option. If setting up a new data store is expensive and time-consuming and/or the backend API is well tested, there is at least an option to mock data. Another reason to use a mock backend is to learn about the mocking capabilities of Angular in the context of E2E testing.

The service that is again going to help in this case is `$httpBackend`, but this time the service comes from the `ngMockE2E` module, instead of `ngMock`.

Setting up the HTTP mock backend is an intrusive process and requires some changes to the existing application code. To plug in a mock backend we need to perform the following steps:

1. Create a new module with dependency on the main app module (named app) and the `ngMockeE2E` module.

2. Add the mock HTTP implementation in this module using the `$httpBackend.when*` functions. These methods are similar to the ones we used in unit tests.

3. Rewire the `ng-app` declaration in `index.html` to use the new `ngMockeE2E` module instead of the existing app module. The app bootstrapping process will use `ngMockeE2E` now, and the mock backend setup in the `ngMockeE2E` module will override the standard HTTP requests that the app makes to get data.

The overall process explained in the preceding steps is intrusive, because it rewires the app to use the mock backend with mock data. To revert to the original backend, we need to reconfigure the app.

This may seem to be a deal breaker, but most modern build systems (such as *Grunt*) allow us to do dynamic file transformations based on build deployment configurations.

Let's rewire our app to use mock backend. Copy `appe2e.js` from `chapter7/checkpoint2` into the same location where `app.js` resides. This file declares the new module that we use (`appe2e`). It also contains a mock data setup for our backend, which is nothing but a series of `$httpBackend.when*` calls to set up the backend endpoint to respond to and the data to return.

`$http` in Angular is used for all types of HTTP communication. This includes loading view partials too. We do not want to mock such requests to our backend. The good thing about the when API is that it does allow us to pass through any request to the real backend if desired, and the following command does just that:

```
$httpBackend.whenGET(/^partials///).passThrough();
```

Any request made to the `/partials` path is served from the real backend; in this case, this is the path to our HTML partials views. This is possible due to the fact that the URL to the when function allows regex pattern matching.

Even the `index.html` file needs to change as we need to use the new module now. Update the existing `ng-app` declaration in `index.html` to:

```
<body ng-app="appe2e" ng-controller="RootController">
```

Add the following two script references in the script section:

```
<script src =... angular-animate.js"></script>
<script src = "http://ajax.googleapis.com/ajax/
    libs/angularjs/1.3.3/angular-mocks.js"></script>
//Other scripts
<script src="js/app.js"></script>
<script src="js/appe2e.js"></script>
```

We add references to `appe2e.js` and `angular-mocks.js` that contain the `ngMockE2E` module definition.

Load the app again! If the app start page (`/start`) loads correctly and shows two workouts, then the mock backend is working fine. Check out the following screenshot:

The app is now working on mock data and is ready to be tested.

More E2E tests

Let's get back to testing workout search features on the start page. Our mock backend returns two fixed workouts and we can assert search behaviors against these. Add this test after the existing test in `workout-runner.spec.js`:

```
it("should search workout with specific name.", function () {
var filteredWorkouts = element.all(by.repeater("workout in
  workouts"));
expect(filteredWorkouts.count()).toEqual(2);

var searchInput = element(by.model("workoutSearch"));
  searchInput.sendKeys("test");

  expect(filteredWorkouts.count()).toEqual(1);
    expect(filteredWorkouts.first().element(by.css(".title")).
getText(
  )).toBe("A test Workout");
});
```

The test uses `ElementFinder` and *Locator* API to look for elements on the page. Check the first line; there is a locator for ng-repeat: `by.repeater`! The `by.repeat` locator together with the `element.all` function does a multi-element match and the next line asserts the element count.

The test then gets hold of the search input, but uses another Angular-specific locator `by.model` that looks for the `ng-model` binding. The `sendKeys` function is used to simulate data entry in the search `input`.

The last two expect operations check for the count of elements in `ng-repeat` again, and they check whether the correct workout is filtered based on the span text. The last `expect` statement also highlights how we can chain element filtering and get hold of child elements in HTML.

Run the test again (`protractor tests/protractor.conf.js`) and once again observe the magic of browser automation as two tests run one after another.

Can we automate E2E testing for *Workout Runner*? Well, we can try.

Testing Workout Runner

One of the major challenges with testing *Workout Runner* is that everything is time-dependent. With unit testing, at least we were able to use the mock `$interval` service—but not anymore. Testing exercise transitions and workout completion is definitely difficult.

However, before we tackle this problem or try to find an acceptable workout, let's digress and learn about an important technique to manage E2E testing: page objects!

Page objects to manage E2E testing

The concept of page objects is simple. Encapsulate the representation of page elements into an object so that we do not have to litter our E2E test code with `ElementFinder` and *locators*. If any page element moves, we just need to fix the page object.

Here is how we can represent our *Workout Runner* page:

```
var WorkoutRunnerPage = function () {
this.description = element(by.binding(
  "currentExercise.details.description"));
this.steps = element(by.binding(
  "currentExercise.details.procedure"));
this.videos = element.all(by.repeater(
  "video in currentExercise.details.related.videos"));
this.pauseResume = element(by.id("pause-overlay"));
  this.exerciseHeading = element(by.binding(
  "currentExercise.details.title"));
this.workoutTimeRemaining = element(by.binding(
  "workoutTimeRemaining"))
this.exerciseTimeRemaining = element(by.binding(
  "currentExercise.duration-currentExerciseDuration"));
};
```

This page object now encapsulates all the elements that we want to test. By organizing the element selection code in one place, we increase the readability and hence maintainability of E2E tests.

Add the `WorkoutRunnerPage` function inside the `describe` block of *Workout Runner* at the top and we can now add a test for *Workout Runner*.

Add the following `describe` block as a nested child of `describe( "Workout Runner")`:

```
describe("Workout Runner page", function () {
    beforeEach(function () {
        browser.get("#/workout/testworkout");
    });

    it("should load workout data", function () {
        var page = new WorkoutRunnerPage();
        expect(page.description.getText())
.toBe("The basic crunch is a abdominal exercise in a
strength-training program.");
        expect(page.exerciseHeading.getText())
```

```
        .toBe("Abdominal Crunches");
            expect(page.videos.count()).toBe(2);
        });
    });
```

The workout that we load for this test is **testworkout**. This workout has two exercises with a 5-second duration and the rest period is 5 seconds too. The overall duration is 15 seconds! This workout was set in appe2e.js while setting up the mock backend earlier in the chapter.

The test verifies that the workout is loaded and the correct data is shown. We make full use of the page object that we defined earlier. Run the test and verify whether it passes.

Let's get back to the challenge of testing code based on $interval or $timeout. Add the following test to the current test suite:

```
it("should transition exercise when time lapses.", function () {
    var page = new WorkoutRunnerPage();
    browser.sleep(5000);
    page.pauseResume.click();
    expect(page.videos.count()).toBe(0);
    expect(page.description.getText()).toBe("Relax a bit!");
    expect(page.exerciseHeading.getText()).toBe("Relax!");
});
```

This test checks whether the exercise transition happened. It does so by adding a browser.sleep function for 5 seconds, and then verifying from the UI state whether exercise-related content of Rest is visible. The problem with this test is that it is not very accurate. It can confirm the transition is happening but cannot confirm it happened at the right time.

A plausible explanation for this behavior is in the way Protractor works. Before Protractor can start a test, it first waits for the page to load. If the test involves any action (such as getText), it again waits till Angular synchronizes the page. During page synchronization, Angular waits for any pending HTTP requests or any timeout-based operations to complete before it starts the test. As a result, when the browser. sleep function is invoked and when the browser actually goes to sleep cannot be predicted with great accuracy.

 We can disable this synchronization behavior by setting browser. ignoreSynchronization to true, but we should avoid this as much as possible. If we set it to true, the onus is on us to determine when the page content is available for making assertions.

As described earlier, Angular waits for any operation based on $timeout to lapse before starting the test. If you do want Angular to wait for the timeout, use the $interval service: $interval(fn, delay,1).

The bottom line is that the *Workout Runner* app workflow is indeed difficult to test. Compared to *Workflow Runner*, other things are far easier to test as we saw with the start page testing.

> The companion codebase in the chapter7/checkpoint2/tests/e2e contains some more tests created for other parts of the application. The *GitHub branch* is checkpoint7.2 and the folder is trainer.

It's time now to wrap up the chapter and summarize our learning.

Summary

We do not need to reiterate how important unit and E2E testing are for any application. The way the Angular framework has been designed makes testing the Angular app easy. In this chapter, we covered how to write unit tests and E2E tests using libraries and frameworks that target Angular.

For unit testing, we used Jasmine to write our tests and Karma to execute them. We tested a number of filters, controllers, services, and directives from *Personal Trainer*. In the process, you learned about challenges and techniques to effectively test these types.

For E2E testing, the framework of choice was Protractor. We still wrote out tests in Jasmine but the test runner this time was Protractor. You learned how Protractor automates E2E testing using Selenium WebDriver, as we did some scenario testing for the *Start* and *Workout Runner* pages.

If you have reached so far, you are getting closer to becoming a proficient Angular developer. The next chapter reinforces this with more practical scenarios and implementations built using Angular. We will touch upon important concepts in the last chapter of this book; these include multilingual support, authentication and authorization, communication patterns, performance optimizations, and a few others. You sure do not want to miss them!

8

Handling Common Scenarios

With seven chapters under our belts, it should feel nice. What we have learned thus far is a direct consequence of the apps we have built in the last few chapters. I believe we now have an adequate understanding of the framework, how it works, and what it supports. Armed with this knowledge, as soon as we start to build some decent-sized apps, there are some common problems/patterns that will invariably surface, such as:

- How to authenticate the user and control his/her access (authorization)?
- How to make sure that the app is performing enough?
- My app requires localized content. What should I do?
- What tools can I use to expedite app development?

And many more!

In this chapter, we try to address such common scenarios and provide a working solution and/or prescriptive guidance to help you handle such use cases.

The topics we cover in this chapter include:

- **Angular seed projects**: You learn how some seed projects in Angular can help us when starting a new engagement.
- **Multilocal/lingual support**: AngularJS has decent support for app localization. We cover the Angular constructs that help us localize an application and some libraries that extend multi-locale support in Angular.
- **Authenticating Angular applications**: This is a common requirement; we look at how to support cookie- and token-based Authentication in Angular.

- **Communication and data sharing patterns**: You learn how to share data and communicate across controllers, directives, filters, and services.

- **Angular performance**: A customary performance section is a must as we try to layout some tips and guidelines on how to make our Angular more performant with regard to apps.

Let's start from the beginning!

Building a new app

Image a scenario here. We are building a new application and given the super awesomeness of the Angular framework, we have unanimously decided to use Angular. Great! What next? Next is the mundane process of setting up the project.

Although setting up a project/codebase may be a mundane activity, it's still a critical part of any engagement. This activity typically involves:

- Creating a standard folder structure. This is at times influenced by the server framework (such as RoR, ASP.Net, NodeJS, and others).

- Adding some standard assets to specific folders.

- Including any third-party dependency upfront.

- Setting up unit/E2E testing.

- Setting up app builds for different environments such as dev, test, and production, again influenced by the server technology involved.

What if we can short-circuit the setup process? This is indeed possible; we just need a seed project or a starter site.

Seed projects

AngularJS has a number of seed projects that can get us started in no time. Some seed projects integrate an Angular framework with a specific backend and some only dictate/provide Angular-specific content. Some come preconfigured with vendor-specific libraries/frameworks (such as *LESS*, *SASS*, *Bootstrap*, and *Fontawesome*) whereas others just provide a plain vanilla setup.

Two of the notable seed projects that are not tied to a backend but are pretty useful are:

- `angular-seed` (`https://github.com/angular/angular-seed`): This is a prescriptive guide for the Angular team itself. It specifically targets how to set up code for development and unit testing an Angular application. It does not come with any third-part integration. Download/clone it and we are ready to go.

- `ng-boilerplate` (`http://joshdmiller.github.io/ng-boilerplate/`): This is a more complete and a very useful seed project. The project structure we have used for our apps derives heavily from `ng-boilerplate`. It has basically everything and uses LESS for CSS, Twitter Bootstrap for views, Font Awesome for icons/images, and the ever awesome `angular-ui` for some handy directives. It even comes with a predefined build setup using Grunt.

These projects provide a head start when building with Angular.

If the app is tied to a specific backend stack, you have two choices:

- To use one of these seed projects and integrate it with the backend manually.

- To find a seed project/implementation that does it for us. Angular has been there for a long time. There is a good probability that we can find an integrated solution.

 Dan Cancro did a comprehensive study on available starter/seed projects and has made it available on his blog. Check it out here at `http://www.dancancro.com/comparison-of-angularjs-application-starters/`.

This discussion cannot be complete without mentioning Yeoman. If we want a bit more automation, a standardized build, tests, and a release workflow, Yeoman is a good choice.

Yeoman

Yeoman (`http://yeoman.io/`) is a suite of tools targeted toward web application development. It defines a workflow to build modern web applications. Yeoman consists of:

- **yo**: This is a scaffolding tool to generate code on the fly.

- **Grunt**: This is one of the most popular build systems on Node.

- **Bower**: This is a package manager for the Web. We have already used it while testing our application with the Karma test runner in the previous chapter.

The scaffolding component of Yeoman is quite interesting. *yo* as it is named uses the concept of a generator to achieve scaffolding.

> *Scaffolding* is the process of generating a code skeleton that can be built upon. Using scaffolding, we can save some initial effort and provide some guidance around how the overall structure of any coding artefact should look.

Generators in Yeoman are used to set up the initial seed project and later, for individual script generation too. Since Yeoman is not targeted specifically towards Angular, there are generators for various client and server stacks. There are also generators for Angular, Angular + *Express* (the *Node* web framework), mobile apps, and many more.

> Checkout `http://yeoman.io/generators/` for an exhaustive list of generators supported on Yeoman!

Let's try to understand the Yeoman workflow from the Angular perspective. Before we start, make sure you have *Yeoman*, *Bower*, and *Grunt* installed on your machine:

1. Our first task is to select a generator. Since we are targeting Angular, our choices are limited to generators that support Angular. For this quick walkthrough, we will use the Angular generator (`https://github.com/yeoman/generator-angular`), which is the official Angular generator supported on Yeoman.

2. Install the generator from the command line:

   ```
   npm install -g generator-angular
   ```

3. Post-installation creates a project directory that hosts the project. Then, navigate to the directory and run the generator:

   ```
   mkdir angularApp
   cd angularApp
   yo angular
   ```

4. Follow the wizard and within no time a seed project is generated. Depending upon the generator used, the final code may vary, but the resultant project code uses Bower to manage script dependency and comes preconfigured with Grunt build tasks.

5. It is easy to verify that everything was set up correctly. Just run Grunt from the command line to compile and build the application, and it serves to see the new app in action.

6. Once the app is set up and running, we can use the yo subgenerators to generate routes, controllers, views, directives, and services. And the awesome part is that they are all included in the build automatically. No more updating the `index.html` file and adding dependencies; everything is taken care by Grunt. Pretty awesome!

> What all artefacts can be generated by *yo* subgenerators is dictated by the Yeoman generator we chose initially.

7. If not already started, start the newly created app using Grunt, open another command window, and run the following command:

    ```
    yo angular:route exercise
    ```

8. The Angular generator generates a view, a controller, and a controller test spec and also sets up the route for exercise. Grunt is watching and automatically picks the changes and refreshes the app. We can now load the page #/exercise and a standard view template is loaded. Automation at its very best!

A word of caution here! What Yeoman generators create is opinionated to say the least. It may or may not fit the app requirements. Some aspects of the generated code can be tweaked easily, for example, we may be able to tweak the Grunt configuration file and adapt it to our project needs. But things like the default generated code, the organization of files and folders, and the result of code generated using subgenerator may require us to tinker with the generator implementation, not a trivial affair by any stretch of the imagination.

> I suggest that when planning to use Yeoman, you try out different generators and see the mileage you can derive from each one of them before committing to a specific generator.

Building multilingual apps (internationalization)

English is not the first language for a sizable population of the world, therefore building an app that just renders in English may not be a very wise idea. Imagine, with just some content localization, how much we can gain in terms of application reach. Internationalization is all about designing our app so that anyone in any region of the world can use the app in their native locale.

Before we delve deeper into this topic, why not address a common confusion between what internationalization (I18n) and what localization (L10n) is?

Internationalization (I18n) is the process of making sure that the application has elements that can help it render locale-specific content, in other words, the application is adaptable to different locales.

Localization (L10n) on the other hand, is the actual process of adapting parts of the application to specific locales. These could be the text shown, the date, the time, the current formatting, and other such content that is affected by locale change.

 This overall process of I18n and L10n is, at times, referred to as **globalization**.

It is a normal tendency to just overlook this topic and believe that the app we are building does not need to handle I18n concerns. But even apps targeted at an English language audience need to manage locale variations that are country-specific. We may be able to work with the text content, but we still need to handle date, number, and currency variations.

For example, en-us (language code, English: United States) and en-gb (English: United Kingdom) have variations. The US date format is MM/DD/YY whereas for the UK, it is DD/MM/YY. The same holds true for currency formatting too.

 en-US, *en-GB*, and *es-ES* are ISO 639-1 language codes to denote a locale. Left part of - (the dash) signifies the language and the right part, the country.

Angular too supports internationalization; let's see how.

Angular I18n support

AngularJS comes with support for I18n and L10n for date, number, and currency. No surprises here! Angular's filters currency, date, and number are locale-aware.

To make these filters work according to a specific locale, we need to do some locale-specific configurations. AngularJS comes with more than 250 locale files that contain rules for formatting currency, dates, or numbers in specific locales. We need to include the locale-specific script file for every locale that we want to support.

For example, say we want to support the German locale. We first include the locale-specific script file in our main page (`index.html`):

```
https://code.angularjs.org/1.2.15/i18n/angular-locale_de-de.js
```

Every one of these script files declare a module `ngLocale` and contains configurations specific to that locale. To utilize the locale specific module, we need to reference the `ngLocale` module in our application:

```
angular.module('app',['ngLocale'])
```

And that's it! We have altered the currency, date, and number filters behavior in accordance with the German locale. Look at the jsFiddle link at `http://jsfiddle.net/cmyworld/f46aLar2/`, which is a working version of what we have highlighted earlier. Go ahead and tinker with it to understand what is possible with Angular's localized filters.

> Look at the content of these locale files. It's always interesting to know what is happening under the hood!

If we play around with the preceding jsFiddle page, and read some documentation on Angular I18n support (`https://docs.angularjs.org/guide/i18n`), we will soon realize that it has some notable limitations. There are two major shortcomings:

- Firstly, we cannot change the current locale at runtime without a complete page reload
- Secondly, there is no service/guidance available for localizing text content, which is a major disappointment

A good framework attracts great developers and great developers fill the gaps left by the framework. There are some good community projects to make Angular localization easy. We are going to discuss two of those here: one that targets the dynamic locale change, and the other that helps with content localization.

Locale changes using angular-dynamic-locale

To tackle the first limitation related to changing the locale on the fly, there is a community project `angular-dynamic-locale` (`http://lgalfaso.github.io/angular-dynamic-locale/`). This module allows us to dynamically change the locale once the application has been bootstrapped.

Installing and using `angular-dynamic-locale` is easy. As with any third-party module, reference the script in `index.html` and add the module dependency `tmh.dynamicLocale` to the app's main module.

It exposes two services: `tmhDynamicLocale` and `tmhDynamicLocaleCache` to manage dynamic locale changes. The only function available on the `tmhDynamicLocale` service is `set(newLocale)` that changes the actual locale (for example, `tmhDynamicLocale.set('es-es')`).

The `tmhDynamicLocaleCache` function is used for caching the locale file and service downloads.

Look at the documentation for `angular-dynamic-locale` to know more about the service and how it works. From a usage perspective the service is quite simple.

The second library that we are going to talk about is the angular-translate library. This is a library targeted towards content/text translations.

Using angular-translate for text translations

Content translation may seem simple but there are some technical challenges here too. To understand these challenges, you need to understand how the process of content translation works. The task of content/text translation begins with identifying what content should be translated. Such content can broadly be classified in two categories:

- **Fixed string literals**: In any HTML page, there are parts that are dynamic and parts that are fixed. If we hardcoded strings anywhere in the view, those are fixed-string literals and are potential candidates for localization.
- **Dynamic string literals**: Any string/text fragments retrieved from the server and rendered in the view are dynamic string literals. The exercise name shown during workout execution is a good example of this.

Localizing fixed string literals is comparatively easy. Depending upon the number of locales to support, the content is generated for each locale and is made available to a tool/library. The library then based on the locale requested embeds the locale-specific content in the HTML. You will shortly learn how to do this with angular-translate.

Localizing dynamic string literals is a tricky affair and requires a good amount of design effort upfront. Take the example of *Workout Builder*; while creating a new workout or an exercise, there is no provision in the application to support localized content addition. We cannot add the locale-specific title of a workout in *Workout Builder*. We cannot define the exercise steps in different languages. Neither the user interface nor our data store supports saving multi-locale data.

This clearly means that in its current state we cannot use the *Workout Builder* app to create multilingual workout content. There is a decent amount of refactoring effort required and hence we will skip it for now and focus our efforts on localizing static content for our apps using angular-translate.

Angular-translate (`http://angular-translate.github.io/`) does a great job in supporting content/text localization. It has a number of features including asynchronous loading of I18n data, changing locale on the fly, filters, directives, and a service to localize content.

To use angular-translate, the first thing that we do is look for all HTML elements in the page that have string literals. These string literals will be replaced with keys that angular-translate uses to localize the content.

Once the string literals are identified and replaced with keys, translation mapping that maps keys to translated content is created. In angular-translate, this mapping is nothing more than a JavaScript object, with the name of the property as the key and the value as the localized content. For example, this is the German translation mapping for the *Start* page:

```
var translations = {
    "START": {
        "HEADER":"Bereit für ein Workout?",
        "SELECT":"Wählen Workout",
        "WORKOUTS":"Workouts",
        "SEARCH":"Suchen Sie nach dem Training"
    }
};
```

The translations object is then registered with the angular-translate $translate service during the configuration stage:

```
$translateProvider.translations('de', translations);
```

This example sets up the German-language translation:

 Remember, before using $translate, like any other Angular module we need to first add the reference of angular-translate to index.html and include the module dependency pascalprecht.translate.

On the same lines, other translations can be registered if desired.

We can see that translation also allows us to maintain hierarchy and we can have any level of object hierarchy to compartmentalize the translations. For example, if the *Start* page has a large number of translations, we could add subobjects to the START property to segregate sections further.

Once the translations are registered, we are ready to use these translations in our app. There are three ways to use them:

- **Using the $translate service**: We can retrieve a specific translation in the controller using the $translate service. Although not used much, it allows us to get the localized version of a translation key. For example:

```
$translate('START.HEADER').then(function (header) {
$scope.header = header;
});
```

  The retrieval syntax is promise-based, and there is a reason for this. The library also allows asynchronous loading of localization content from remote locations.

- **Using the translate filter**: Replace the literal string with a translation key and apply the translate filter; we are done:

```
<h1>Ready for a Workout?</h1> // Replace this
<h1>{{'START.HEADER'|translate}}</h1>  // With this
```

  Using the START.HEADER key, the translate filter replaces the interpolation with the localized version of the content from the registered translations.

  Remember, every translation filter adds to the number of watches on the page. The static content now becomes dynamic and for a large page there may be a performance impact due to this. A better but restricted approach is to use a directive for translations.

- **Using the translate directive**: The `translate` directive does something similar to the `translate` filter. The directive replaces the inner content of HTML on which it is declared with the translated text. This is how we use directives for translations:

```
<h2 translate>START.WORKOUTS</h2>
<-- OR -->
<h2 translate="START.WORKOUTS"></h2>
```

  The nice thing about the `translate` directive is that it supports interpolations too, allowing a dynamic translation key. For example, look at this:

```
<h2 translate>{{scopeVariable}}</h2>
```

  OR

```
<h2 translate="{{scopeVariable}}"></h2>
```

  Prefer the directive version over filter version as the directive does not create a watch-like filter. But remember, the `translate` directive may not work everywhere and in such scenarios, the filter is the only choice. A good example of this is an attribute that needs localization:

```
<input type="text"
  placeholder="{{'START.SEARCH'|translate}}" />
```

  The directive version cannot handle this.

So far, we have looked at how to define translations and how to use them in views and otherwise. The last thing that you need to understand is how the `$translate` service selects the default locale and how we specify which locale to use for the translation.

We can set the default locale during the configuration stage using this:

```
$translateProvider.preferredLanguage('en');
```

This sets the default locale to en (English) and if the locale is never set during app execution, the en locale is used.

To actually change the locale any time during the app execution, we can call the following code:

```
$translate.use('de'); // Change locale to German
```

And magically, the locale changes!

Angular-translate is a mature library and we have just scratched the surface in terms of its capabilities. Look at the angular-translate documentation to learn more about the library.

Have a look at the updated *Personal Trainer* app available in the `checkpoint1` folder under `chapter8`. Some parts of the app have also been made locale-aware using the `angular-translate` library. The *Index* page container (`index.html`), the *Start* page, and the *Workout Runner* page have been localized to support two languages, English and German. Also, to showcase an advance scenario and optimize the app experience, the translations are being loaded from a remote server (defined in locale-specific files) instead of defining them inline at the configuration stage.

> The code is also available on GitHub (`https://github.com/chandermani/angularjsbyexample`) for everyone to download. Checkpoints are implemented as branches in GitHub. The branch to download is:
>
> *GitHub branch: checkpoint8.1 (folder: trainer)*

As we can see that the Angular's inbuilt support for localization may not be first class but the community more than makes up for it with these great modules.

Next we have a look at another common requirement that invariably most apps have, authenticating its users.

Handling authentication and authorization

Most, if not all, apps have a requirement to authenticate/authorize user access. We may argue that authentication and authorization are more of a server concern than a client concern, and that is correct. Still, the client side needs to adapt and integrate with the authentication and authorization requirement imposed by the server.

Any typical Angular application first loads partial views and then makes calls to pull data from the server and binds them to the views. Clearly, the views and the remote data API are the two assets that need to be secured.

To guard these resources, you need to understand how a typical application is secured on the server. There are primarily two broad approaches for securing any web applications: cookie-based authentication and token-based authentication. Each of them requires different handling on the client part. The next two sections describe how we can integrate with either of these approaches.

Cookie-based authentication

This authentication mechanism is the easiest to implement if the server stack supports it. It's non-intrusive and may require the bare minimum of changes to the Angular application. Cookie-based authentication involves setting the browser cookie to track the user authentication session. The following sequence diagram explains a typical cookie-based authentication workflow:

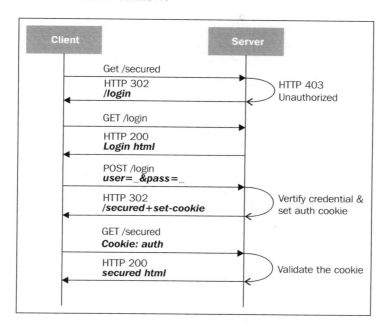

Here is how a typical authentication workflow works:

- When trying to access a secured resource from the browser, the server sends a HTTP 401 Unauthorized status code if the user is not authenticated,. As we see later, a user request is an unauthorized request if there is no cookie attached to the request or the cookie is expired/invalid.

- This unauthorized response is intercepted by the server or, at times, by the client framework (Angular, in our case) and it typically results in a 302 redirect (if intercepted by the server). The redirect location is the URL to the login page (the login page allows anonymous access).

- The user then enters the username and password on the login page and does a POST to the login endpoint.

- The server validates the credentials, sets a browser cookie, and redirects the user to the original requested resource.

- Henceforth, the authentication cookie is a part of every request (added by the browser automatically) and the server uses this cookie to confirm its identity and whether the user is authenticated.

 This scenario assumes that the HTML and API exist under a single domain.

As we can see, with this approach the Angular infrastructure is not involved or the involvement is minimal. Even the login page can be a standard HTML page that just sends data to the login endpoint for authentication. If the user lands on the Angular app, it implicitly means that the user has already been authenticated.

 The cookie-based authentication flow may vary depending on the server framework, but the general pattern of setting a cookie and attaching a cookie with every subsequent request, remains the same.

In a cookie-based application authentication, if the application wants to get the user context, a server endpoint (such as /user/details) is exposed that returns the logged in user-specific data. The client application can then implement a service such as UserService that loads and caches the user profile data.

The scenario described here assumes that the API server (the server that returns data) and the site where the application is hosted are in a single domain. That may not be the case always. Even for *Personal Trainer,* the data resides on the MongoLab servers and the application resides on a different server (even if it is local). And we already know that this is a cross-domain access and it comes with its own set of challenges.

In such a setup, even if the API server is able to authenticate the request and send a cookie back to the client, the client application still does not send the authentication cookie on a subsequent request.

To fix this, we need to set a Boolean variable with credentials to true on the $http configuration object:

```
$http.get('api/users',{ withCredentials : true});
```

And the client will start attaching the authentication cookie for the cross-domain requests.

The server too needs to have **cross-origin resource sharing (CORS)** enabled and needs to respond in a specific manner for the request to succeed. It should set the access-control-allow-credentials header to true and the access-control-allow-origin header to the host site making the request.

Check the MDN documentation (`https://developer.mozilla.org/en/http_access_control#section_5`) to learn more about this scenario in detail.

Cookie-based authentication is definitely less work on the client side, but there are times when you have to revert to token-based access. This could be because:

- Cookies and cross-domain requests do not play nicely across browsers. Specifically, IE8 and IE9 do not support it.
- The server may not support generating cookies or the server only exposes token-based authentication.
- Token-based solutions are easy to integrate with native mobile applications and desktop clients.
- Tokens are not susceptible to **cross-site request forgery (CSRF)** attacks.

 To know more about CSRF, look at the CRSF Prevention cheat sheet here at `https://www.owasp.org/index.php/Cross-Site_Request_Forgery_%28CSRF%29_Prevention_Cheat_Sheet`.

The next section talks about supporting token-based authentication.

Token-based authentication

Token-based access is all about sending the token (typically in HTTP headers) with each request instead of a cookie. A simplified token-based workflow looks something like this:

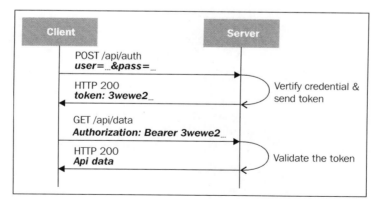

Many public APIs (such as *facebook* and *twitter*) use token-based authentication. The format of the token, where it goes, and how it is generated depend upon the protocol used and the server implementation. Popular services that use token-based authentication implement the *OAuth 2.0* protocol for token generation and exchange.

In a typical token-based authentication setup, the views are available publically, but the API is secured. If the application tries to pull data through API calls without attaching the appropriate token to the outgoing request, the server returns the HTTP 401 Unauthorized status code.

Integrating with a token-based authentication system requires a decent amount of setup on the client side too. Let's take a simplified example of a **Human Resource (HR)** system that supports token-based authentication and so that you understand how the authentication workflow works with the Angular application as a client.

The HR system has a page showing the list of employees and a login page. It also has API endpoints to get the list of employees and generate access tokens. The API endpoint that returns the employee list is secured by token-based access.

The workflow starts with the user loading the employee list page. The view is loaded but the API call fails with the server returning HTTP 401 Unauthorized.

On receiving a 401 HTTP error code, the app should respond by either routing the user to a login view (remember this is an SPA) or opening a login popup.

A naive implementation for this could be:

```
$http.get('/api/employees').then(function (employees) {}, function
(error) {
    if (error.status === 401) {
        $scope.unauthorized = true; //Triggers login popup
        //$location.path('/login'); // or redirect to login.
    }
});
```

The biggest problem with the preceding implementation is that we need to add this code to every controller that requires remote data access as the call may fail. Not very smart!

The correct way to handle this scenario is to use the Angular HTTP interceptor and events. The HTTP interceptor intercepts all 401 errors and raises a global unauthorized event. The interceptor (oversimplified) looks like this:

```
function ($rootScope, $q, ) {
return {
```

```
responseError: function (error) {
if (error.status === 401)
 $rootScope.$broadcast('unauthorized', error);
    return $q.reject(rejection);
   }
  }
 }
```

With such an interceptor in place, any remote request that results in a 401 response is caught by the interceptor and an unauthorized event is raised.

Now it's just a matter of catching this event in some type of global controller (such as RootController in *Personal Trainer*) and reacting to it. We use something like this where we set a Boolean variable true, triggering a modal username/password dialog:

```
$scope.$on("unauthorized",function(evt,err){
    $scope.showLoginDialog=true;
});
```

The user then enters his/her username/password to authenticate himself with the server. As part of the authentication process, the server validates the credentials, creates a token, and sends it back to the client app.

On the client side, we need to create a service that can send the username/password to the authentication endpoint, and manage the token returned as part of a successful authentication. A sample AuthService implementation might look like this:

```
angular.module('app').factory("AuthService", function ($q,
localStorageService, $http, $rootScope) {
    var service = {};
    service.authenticate = function (userName, password) {
        $http.post('/authenticate', {
            user: userName,
            password: password
        }).then(function (data) {
            localStorageService.add('authToken', data.token);
            $http.defaults.headers.common['Authorization'] =
              'Basic ' + data.token;
            $rootScope.$broadcast('userAuthenticated');
        });
    }
    service.useTokenFromCache=function() {
        var token=localStorageService.get('authToken');
        if(token)
```

```
        $http.defaults.headers.common['Authorization']
            = 'Basic ' + data.token;
    }
return service;
});
```

The `AuthService.authenticate` function basically invokes the server endpoint to verify credentials, parse the token received from the server, save the token to the local storage/session storage for future use (if there is a page refresh), set the appropriate HTTP header (so that the token is sent on all subsequent requests), and finally broadcast the authentication-complete event.

The following statement actually sets the `auth` header for all subsequent requests:

```
$http.defaults.headers.common['Authorization']
= 'Basic ' + data.token;
```

Without this, the complete login process described here will be repeated and we will be stuck in a loop.

This statement also highlights how we can use `$http.default.headers` to set common headers for all outgoing requests. Angular shows us how to be more specific and that we can alter specific verbs:

```
$http.defaults.headers.post['some-header']=value;
$http.defaults.headers.put['some-header']=value;
$http.defaults.headers.get['some-header']=value;
```

 These headers can also be set during the configuration stage of the Angular application, by injecting `$httpProvider`.

The `AuthService.useTokenFromCache` function is useful in case of a page refresh scenario. This function can be invoked during the module run phase:

```
angular.module('app').run(function(AuthService){
    AuthService.useTokenFromCache();
});
```

If the token is found in local storage, the login workflow is avoided.

 If the token in location storage expires (remember, each token has a lifetime) the authentication will fail with HTTP 401, and we will need to repeat the login flow.

The walkthrough here just outlines one mechanism to send a token to the server but the process may vary based on the server stack too. Always refer to the backend/server documentation before implementing a token-based authentication in Angular.

Two of the notable modules/libraries that we should mention here are:

- `angular-http-auth` (`https://github.com/witoldsz/angular-http-auth`): The preceding walkthrough can be easily implemented using this library, as it already has the http interceptor and events to support what we have described earlier.

- `ng-token-auth` (`https://github.com/lynndylanhurley/ng-token-auth`): This is a comprehensive library that does much more than just authentication.

Both these libraries can help us get started with token-based authentication.

We have taken care of authentication but what about authorization? Once the user context is established we still need to make sure the user is only able to access the parts that he/she is allowed to. *Authorization* is still missing.

Handling authorization

Like authentication, authorization support too needs to be implemented on both the server and client side; more so, on the server than the client. Remember, anyone can hack into the JavaScript code and circumvent the complete authentication/authorization setup. So always tighten your server infrastructure irrespective of whether the client has the necessary checks in place or not.

This still does not mean that we do not do an authorization check on the client. For standard users, this is the first line of defense against unwarranted access.

When working on an authorization requirement for any application, there are three essential elements that are part of the setup:

- The resources that need to be secured/authorized
- A list of roles and users that are part of these roles
- A mapping between the resources and the roles that defines who can access what

From an Angular app perspective, the resources are the pages, and sometimes sections of pages, that need to be restricted to specific roles. If the user is in a specific role, depending upon the role-resource mapping he/she gets access to some pages, else he/she is denied access.

While authorization in Angular applications can be implemented in a number of ways, we will outline a generic implementation that can be further customized to suite our needs in the future.

Adding authorization support

To enable authorization, the first thing that we need to do is to expose the logged-in user data including roles throughout the application.

Sharing user authentication context

Using the Angular service to share the authentication context perfectly fits the bill. Look at the outline of the service here:

```
angular.module('app').factory('sessionContext', function () {
    var service;
    service.currentUser = function () {...}
    service.isUserInRole = function (roles) {...}
    service.authenticated = false;
    return service;
});
```

The `sessionContext` service tracks the user login session and provides details such as the logged-in user (`currentUser`), whether the user is authenticated (`authenticated`), and the `isUserInRole` function that returns `true` or `false` based on whether the user is part of any of the roles passed into the `roles` parameter.

With this service in place, we can add authorization for routes (views), thereby restricting access to some routes to specific roles only.

Restricting routes

To restrict route access, we can use the route configuration to define what roles have access to which routes, and hence views. Here is how a sample route configuration with role-access defined looks:

```
$routeProvider.when('/admin', {
    templateUrl: 'admin.html',
    controller: 'AdminController',
    roles:['admin']
});
$routeProvider.when('/home', {
    templateUrl: 'home.html',
    controller: 'HomeController',
    roles:[ 'admin', 'user']
});
```

The new `roles` property on the route declares who has access to the specific view. This sets up the mapping between role and view access, but it still needs to be enforced.

To make sure the route is not loaded for an unauthorized user, we can catch the `$routeChangeStart` event in either a root controller or the module `run` function and redirect the user to an unauthorized page appropriately. This is a rough draft of how the code that does this redirection should look:

```
angular.module('app').run(function ($rootScope, $location,
SessionContext) {
    $rootScope.$on('$routeChangeStart', function (event, next) {
        if (next.roles && !SessionContext.authenticated) {
            $location.path('/login');  //needs to login
        }
        if (next.roles && SessionContext.authenticated &&
        !SessionContext.isInRole(next.roles)) {
            $location.path('/unauthorized'); //un-authorized
        }
    });
});
```

We subscribe to the `$routeChangeStart` event and in the event handler look at the `roles` property of the `next` route to establish whether the user is allowed to access the route or not. If not, we redirect the user to either the login or unauthorized page.

This fixes the routes, but there is one more thing to fix. What happens when a page has view elements that are rendered based on the user's role?

Conditionally rendering content based on roles

Conditionally rendering content is easy to implement. We just need to show/hide HTML elements based on the user role. Something like this works:

```
<div  id='header'>
    <div> Welcome, {{userName}}</div>
    <div><a href='#/setting/my'>Settings</a></div>
    <div ng-if='isUserInRole(["admin"])'>
<a href='#/setting/site'>Site Settings</a>
</div>
</div>
```

The preceding code checks whether the user is in an admin role before rendering a `Site Setting` hyperlink.

What we have previously outlined is a reference implementation to achieve authentication and authorization. With this basic understanding in place, any setup can be tweaked to handle other custom authentication/authorization scenarios.

Communication and data sharing patterns

A typical Angular app employs a number of framework artefacts to achieve any functionality. Any Angular app has multiple *views*, *controllers*, *services*, *filters*, and also *directives*, all working together in unison. The need for communication between these constructs thus becomes imperative.

This section highlights how communication can happen among these constructs and how data is shared. It tries to address scenarios such as:

- How to send data from one view to another on page transition
- How to communicate and or share data:
    - Between controllers
    - Between controllers and services, other controllers, or directives
    - Via inter-directive communication and even inter-service communication

We have used patterns at various times throughout the book. The aim here is to consolidate our learning and provide a quick reference.

Using a URL to share data across pages

If data needs to be shared across pages, it can be done using route URLs. A route definition is something like this:

```
/builder/workouts/:id
```

It allows setting the id fragment (on the source page) to a value that is available on the target view controller, and other controllers that are available when the route is loaded using $routeParams.id.

Passing data using a route is simple but the capability is limited to passing only string parameters. This approach seems similar to the process of using query strings when working with standard web applications with multiple pages.

In spite of this limitation, a lot can be achieved by passing data using routes. Data passed in the URL (using `$routeParams`) can be used by the target page to retrieve more content based on what is passed in the URL.

Look at the route example outlined previously, it is from the *Workout Builder*. Clicking on a specific workout tile in *Workout List* takes us to the workout edit page with the workout name embedded in the URL (`/builder/workouts/7minworkout`). The `WorkoutController` object then uses `$routeParams.id`/`$route.current.params.id` to actually retrieve the selected workout from the server (using the `WorkoutService`).

Using $scope

Scopes are a ubiquitous mechanism for communication and data sharing. Scopes are used so often that we do not put much thought into *how* and *what* we are actually sharing.

To reiterate how scopes work in Angular, look at this:

- Scopes are created as part of the directive execution, or as part of the application bootstrapping process when an application starts
- At any given time in the application, one or more scopes are active
- Scope hierarchy is driven by the HTML element hierarchy
- A child scope inherits from its parent scope (the prototypal inheritance) and hence can access all properties of the parent scope (isolated scope is an exception).

Given how scopes work, parent/child views can implicitly communicate with each other using the associated parent scope.

The *Workout Runner* app is an excellent example of this. It has a *workout videos* view and a *description panel* that derive their content from the parent scope.

Scopes as a data sharing mechanism have their limitation too.

The very fact that scopes share data with a child scope through inheritance implies two unrelated scopes or sibling scopes cannot share data/communicate directly. In such a scenario, we need one of the following:

- Use the parent scope as a communication channel. This parent can be an immediate parent in the case of sibling scopes or a parent scope up higher in the hierarchy.

- Or as a special case, we can use $rootScope to communicate and share data. Since $rootScope is the root for the complete application scope hierarchy, any data set on $rootScope can be accessed throughout all scopes.

- Use services to communicate between such scopes. This is possible because services by nature are singleton.

While all these methods try to solve the same problem, there are some that are preferable to others. $rootScope should be avoided as this results in the creation of a global state, which is never a good thing.

Prefer services over parent scopes when it comes to sharing data. The disadvantage of the parent scope is that, just by looking at variables defined on the parent scope, one cannot determine who is consuming them, whereas services makes this dependency explicit.

This also happens when we break a large view into multiple smaller manageable views. We may be taking dependency implicitly on the scope that these new views inherit. In such a case, too, we should try to evaluate whether a service can be used.

Using $rootScope

Since there is a single $rootscope service created for any Angular application, $rootScope can be used to share data. Anything added to $rootScope is accessible throughout the app.

Using $rootScope just to share data among controllers should be avoided. In fact, any global state can easily be managed using services as they too are singleton in nature.

The only reason $rootScope is useful is that it can be injected into services and can be used to broadcast/emit events at a global level.

Using services

The original intent of services is not to share data. Services allow us to encapsulate data and behavior that is not coupled with the view and can be used across the application. But since services are singleton in nature, they can very well be used to share data among Angular constructs.

Create a service and inject it into a controller, directive, or other service itself and you have a working communication channel. When service functions are invoked or data is manipulated, the changes are automatically available to any component that has the service dependency.

When writing services to communicate and share data, write them from a behavioral perspective, without thinking of them as a mere data store (shared).

Inter-directive communication

How can two directives interact? If they are defined on the same HTML tag or follow a parent-child hierarchy, we can use the `require` attribute of the directive definition object.

To reiterate what you learned in the chapter on directives, use this:

```
require: ['ngModel'],
```

To take dependency on another directive (the preceding `ngModel`) defined on the same element, use this:

```
require: ['?^busyIndicator'],
```

This takes dependency on a directive defined on the parent (`busyIndicator`).

> Remember, directive dependency is about taking dependencies on the directive's controller function.

When `require` is `true`, the directive controller dependency is injected into the link function of the dependent directive, as shown here:

```
link: function (scope, elm, attr, ctrl) {
ctrl.$setValidity(validatorName, data);
}
```

But if the directives are not defined on the same HTML hierarchy or are not using directive controllers, then they can communicate using either the parent scope, the `$rootScope`, services, or through events. For directives with isolated scopes, the options are further limited to services, `$rootScope`, or events. Avoid `$rootScope` and stick to the service or event broadcast/subscribe in such a case.

Using events

Events are a great mechanism for communicating between components and while keeping them decoupled. A publisher component raises an event, and one or more subscribers can listen to the events and react to them. Events can be used across controllers, directives, filters, or services for communication.

Angular eventing infrastructure is set up using three functions defined on the scope object:

- To publish $broadcast and $emit: $broadcast sends a message down the scope hierarchy and $emit sends a message up the hierarchy.
- To subscribe $on.

When using $broadcast or $emit from a scope to raise an event, we need to be aware of where the subscribers are. To reiterate what you learned about eventing in *Chapter 3, More AngularJS Goodness for 7 Minute Workout,* have a look at this:

- With $scope.$emit, event messages travel up, hence any upstream parent scope can subscribe to these event messages
- With $scope.$broadcast, event messages travel down, hence any downstream child scope can subscribe to these messages

But if the publisher and subscribers do not share a parent-child hierarchy, then the publisher can use $rootSope.$broadcast to communicate. $rootScope.$broadcast propagates the event through every available scope in the application.

While $emit and $broadcast are great mechanisms for communicating, we should be careful not to overuse them. Too many events can make an application difficult to understand and debug as the flow of the application is not linear any more.

With this we have covered every communication mechanism/pattern available.

 As far as possible, stick to services to share data and the events to publish important changes that happen during the execution of the app.

Let's focus our attention on another critical area of Angular apps: performance!

Performance

From what we have seen and built so far, we can all agree that AngularJS is insanely fast. For standard size views, we rarely see any performance bottlenecks. But many views start small and then grow over time. And sometimes the requirement dictates we build large pages/views with a sizable amount of HTML and data. In such a case, there are things that we need to keep in mind to provide an optimal user experience.

Take any framework and the performance discussion on the framework always requires one to understand the internal working of the framework. When it comes to Angular, we need to understand how Angular detects model changes. What are watches? What is a digest cycle? What roles do scope objects play? Without a conceptual understanding of these subjects, any performance guidance is merely a checklist that we follow without understanding the *why* part.

We have covered concepts behind the digest cycle and dirty checking in *Chapter 3, More AngularJS Goodness for 7 Minute Workout*, while implementing audio playback support for the *7 Minute Workout* app.

To summarize that discussion here, we saw the following:

- The live binding between the view elements and model data is set up using *watches*. When a model changes, one or many watches linked to the model are triggered. Angular's view binding infrastructure uses these watches to synchronize the view with the updated model value.

- Model change detection only happens when a *digest cycle* is triggered.

- *Angular does not track model changes in real time*; instead, on every digest cycle, it runs through every watch to compare the previous and new values of the model to detect changes.

- A digest cycle is triggered when `$scope.$apply` is invoked. A number of directives and services internally invoke `$scope.$apply`:
    - Directives such as `ng-click`, `ng-mouse*` do it on user action
    - Services such as `$http` and `$resource` do it when a response is received from server
    - `$timeout` or `$interval` call `$scope.$apply` when they lapse

- A digest cycle tracks the old value of the watched expression and compares it with the new value to detect if the model has changed. Simply put, the digest cycle is a workflow used to detect model changes.

- A digest cycle runs multiple times till the model data is stable and no watch is triggered.

Once you have a clear understanding of the digest cycle, watches, and scopes, we can look at some performance guidelines that can help us manage views as they start to grow.

Performance guidelines

When building any Angular app, any performance optimization boils down to:

- Minimizing the number of binding expressions and hence watches
- Making sure that binding expression evaluation is quick
- Optimizing the number of digest cycles that take place

The next few sections provide some useful pointers in this direction.

 Remember, a lot of these optimization may only be necessary if the view is large.

Keeping the page/view small

The sanest advice is to keep the amount of content available on a page small. The user cannot interact/process too much data on the page, so remember that screen real estate is at a premium and only keep necessary details on a page.

The lesser the content, the lesser the number of binding expressions; hence, fewer watches and less processing are required during the digest cycle. Remember, each watch adds to the overall execution time of the digest cycle. The time required for a single watch can be insignificant but, after combining hundreds and maybe thousands of them, they start to matter.

 Angular's data binding infrastructure is insanely fast and relies on a rudimentary dirty check that compares the old and the new values. Check out the **stack overflow (SO)** post (http://stackoverflow.com/questions/9682092/databinding-in-angularjs), where *Misko Hevery* (creator of Angular) talks about how data binding works in Angular.

Data binding also adds to the memory footprint of the application. Each watch has to track the current and previous value of a data-binding expression to compare and verify if data has changed.

Keeping a page/view small may not always be possible, and the view may grow. In such a case, we need to make sure that the number of bindings does not grow exponentially (linear growth is OK) with the page size. The next two tips can help minimize the number of bindings in the page and should be seriously considered for large views.

Optimizing watches for read-once data

In any Angular view, there is always content that, once bound, does not change. Any read-only data on the view can fall into this category. This implies that once the data is bound to the view, we no longer need watches to track model changes, as we don't expect the model to update.

Is it possible to remove the watch after one-time binding? Angular itself does not have something inbuilt, but a community project **bindonce** (`https://github.com/Pasvaz/bindonce`) is there to fill this gap.

 Angular 1.3 has added support for *bind* and *forget* in the native framework. Using the syntax `{{::title}}`, we can achieve one-time binding. If you are on Angular 1.3, use it!

Hiding (ng-show) versus conditional rendering (ng-if/ng-switch) content

You have learned two ways to conditionally render content in Angular. The `ng-show/ng-hide` directive shows/hides the DOM element based on the expression provided and `ng-if/ng-switch` creates and destroys the DOM based on an expression.

For some scenarios, `ng-if` can be really beneficial as it can reduce the number of binding expressions/watches for the DOM content not rendered. Consider the following example:

```
<div ng-if='user.isAdmin'>
    <div ng-include="'admin-panel.html'"></div>
</div>
```

The snippet renders an admin panel if the user is an admin. With `ng-if`, if the user is not an admin, the `ng-include` directive template is neither requested nor rendered saving us of all the bindings and watches that are part of the `admin-panel.html` view.

From the preceding discussion, it may seem that we should get rid of all `ng-show/ng-hide` directives and use `ng-if`. Well, not really! It again depends; for small size pages, `ng-show/ng-hide` works just fine. Also, remember that there is a cost to creating and destroying the DOM. If the expression to show/hide flips too often, this will mean too many DOMs create-and-destroy cycles, which are detrimental to the overall performance of the app.

Expressions being watched should not be slow

Since watches are evaluated too often, the expression being watched should return results fast.

The first way we can make sure of this is by using properties instead of functions to bind expressions. These expressions are as follows:

```
{{user.name}}
ng-show='user.Authorized'
```

The preceding code is always better than this:

```
{{getUserName()}}
ng-show = 'isUserAuthorized(user)'
```

Try to minimize function expressions in bindings. If a function expression is required, make sure that the function returns a result quickly. Make sure a function being watched *does not*:

- Make any remote calls
- Use `$timeout`/`$interval`
- Perform sorting/filtering
- Perform DOM manipulation (this can happen inside directive implementation)
- Or perform any other time-consuming operation

Be sure to avoid such operations inside a bound function.

To reiterate, Angular will evaluate a watched expression multiple times during every digest cycle just to know if the return value (a model) has changed and the view needs to be synchronized.

Minimizing the deep model watch

When using `$scope.$watch` to watch for model changes in controllers, be careful while setting the third `$watch` function parameter to `true`. The general syntax of watch looks like this:

```
$watch(watchExpression, listener, [objectEquality]);
```

In the standard scenario, Angular does an object comparison based on the reference only. But if `objectEquality` is `true`, Angular does a deep comparison between the last value and new value of the watched expression. This can have an adverse memory and performance impact if the object is large.

Handling large datasets with ng-repeat

The `ng-repeat` directive undoubtedly is the most useful directive Angular has. But it can cause the most performance-related headaches. The reason is not because of the directive design, but because it is the only directive that allows us to generate HTML on the fly. There is always the possibility of generating enormous HTML just by binding `ng-repeat` to a big model list. Some tips that can help us when working with `ng-repeat` are:

- **Page data and use limitTo**: Implement a server-side paging mechanism when a number of items returned are large.

  Also use the `limitTo` filter to limit the number of items rendered. Its syntax is as follows:

  ```
  <tr ng-repeat="user in users |limitTo:pageSize">...</tr>
  ```

   Look at modules such as `ngInfiniteScroll` (`http://binarymuse.github.io/ngInfiniteScroll/`) that provide an alternate mechanism to render large lists.

- **Use the track by expression**: The `ng-repeat` directive for performance tries to make sure it does not unnecessarily create or delete HTML nodes when items are added, updated, deleted, or moved in the list. To achieve this, it adds a `$$hashKey` property to every model item allowing it to associate the DOM node with the model item.

  We can override this behavior and provide our own item key using the track by expression such as:

  ```
  <tr ng-repeat="user in users track by user.id">...</tr>
  ```

  This allows us to use our own mechanism to identify an item. Using your own track by expression has a distinct advantage over the default *hash key* approach. Consider an example where you make an initial AJAX call to get users:

  ```
  $scope.getUsers().then(function(users){ $scope.users  = users;})
  ```

  Later again, refresh the data from the server and call something similar again:

  ```
  $scope.users = users;
  ```

With `user.id` as a key, Angular is able to determine what elements were added/deleted and moved; it can also determine created/deleted DOM nodes for such elements. Remaining elements are not touched by `ng-repeat` (internal bindings are still evaluated). This saves a lot of CPU cycles for the browser as fewer DOM elements are created and destroyed.

- **Do not bind ng-repeat to a function expression**: Using a function's return value for `ng-repeat` can also be problematic, depending upon how the function is implemented.

  Consider a repeat with this:

  ```
  <tr ng-repeat="user in getUsers()">...</tr>
  ```

  And consider the controller `getUsers` function with this:

  ```
  $scope.getUser = function() {
      var orderBy = $filter('orderBy');
      return orderBy($scope.users, predicate);
  }
  ```

  Angular is going to evaluate this expression and hence call this function every time the digest cycle takes place. A lot of CPU cycles were wasted sorting user data again and again. It is better to use scope properties and presort the data before binding.

- **Minimize filters in views, use filter elements in the controller**: Filters defined on `ng-repeat` are also evaluated every time the digest cycle takes place. For large lists, if the same filtering can be implemented in the controller, we can avoid constant filter evaluation. This holds true for any filter function that is used with arrays including `filter` and `orderBy`.

Avoiding mouse-movement tracking events

The `ng-mousemove`, `ng-mouseenter`, `ng-mouseleave`, and `ng-mouseover` directives can just kill performance. If an expression is attached to any of these event directives, Angular triggers a digest cycle every time the corresponding event occurs and for events like mouse move, this can be a lot.

We have already seen this behavior when working with *7 Minute Workout*, when we tried to show a pause overlay on the exercise image when the mouse hovers over it.

Avoid them at all cost. If we just want to trigger some style changes on mouse events, CSS is a better tool.

Avoiding calling $scope.$apply

Angular is smart enough to call `$scope.$apply` at appropriate times without us explicitly calling it. This can be confirmed from the fact that the only place we have seen and used `$scope.$apply` is within directives.

The `ng-click` and `updateOnBlur` directives use `$scope.$apply` to transition from a DOM event handler execution to an Angular execution context. Even when wrapping the jQuery plugin, we may require to do a similar transition for an event raised by the JQuery plugin.

Other than this, there is no reason to use `$scope.$apply`. Remember, every invocation of `$apply` results in the execution of a complete digest cycle.

The `$timeout` and `$interval` services take a Boolean argument `invokeApply`. If set to `false`, the lapsed `$timeout`/`$interval` services does not call `$scope.$apply` or trigger a digest cycle. Therefore, if you are going to perform background operations that do not require `$scope` and the view to be updated, set the last argument to `false`.

 Always use Angular wrappers over standard JavaScript objects/ functions such as `$timeout` and `$interval` to avoid manually calling `$scope.$apply`. These wrapper functions internally call `$scope.$apply`.

Also, understand the difference between `$scope.$apply` and `$scope.$digest`. `$scope.$apply` triggers `$rootScope.$digest` that evaluates all application watches whereas, `$scope.$digest` only performs dirty checks on the current scope and its children. If we are sure that the model changes are not going to affect anything other than the child scopes, we can use `$scope.$digest` instead of `$scope.$apply`.

Lazy-loading, minification, and creating multiple SPAs

I hope you are not assuming that the apps that we have built will continue to use the numerous small script files that we have created to separate modules and module artefacts (*controllers*, *directives*, *filters*, and *services*). Any modern build system has the capability to concatenate and minify these files and replace the original file reference with a unified and minified version. Therefore, like any JavaScript library, use minified script files for production.

The problem with the Angular bootstrapping process is that it expects all Angular application scripts to be loaded before the application can bootstrap. We cannot load modules, controllers, or in fact, any of the other Angular constructs on demand. This means we need to provide every artefact required by our app, upfront.

For small applications, this is not a problem as the content is concatenated and minified; also, the Angular application code itself is far more compact as compared to the traditional JavaScript of jQuery-based apps. But, as the size of the application starts to grow, it may start to hurt when we need to load everything upfront.

There are at least two possible solutions to this problem; the first one is about breaking our application into multiple SPAs.

Breaking applications into multiple SPAs

This advice may seem counterintuitive as the whole point of SPAs is to get rid of full page loads. By creating multiple SPAs, we break the app into multiple small SPAs, each supporting parts of the overall app functionality.

 When we say app, it implies a combination of the main (such as `index.html`) page with `ng-app` and all the scripts/libraries and partial views that the app loads over time.

For example, we can break the *Personal Trainer* application into a *Workout Builder* app and a *Workout Runner* app. Both have their own start up page and scripts. Common scripts such as the Angular framework scripts and any third-party libraries can be referenced in both the applications. On similar lines, common controllers, directives, services, and filters too can be referenced in both the apps.

The way we have designed *Personal Trainer* makes it easy to achieve our objective. The segregation into what belongs where has already been done.

The advantage of breaking an app into multiple SPAs is that only relevant scripts related to the app are loaded. For a small app, this may be an overkill but for large apps, it can improve the app performance.

The challenge with this approach is to identify what parts of an application can be created as independent SPAs; it totally depends upon the usage pattern of the application.

For example, assume an application has an admin module and an end consumer/ user module. Creating two SPAs, one for admin and the other for the end customer, is a great way to keep user-specific features and admin-specific features separate. A standard user may never transition to the admin section/area, whereas an admin user can still work on both areas; but transitioning from the admin area to a user-specific area will require a full page refresh.

If breaking the application into multiple SPAs is not possible, the other option is to perform the lazy loading of a module.

Lazy-loading modules

Lazy-loading modules or loading module on demand is a viable option for large Angular apps. But unfortunately, Angular itself does not have any in-built support for lazy-loading modules.

Furthermore, the additional complexity of lazy loading may be unwarranted as Angular produces far less code as compared to other JavaScript framework implementations. Also once we *gzip* and *minify* the code, the amount of code that is transferred over the wire is minimal.

If we still want to try our hands on lazy loading, there are two libraries that can help:

- `ocLazyLoad` (`https://github.com/ocombe/ocLazyLoad`): This is a library that uses `script.js` to load modules on the fly

- `angularAMD` (`http://marcoslin.github.io/angularAMD`): This is a library that uses `require.js` to lazy load modules

With lazy loading in place, we can delay the loading of a controller, directive, filter, or service script, until the page that requires them is loaded.

The overall concept of lazy loading seems to be great but I'm still not sold on this idea. Before we adopt a lazy-load solution, there are things that we need to evaluate:

- **Loading multiple script files lazily**: When scripts are concatenated and minified, we load the complete app at once. Contrast it to lazy loading where we do not concatenate but load them on demand. What we gain in terms of lazy-load module flexibility we lose in terms of performance. We now have to make a number of network requests to load individual files.

  Given these facts, the ideal approach is to combine lazy loading with concatenation and minification. In this approach, we identify those feature modules that can be concatenated and minified together and served on demand using lazy loading. For example, *Personal Trainer* scripts can be divided into three categories:

  - **The common app modules**: This consists of any script that has common code used across the app and can be combined together and loaded upfront

  - **The Workout Runner module(s)**: Scripts that support workout execution can be concatenated and minified together but are loaded only when the *Workout Runner* pages are loaded.

  - **The Workout builder module(s)**: On similar lines to the preceding categories, scripts that support workout building can be combined together and served only when the *Workout Builder* pages are loaded.

As we can see, there is a decent amount of effort required to refactor the app in a manner that makes module segregation, concatenation, and lazy loading possible.

- **The effect on unit and integration testing**: We also need to evaluate the effect of lazy-loading modules in unit and integration testing. The way we test is also affected with lazy loading in place. This implies that, if lazy loading is added as an afterthought, the test setup may require tweaking to make sure existing tests still run.

> The *Personal Trainer* implementation has been altered to showcase the lazy-loading approach using *ocLazyLoad*. The implementation is available in the `checkpoint2` folder under `chapter8`.
>
> *GitHub branch: checkpoint8.2 (folder – trainer)*

Given these facts, we should evaluate our options and check whether we really need lazy loading or we can manage by breaking a monolithic SPA into multiple smaller SPAs.

Caching remote data wherever appropriate

Caching data is the one of the oldest tricks in the book to improve any webpage/application performance. Analyze your GET requests and determine what data can be cached. Once such data is identified, it can be cached from a number of locations.

Data cached outside the app can be cached in:

- **Servers**: The server can cache repeated GET requests to resources that do not change very often. This whole process is transparent to the client and the implementation depends on the server stack used.

- **Browsers**: In this case, the browser caches the response. Browser caching depends upon the server sending **HTTP cache headers** such as *ETag* and *cache-control* to guide the browser about how long a particular resource can be cached. Browsers can honor these cache headers and cache data appropriately for future use.

If server and browser caching is not available or if we also want to incorporate any amount of caching in the client app, we do have some choices:

- **Cache data in memory**: A simple Angular service can cache the HTTP response in the memory. Since Angular is SPA, the data is not lost unless the page refreshes. This is how a service function looks when it caches data:

```
var workouts;
```

```
service.getWorkouts = function () {
    if (workouts) return $q.resolve(workouts);
    return $http.get("/workouts").then(function (response)
 {

        workouts = response.data;
        return workouts;
    });
};
```

The implementation caches a list of workouts into the workouts variable for future use. The first request makes a HTTP call to retrieve data, but subsequent requests just return the cached data as promised. The usage of $q.resolve makes sure that the function always returns a promise.

- *Angular $http cache*: Angular's $http service comes with a configuration option cache. When set to true, $http caches the response of the particular GET request into a local cache (again an in-memory cache). Here is how we cache a GET request:

```
$http.get(url, { cache: true});
```

Angular caches this cache for the lifetime of the app, and clearing it is not easy. We need to get hold of the cache dedicated to caching HTTP responses and clear the cache key manually.

The caching strategy of an application is never complete without a cache invalidation strategy. With cache, there is always a possibility that caches are out of sync with respect to the actual data store.

We cannot affect the server-side caching behavior from the client; consequently, let's focus on how to perform cache invalidation (clearing) for the two client-side caching mechanisms described earlier.

If we use the first approach to cache data, we are responsible for clearing cache ourselves.

In the case of the second approach, the default $http service does not support clearing cache. We either need to get hold of the underlying $http cache store and clear the cache key manually (as shown here) or implement our own cache that manages cache data and invalidates cache based on some criteria:

```
var cache = $cacheFactory.get('$http');
cache.remove("http://myserver/workouts"); //full url
```

Using Batarang to measure performance

Batarang (a Chrome extension), as we have already seen, is an extremely handy tool for Angular applications. Using Batarang to visualize app usage is like looking at an X-Ray of the app. It allows us to:

- View the scope data, scope hierarchy, and how the scopes are linked to HTML elements
- Evaluate the performance of the application
- Check the application dependency graph, helping us understand how components are linked to each other, and with other framework components.

If we enable *Batarang* and then play around with our application, Batarang captures performance metrics for all watched expressions in the app. This data is nicely presented as a graph available on the **Performance** tab inside Batarang:

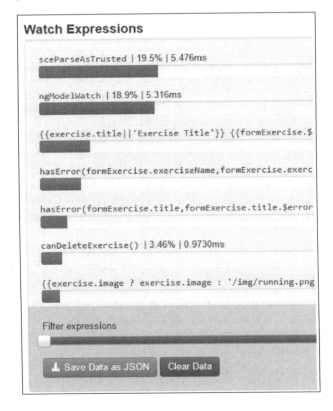

That is pretty sweet!

When building an app, use Batarang to gauge the most expensive watches and take corrective measures, if required.

Play around with Batarang and see what other features it has. This is a very handy tool for Angular applications.

This brings us to the end of the performance guidelines that we wanted to share in this chapter. Some of these guidelines are preventive measures that we should take to make sure we get optimal app performance whereas others are there to help when the performance is not up to the mark.

Useful third-party libraries

In the Angular world, there are some third-party libraries/modules that we need to highlight as they have become the *de facto* choice in their respective problem domain. These libraries include:

- `ui-router` (https://github.com/angular-ui/ui-router): Angular routing allows us to define a single main view (using `ng-view`) and drive the view through route changes. For some applications, this may be too limiting and hence they require a more capable routing infrastructure. The `ui-router` library overcomes this limitation, allowing us to define multiple siblings and nested views and link them through routes (referred to as `states` in the `ui-router` vocabulary). Any time the standard routing infrastructure is not working, we should explore the `ui-router` capabilities.

- AngularUI (http://angular-ui.github.io/): This is a suite of tools for Angular. It has a number of gems such as `ui-bootstrap`, a drop-in replacement for Bootstrap JavaScript components; `ng-grid`, a grid component; and `ui-router`, that we have discussed already; and many more.

- `ng-grid` (http://angular-ui.github.io/ng-grid/): If we are looking for a grid for Angular, this is the one to use. This is a feature-rich and highly customizable grid.

 There are efforts being made to rewrite `ng-grid` as `ui-grid`. Do check it out too (http://ui-grid.info/).

- Restangular (https://github.com/mgonto/restangular): This is a replacement for the `$resource` service. A feature-rich service that is totally promise–based and supports nested resources, custom functions, and many more features.

- Ionic Framework (http://ionicframework.com/): Ionic is a hybrid mobile app framework that allows us to build apps that target mobile devices. It uses HTML, CSS, and JavaScript, and has been optimized for AngularJS development.

These are just a few libraries that we have highlighted; there are many more useful modules/libraries out there that can save our precious development time. Always search before implementing your own!

With this, we have reached the end of this chapter and the book. Awesome! It's time to summarize your learning.

Summary

In this chapter, we gained some useful insight into a number of practical issues surrounding AngularJS development. These tips and guidelines can be extremely handy when building real-life applications using the framework.

We started the chapter by exploring the concept of seed projects and how these projects can get us up and running in no time. We looked at some popular seed projects that can serve as a base for any new Angular app development. We also touched upon Yeoman, a suite of tools that helps us kick-start new projects.

Next you learned about multilingual apps and some common concerns surrounding internationalization. We explored the localization support that Angular provides and its shortcomings. We also localized some of our app content in the US and German locales.

In spite of being a server side concern, authentication and authorizations do affect client implementation. The section on authentication/authorization covered how to handle authentication in a cookie- and token-based setup.

We then covered a number of useful patterns for communication and data sharing among various Angular constructs. This section covered scope, service, and event-based communication with their merits and shortcomings.

Lastly, we looked at the ever-so-important topic of performance, where you learned ways to optimize an Angular app performance.

The book is coming to a close, but for everyone reading it the journey has just begun. It's time to put theories into practice, hone our newly acquired skills, build something useful with Angular, and share it with the world. The more you invest in Angular the more rewarding the framework is. Let's get started!

Index

B

Batarang
   about 25, 29, 420
   URL 29
   using 25, 420
Bootstrap progress bar
   ng-style, used with 63
   URL 63
Bower
   about 340
   script dependencies, managing
      with 340, 341
browser storage
   workout history, persisting in 148, 149
busy-indicator 302

C

callback functions
   arguments 226
codebase download 35
code organization
   about 36
   JavaScript code, organizing 36-39
communication pattern 404
compile function
   attr 284
   element 284
config phase 66
constant services
   services, creating with 133
controller
   about 8, 12, 13, 37
   dependencies, setting up 345-348
   refactoring 116, 117
   revisiting 23, 24
   unit testing 344, 345
   WorkoutHistoryTracker service,
      integrating with 139
controller dependencies
   $interval 346
   $location 346
   $routeParams 347
   $scope 346
   appEvents 347
   Exercise 347

   setting up 345-348
   WorkoutHistoryTracker 346
   WorkoutService 347
controller implementations
   about 47-50
   exercise duration tracking,
      $interval service used 50, 51
   verifying 51-53
cookie-based authentication 395, 396
cross-domain access 249, 250
cross-domain requests
   creating, JSONP used 250, 251
cross-site request forgery (CSRF) 397
cross-site scripting (XSS) 91
CRUD 245
CRUD, on exercises/workouts
   AngularJS 249, 250
   cross-domain access 249, 250
   cross-origin resource sharing (CORS) 252
   JSONP used, for creating cross-domain
      requests 250, 251
   performing 245
   workout, creating 246-249
   workout, fixing 246-249
CSS class
   manipulating, ng-class directive used 112
custom promises
   $q.when function 243, 244
   creating 242, 243
   resolving 242, 243

D

data
   browsers 418
   servers 418
database
   seeding 224, 225
data binding, AngularJS
   URL 104
data, of exercise step
   ng-bind-html directive, using with 93, 94
data sharing pattern 404
dependency annotations
   $inject annotation 46
   about 46
   inline annotation 46, 47

invalid route
  resolving 174
isolated scopes 313

J

Jasmine Spies
  used, for verifying dependencies 352, 353
JavaScript-based animation, jQuery
  URL 127
JavaScript code
  organizing 36-39
jQuery plugin
  URL 324
jsFiddle
  about 29
  URL 29
jsPerf
  URL 145

K

Karma
  setting up, for unit testing 338, 339
  unit tests, debugging 349-351
  URL 339
keyboard
  used, for pausing exercises 114, 115
  used, for resuming exercises 114, 115
keyboard events
  references, for capturing 115

L

lazy loading modules
  about 417
  angularAMD 417
  ocLazyLoad 417
left nav
  building 168, 169
left navigation
  and top navigation, integrating 162-164
link function 292-294

M

media-player directive 101
minification
  about 45
  handling 45
model data
  and server data, differences 234
model update, on blur
  about 296
  directive, life cycle 299-301
  multiple directive, on single element 302
  priority directive, on single element 302
  remote validation, performing 297, 298
model updates
  controlling, with ng-model-options
    (Angular 1.3) 181, 182
Model View Controller. *See* **MVC**
module 14, 343
module initialization 66-69
MongoDB
  URL 222
MongoLab
  URL 222
mouse events
  used, for pausing overlays 110, 111
  used, for resuming overlays 110, 111
multi-lingual apps
  Angular I18n support 389
  building 388
multiple SPAs
  creating 416
MVC 7, 8

N

NaN (not a number) 187
navigation pattern
  routes 161
newCollection parameter 57
ngAnimate module
  URL 128
ng-annotate
  URL 47

About Packt Publishing

Packt, pronounced 'packed', published its first book, *Mastering phpMyAdmin for Effective MySQL Management*, in April 2004, and subsequently continued to specialize in publishing highly focused books on specific technologies and solutions.

Our books and publications share the experiences of your fellow IT professionals in adapting and customizing today's systems, applications, and frameworks. Our solution-based books give you the knowledge and power to customize the software and technologies you're using to get the job done. Packt books are more specific and less general than the IT books you have seen in the past. Our unique business model allows us to bring you more focused information, giving you more of what you need to know, and less of what you don't.

Packt is a modern yet unique publishing company that focuses on producing quality, cutting-edge books for communities of developers, administrators, and newbies alike. For more information, please visit our website at www.packtpub.com.

About Packt Open Source

In 2010, Packt launched two new brands, Packt Open Source and Packt Enterprise, in order to continue its focus on specialization. This book is part of the Packt Open Source brand, home to books published on software built around open source licenses, and offering information to anybody from advanced developers to budding web designers. The Open Source brand also runs Packt's Open Source Royalty Scheme, by which Packt gives a royalty to each open source project about whose software a book is sold.

Writing for Packt

We welcome all inquiries from people who are interested in authoring. Book proposals should be sent to author@packtpub.com. If your book idea is still at an early stage and you would like to discuss it first before writing a formal book proposal, then please contact us; one of our commissioning editors will get in touch with you.

We're not just looking for published authors; if you have strong technical skills but no writing experience, our experienced editors can help you develop a writing career, or simply get some additional reward for your expertise.

AngularJS Web Application Development Blueprints

ISBN: 978-1-78328-561-7   Paperback: 300 pages

A practical guide to developing powerful web applications with AngularJS

1. Get to grips with AngularJS and the development of single-page web applications.

2. Develop rapid prototypes with ease using Bootstraps Grid system.

3. Complete and in depth tutorials covering many applications.

Mastering Web Application Development with AngularJS

ISBN: 978-1-78216-182-0   Paperback: 372 pages

Build single-page web applications using the power of AngularJS

1. Make the most out of AngularJS by understanding the AngularJS philosophy and applying it to real-life development tasks.

2. Effectively structure, write, test, and finally deploy your application.

3. Add security and optimization features to your AngularJS applications.

Please check **www.PacktPub.com** for information on our titles

Mastering AngularJS Directives

ISBN: 978-1-78398-158-8   Paperback: 210 pages

Develop, maintain, and test production-ready directives for any AngularJS-based application

1. Explore the options available for creating directives, by reviewing detailed explanations and real-world examples.

2. Dissect the life cycle of a directive and understand why they are the base of the AngularJS framework.

3. Discover how to create structured, maintainable, and testable directives through a step-by-step, hands-on approach to AngularJS.

Learning AngularJS [Video]

ISBN: 978-1-78398-506-7   Duration: 02:00 hrs

A fast, easy and rewarding way to create web applications with AngularJS

1. Create simple and powerful web applications and learn to make your code reusable.

2. Add resources, directives, services, and factories to increase the efficiency of your app.

3. Get a spectacular and interactive visualization for your app through third party components such as D3.js, and Bootstrap.

4. Use CSS and animations to make your app look good.

Please check **www.PacktPub.com** for information on our titles

23324342R00255

Made in the USA
San Bernardino, CA
13 August 2015